200,000 Miles aboard the Destroyer *Cotten*

200,000 Miles

Miles

ABOARD THE

DESTROYER

COTTEN

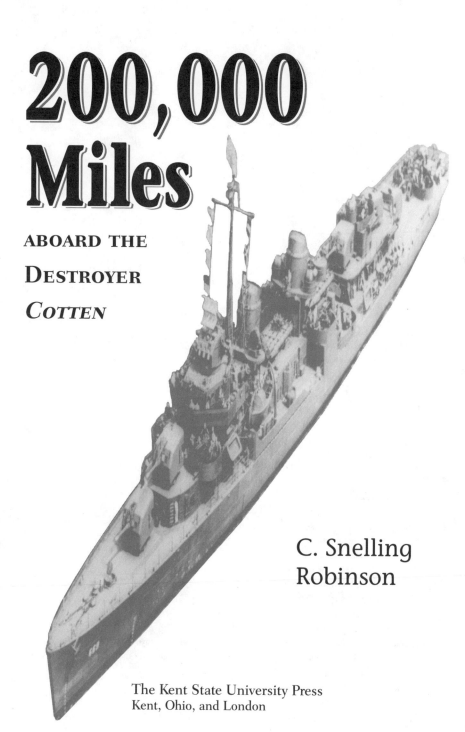

C. Snelling Robinson

The Kent State University Press
Kent, Ohio, and London

© 2000 by the The Kent State University Press, Kent, Ohio 44242
All rights reserved
Library of Congress Catalog Card Number 99-21394
ISBN 0-87338-645-0 (cloth)
ISBN 0-87338-698-1 (paper)
First paper edition 2000.
Manufactured in the United States of America

06 05 04 03 02 01 00   5 4 3 2

Library of Congress Cataloging-in-Publication Data
Robinson, C. Snelling (Charles Snelling), 1922–
    200,000 miles aboard the destroyer Cotten / C. Snelling Robinson.
        p.   cm.
    Includes bibliographical references and index.
    ISBN 0-87338-645-0 (cloth: alk. paper) ∞
    ISBN 0-87338-698-1 (paper: alk. paper) ∞
    1. Robinson, C. Snelling (Charles Snelling), 1922–   . 2. World War, 1939–1945—Naval
operations, American.   3. Cotten (Destroyer)   4. World War, 1939–1945—Personal narratives,
American.   5. United States. Navy Biography.   6. Sailors—United States Biography.   I. Title.
D774.C868R63   1999
940.54'5973—dc21   99-21394

British Library Cataloging-in-Publication data are available.

Contents

Illustrations

Photographs

Maps

Preface

I started to write this book after retiring from a thirty-nine-year business career in Chicago real estate and moving with my wife, Carolyn, and our then four-year-old daughter, Mary, from Lake Forest, Illinois, to our present home in Asheville, North Carolina. With the pressures of a business life removed, I had the time and energy for what was to become an enterprise that lasted, on and off, for the better part of eight years.

The first task entailed obtaining photocopies of the complete deck logs of the *Cotten* from November 1, 1943, until August 31, 1945, from the Operational Archives of the Naval Historical Center. The logs for 1943 were handwritten, those where I had been the junior officer of the watch being in my own handwriting. Beginning in January 1944, the logs were typed by the ship's office. In the instances where I was the officer of the deck, my signature appears under each of the summaries of my watches; after I became navigator, my signature appears with that of the captain at the bottom of each page, in effect certifying that the facts had been checked and found correct. Studying these terse and formal recitations of the pertinent events, set forth in the sequence that they occurred, brought the scenes themselves vividly back to life.

After starting the drafting process proper, I found it desirable to obtain microfilm copies of the war diaries of the several commanders of Destroyer Squadron 50, also from the Naval Historical Center. These diaries covered the period when the squadron existed as an entity—from January 1, 1944, through December 1, 1945—and provided an overview of its wartime activities.

After the deaths of my parents, the fifty-five letters I had written to them while I was aboard the *Cotten* were returned to me. Of these, eight lengthy letters were vital in reconstructing my experiences ashore in Japan during the first months of the occupation. The others, covering the war period proper, had been censored and mainly conveyed my personal feelings and some vignettes of friends in the wardroom. Nonetheless, they were important in recapturing the spirit of the wartime environment.

As the actual drafting progressed, I felt that an overall structure was emerging, one that was the result of rediscovering my strong personal objectives and my pursuit of the same in 1943–45. I kept this structure in mind during the laborious editing and reediting that followed the first complete draft. At least for me, the memoir now stands as an entity rather than a loosely connected series of scenes, and I hope it is more interesting as a result.

Over the past fifty years, I have read countless memoirs and histories of the World War II era, but only a few, covering particular segments of the Pacific War, were of direct use to me in writing the story of the *Cotten*. These references are listed in the bibliography. They were helpful in understanding the political environment, fleet statistics, and enemy tactics, all of which are critical background for an appreciation of what the *Cotten* and its companions in the various task forces faced.

Shortly after completion of the first draft of my manuscript, I met Col. Joseph H. Alexander, USMC (Ret.), currently the best known author writing about the history of the United States Marine Corps. After having read my manuscript, Colonel Alexander suggested I send several chapters and an outline to The Kent State University Press, which he had heard was interested in well written military history. I followed his suggestion, and that turned out to be a critical first step in the publishing of this volume. He also recommended that I ask Mary Craddock Hoffman to assist in the preparation of the six maps that appear in the book. Her skill is evident in the clarity of the result.

I wish to express my thanks to John Hubbell, director of The Kent State University Press, whose encouragement and subsequent skillful editing brought the manuscript up to the publisher's high standards; and also to Joanna Hildebrand Craig, managing editor, and her crew for the careful

PREFACE

and constructive job they performed in the final editing. And finally, I thank my wife, Carolyn, whose valiant and protracted efforts brought my many pen-and-paper drafts to manuscript status.

1

Fitting Out

Departure Day. Robinson family (left to right): Ralph, Evelyn, author, Snelling S. and Keith

The two-week holiday that followed my graduation from Harvard University and receipt of a commission as an ensign in the U.S. Naval Reserve came to an end on June 13, 1943. My imminent departure for active duty had been the motivation for a family reunion, held in our family's summer cottage on the east coast of Penobscot Bay in Maine with my parents and two younger brothers—a happy and warm occasion for all of us.

After lunch on the day of departure, I put aside civilian clothes and dressed in a khaki uniform, one of the outfits I had recently purchased with an allowance the navy had given to each of its thousands of newly commissioned officers. The balance of the new wardrobe had been neatly packed in a sea chest by my mother, as her final maternal contribution to her firstborn son's leaving home.

I was driven to Rockland, Maine, to catch the afternoon train for Boston, the first leg of a trip to New York, and said farewell to my family before climbing aboard. Once the train had started on its way, I sat back to take stock of myself as an officer on active duty for the duration of the war, and to evaluate how I had managed to arrive in such a situation.

The naval training I had received had been a large part of my college undergraduate curriculum. I had enrolled in the Harvard unit of the Naval

Reserve Officers Training Corps in September 1940, with the result that one-quarter of my college courses had been in the required indoctrination and professional subjects collectively known as Naval Science. In addition to the classroom requirements of the program and the practical drilling under the supervision of chief petty officers and marine drill sergeants, the NROTC cadets were obligated to go to sea for training each summer while in college.

During our freshman year, 1940–41, we had still been under the delusion that the war in Europe was neither a vital concern for the United States nor something in which we would become involved. The Japanese were hardly considered at all and certainly not taken seriously. None of us believed that there was any likelihood of our being in a war in the Pacific.

In June of 1941 the required midshipman's cruise for the Harvard unit was aboard the USS *St. Augustine,* a three-hundred-foot former yacht converted into a naval patrol ship. The day after we boarded, in Boston Harbor, the *St. Augustine* headed out alone to the mid-Atlantic to meet up with the British battleships *King George V* and *Rodney,* escorted by two British destroyers. After the rendezvous the British destroyers returned to England, and the *King George V* and *Rodney*, now escorted solely by the *St. Augustine*, continued to Boston. There the battleships went to the Boston Navy Yard for major structural repairs. This escort duty accomplished, the *St. Augustine* returned to sea to patrol between Provincetown, at the tip of Cape Cod, and Cape Ann, with the midshipmen standing watches and conducting drills.

This cruise was under old-time reserve officer supervision, which seemed professional to those of us who had no prior sea experience, and it was a well-organized introduction to shipboard routine and naval discipline. The cruise did not by any measure end the midshipmen's first enthusiasm for sea duty, though intermittent bouts of seasickness may have muted some of it. However, there is no getting around the fact that it constituted a minimal exposure to life at sea.

We started our sophomore year in September of 1941 still in a civilian environment, on balance, but there had been a subtle change in the political climate. During the presidential campaign of 1940, all the candidates, including President Franklin Roosevelt, had solemnly vowed that no American boy would ever fight on foreign soil in a foreign war. By the fall of 1941, however, Mr. Roosevelt's administration had begun to prepare the country for a different role than continuing the isolationism that had been the cornerstone of American policy since the end of World War I.

In the first place, the Soviet Union was being torn apart by a German invasion, and sympathies were being extended in the Russians' direction, as well as toward our avowed friends, the British. Secondly, Roosevelt and his secretary of state, Cordell Hull, were attempting to curtail the Japanese invasion of China, which had been going on for almost eight years, by threatening to cut off our exports to Japan of oil and iron—apparently a very serious matter for the Japanese. In brief, our government had been making motions toward becoming involved in the affairs of a warring world, something that would have been impossible in the isolationist environment of the previous year.

A bit after noon on Sunday, December 7, 1941, I was playing bridge at the home of cousins, listening with them to music on the radio. The program was interrupted to report that the U.S. fleet and base at Pearl Harbor had been bombed by planes of the Japanese navy and that the report "was not a drill." Our two-decade-long experiment with isolationism had come to an end.

Of the many misdirected moves made in history, the Japanese surprise attack on Pearl Harbor without a prior declaration of war was perhaps the worst. Nothing else could have more effectively produced an overwhelming unity of purpose among the American people, including the young men of military age, to avenge this single act by committing themselves to the total defeat of the Japanese Empire.

Within two months the Naval ROTC program had put together a revised schedule for my class, that of 1944. We were ordered to enroll in a summer session at Harvard in 1942, forgoing a second summer cruise, to earn enough credits for early graduation, and we were requested to take both the junior and senior Naval Science courses during the academic year 1942–43, in order to graduate and be commissioned a year early. I altered my plans to conform to this accelerated schedule.

We graduated from Harvard at the end of May 1943, and on May 27, 1943, we received our commissions as line ensigns (that is, not in one of the several staff corps) in the United States Naval Reserve. At the same time, we each received orders to report on June 14 for active duty. I was to report to the Federal Shipbuilding and Dry Dock Company in Kearny, New Jersey, to be attached to the precommissioning crew of the USS *Cotten* (DD 669), a destroyer of the *Fletcher* class currently under construction. The ship had been named for Capt. Lyman A. Cotten, U.S. Navy. Cotten graduated from the U.S. Naval Academy with the Class of 1898. After service at sea, he attended the Naval War College and later served as naval attaché to Japan and China prior to World War I. During World War I, he established and commanded the U.S. naval base at Plymouth, England, for which he received the Distinguished Service Medal. He died in 1926.

When I reached Boston after my leave in Maine, I switched to a train bound for New York, the sea chest having already been checked through to that destination. On the ride to New York, mulling over the adequacy of my training for what now lay immediately ahead, I concluded that I really had no idea what faced me and therefore was in no position to judge whether I was well or poorly prepared. I ended the intellectual torture by deciding that there was nothing I could now do that would serve me better than to take one day at a time. At the very least, I believed, my own training, whether adequate or not, was as good as that of anyone else in my position.

When the train reached New York that evening, I was met by family friends. They took me to their home in Englewood, New Jersey, where I was invited to stay until the navy revealed what it ultimately intended to do with me. The next morning I took a bus to New York City, a subway to the ferry landing at the end of Manhattan Island, a ferry back across the Hudson River to New Jersey, and a streetcar to the Federal Shipbuilding and Dry Dock Company in Kearny.

The shipyard had contracts with the government to build *Fletcher*-class destroyers and Victory ships as fast as they could be turned out. There were numerous dry docks for the Victory ships and ways for the destroyers, with cranes, derricks, and scaffolds all about in seeming confusion; the noise of the riveting and general clanging of metal on metal was all but deafening. I found my way to the office that had been assigned to the precommissioning officers and crew of the USS *Cotten* and duly presented my official orders to a yeoman seated at a desk near the entrance.

The supply officer, Lt. (jg) Fred Butler, took me over, and after getting me entered on the books, he introduced me to the other officers who were present at the time. Lt. Augustine T. Smythe Jr. was the senior officer present, and after a chat that summarized my training history and education, he inquired if I would like to be his assistant, he being the prospective first lieutenant and the senior officer after the executive officer, Lt. Cdr. Joseph Wesson. I accepted his suggestion immediately and with as much enthusiasm as I could muster; having a definite job, even if I had no idea what it entailed, was somehow reassuring. Smythe said that he had been on active duty for over two years and had spent his time on destroyers in the Atlantic convoy system. He was a graduate of Yale University, a member of an old Charleston, South Carolina, family, and a capable and gracious gentleman.

I learned that I was the last and most junior of the ship's fifteen officers to report for duty, that the others had already obtained living quarters in

New York, that I was going to have to find accommodations on my own, and that a cash allowance would be provided by Fred Butler in advance for both room and board. Smythe told me to take the afternoon off, directing me to the facility of the United Service Organizations—the nonprofit association formed in 1941 to assist servicemen, and universally known as the USO—situated near Grand Central Station in the Commodore Hotel. After meeting the other officers at lunch, including the prospective commanding officer, Frank Sloat, and the executive officer, Joe Wesson, I returned to New York, heading for the patriotic ladies at the USO who ran the desk that located temporary housing for officers in New York City.

I was offered and accepted a furnished, two-room, fifth-floor walkup apartment on Madison Avenue about five blocks from the station. I paid six weeks' rent in advance, which covered the time until the *Cotten*'s commissioning, when I would first be able to move aboard. It took me until noon the next day to remove my clothes from my friend's house in New Jersey and to get settled in the apartment. I reported back to the shipyard and the new job as assistant to the first lieutenant the next morning.

Gus Smythe showed me the plans of the *Cotten*, including the piping diagrams for the entire ship outside the engineering spaces, and explained how the highest condition of watertight integrity of each compartment was established. The two of us then toured the ship, crawling through the compartments and checking each "fitting"—valve or hatch—as we went. It was the first lieutenant's responsibility to have each fitting labeled so that it would be properly set—shut or left open, as required—by the damage control parties when the ship went to general quarters. At this stage of the shipbuilding process, it was impossible for me to visualize that the end result was going to be a beautiful destroyer, as it was still only a steel frame enclosed by thin steel plates with many bulkheads not yet in place, encompassing miles of wires, ventilation ducts, pipes, and some recognizable pieces of major machinery. I was grateful that the only physical things I needed to concern myself with at the moment seemed to be the fittings of the firefighting and fresh-water lines, the ventilating ducts, and the watertight doors and hatches.

Lunch was available to us at a shipyard cafeteria, where the food was both excellent and cheap. It made good sense to eat as much as possible at a cost of twenty-nine cents per meal, so that breakfast and supper could be a minimal expense—saving the ensign's pay of $150 per month for more important events, such as an occasional date in New York.

After lunch Wesson and Smythe had another chat with me, to review my background in more detail, including the Harvard ROTC training and the one midshipmen's cruise on the *St. Augustine*. After this interview they decided to assign me to the *Cotten*'s heavy machine guns for a battle station and arranged for me to attend the antiaircraft school aboard the USS *Wyoming* from June 25 until July 11. The *Wyoming*, based in Chesapeake Bay, was an old battleship that had been converted into the Atlantic Fleet's principal school for 20-mm and 40-mm heavy automatic antiaircraft ordnance. Because of this school assignment, I did not have time to contribute to the organization of the first lieutenant's department, but my usefulness would have been limited in any case.

Every afternoon at the close of the day, the officers would gather at the *Cotten*'s office and listen to stories told by Frank Sloat and Ens. Leo Howard. Howard had been commissioned from the ranks, having been aboard a destroyer in the Solomon Islands as a gunner's mate first class. Leo's favorite stories were about the early attempts by the Japanese to land reinforcements by barge on Guadalcanal. On one such occasion, a barge had been sunk at night, and Leo's destroyer had picked up some Japanese soldiers from the water. The Japanese would not willingly surrender, so Leo's men had had to use force to get them up the nets to the deck, there to be shackled to stanchions so that they could not jump back into the water to drown themselves. The next morning the commander of the naval forces in the area ordered Leo's destroyer to take their prisoners to Guadalcanal and deliver them to the marines for interrogation. Leo's destroyer complied promptly, approaching the shore and contacting the marines, requesting them to come for the prisoners. The marines motored out in a landing craft, came alongside the destroyer, signed for the prisoners, roughly threw them into the landing craft, and headed back for the shore.

The next day Leo's ship was reprovingly advised by the admiral that all of the prisoners had been machine-gunned by the marines while attempting to escape, which Leo told us was impossible, as the Japanese had been securely bound when they had been handed over. However, Leo said, no one was surprised, as the marines did not believe in taking prisoners any more than did the Japanese. Leo was a pragmatic man, not likely to exaggerate a story that already was sure to hold his audience's attention. The bloodthirsty nature of the fighting in the Solomon Islands became more personal when Leo told his sea stories.

Captain Sloat's training, experience, and status were far above those of the gunner's mate Leo at the time of his tales. As a result, the captain's stories were very different in their perspective. He was a 1930 graduate of the U.S. Naval Academy, with extensive destroyer duty during the thirteen years since. He had been the chief engineer aboard the destroyer USS *Benham* before becoming its executive officer in 1942.

The *Benham* had been one of the screening destroyers in Rear Adm. Frank Jack Fletcher's carrier task group during the Battle of Midway (June 1942). In that pivotal battle the American carrier USS *Yorktown* had been lost, but the Japanese navy had lost four of its major carriers, along with its most experienced carrier pilots—who at that time had been the equal of any naval pilots in the world. Captain Sloat's tale of this epic battle, especially the events leading up to the sinking of the *Yorktown*, helped bond his young and inexperienced officers with the closeness that became characteristic of the officer corps aboard the *Cotten*.

Captain Sloat also took pleasure in relating the *Benham*'s part in the nighttime surface battle that had taken place around and between Savo Island and Guadalcanal during the night of November 14–15, 1942, when his ship had been sunk. This battle had been between the U.S. battleships *Washington* and *South Dakota* and four destroyers, including the *Benham*, which had been stationed in line ahead of the battleships, and a Japanese bombardment task group consisting of one battleship, two heavy cruisers, two light cruisers, and nine destroyers. Rear Adm. Willis A. Lee had been in command of the United States forces, and Vice Adm. Nobutake Kondo had commanded the Japanese.

According to Captain Sloat, this battle was similar to other nighttime surface battles of the Guadalcanal campaign: confusing, fought at relatively close range, and lethal. During the early stages of the engagement, the *Benham* was steaming at flank speed with the other three screening destroyers ahead of our battleships when it was struck in the bow by a Japanese torpedo, which exploded with such violence that the ship was brought to a stop from a speed of thirty knots in a fraction of a minute. Captain Sloat was uncertain of the source of the torpedo, as the *Benham* had just opened gunfire on unseen radar targets ahead when disaster struck. Within minutes, two of the other destroyers were also hit by torpedoes, leaving our battleships to continue the engagement with a screen of but one destroyer. The battleships, especially the *Washington*, continued the fight on their own, with impressive success. Vice Admiral Kondo lost the battleship *Kirishima* and was completely frustrated in his attempt to bombard the U.S. marine positions on Guadalcanal, which had been his objective. Captain Sloat attributed our overall success that night, despite his own discomfiture and his ship's loss, to the tactical ability of Rear Admiral Lee, who had admittedly been blessed with some good luck.

The destroyermen were not so lucky. The *Benham* ultimately went down with few casualties, but the many remaining crew members, Captain Sloat among them, were compelled to abandon ship and trust their lives to the waters of "Iron Bottom Sound." The other two torpedoed destroyers also sank, so the attrition rate that night for the destroyers of Admiral Lee's force was 75 percent.

Captain Sloat enjoyed telling us this story, at the same time leaving his audience with the feeling that he had been confused by the battle. This touch of uncertainty was something that the inexperienced young officers could relate to.

During the two weeks that I was aboard the *Wyoming* in Chesapeake Bay, the *Cotten* was launched and began rapidly acquiring the finishing details at the shipyard. As for me, life aboard the *Wyoming* persuaded me that sea duty had its advantages, one being that you could not spend any money aboard ship, so that your wages seemed more than adequate when you finally went ashore on liberty. Secondly, the antiaircraft battery fire was both noisy and a challenge; it gave the young participants the feeling that they were involved in a combatlike activity, even when the target of the moment was a red sleeve towed past the guns by an aircraft. At the conclusion of the school I was qualified as an instructor in the operation of twin and quadruple 40-mm gun mounts and the Mark 49 directors controlling those mounts.

When I returned to the shipyard on July 12, Mr. Wesson placed me in charge of the after heavy machine gun battery for my general quarters station, so recorded on the watch, quarter, and station bill, the document that assigns every officer and member of the crew of a naval ship to their regular watches at sea and in port, and to battle stations. Otherwise, I returned to the deck force duties assigned me by Gus Smythe as his assistant.

The mood of the nation during the early summer of 1943, even in cosmopolitan New York, was highly charged; there was a pervasive feeling of being in a whirlwind of history in the making. This was a dramatic change from ten years of dreary economic depression and from the first years of the war, during which the well-trained military machines of Germany and Japan had given first our Allies, and later ourselves, a thorough drubbing. For the young men who were preparing for sea duty—yet were still safely in circumstances little changed from a collegiate environment, except that they now had more money in their pockets—it was a time to dream of future heroics, while sublimating the fact that they had utterly no concept of what active wartime military life would demand of them or what a protracted life at sea would be like.

While the Allied strategy was an unknown to the naval personnel based in the United States, and in fact may not yet have been resolved by our high command, the general belief was that somehow the war had just entered a new phase and that the forces of America's enemies had seen the last of their notable victories. On July 10, 1943, just prior to my return to New York from the *Wyoming*, the Allies had landed a major invasion force on Sicily, capturing the attention of the American public. The enthusiasm for the war effort was heightened, and untested young military men were eager to enter the fray before it was too late. It is hard to imagine how the national mood could have been more sharply focused.

In the eyes of the destroyer's fifteen original officers, the *Cotten* was finally becoming a thing of considerable beauty—long and sleek, smooth and functional, crammed with intricate machinery, and possessed of a variety of weapons of considerable power. While common sense cautioned everyone that wars are very chancey and dangerous, this factor only served to add spice to the times. It was felt that to be among those selected to head for battle, where dangers could be faced, was in itself commendable, the highest prospect that one could hope for.

In this mood, the officers of the *Cotten* were in a transitory no-lose environment, enjoying an undemanding life in one of the great cities of the world without actually being subject to the routine of military life, much less to the hazards of combat.

2

Shakedown Cruise

USS Cotten (DD669) under way from Kearny, New Jersey, to Brooklyn Navy Yard, July 20, 1943. Courtesy of United States Naval Institute (USNI).

Just prior to being placed in commission, the *Cotten* was moved under its own power from the shipyard in Kearny, New Jersey, where it had been completed according to the contract specifications, to the Brooklyn Navy Yard, where alterations were to be made before the ship went to sea.

The most important change involved the creation of a small compartment for a combat information center, known as CIC, located in the forward deckhouse on the port side near the wardroom. CIC contained a large plotting table in the center surrounded by repeaters for the air search (SC) and surface search (SG) radars, plotting boards, speakers, and transmitters for the short-range tactical radio circuits (known as TBS and TBC). A CIC existed in each ship of a task group and was manned during regular watches while under way, as well as during general quarters; every unit could now keep track of the tactical situation, something that had been sorely lacking during nighttime operations in the initial stages of the war.

On July 23, 1943, the officers and leading petty officers moved aboard the *Cotten*, now moored alongside a dock in the Brooklyn Navy Yard. They were joined by the remainder of the crew on July 24, the day that the ship was placed in commission at a noontime ceremony, with the crew standing at attention at quarters in dress uniform, according to custom. The members of the crew were in large part directly from "boot" (recruit) training, with a sprinkling of junior petty officers and seamen first class who had either had some previous shipboard service or had attended schools for a particular specialty. The three hundred crew members were each assigned a bunk, arranged in vertical tiers of three, with a small locker for uniforms and personal possessions located directly underneath the bunks.

The officers were quartered in an area below and forward of the wardroom, consisting of ten two-officer staterooms, each containing two bunks and two wardrobes with chests of drawers. The chief petty officers had living quarters in a compartment located directly forward of the officers' quarters and similar to them in layout. The captain had a private cabin on the main deck, as well as a small sea cabin behind the pilothouse, for use when the ship was under way.

The wardroom was on the main deck in the forward deckhouse; it contained a dining table large enough for all the officers at one sitting, with a small, adjacent galley, where meals were warmed for serving by the mess attendants. The wardroom furnishings were adequate but utilitarian, except for a set of the *Encyclopaedia Britannica* in a small bookcase, a gift of the Federal Shipbuilding and Dry Dock Company. Of interest were steel stanchions that could be fitted into the deck and overhead (ceiling) between the chairs around the wardroom table. These were stored in a locker for use when it was so rough that normal sitting at the table became impossible. The stanchions were then installed, and the diners could hook their arms around them and eat without difficulty, with one hand on the plate and the other on a fork. The newly commissioned officers viewed this aspect of their future with some apprehension.

As soon as the ship had been placed in commission, formal military routine was put into effect. The twenty-four-hour day is divided into five four-hour watches and two two-hour "dog watches," the latter being the 1600–1800 and the 1800–2000 periods. The officer of the deck is in direct charge of the ship, in port or at sea, and among his responsibilities is carrying out the ship's routine. Hours for sleeping, "tricing up" all bunks, meals, drills, and special details, and the hours set for ship's work, instruction periods, and "liberty" parties are all covered by the orders of the day, which are prepared by the executive officer. Of all of these aspects of shipboard routine while the *Cotten* was in the Brooklyn Navy Yard, the most important to its personnel was liberty—when men not in the "duty section" could go ashore.

While the destroyer was berthed in the navy yard, it took a major effort just to keep it from becoming a filthy mess, let alone to make it a spit-and-polish warship. The yard workers were not motivated to clean up after

11

themselves, and Brooklyn was not a clean environment. The largely bewildered crew of the *Cotten* had its hands full keeping the areas it was responsible for shipshape and clean enough to stay out of trouble with the petty officers, who themselves did not want to get in trouble with their chiefs. The latter were experienced enough not to be at cross-purposes with their officers, who certainly did not wish their divisions to be a source of irritation to Mr. Wesson. Discipline during this early period was therefore not strictly military as much as it arose from the crew members' universal motivation to remain on the "liberty list" every other day. The threat of restriction aboard ship was enough to make a conformist out of the wildest rebel.

The navy yard completed the required alterations on August 12, and the next day the *Cotten* put to sea, heading for the island of Bermuda, the training base for newly constructed destroyers and destroyer escorts in the Atlantic area. The *Cotten* remained at Bermuda for two weeks, between August 15 and August 29. Each day it put to sea early in the morning for day-long drills under the direction of the representative of the commander of destroyers, Atlantic Fleet, based on Bermuda. The exercises consisted of antisubmarine attacks on a submerged American submarine, permitting Captain Sloat, the sonar team, and CIC to make simulated depth charge attacks. There were daily exercises of the main and secondary gun batteries, the targets being sleeves towed by aircraft; live torpedo firing exercises; and some practice at destroyer division tactics, in company with other destroyers. Each day in late afternoon, the *Cotten* returned to anchor off Bermuda. Both sections of the crew were permitted liberty ashore for two evenings during the two-week period.

During the Bermuda phase of the shakedown cruise, the officers and crew of the *Cotten* began to make progress toward becoming team players. Working for a common purpose does not produce results overnight, but a well-designed shakedown cruise starts the process.

When the Bermuda phase was completed, the *Cotten* was ordered to Portland, Maine, for the next series of training exercises, which required three more weeks, including three days in transit. Live shore bombardment gunnery exercises for the 5-inch main battery were conducted against targets on Seal Island, one of the outermost islands of Penobscot Bay, which is about one hundred miles northeast of Portland. While the *Cotten* remained in the harbor at Portland, groups of the crew went to various schools ashore. The officers who were to stand watches on the bridge when the ship was under way were sent ashore to practice antisubmarine attack procedures on a new device called an Attack Teacher. On this equipment, each officer, including the junior officers of the watch, as well as the four regular officers of the deck, the executive officer, and the captain, "took the conn" (that is, control of the "ship") to direct a simulated depth charge attack on an enemy submarine, using simulated sonar echoes for tactical data. The *Cotten's* speed, course, and maneuvering characteristics (such as its thousand-yard turning radius), as well as the superior maneuvering capability of a submerged sub, were mechanically simulated. Because the sonar beam leaves the transmitter at an angle from the bottom of the destroyer, a submarine target slips under this beam when the attacking ship closes on the sub's position. The deeper the submarine descends, the sooner it slips under the sonar signal and the sooner the return signal is "lost." This characteristic was included in the design of the Attack Teacher, further complicating the lesson. However, analysis of the distance at which sound contact was lost was the only way the destroyer conning officer could estimate the sub's depth, knowledge vital to the proper setting of the depth charges prior to dropping a pattern. As a result of these variables, the Attack Teacher allowed the conning officer complete discretion in carrying out a depth charge attack and demonstrated how difficult it was to make an effective, killing attack on a submarine with depth charges, given the *Fletcher*-class destroyer's cumbersome maneuvering characteristics and the three dimensions of the battle problem.

Both the shore bombardment and the instruction on the Attack Teacher showed that the *Cotten's* weapons were far from accurate, at least in the hands of its officers and men, and that great care, practice, and concentration would be necessary if any improvement was to be achieved. This was discouraging, as was the realization that becoming a useful destroyer officer or crew member would require much more than simply wearing a uniform.

At the conclusion of the shakedown cruise on September 22, awareness that the routine and duties aboard a destroyer at sea are confining, regimented, and at times uncomfortable had worked itself into the psyche of the *Cotten's* complement, along with the realization that the learning process had just begun. It was not quite as easy to dream about future feats of heroics, and the possibility that the real future might hold some uninviting elements began to sink in. Thus, while the officers and crew had begun the slow process of uniting in spirit to form a close-knit team, the awareness of downside aspects of destroyer duty had also appeared.

3

To Pearl Harbor and the Pacific Fleet

The *Cotten* completed the shakedown cruise by September 22, and it returned to the Brooklyn Navy Yard for maintenance and some minor alterations. Despite the fact that our country was in the midst of a total war effort supported by an overwhelming majority of the American people, the draftees aboard the *Cotten*, who exceeded the volunteers in number, were not completely resigned to military discipline. Some of the crew gave an extension of their time ashore more weight than the prospect of court-martial, as evidenced by the seventeen who were reported as "absent without leave" (AWOL) on October 4, the eve of the ship's departure for the Pacific. They were in addition to approximately the same number of AWOLs who had already been returned to the ship by armed guard. The administrative requirements of garnering the facts and then trying these wayward souls at "captain's mast" or summary court-martial had consumed an inordinate amount of Mr. Wesson's time during the shakedown period. The extent of this disdain for military discipline came as a surprise.

On October 5, the *Cotten* was released from the Brooklyn Navy Yard and proceeded to Norfolk, Virginia. Four days later it departed for the

Pacific, by way of the Panama Canal and San Francisco, with orders to report to the commander of destroyers, U.S. Pacific Fleet, at Pearl Harbor.

On October 12, the *Cotten* was steaming alone in the Windward Passage, between Cuba and Haiti. It was a beautiful day, with a wind of about fifteen knots, a moderate sea, and a sky studded with cumulus clouds. The spectacular weather and the fact that the U.S. east coast was behind and already forgotten seemed to erase some of the apprehension that had developed during the shakedown cruise. At least the future looked more interesting, if no less obscure, and the ship was beginning to feel a bit more like home. During the morning watch, the *Cotten* received a radio message from the commander of destroyers, Atlantic Fleet, advising that one of the top captains of the German U-boat fleet had been located with his sub in the Windward Passage and that we should be on the lookout for him. The U-boat campaign against Allied shipping was still the major part of the war in the Atlantic at this time, and memories of the previous German successes remained vivid, despite recent evidence that the antisubmarine efforts were becoming effective.

This contact report was delivered to Captain Sloat, who enjoyed sitting in his chair on the bridge when the weather was as pleasant as it was on this particular morning. He passed the message sheet around to the officer of the deck with an appropriate comment before returning to his position in silent contemplation. The watch returned to its peaceful routine and individual appreciation of the brisk beauty of the Windward Passage—for about one hour.

Suddenly the atmosphere was changed by a call to the bridge from the sonar operator, who reported that he had a strong contact fifteen hundred yards on the port bow. The captain came to life, bellowing, "Call general quarters!" It was done in an instant. Hearing the general alarm, I ran to my battle station, Sky 2, where I was in charge of the after 40-mm and 20-mm batteries. Everyone was at his battle station two and one-half minutes after the report of the sound contact. As soon as all automatic weapons were manned, I advised the gun captains of the tactical situation and directed that they keep their eyes open for a periscope, as the presumed U-boat was less than a mile away.

This done, and convinced that an engagement was imminent, I contemplated what would happen to the *Cotten* when the Germans' torpedoes hit home. My next thought projected the destroyer sinking under me, and then me swimming around with fellow crew members in an ocean filled with sharks. At this juncture, my knees started to shake uncontrollably. In order to maintain a semblance of a military posture, I grabbed hold of the steel railing of my station with all my strength and did my best to look intently in the reported bearing of the submarine.

Suddenly the surface of the sea was broken, and a large whale showed his back and flippers while he took a good gulp of air. My knees immediately stopped shaking, and self-control returned. Subsequently, reviewing what had happened, everyone expressed disappointment that the U-boat had not been encountered. I joined the consensus without qualification, feeling that self-inflicted buck fever was my own private concern. The whale was given due credit for having made a vivid impression on everyone and for conditioning the *Cotten*'s crew to the feel of combat.

On the morning of October 14, the *Cotten* was located somewhere in the vicinity of the Atlantic entrance of the Panama Canal but still in the deep waters of the Caribbean Sea. The regular ship's navigator, Ens. Norman Campbell, who had reported for duty during the shakedown cruise, was ashore to recuperate from an appendectomy. His duties as navigator had been taken over temporarily by Mr. Wesson, on top of everything else he had to do. Complicating his troubles was the fact that the chief quartermaster, whose assistance he needed for celestial navigation, had then turned up sick, so there had been no accurate navigational fixes since leaving the island of Jamaica. The landfall on the Atlantic side of the canal can be confusing, as there are no easily recognizable headlands. All of this resulted in Mr. Wesson's being somewhat unsure of our position. After debating the matter for a few minutes, the captain, observing some fishing vessels a mile or so away, came to a practical conclusion. In his customary easily heard and far-carrying tones, he turned to his capable and hardworking "exec" and bellowed, "For Christ's sake, Joe, ask one of those goddamn fishermen over there where the hell the Panama Canal is!" The *Cotten* was maneuvered over to the closest fisherman, of whom Mr. Wesson inquired in Spanish where the canal was. A respectful response and an accurate bearing were given, permitting the destroyer to proceed to the canal entrance on the Atlantic Ocean side without further incident, other than passing within sight of two waterspouts as it neared the land.

Before entering the canal proper, the *Cotten* took aboard a pilot, who conned the ship for the fifty-mile passage to the Pacific Ocean. The route lay first through the set of locks that raise ships some eighty-five feet to the level of Lake Gatún, then through the two sets of locks that between them lower ships back down to the Pacific Ocean level, near the city of Balboa in the Republic of Panama.

Mr. Wesson knew full well that in the months to come the *Cotten* and its crew would be far removed from the pleasures of civilization. He encouraged the officers to divide up in two groups to take turns ashore on the

Cotten officers at cabaret "Shelter," Balboa, Panama, October 1943. From left: Lt. (jg) Wayne Dorman, Lt. Augustine Smythe Jr., Ens. Carl Holthausen, Lt. (jg) Herbert Kanter, Lt. (jg) Frederick Butler, Lt. W. L. Hadley Griffin, and Ens. C. Snelling Robinson

two nights the *Cotten* was scheduled to remain alongside a dock near Balboa. From personal experience he possessed a list of the more prominent bars and cabarets in that city; he handed it over to Gus Smythe, who was designated to lead the first contingent of seven ashore.

One establishment, the Shelter, remained fixed in the minds of our first group. It was a typical "Blue Moon" establishment—young bar girls were available to dance with the customers, and they were happy to do so as long as their companions bought them drinks, known as Blue Moons, between dances. Since their drinks, unlike those of their customers, contained no alcohol, the girls' ability to down them resulted in our drinking an unusual amount even for us, at a cost several times more than we had anticipated. Despite the fact that this was an expensive enterprise, all seven officers had a memorable evening, due mostly to one of the entertainers, a beautiful Eurasian girl named Lily Wong, who performed an exotic strip dance during the floor shows as the feature act. When not performing she sat at the *Cotten* table, dancing with each of the group in turn and captivating them all. No one considered the money spent as wasted, and the camaraderie of the evening was of especially great value to the morale of the younger officers.

On the morning following the second night's liberty, the *Cotten* set forth for San Francisco, some thirty-five hundred nautical miles to the northwest. This is a long distance for destroyers, whose modest fuel capacity makes them notoriously "short legged." In order to limit fuel consumption, the ship's speed was lowered to thirteen knots, which seemed to be no movement at all in the windless, oily Pacific waters of the lower latitudes. In all, the trip took a bit over eleven days, which was the longest the *Cotten* had yet been at sea without anchoring or docking. For this reason, in addition to the fact that the ship was steaming alone without even any interesting weather for company, this particular trip seemed to last an inordinately long time.

When the *Cotten* finally arrived in San Francisco Bay, it was allowed to remain only long enough to fuel and take on some passengers and a few fresh provisions. No liberty for a restless crew at least meant no desertions, but at the time that did not seem to be an equitable trade-off.

The next morning, the *Cotten* headed westward under the Golden Gate Bridge in company with two other destroyers and two cruisers en route to Pearl Harbor, into the teeth of a northwesterly Pacific storm. The gale persisted for almost two days, and coming in as it did on the starboard bow, caused the *Cotten* to heave, pitch, and roll as it had not done previously. A four-hour watch on the bridge, holding on to a railing at all times to keep from being hurled from one side to another, was physically demanding. Watching the bow plunge deep into an oncoming wave, cover itself with solid ocean, then rise far up out of the water, only to slam into the sea once again, seemingly headed for the bottom, was demoralizing to those who had not experienced a storm aboard a small ship before. The other destroyers fared no better, of course, and during the worst of the gale we saw their propellers come clear of the water when the bows were down. Even the cruisers seemed to toss about like chips of wood in a rapids.

This two-day period reduced me to a seasick wretch; my only respites came at the conclusions of my watches, when I could return to my bunk, after having sneaked to the fantail to be able finally to empty my stomach in privacy. I never admitted to my miseries, which must nonetheless have been evident to anyone from my pallor and my sudden and uncharacteristic lack of interest in food. For all I knew, I might have been the only person aboard who felt tormented by this little gale and the *Cotten*'s antics in making way into it, although this was extremely unlikely.

The gale abated after the second day, the ocean calmed down, and the sky cleared, except for the cumulus puffs chasing each other—now from the northeast, toward our starboard quarter. My own appetite returned in full force, and a renewed interest in life came close behind. By the time we saw the snowcapped peak of Mauna Kea far to the south before making our approach to Pearl Harbor, I even felt excited by the prospect of the experiences that lay in the future. I was now fully acclimated to being aboard the *Cotten*.

4

Tarawa: Operation Galvanic

During the forenoon of October 31, 1943, the formation with which the *Cotten* had been steaming arrived outside Pearl Harbor. The ships entered the harbor individually, proceeding to assigned berths. Although December 7, 1941, was now just a month shy of two years in the past, one's first entry into Pearl Harbor was an emotional experience. There were still abundant signs of the Japanese attack, the most notable being the listing, scorched mast of the sunken *Arizona*, which had eleven hundred dead crewmen still aboard. The *Arizona* was still technically in commission, and its colors were raised each morning (and still are today) from a small platform that was built on the wreckage for that purpose. This stark reminder of why our country was at war with Japan had a great deal to do with the continuing dedication of the officers and men of the Pacific Fleet to fighting their war.

After the *Cotten* had moored at berth M2 at Merry Point in Pearl Harbor, the initial surge of patriotism gave way to the more familiar urge to enjoy a liberty ashore. However, within the hour the *Cotten* received orders to return to sea with the heavy cruiser *Pensacola* for four days of gunnery exercises. Only then were we to return to Pearl Harbor, for fuel and provisions, some necessary repairs, and finally for two liberties apiece for each officer and member of the crew.

Knowing for certain when I would be free, I telephoned Henry A. Walker Jr., who had roomed next door to me in Winthrop House during our final year at Harvard, to see if we could get together on one of my two coming nights ashore. Henry invited me to come, on my first scheduled liberty, some six days hence, to his family's house in Honolulu for a drink and then to go out for dinner. He also asked if I would like to bring one of my shipmates, and I accepted his suggestion, inviting my boss, Gus Smythe.

The next morning, November 1, we put to sea with the *Pensacola*, a prewar heavy cruiser that was just returning to the fleet after about a year's absence. It had received all but fatal damage on November 30, 1942, in the Battle of Tassafaronga off Guadalcanal, which had occurred two weeks after the *Benham* was sunk. The *Pensacola* had been hit amidships by one of the powerful 24-inch torpedoes of Rear Adm. Raizo Tanaka's justly renowned destroyer squadron; it had been forced to return to the West Coast for an extensive rebuilding. In the four-day practice cruise, the *Cotten* was a mock target for the main batteries of the *Pensacola,* as well as its watchdog and errand boy. The practice the *Cotten* gained in station keeping and maneuvering was advantageous, but it hardly compensated for having a first visit to Honolulu postponed.

Smythe and I had not been ashore since Balboa on October 14, some three weeks past, and in contemplating an evening with Walker in Honolulu, my memories of the beautiful Lily Wong kept coming to the forefront. On the afternoon of our liberty, Gus and I left Pearl Harbor by taxi and checked in at the Moana Hotel, which, along with the Royal Hawaiian, fronts on Waikiki Beach. These two hotels had been taken over by the navy for the duration of the war. The Royal Hawaiian was solely for officers of the submarine service, but the Moana was available to all officers of the Pacific Fleet. After engaging a room for the night and then sprucing up, Gus and I hailed another taxi and were off for the Walkers' home address.

We had not gone much over a mile from the Moana before the taxi driver turned to the left up a long driveway; the house at the end was an attractive and imposing structure. Walker greeted us at the door and ushered us into a drawing room, where we had cocktails. The others present were a friend of Hank's and Mr. and Mrs. Walker senior. After the drinks, Hank and his friend took us to a restaurant for dinner. Because of the curfew in effect on Oahu, we made an early return to the Walkers' house, where we smoked cigars, drank brandy, and played poker. Later in the evening Mr. and Mrs. Walker returned home from a dinner party they had attended, reporting that one of the other guests had been Adm. Chester W.

Nimitz, commander of the United States Pacific Fleet. Suitably impressed and somewhat numbed by food and drink, Gus and I were returned to the Moana Hotel near midnight. Early next morning we returned to the *Cotten* and duty. I admitted to myself that while the evening had been pleasant enough, it had not compared to the standard that had been set in Balboa, particularly with respect to the company of cabaret girls.

Four days later, during the afternoon of November 9, the *Cotten* received a copy of Vice Adm. Raymond Spruance's Commander Fifth Fleet Operation Order 1-43. Every officer who stood bridge or CIC watches was required to read the complete operation order as quickly as it could make the rounds. All members of the crew were restricted on board, as we were assigned a departure time of 0700 of the following morning, November 10, with the other units of the newly formed Task Force 52.

The first part of the operation order defined the "Objective," which was the seizure, occupation, and development of the islands of Tarawa and Makin in the Gilberts. This was followed by the admiral's "Estimate of the Situation," an outline of the relative strength, capabilities, and intentions of the enemy forces that either would or could oppose the naval and landing forces of the Fifth Fleet. The balance of the operation order covered the details, including the assignment of ships to the various task forces of the Fifth Fleet, the composition of the landing forces, the prelanding naval gunfire, and aircraft bombing targets. Supporting material consisted of charts, designations of landing areas, boat lanes for the landing craft, and estimates of low and high tides for D day. It seemed to me that the operation order covered every contingency. It also seemed as though the landings could be accomplished successfully and on schedule, my assumption being that the defenders would be crushed by the massive gunfire and bombing attacks to be made on the target areas before D day.

The *Cotten* got under way as scheduled, sortied from Pearl Harbor, and joined the antisubmarine screen of Task Force 52. Our formation, which was heading for the Makin landings, and Task Force 53, which was heading for Tarawa, were sailing in "tactical concentration"—which meant in close proximity although maneuvering independently. The formations each consisted of the attack transports carrying the troops who would make the landings, four escort carriers to provide direct air support for the landings, and a battleship to furnish heavy gunnery "preparation" of the enemy's fortified areas immediately before the landings. In addition, there were the heavy cruisers *Indianapolis* (flagship of Admiral Spruance, the Fifth Fleet commander) and the newly constructed *Baltimore*.

The first sight of so many warships in a task group formation was breathtaking. Most of the time, the destroyers were in a circular screen around the heavy ships and transports. This was the *Cotten's* basic duty, and it required maintaining position on a given bearing and at a given distance from a major unit, designated as the "guide," at the formation's center. The destroyers' stations were changed several times each day, requiring a graphical maneuvering-board calculation to accomplish the change in relative position. The sound gear of each destroyer continuously searched through an outboard arc covering its section of the screen, so that an effective antisubmarine search could be maintained around the entire task group. Each task group changed course on a prearranged schedule, called a zigzag plan, as was standard doctrine for the Pacific Fleet.

The junior officer of the watch, or JOOW, which was the training position for bridge officers (and my own watch assignment), actually directed the heading and speed adjustments necessary to keep proper station and to make the required course changes. In addition, the junior officer worked out a maneuvering-board solution for each change in station, kept the rough bridge log, and wrote up the smooth deck log when the watch was over. Hadley Griffin, the gunnery officer, was the officer of the deck, or OOD, during my watches at this time, which gave him responsibility for the operation and maneuvering of the ship and for my training. Whenever the ship was maneuvered from one position to another in the task force, Griffin would take the conn until the new position had been reached and we were on the new station.

From Pearl Harbor to the Gilbert Islands it was nineteen hundred miles, which took the task group nine days to cover. Once each day the battleships, cruisers, and destroyers maneuvered separately from the transports and escort carriers for several hours in order to conduct fleet tactical exercises for training. These exercises generally required about half of the destroyers to leave the screen and form up in column in division order, with three hundred yards between each destroyer of a three or four-unit division. In a typical exercise, the destroyer divisions, after moving some ten miles from the battle line, would make a high-speed simulated torpedo attack on the heavy ships, giving the latter the opportunity to simulate firing their main batteries—15-inch guns for the battleships and 8-inch guns for the heavy cruisers.

On one of these exercises, I was on the bridge as the junior officer of the watch, Griffin, was OOD, and the captain had taken the conn. We were closing the two heavy cruisers at a speed of twenty-seven knots, and because we were approaching their column from about fifteen degrees forward of their starboard beams, the relative speed of our approach was close to forty knots. In my view we had gotten far too close for comfort when the captain hollered the command "right full rudder" to turn the *Cotten* to

22

starboard, in the direction of the leading cruiser, but with less than a right angle in which to come around to a parallel course. I asked the captain if he meant "right full rudder." In full voice the captain shouted, "Yes, goddamn it, I said right full rudder!" The *Cotten* turned right, missing the cruiser *Baltimore* by three hundred yards, far enough away that no one was upset by the maneuver, except me. In the first place, three hundred yards at the speed we were going had seemed dangerously close, at my minimal level of experience. In the second place, it was the first time an oath had been fired at me by the captain. The verbal exchange was so routine for Captain Sloat, Mr. Wesson, and Griffin that what had transpired was not worth their noting.

However, little incidents like this made a deep impression on me, and doubtless on the other junior watch officers, who were also trying to learn the tactical requirements laid upon a destroyer, which sometimes included high-speed maneuvers with only three hundred yards between ships. There is but one way to learn how this should be done, and that is first to observe it being done by others and then to do it yourself (under watchful eyes). This type of maneuvering requires precise timing and quick decisions, and it leaves minimal opportunity for deliberate consideration of alternatives. For example, in the maneuver just described, had we turned left instead of right, we would have passed down the cruiser column in the opposite direction, with a speed differential of fifty-four knots, instead of finishing as we did on a parallel course with no relative speed at all. My instinctive concept of the proper maneuver did not take into consideration how the *Cotten* should end up, which was a very bad mistake. A maneuver must place your ship in the intended position, something that is instinctive to an experienced officer. I reflected on this particular sequence for some time afterward.

As Task Forces 52 and 53 progressed toward the equator in the voyage from Pearl Harbor, the weather conditions changed on a day-by-day basis. The island of Oahu is at 21° 30' north latitude, about the same as the south half of Cuba, and is generally favored by the northeast trade winds. The ocean temperature around the Hawaiian Islands hovers around seventy-five degrees, giving the climate its benign, semitropical temperature range. The course of the Fifth Fleet was generally to the southwest, the latitude decreasing a little more than two degrees every day. At about ten degrees north latitude, the trade winds were left behind for good. As the sun rose higher and higher, the surface temperature of the ocean rose steadily as well, until it was in excess of eighty degrees. The ocean was often almost dead calm, disturbed only by gentle breezes at best.

Fresh water aboard a naval vessel at sea must be made from ocean water by the ship's evaporators, which have to produce enough for the boilers, for drinking, and for washing bodies and clothes. When the seawater rises to the temperatures encountered near the equator, the evaporators' condensers, which are cooled by seawater, become much less efficient. Fresh water use for washing purposes must then be sharply reduced, in order to have enough to run the boilers and to provide drinking water for the crew.

Destroyers' steel hulls and decks were made without any insulating or protective coating except camouflage paint. After being under the equatorial sun for twelve hours, this steel became blistering hot to the touch and even uncomfortably warm through the soles of one's shoes. The heat worked itself into the compartments themselves, so that eventually all the living quarters became tropically hot. The heat was unrelieved by the ship's ventilating system, there being, of course, no air-conditioning. Since the ventilating system was turned off when the ship went to battle stations every morning and evening (the mostly likely times for air attacks, with the sun on the horizon, in the eyes of lookouts), the humidity level built up to the point that nothing could ever really dry out, whether it was your body, your clothes, or, most noticeable of all when you first climbed into it, your bunk.

This negative change in living conditions aboard the ship was, like every such change, very noticeable at first, so that it stood out in one's memory of this particular operation. In time, the same shipboard circumstances would lose their novelty and seem to approach normality, if not desirability.

On November 15, Task Force 52 crossed the equator. This was the first such crossing for most of the officers and men aboard the various ships, and long-standing naval tradition called for a ceremony in which the "shellbacks," already enrolled in the domain of King Neptune, initiated the "polliwogs," who were not. This ceremony is akin to a fraternity initiation in form, with novel indignities visited upon the inductees, the routine of naval discipline being temporarily set aside. However, in this instance the Fifth Fleet was within range of the Japanese air forces based in the Gilbert Islands. Admiral Spruance felt it prudent to proclaim officially that all who had not previously crossed the equator were to be elevated to shellback status without the rites, which were forever waived in their cases. This was doubtless a sensible order, but it was disappointing for everyone, even those who were preparing to be hazed.

On the morning of November 16, the special sea details were set, and the captain maneuvered the *Cotten* alongside the *Baltimore* to refuel, both ships steaming at nine knots. Our men manhandled two fuel oil hoses across the forty feet separating the two ships and secured them to the respective fuel-oil intake receptacles. My station during the refueling operation was with the second deck division, which was responsible for the after-fueling hose. The *Baltimore* then started pumping heated fuel oil,

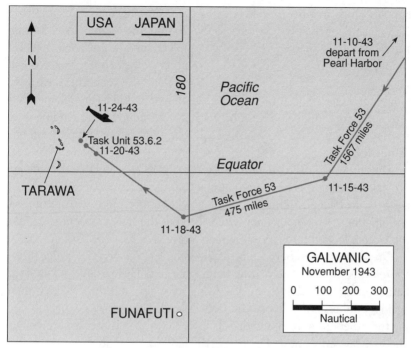

USA   JAPAN

11-10-43
depart from
Pearl Harbor

N

180

Pacific
Ocean

11-24-43

Task Unit 53.6.2
11-20-43

Equator

Task Force 53
1567 miles

TARAWA

Task Force 53
475 miles

11-15-43

11-18-43

GALVANIC
November 1943

0   100   200   300

Nautical

FUNAFUTI ○

Track of Cotten from Pearl Harbor to Tarawa, November 10–24, 1943. (See Appendix C.)

completing in about thirty minutes. The captain was at the conn through-out, and the steersman was R. O. Brockway, QM2c. Maintaining exact sta-tion alongside another ship required experience and talent, as well as strict concentration.

On November 18, the *Cotten* left Task Force 52 and joined Task Force 53, the Southern Attack Force, which was assigned to the Tarawa landings. The old battleship *Maryland* and Admiral Spruance's flagship *Indianapolis* also made this change, so that Task Force 53 in its final approach con-tained the heavy ships, the Tarawa marine landing forces, the gunfire sup-port ships, the four escort carriers providing direct air support for the operation, and the screening destroyers.

On November 19, Task Force 53 reached the vicinity of Tarawa Atoll, close enough that air operations from the escort carriers could be carried out against Betio Island, which was the southwestern extremity of the atoll. On two occasions Japanese island-based aircraft attempted to close on our ships, but without success; they were turned away by the combat air patrol (CAP) from the escort carriers. At this point the tension rose, as the land-ings on Betio were scheduled for the next morning. During the day of November 19, the *Cotten* went alongside all of the escort carriers and gunfire support ships in turn to deliver last-minute intelligence photographs of Betio Island taken at low altitude by planes from the escort carrier *Suwannee*. The *Cotten*'s messenger duty was completed by late afternoon, at which time Admiral Spruance ordered the formation of Task Unit 53.6.2, consisting of the escort carriers *Nassau* and *Barnes* and the screening destroyers *Cowell* and *Cotten*. Our task unit was stationed within a general operating area some fifty miles northeast of the Betio Island (Tarawa) landing area, so that air support for the marines could be provided on a direct-call and as-needed basis.

The consensus was that Tarawa was not heavily held and that the strength of Task Force 53 was so overwhelming that the marines would be able to seize Betio Island in short order. It was therefore more with optimistic anticipation than nervous apprehension that the new crews of ships like the *Cotten* looked forward to the next morning.

On D day, November 20, one of the radio speakers on the bridge of the *Cotten* was tuned to the marine landing circuit. This circuit included the battleship *Maryland* when it was firing its main battery of 15-inch guns against bunkers and pillboxes on Betio Island. This fire was delivered during the ninety minutes immediately prior to the first wave of marines, but due to delays encountered in getting the landing craft into the water and in position to proceed to the beaches, the fire had stopped twenty minutes before the marines could get started into the lagoon. The *Maryland* had been fairly close to the beachhead while firing its main battery. Because Betio Island was only twenty feet or so above sea level at its highest, every two-gun salvo produced at best one hit on the island; the other round either fell short in the lagoon or passed over into the reef area on the seaward side. On top of this, only one shot in about ten that actually landed on Betio was observed to hit a bunker, pillbox, or artillery emplacement. While it was the impression aboard the *Maryland* that this prelanding gunfire caused extensive damage to the Japanese defensive positions, it actually was of very limited effect, due to its imprecise nature, the short time of the bombardment, and the low profile of the targets.

The waves of marines, twenty minutes behind schedule, were in landing craft, which required several feet of water, or in amphibious tractors, "amtracs," tanklike seagoing vehicles that could travel over reefs and up onto the beach. The waves of these landing craft were now proceeding into Tarawa Lagoon toward low-lying Betio Island during an ominous lull, with the amtracs in the first wave.

Those listening on the *Cotten*'s bridge to the tactical radio circuit used by the marines now heard reports back to the commanders that the depth of water in the lagoon seemed to be much less than forecast in the operation order. The landing craft behind the amtracs were stranding on coral reefs some five to eight hundred yards short of the beach and were grinding to a halt. These voice radio conversations to and from the landing craft were listened to in silence as the scene unfolded.

The Fifth Fleet intelligence estimate had predicted that there would be a sufficiently high tide during the morning of November 20 in the Tarawa lagoon to permit the landing craft to proceed practically all the way to the Betio Island beach, there to unload the marines. According to the plan, the first wave of tracked assault craft were supposed to be able to get to the beach and then bring their troops to the protection of the first low-lying dunes. What was heard over the radio contrasted sharply with these optimistic assumptions. When the landing craft grounded on the coral far short of the beach, the marines were forced to get out of the boats and wade ashore through a quarter to a half-mile of water, subjected to intense rifle, machine-gun, and artillery fire. The Japanese lagoon-oriented defenses were now revealed to be still largely undamaged and fully manned, in spite of the prelanding gunfire and air bombardments.

The marines who made it to the beach in amtracs with the first wave were the only ones not to be shot to pieces during the morning hours. The boat crews of the landing craft stuck on the coral reefs called incessantly for gunfire support over their radio circuits. Their voices were more often than not high-pitched and impassioned, crying that their passengers were being cut to ribbons by withering fire from the Japanese positions.

This desperate situation continued throughout the day of November 20, although by late afternoon several thousand marines were finally able to reach the beach, enough to constitute a foothold. They suffered a casualty rate of almost a third in the process. The completely unexpected carnage of November 20 stunned the officers and men of the *Cotten*. There was unreserved respect for the men of the Marine Corps, and in a different way, for their enemy as well.

The two escort carriers that the *Cowell* and *Cotten* were escorting pulled away from Tarawa after nightfall as a defensive measure against Japanese submarines, which were presumed to have been sent to the Gilbert Islands. As a result of the increase in distance from the beachhead, it was not possible to hear any further marine tactical conversations. In any case, Mr. Wesson decided that monitoring this circuit on the bridge was disturbing the concentration of those on watch, and he had it turned off.

During the next day, continuous cover for the marines was again provided by the air groups of the *Nassau* and *Barnes*. This required radical maneuvering by the *Cotten* and *Cowell* before and after each flight operation in order to stay ahead of the carriers so as to maintain an antisubmarine defense. Every time the carriers reversed course, which was done before and after each set of flight operations (since aircraft had to take off and land into the wind), the two destroyers had to come about and go to flank, or maximum, speed in order to regain their positions twenty-five hundred yards ahead of the leading carrier. With only the two destroyers, this meant minimal antisubmarine protection at best; since the underwater sound equipment was not effective while the destroyers were at high speed, due to the increased water-flow noises, there was no real antisubmarine screen at all during the maneuvering periods.

During the daylight hours of November 21, the *Cotten*'s CIC was able to keep rough track of the Betio landing forces by monitoring their voice radio channels. A decision had been made by Adm. Richmond K. Turner, who commanded the landing force, to land the reserve force; it was able to get ashore with one-fifth of the rate of casualties suffered on D day. This still represented an unacceptably high casualty rate, but rapid progress was now being made. Despite their resolve, the Japanese defenders, some forty-eight hundred in all, were eliminated by the end of November 23, and the Tarawa airstrip received its first U.S. plane. In three days this nightmare was over and the objective taken.

During the morning watch of November 24, it was learned that the escort carrier *Liscome Bay* of the Northern Attack Force, one of two carriers providing support for the Makin landings, had been torpedoed in the early morning. The casualties had been enormous, as a result of an explosion of the ship's magazines and aircraft fuel that had blown it to pieces. While half as many sailors of the *Liscome Bay* had died in seconds as the marines had just lost over three days, it did not seem as traumatic an event, sudden death being more easily accepted than the prolonged slaughter of the assault on Betio Island.

At breakfast that morning Captain Sloat commented on the loss of the *Liscome Bay*, remarking that he would hate to have been the captain of either of the two destroyers in the antisubmarine screen; the loss of a carrier and its crew would be a heavy burden on the consciences of the men assigned to protect them. Of course, we realized he had been through this himself, when the *Yorktown* had been lost at Midway and he was the executive officer of the *Benham*. The captain emphasized that destroyers were not supposed to win the war, but that they damn well were supposed to protect the carriers, which *would* win the war.

I had been recently reassigned to be the junior officer of the watch under Roger Stokey, assistant gunnery officer and one of the four qualified as OOD when under way. On this day the two of us were standing the

28

forenoon watch, from 0800 until noon. At 1120 the sonar operator called the bridge to report a sound contact bearing twenty-five degrees on the starboard bow at a range of one thousand yards. If this were a submarine (there were no whales on the equator), it was perfectly positioned to launch torpedoes against our two carriers, being only three thousand yards ahead of the *Nassau*. Captain Sloat was in his chair on the bridge, and he immediately jumped to his feet and took the conn from Stokey.

The captain ordered "right full rudder, all ahead full," giving a course directly for the contact. He told Stokey to call the task group commander on the *Nassau* to tell him we had a submarine on the sound gear, giving its range and bearing, and that we were headed for an immediate attack. Stokey grabbed the radiotelephone and made the report. In two and a half minutes we were over the contact, and the captain bellowed, "Fire depth charges!" His immediate concern was more to disrupt the presumed sub captain's effort to launch torpedoes against the carriers than to make a precise attack, as he understood what the effect on his own career would be if he were to permit the sub to fire.

Because the captain was attacking at a twenty-knot speed, the torpedomen had not had time to arm the firing mechanisms of all of the three-hundred-pound depth charges on the K-guns, or any of the six-hundred-pound depth charges on the stern. As a result, when the firing buttons were pressed on the bridge at the captain's command, only two of the K-guns on either side responded, sending two charges to both port and starboard, set for detonation at shallow depth. A torpedoman on the starboard battery was bruised by the firing, as he had just armed the depth charge and had not had time to pull away. He was knocked flat, but fortunately no bones were broken.

The four depth charges exploded properly, and the captain ordered the ship slowed to ten knots and made a wide circle to starboard to regain sound contact and prepare for a second and more organized attack. At this point he realized he had not ordered the ship to general quarters, an oversight he immediately rectified. When relieved by the "GQ" officer of the deck, Stokey and I ran to our own battle stations.

As soon as the presence of the submarine had been reported, the admiral had ordered the task group turned directly away from the bearing of the contact, and he had increased speed to head his two carriers, now screened by *Cowell* alone, to safety.

At 1143 sound contact was regained, at a range of twenty-two hundred yards. All depth charges were now armed, and the ship was at battle stations. Captain Sloat increased speed to fifteen knots and approached the apparent sub again, noting a gradual change in bearing to starboard. He compensated with a course change, assuming that the sub was making two knots at right angles to our course. At a range of four hundred yards sound contact was lost, and the captain ordered the depth charges reset to explode at a depth of two hundred feet, speculating that the enemy captain had taken his boat down to that depth after the *Cotten*'s original attack.

At 1150 he ordered the firing of an eleven-depth-charge pattern, having reached his best estimate of the proper place for a killing attack. This full pattern contained five depth charges of six hundred pounds of TNT dropped over the stern and six depth charges of three hundred pounds of TNT hurled by the K-guns, three to port and three to starboard, for a total of forty-eight hundred pounds of explosive. After this second attack, the captain turned the *Cotten* again and reduced speed to ten knots to begin a search with the sound gear in the area roiled by the recent explosions of the depth charges. At 1205, fifteen minutes after the second attack, sonar regained sound contact with the sub, at a range of 950 yards. The captain immediately increased speed to fifteen knots for the third attack and at 1212 dropped another eleven-depth-charge pattern at a depth setting of two hundred feet, right on top of his predicted location of the sub.

About two minutes after the last depth charge had detonated, all of us heard and felt a very large underwater explosion. Two minutes later a gigantic air bubble, filled with oil and the debris of wooden decking, came to the surface where the last depth-charge pattern had been dropped. Eager now for the kill, the captain turned the ship toward the oil slick and debris and ordered a fourth depth-charge attack dropped on the area, another eleven-charge pattern with a two-hundred-foot setting.

After this attack the captain slowed the *Cotten* to resume a careful sound search, maneuvering in a circle around the point where the debris had surfaced. A radio report of the action was made to the task group commander in the *Nassau*, who ordered us to continue the search. The *Cotten* secured from general quarters, set the regular watch, and instituted the search plan required by doctrine. It consisted of searching along a continuously enlarging circle, the radius of which is the submarine's assumed escape speed multiplied by the time elapsed since the last contact. This tactic assumes that the submarine had not been sunk, which was contrary to the view held by the officers and men of the *Cotten*. The fruitless search for the submarine continued until 0800 of the next day, November 25, when the *Cotten* was ordered to rejoin the task group.

While the *Cotten* had been searching for the submarine, the two task units of Escort Carrier Task Group 53.6 had reconsolidated, so that when we rejoined there were now four escort carriers, an oiler, and five destroyers,

Cotten included. During the day, the destroyers were refueled and reprovisioned at sea from the oiler, after which planes were sent off from the carriers to land on the Tarawa airstrip. Tarawa was now officially designated an advance air base, and its expansion and improvement by construction units were given a top priority.

Task Group 53.6 remained in the vicinity of Tarawa for the next twelve days, until December 8, providing air cover while the airstrip was being expanded and improved, and support facilities for aircraft were constructed and supplied. During this period the *Cotten* continued to screen the carriers, a duty with which the junior officers of the watch were becoming more familiar day by day.

On November 28, at 0855, Stokey and I again on watch, another sound contact was reported by the sonar crew, at a range of twenty-five hundred yards on our port beam. This time Captain Sloat ordered the crew to general quarters instantly, reported the contact to the task group commander, and taking the conn, increased speed to twenty knots while heading for the contact for an immediate attack. At 0858 contact was lost at a range of 150 yards; at 0859 an eleven-depth-charge pattern was dropped with a shallow setting.

The captain slowed the ship and circled; contact was regained at 0902 at a range of two hundred yards. The task group commander had ordered the destroyer *Monaghan* to join the *Cotten* to take over the attack, as we had by now dropped all of our depth charges except enough for one full pattern. The *Monaghan* made sound contact at 0909 and made a full depth-charge attack, after which the *Cotten* was ordered back to its screening station, leaving the sub to the *Monaghan*.

On the following day, one of the crew, a seaman named Zimmer, came down with severe appendicitis. The *Cotten* was released from the screen for two hours so that it could slow down and take a heading for minimum roll and pitch while Dr. Howard Spindler successfully performed the operation on the wardroom table. As soon as Zimmer had been sewn back up, the *Cotten* rejoined the task group.

On November 30, while fueling and taking aboard some dried provisions from the oiler *Sangamon*, the *Cotten* received eleven replacement depth charges, thereby doubling its antisubmarine ordnance.

On December 3, the destroyer *Caperton*, our sister ship and the second unit of Destroyer Squadron (DesRon) 50 to join the Fifth Fleet, reported for duty. Five days later, the *Cotten* was detached from the task group and directed, along with the *Caperton*, to report to the senior officer present at Tarawa and form an antisubmarine patrol outside the lagoon entrance. With the exception of the *Cotten, Caperton,* and a few destroyer escorts (DEs) and other destroyers, the Fifth Fleet now departed from the Gilberts, signifying the completion of Operation Galvanic.

Galvanic had again demonstrated how formidable Japanese troops could be. When in well-designed, dug-in fortifications, they could only be overcome by faultless planning, overwhelming and persistent firepower, and in the end, the heroic determination of the United States Marines. In the case of Tarawa, the first two of these requirements had been flawed, so that the marines had had to pay a fearful price to secure the objective.

5

Independent Duties in the Gilbert and Ellice Islands

The *Cotten* arrived at Tarawa during the early morning of December 8 and started patrolling outside the lagoon entrance, along with the destroyers *Caperton, Black, Franks,* and *Walker* and three destroyer escorts, *W. C. Miller, LeHardy,* and *Whitman*. Inside the lagoon, supply ships, oilers, and landing craft were moored, supporting what was now intense construction activity in connection with the airstrip.

The screening destroyers and destroyer escorts were the only combat ships remaining in the Gilbert Islands, which were some six hundred miles southeast of the nearest Japanese advance base, on Eniwetok Atoll in the Marshall Islands. It was believed that while the landings had been under way in the Gilberts, the Fifth Fleet Fast Carrier Task Force had taken out the offensive capabilities located on Eniwetok and the other islands of the Marshalls occupied by the enemy. On the other hand, the Japanese were fully capable of sending in reinforcements by air and submarine, so some air surveillance was expected from those islands.

This being the situation, it did not come as a surprise when at twilight of the first day of our stay at Tarawa, a Japanese patrol plane from the Marshall Islands flew leisurely circles some fifteen thousand feet above the Tarawa lagoon, checking out the construction activities and our shipping, and sending everyone on the ships below to general quarters. The snooper was too high for our 5-inch guns, and there were no night fighters yet on Tarawa, so the effect of the event was nil from our point of view. This visitation from the Marshalls became a routine, nightly event.

By the next morning, the recent change in our circumstances had begun to sink in. The *Cotten*'s involvement in Operation Galvanic had made the ship a part of a very large entity, one that had a well-defined objective. Although Captain Sloat remained the personification of naval authority as far as the personnel of the *Cotten* were concerned, it had been readily apparent that both he and the ship itself were but small cogs in the organization of the fleet, and specifically in the task group and units with which we were operating. As a result our attentions had been directed toward the guide at the hub of the task unit, to the flight schedules of the carriers, to the continuous "pinging" of our sonar gear, and, when we were peripherally privy to them, to the trials and agonies of the assault forces. This had been a more stimulating psychological environment for the crew than the ship alone had provided during the shakedown period and the independent cruise from New York to Pearl Harbor.

Once committed to patrol duty outside the Tarawa lagoon, however, we were no longer part of a large fleet with an objective, and our horizon seemed to revert to the confines of life aboard our individual destroyer. We remained continuously under way, standing regular Condition III watches, with one-third of the armament manned and ready twenty-four hours a day, seven days a week. There were morning and evening calls to battle stations, but there was no enemy to shoot at except for the nightly snoopers from the Marshall Islands, who were still flying above our effective range of fire. There was enough to eat, though the food was either canned or dehydrated, as it had been since we were but two weeks out of Pearl Harbor. In addition to regular watches to stand, there was divisional work to do, including professional on-board courses for the junior officers, division supervision, and instruction of petty officers in courses necessary for their advancement in rating.

On a personal basis, letter writing was a ritual to which the men gave universal devotion. Letters home had to be censored; any mention of the *Cotten*'s activities had to be excised from the text by the junior officers, of whom I was still the most junior. The letters were therefore either romantically slanted or carefully "coded" in an effort to sneak some war-zone background past our scrutiny. There was time for the officers to socialize, which largely meant playing acey-deucey in the wardroom during daytime free periods or playing poker in the evening, a pastime that the captain, the chief engineer, Roy Blackburn, and the communications officer, Herb Kanter, relished.

I had allotted all but thirteen dollars per month over the monthly mess bill to be automatically sent to my parents, so I entered the poker games once a week with a working capital of three dollars. By folding on every weak hand and staying in the game only on those that contained at least two pairs, I usually managed to keep my stake intact for about an hour and a half, when it was time for the "sack" in any event.

On one memorable hand, only two players (of whom I was one) folded after the opening, and five players stayed in. Four players drew one card each; the fifth drew two cards. Bob Drake, assistant engineering officer, drew one card, having held four aces at the start of the hand. Captain Sloat held two kings and two fours, drawing the third king for a very respectable full house. The chief engineer filled out a flush, and the heavy betting by these three drove out the others. When the hand ended with a substantial pot, Drake was momentarily the happiest man aboard, oblivious to the look on the "Old Man's" face. As I excused myself from the table, I made a mental note to be very unobtrusive in the captain's presence for the next twenty-four hours.

There were no apparent wardroom rivalries on the *Cotten*, only a hierarchy dependent on rank, date of rank, and assignment in the ship's organization. Because advancement in rank was controlled by the Navy Department in Washington, one was resigned to receiving promotion only with the passage of time. As far as the ship's organization was concerned, my personal goal had crystallized: I was determined to become one of the four officers of the deck under way. You could only become qualified as an OOD by the captain, after he had observed your conduct as a junior officer of the watch over the months. Only the top four so qualified, in the captain's and exec's judgment, were given the responsibility of actually standing the regular watches when at sea. Ever since the ship's commissioning, the four watch officers of the *Cotten* had been my boss Gus Smythe, Had Griffin, the gunnery officer, Alex Early, the sonar officer, and Roger Stokey, who was Griffin's top assistant. I was still far enough away from deserving qualification, even in my own estimation, that serious effort, over several months, was required to gain ground toward my goal. My spirits benefited from this strong desire to improve my watch-standing skills and with them my self-esteem, especially as it seemed that success was far from assured.

The *Cotten* received a break from the monotonous patrol when on December 11 it was ordered to sail alone to Funafuti in the Ellice Islands, some 750 miles south-southeast of Tarawa, for fuel and provisions. The trip took two and a half days, at the end of which we made our way into Funafuti Lagoon and moored alongside the commercial tanker SS *Esso Annapolis*.

In addition to taking aboard enough fuel to top off the tanks, we received a full reprovisioning of food, including frozen meat from Australia. This operation took over three hours, with all hands employed in "striking down" the provisions into the storerooms. This procedure always entailed the loss of some stores, the most noticeable disappearance being grapefruit. Their skins were vital in the process of filtering enough of the poisons from torpedo alcohol (used for fuel) to make it potable for certain chief petty officers whose stomachs were strong enough to cope with the remaining toxins. When the fueling and reprovisioning had been completed, the *Cotten* moved to an independent berth and anchored.

Funafuti is composed of a circle approximately five miles in diameter of small, low-lying coral islands, islets, and reefs. The entrance to the lagoon is very restricted and tricky, which made it an anchorage safe from penetration by enemy submarines. It was not likely they would make the attempt, as they could not get through either submerged by day or on the surface in the dark without running onto a reef. Because the height of the islands above sea level is minimal, from the deck of the *Cotten* you might think you were anchored in the middle of the Pacific Ocean, when in fact you were inside the lagoon.

During the morning of the next day, Griffin, Stokey, and I took the opportunity to go ashore in the small boat provided for the captain, known as the gig. The wardroom encyclopedia advised that the natives in the Ellice Island chain were almost pureblooded Polynesians and that the islands themselves were completely made of coral, the major vegetation being coconut trees. It sounded inviting.

It was a long, wet, three-mile trip in the gig before we were let off at a concrete jetty. We were free to walk about for two hours, enough time to cover most of the largest island of the atoll on foot. We learned from a young marine that (a) the natives had all been removed from Funafuti and placed on their own private island to keep their Polynesian blood pure, so no native women were available; and (b) there was no beer or any other alcoholic beverage. Putting the best light on our circumstances, we decided to hike around the island, this being the only activity that was available. Accordingly, we set forth on foot down a coral-surfaced road toward the air base, some half a mile from the jetty.

The airstrip was surfaced with tightly compressed coral. It was about a mile long and five hundred yards wide. The aircraft in view consisted of some thirty air force B-25 medium bombers, with a lesser number of marine F4U Corsairs, the standard marine fighter, all tied down in individual revetments. The bombers had been occupied in attacking the Gilbert Islands prior to Operation Galvanic, presumably to prevent an even larger enemy buildup than had existed. While the three of us were standing and looking, four Corsairs took off. They had a struggle to get airborne, coming down the runway at one hundred knots, shuddering and shaking until they managed to take off. We supposed that their ordnance load, plus additional fuel tanks under the wings, added up to the maximum weight allowable. This takeoff routine constituting the sole tourist entertainment, we continued down the road for a bit, coming to the inevitable conclusion that there was nothing else to look at.

This hike was the entirety of our visit to Funafuti Atoll. From a distance it looks charming—glimmering white beaches with waving palms above. Far from being sand beaches, however, seen from close aboard they revealed themselves to be lethal piles of coral blocks, and the palm trees were but poor relations of the magnificent royal palms lining the Walkers' driveway in Honolulu. We returned in the gig across the three miles of lagoon to the *Cotten*'s anchorage, satisfied that we had savored the full measure of the available possibilities ashore. Two days later we headed back for Tarawa, arriving there on the afternoon of December 19 to resume the somnambulant patrol outside the lagoon.

On December 22, a New Zealand harbor pilot came aboard to conn the *Cotten* into Tarawa Lagoon for our first visit to Betio Island. Because the lagoon had been incorrectly charted, during the early stages of the battle ashore the destroyer *Hoel* had slammed into a coral reef while providing direct fire support for the marines. As a result no naval vessel made its first venture into the lagoon thereafter without the services of the pilot, Lieutenant Page, Royal New Zealand Naval Reserve (RNZNR), a grizzled old-timer who could read the tints of a coral bottom like an open book. We moored alongside the merchant vessel SS *Carey*, topped off our fuel tanks, and took aboard a Japanese aerial torpedo that had been retrieved intact from the airstrip. We were then given orders to deliver the torpedo to the Pearl Harbor Navy Yard, an assignment that was enthusiastically received by all hands.

Because the *Carey*'s oil flowed like molasses, there was time for several of us to visit the Tarawa beachhead, which had theoretically been secured some four weeks previously. The battleground was still in complete disarray. There was live ammunition of all calibers, both American and Japanese, lying about in profusion. There were boxes and crates strewn amongst the ordnance, with descriptive markings in two languages and alphabets.

Last but most definitely not least were the rotting remains of some of the combatants; most of the corpses had no skin left and were crawling with blue-faced flies and gray maggots. Acting like scavengers ourselves, we picked up a few samples of ordnance memorabilia and returned silently to the ship.

The memory of the voices from the landing craft stuck on the reefs, desperately calling for assistance, was given another dimension by the sight of the battleground, even a month after the fact. The marines in the waves after the amtracs, for managing to reach the beach at all through the hail of steel thrown at them, deserved our lifelong gratitude and admiration. The next day we left the lagoon, this time Mr. Wesson piloting us through the lagoon and the reef (without a scratch), and returned to the antisubmarine patrol outside.

On Christmas Day, the officers and the entire crew put on dress white uniforms for a noontime Christmas feast that included roast turkey, cranberry sauce, and pumpkin pie, furnished courtesy of Admiral Nimitz and delivered to us via the SS *Carey*. The wardroom tablecloth was clean, as were the officers' napkins, even though this had required an extra laundry day. None of the officers had worn their whites since the liberty in Panama City, the recollections of which added a festive dimension to what was otherwise a thoughtful and dignified dinner.

After five more days on patrol, we were back inside the Tarawa lagoon, this time to pick up eighteen passengers for Pearl Harbor and to receive a final infusion of fuel oil for the trip back. We received our sailing directions and got under way, steaming first to Apamama Atoll. There we met SS *Rutilicus*, which we were to screen for two days of the trip back to Pearl Harbor.

The voyage to Pearl Harbor lasted one week and was uneventful, with one major exception. During this passage I, along with Herb Kanter, Wayne Dorman, Spencer Beresford, and Walter Walborn, took turns standing our first independent officer of the deck watches, patrolling back and forth across the bows of *Rutilicus* as an antisubmarine screen. For me, this compensated for the month spent steaming back and forth across the entrance to Tarawa Lagoon. On January 7, 1944, we arrived at Pearl Harbor and moored in berth C-6, a little after midday.

6

Operation Flintlock

From January 7 until January 16, 1944, the *Cotten* was in Pearl Harbor, except for a two-day training cruise with the newly arrived DesRon 50 destroyers *Knapp* and *Cogswell* and the *Essex*-class fleet carrier *Intrepid*. While we were in port, personnel from the fleet ordnance depot picked up the Japanese aerial torpedo we had brought from Tarawa.

I had two nights ashore, the first of which I spent at the Moana Hotel catching up on some socializing with fellow officers and taking aboard a reasonable amount of scotch whiskey. In the morning I took a bus back to the navy yard and found myself sitting next to an attractive woman who was perhaps in her thirties. Screwing up my courage, I engaged her in conversation. She had been born in Korea, a Japanese colony, and had emigrated to Honolulu prior to the war to seek employment, if not her fortune. She now worked in the navy yard and had a small apartment in Honolulu, all of which I learned on the bus ride. Her English was understandable although accented. Before the bus got to the navy yard gates, I asked her for a date for supper two nights hence, on the next liberty for my section. She said that would be fine, and we agreed to meet at the gate at six o'clock, when she would be finished with her work. This would be the first date for me since leaving New York some three months earlier.

Two days later at the appointed hour and place we met and got into the first available taxi. My plan was to head for the Moana to engage a room for the night and have a few encouraging get-to-know-each-other drinks, but she demurred and directed the taxi driver to another address, which turned out to be her apartment house. She then told me that she had made reservations at a nearby oriental restaurant for supper and that I would spend the night with her in her apartment, provided I would promise not to press her for sexual favors, as she was married—a fact not previously discussed. Her husband was away in the army; she told me with firmness that she fully intended to be faithful to him. This was quite a lot for a twenty-one-year-old to absorb, but I accepted her conditions, my desire for feminine companionship being at such an elevated state that I would have agreed to anything to let the adventure proceed.

The evening unfolded as the lady had planned, and I enjoyed every minute of it. When supper was over we returned to her apartment, conversed amiably on small subjects, and in due course retired, sleeping together in a double bed that belonged in part to someone other than myself. I did not press her, as promised, and to my chagrin she did not change her mind. Except for this lack of physical fulfillment, the pleasant evening and feminine companionship were just what I needed; the two of us returned to the navy yard in the morning and parted as good friends. This was my last liberty before the ship was to leave, and I never saw or communicated with her again.

I did not expound upon this adventure in the wardroom. While in theory allusion to affairs with women was one of the areas forbidden to naval officers in their wardroom society, this prohibition was occasionally breached, which was hardly a surprise. However, my very junior status and the unusual nature of the adventure seemed to rule out any reference to the last night ashore. I took some solace in the fact that it was reasonably certain no one else had even been able to get a date during this short layover in Honolulu.

While we were in port, rumors were circulating that a new operation was being planned for the Central Pacific. It seemed that the Pacific Fleet had been built up by the arrival of newly constructed warships like the *Cotten* to the point that it would be able to meet the Japanese fleet with a decisive superiority. The top naval leaders planned to apply this new naval superiority against enemy advance bases that were not only far apart but also far from the major bases of the enemy fleet. An amphibious offensive in the Central Pacific would also be the direct route westward to the Ryukyu Islands and Formosa, seizing which would separate Japan from its sources of natural resources and render it helpless.

With this background in mind, it did not come as a surprise when in the late afternoon of January 15, 1944, guard mail was delivered to the

Cotten from Admiral Nimitz, following the receipt of which the entire complement of officers and men was restricted aboard ship. As had been the case with Operation Galvanic, the officers who stood bridge, CIC, and main battery director watches convened in the wardroom. There Mr. Wesson conducted a briefing on two new operation orders, one from Admiral Spruance, the Fifth Fleet commander, and the second from Rear Adm. Marc Mitscher, the commander of Task Force 58, which was the Fast Carrier Task Force and the major strike force of the Pacific Fleet. These orders defined the next objective of the Fifth Fleet, established the fleet organization of task forces and task groups, and set the timetable for the operation, which was to consist of three separate landings.

Operation Flintlock called for landings on Majuro and Kwajalein in the Marshall Islands. Majuro was undefended and lay 450 miles north-northwest of Tarawa; heavily defended Kwajalein was 350 miles northwest of Majuro. After these two atolls were secured, landings would be undertaken on Eniwetok Atoll, also believed to be heavily defended. It lay 720 miles northwest of Majuro and 560 miles northwest of Kwajalein. Admiral Spruance pointed out that Truk Atoll was six hundred miles southwest of Kwajalein and that a substantial number of Japanese warships were known to be based there. He also estimated that strong enemy air groups could be deployed to the Marshalls from Truk via the Mariana Islands, the latter being the major Japanese island defense position south of the home islands.

The Fast Carrier Task Force, or TF 58, was composed of the veteran fleet carrier *Enterprise*, four new *Essex*-class fleet carriers, six new *Independence*-class light carriers (built on heavy cruiser hulls), eight new fast battleships (including the latest super-battleships, the *Iowa* and *New Jersey*), six new cruisers, and four squadrons of new *Fletcher*-class destroyers (including our own Destroyer Squadron 50, all nine ships of which had finally arrived at Pearl Harbor). Admiral Mitscher had organized these ships into three equal task groups, designated TG 58.1, TG 58.2, and TG 58.3. The *Cotten* and DesRon 50 were assigned to Task Group 58.1, which was built around the fleet carriers *Enterprise* and *Yorktown* (Admiral Mitscher's flagship), light carriers *Cowpens* and *Belleau Wood*, and cruisers *Wichita* and *Oakland*. The commander of Task Group 58.1 was Rear Adm. John W. Reeves, in his flagship *Enterprise*.

The Fifth Fleet amphibious forces were commanded by Vice Admiral Turner and were completely separate from Task Force 58. They consisted of the attack transports, escort carriers (built on oiler hulls) for direct air support, older combatants for shore bombardment of the landing areas, logistical shipping, and a large number of screening destroyers and destroyer escorts.

The dangerous period for Flintlock would be from D day until the beach-heads had been secured and sufficient supplies and equipment landed so that the troops could survive independently from their shipping. The major threat to the success of the operation would be a full-scale intervention by the Japanese navy, assessed by Admiral Spruance to be possible, if unlikely. Task Force 58 was to keep the landing forces and their supporting vessels fully protected from this potential danger. To do this, Task Force 58 was to conduct wide-ranging sweeps, in order to destroy enemy aircraft based in the Marshalls, eastern Carolines, and the Marianas. Once that had been accomplished, the task force would remain on hand until all enemy land forces had been destroyed on the three islands on which our marines were to land and the new airstrips were functional.

For six months following the attack on Pearl Harbor, the Japanese navy had enjoyed sufficient superiority to be able to maneuver wherever it chose in the western Pacific, but its fast carrier strike force had been required to provide direct air support for the amphibious operations of the Japanese army. In addition, this strike force had had the strategic responsibility of defending the landing forces against intervention by the U.S. carrier forces. It was this double requirement that had ultimately led to the loss of four of its fleet carriers in the Battle of Midway: the air groups of three American carriers had struck the Japanese carrier force while it was attacking the ground-based facilities on Midway Island.

The organization of the Fifth Fleet for Operation Flintlock, in contrast to the Japanese fleet's organization during the first half of 1942, gave the responsibility for direct air support to the escort carriers attached to the landing forces under Admiral Turner. This freed the commander of Task Force 58 to maneuver wherever he could best defend the operation against enemy forces, whether those located in nearby advance island bases or those deployed from outside the immediate tactical area.

The final elements of the organization of the Fifth Fleet for this operation were the support forces, oilers with their destroyer screens, formed into task groups that were scheduled to meet Task Force 58 in the advance operating areas. These support forces allowed the task force to remain at sea for weeks at a time.

The section of Spruance's operation order on hydrographic data contained references to accurate Japanese charts and tide tables of the Marshall Islands that had been obtained on Tarawa. These would eliminate the possibility of the landing craft going aground before reaching the designated landing areas.

The schedule on prelanding bombardment called for several times the duration and weight of shelling that had been allotted to Betio Island. In addition to the longer bombardment period, reduced charges for the 15-inch guns had been provided to the battleships, which would enable them to fire with a slower-velocity, arched trajectory, as opposed to the usual flat trajectory, thereby ensuring a higher percentage of hits on the low targets of the landing areas.

After going through the details of the operation orders, it seemed to us that the invasion of the Marshall Islands was more carefully organized than the Gilberts operation. We were exhilarated by the *Cotten's* assignment to Task Force 58, which was inescapably the navy's first team. The potential for keeping Task Force 58 at sea in the combat area on a permanent basis was not yet fully comprehended, but it was apparent that a mobile, floating air base that could launch upward of seven hundred combat aircraft would be sufficiently powerful to control the air and the sea below, wherever it presented itself. We knew enough about the theory of sea power to believe that if control of the sea were ours, in time the United States was certain to defeat Japan.

At the time, despite this confidence in ultimate victory, it did not seem possible that the war could be concluded without many more Tarawas. It was not in the nature of the Japanese to surrender or be faint of heart. That in itself made it impossible to believe that the end of the war was anywhere near, with the Japanese fleet still in being and the Japanese homeland as little affected as it was.

On the morning of January 16, the *Cotten* sortied from Pearl Harbor with the heavy cruiser *Wichita*. As soon as all the ships of TG 58.1 had put to sea, the task group formed up in the circular disposition called "5-R." This was the normal cruising formation for fast carrier task groups; the destroyers were equally spaced in a circular screen, the radius of which was six thousand yards, and the four carriers and two cruisers were stationed in the formation's center, within a radius of twenty-five hundred yards. In this formation the task group could change course and speed as a unit without any ship having to change relative position. In this way a task group of Task Force 58 could be maneuvered as an operating entity, exactly as if it were a single ship instead of fifteen or twenty ships.

Task Group 58.1 set course for the Marshall Islands area, zigzagging according to plan, on a base course of 225° true (southwest) and at a speed of sixteen knots. During each day there were fleet exercises, usually consisting of shifting the task group into formation "5-V," which was the special disposition for defending against air attack. In 5-V all ships were stationed more closely together, the destroyers on a circle with a radius of three thousand yards, the heavy ships proportionately closer to the center. When in formation 5-V, the group was maneuvered on an "emergency" basis. The flagship would send a voice command by TBS in the form: "This is [code name of Commander Task Group 58.1]. All ships emergency turn to course [code group for, say, 320 degrees]." At the instant this command was given, all ships were immediately to turn to the new course.

If the word "emergency" was not used, any TBS-transmitted course or speed change was a three-stage affair. First the command was given, qualified by the words "Stand by to execute" followed by a request that certain ships acknowledge receipt. The second step was the acknowledgment by the ship identified in the command, with the words, "This is [code name for, say, *Cotten*]. Roger, over." In the final step the task group commander repeated the command, concluding with the word "Execute"; the order was then put into effect simultaneously by the entire formation.

Because emergency-turn maneuvering required that the watch officers on all ships be familiar with and have complete confidence in the procedure, there were exercises on a regular basis when in formation 5-V. The purpose of emergency signals was to maneuver the task group rapidly as a unit when under actual air attack. At this time the standard attack by the Japanese air forces based on island airstrips was delivered by long-range, two-engine torpedo bombers called "Bettys," typically during late evening twilight. The Bettys would approach low over the water from a position ahead of the ships in order to penetrate the destroyer screen and launch their torpedoes against the carriers in the center from less than a mile away. The task group commander, on the contrary, wanted to keep the Bettys astern of the task group, so that the ships' gunners would have a longer period for antiaircraft fire and the torpedoes would have to catch up with their targets instead of coming in on opposing courses at very high relative speeds. The emergency-turn technique was specifically designed for this kind of situation.

On January 25, TG 58.1 was joined by the battleships *Washington, Indiana,* and *Massachusetts* and the prewar heavy cruisers *Pensacola* and *Salt Lake City.* These ships provided a powerful gunfire capability to the now concentrated nucleus of the formation.

The operation orders for Flintlock called for the marines to be landed on Majuro Atoll on January 31, the assumption being that this atoll was not occupied by the Japanese. The landings on the north end of Kwajalein were also scheduled for January 31; on the south islands of the latter atoll, the landing date was February 1. It was estimated that between eight and nine thousand Japanese troops, or twice the number that had so tenaciously defended Betio Island, were dug in on Kwajalein.

With all three task groups operating in tactical concentration, Task Force 58 approached the Marshall Islands in a roundabout route, first going south of the Gilbert Islands then heading north toward the Marshalls, arriving in the general area by January 28, three days before D day.

On January 29 at early twilight, a small group of twin-engine bombers heading directly for the task group was sighted by the light carrier *Belleau Wood,* which duly reported, "Bogies [enemy aircraft] coming in from 180 degrees." While the button on the radio handset on the bridge of the *Belleau Wood* was depressed, that ship's bugler was sounding the call to battle stations; its stirring strains were heard on the bridges and in the CICs of all ships in the task group. This was the only time I ever heard general quarters announced by anything other than the *Cotten's* electrically powered general alarm, and it was memorable. Everyone in the task group was immediately called to battle stations, and as soon as the twin-engine planes were sighted, the ships in range opened fire. Two of the fighter planes of the task group's combat air patrol also joined in, diving on the bombers with their .50-caliber machine guns blazing away. Two of the bombers were shot down at once, and the others turned away in a hurry. At this juncture, U.S. stars were seen on their wings, and the flagship called out, "All ships, cease firing. Cease firing. Planes are friendly."

This was a very unhappy moment, reminding us that deadly mistakes of the most unlikely nature seem to occur despite the best-laid plans. It turned out that the planes were air force bombers flying back to their base in the Gilbert Islands. Excited at seeing Task Group 58.1, they had come down to give us a friendly buzz. This particular type of interservice camaraderie was thereafter forbidden.

The air force bombers were the same type we had seen in Funafuti; other than having two engines mounted under the wings, they did not look enough like a Japanese Betty to be taken for one. However, the two-engine bomber was not a type used by carrier forces; green crews could be expected to open fire on unusual aircraft in an enemy area, which rendered the incident less culpable, if nonetheless tragic.

During the daylight hours of January 29, 30, and 31, the air groups of Task Force 58 kept an umbrella over the Marshall Islands. All enemy shipping was sunk and all aircraft destroyed, either on the ground or in the air. Because of the separation, both as to command and to distance, between Task Force 58 and the amphibious forces, we could not monitor directly anything of what was transpiring with the marines who had hit their beaches on January 31. We did learn that there was indeed no enemy presence on Majuro; that lagoon immediately became available to the Fifth Fleet as an advance anchorage. The operation plan called for a buildup of facilities to transform Majuro into an advance naval base and airstrip as well, and work to accomplish this was already under way by February 1.

In the nighttime hours of January 31–February 1, there was a scheduled trial fueling of the screen destroyers from the battleships *Massachusetts,*

Washington, and *Indiana.* Because the fueling of destroyers, undertaken at least every other day throughout a combat cruise, took a minimum of two hours, Admiral Mitscher had directed Admiral Reeves and the battleships of TG 58.1 to try a night refueling, which would free the ships of the need for a refueling in daylight for the next two days.

Accordingly, at midnight of February 1, the destroyer *Knapp* started fueling from *Massachusetts, Cogswell* from *Indiana,* and *Dortch* from *Washington.* Two hours later the fueling ceased. At 0355 our task group executed an emergency turn to maneuver clear of a nearby task group of the amphibious forces, TG 52.9. During this turn, improperly executed by either *Washington* or *Indiana* or both, *Washington* rammed into *Indiana's* starboard quarter. Both battleships were forced to slow to six knots, reporting to the task group commander that they were "in difficulty." *Cotten* and *Healy* were then directed to leave the task group to join *Washington* and form an antisubmarine screen on either bow of the "battlewagon." At 0700 *Washington* and *Indiana,* now screened by *Cotten, Healy, Gatling,* and *Caperton* of DesRon 50, formed in column, keeping a generous two-thousand-yard distance.

That afternoon, funeral services were conducted aboard *Indiana,* and colors were half-masted by all ships in our formation in deference to the ceremony. At 1702 the same ceremony, with the same honors, was conducted aboard *Washington.* It was assumed that in both cases the deaths had been a result of the previous night's collision.

The fact that there had been two fatal mistakes in our task group so soon after its creation was indication that there was still a lot to learn, presumably by experience. In this instance, the use of an emergency turn merely to move the task group away from a friendly formation had hardly been consistent with the original concept of the maneuver. If there had been some hesitance on the part of the OOD of the *Washington* because of this, the accident was partially the responsibility of the task group commander's staff officer who had transmitted the order.

During the rest of the day, all four destroyers fueled from the two stricken giants en route to Majuro Atoll. In the late afternoon of February 2, the formation entered the beautiful lagoon of Majuro, the *Cotten* anchoring at dusk.

On February 4, the main body of TG 58.1 entered the lagoon and anchored, and on the next day the other two groups of TF 58 followed suit, bringing the warship population of Majuro Lagoon to a total of five fleet carriers, six light carriers, eight battleships (including the two damaged ones), eight cruisers, and forty destroyers, as well as fleet oilers, minesweepers, destroyer escorts, and numerous auxiliaries. On February 6, Rear

Adm. Willis A. Lee, who was Commander Battleships, Pacific Fleet, transferred his flag from *Washington* to *North Carolina,* in order to have a sound vessel under him.

Task Force 58 remained in the Majuro lagoon until February 12, when all three task groups made their exits for the open ocean. On the previous day, new Fifth Fleet and Task Force 58 operation orders had been distributed to all ships, calling for air raids and surface force sweeps of the eastern Carolines, specifically the major Japanese fleet's advance anchorage in the Truk lagoon, where a number of heavy naval units were believed to be based. Thence Task Force 58 was to head northwesterly to attack the Japanese air bases on Saipan, Guam, and Tinian in the Marianas. This wide-ranging series of attacks was to be conducted while the second stage of the landings in the Marshalls was under way. This was the landing by the marines on the most westerly of the Marshall chain, Eniwetok, scheduled for February 17.

Because the U.S. Pacific Fleet had long believed the Japanese naval base at Truk to be a potent stronghold, the coming operation seemed to be a direct challenge to the enemy. Admiral Spruance was of the opinion that Task Force 58 could expect strong resistance from Japanese air groups both in the vicinity of Truk and, especially, during the sweep through the Marianas. Putting behind us the recent mistakes that had been made, we headed out to sea with expectations of some action.

Our task group (58.1) now contained Cruiser Division 13, consisting of *Santa Fe*, *Biloxi*, and *Mobile*; these ships replaced the missing *Washington* and *Indiana*, now en route to Pearl Harbor for repairs. The balance of the units were the same as before, centering around fleet carriers *Enterprise*, with Admiral Reeves aboard in command of the task group, and the new *Yorktown*, with Admiral Mitscher aboard, commanding Task Force 58 in its entirety.

The voyage to Truk was circuitous, taking some three and a half days. The course was deceptive, in that we headed directly toward the Marianas until the last day, when we turned to make the run south to Truk, hoping to achieve surprise. At dawn on February 16, Task Force 58 launched air strikes against the airfields and anchorage of the Truk naval base. As soon as the planes arrived at the target, the air group commander reported to the *Yorktown* that the heavy units of the Japanese navy were not in the harbor; the only ships present were one cruiser, several destroyers, and cargo ships.

The air groups bombed and strafed the ships and shore facilities throughout the day. Admiral Spruance, aboard the *New Jersey,* detached his flagship and its sister ship *Iowa* from TG 58.3 at noon to circle Truk at high speed (these two battleships could reach an incredible thirty-two knots) and sink any ships that had left the harbor before the air groups arrived.

They were successful in this venture, sinking a cruiser and destroyer in the high-speed sweep.

At 2000 of the same day, in twilight, our task group was attacked by several low-flying Bettys. Gunfire from the screening ships was heavy enough to turn back the attack, and no damage was done. The only Japanese airfield close enough to have launched the aircraft for this attack was at Ponape; it was heavily counterattacked by our air groups the next morning in a predawn launch. On February 18, Task Force 58, now consisting of our task group and TG 58.3 (TG 58.2 having retired to Majuro), met the fueling group in the afternoon.

At this time we heard a persistent clanging along the starboard quarter of the *Cotten*. The sound was determined to be coming from the after fifty feet of the bilge keel, which had somehow come loose from the ship's bottom. Bilge keels are strips of steel running fore and aft on both sides of the hull, some fifteen feet on either side of the true keel. Their purpose is to dampen the roll of the ship when under way, excessive roll being a distinct handicap in "laying" (aiming) the guns in combat. It is obvious that it is hard enough for a gun or director to track a fast-flying aircraft from a stable platform, let alone from one whose plane constantly shifts. The loose section remained attached to the forward 150 feet of keel, which was securely fastened to the hull; as a result the loose end was acting like a steel whip, whacking the hull every minute or so, making a terrible noise. This situation was reported to our squadron commander, who was also serving as the screen commander.

During the morning watch of February 19, some fifty miles from Eniwetok, where the second stage of the amphibious operations was under way, the formation was again ineffectively attacked by long-range torpedo bombers. Considering that all of their air bases within hundreds of miles had been thoroughly bombed and strafed within the past three days, it was somewhat surprising that the Japanese had been able to stage an attack so quickly. However, the attacking planes were so reduced in number that they did not constitute an effective force.

At 1600 on the same afternoon, when the replenishment ships separated from the task group, *Cotten* was ordered to join them to return to Majuro for repairs to our bilge keel. Our task group then turned westward for the Marianas to attack the airfields and installations on Guam, Saipan, and Tinian. We were disappointed not to be with them as we retired to Majuro with the oilers.

Two days later the *Cotten* entered beautiful Majuro Lagoon again and moored alongside the destroyer *Charrette*. Next day we reanchored in a berth adjacent to the destroyer tender USS *Prairie*, which contained within its hull practically all of the facilities of a navy yard, at least with respect to the needs of a destroyer. Because there was no floating dry dock as yet in Majuro, it was up to divers from the *Prairie* to investigate the bilge keel and the hull where it had been banging away. By 1130 of February 23, the divers had removed the loose fifty feet of bilge keel. Their inspection of the hull and the remaining 150 feet of keel found both to be undamaged and in no need of repair. It was decided that the loss of only fifty feet of one bilge keel would not materially affect the *Cotten's* sea-keeping or antiaircraft capabilities, so the ship was returned to full operational status.

When Task Force 58 returned from the raid on the Marianas, it remained in the Majuro lagoon for a full two weeks for maintenance and supplies, interrupted by a one-day practice cruise, primarily for the benefit of new air groups on several of the carriers.

On February 27, Lt. Cdr. Joe Wesson, the *Cotten's* executive officer since precommissioning days, received orders to transfer to the destroyer *Hickox* (DD 673), where he became the commanding officer. At the same time Gus Smythe, the first lieutenant, was appointed executive officer. Because I was Smythe's assistant, the thought occurred to me that I might become the first lieutenant as his successor. He and the captain, however, knew I was too young and inexperienced for the responsibility, with which opinion I came to agree after a few days of disappointment.

There was no other officer aboard the ship, however, who had experience with the ship's deck force, hull maintenance, seamanship, and damage control. The job of first lieutenant was given to Roger Stokey, still the senior assistant gunnery officer, more or less as an expedient until an experienced officer could come aboard to fill the position on a permanent basis. While Stokey knew little about the first lieutenant's responsibilities, he was certain to put forth his best effort in what for him was a diversion from his specialty, the 5-inch guns. I continued as the first lieutenant's assistant and the Second Division officer. Herb Kanter, the communications officer, became a regular officer of the deck under way to replace Smythe, who as exec was relieved of the requirement to stand watches.

From March 1 through March 4, the *Cotten* was moored alongside the *Prairie*, receiving power, water, and steam from the tender. This permitted the boiler and engine rooms to be shut down for a number of repairs to the propulsion plant, to bring us back up to full operational capability. After the various repairs had been completed and our supplies replenished, we returned to the destroyer anchorage, remaining there until March 7.

New orders in dispatch form (speed letter 0041 dated March 5, 1944) from the task group commander advised that the task group was to proceed to Espiritu Santo, the northernmost island of the New Hebrides. It would be under the control of Adm. William F. Halsey but would continue to operate as an independent entity, under the tactical command of Admiral Reeves. Our assignment was to provide air support for Gen. Douglas MacArthur's troops, who had just landed on Manus Island in the Admiralties.

7

To Espiritu Santo

At 0600 on March 7, our task group sortied from Majuro and set a course for Espiritu Santo, some 1,460 nautical miles south. The carriers in the task group had been temporarily reduced to two, fleet carrier *Enterprise* and light carrier *Belleau Wood*. Cruiser Division 13, the light cruiser *Oakland*, and our DesRon 50 made up the balance of the formation.

To those who were interested, this cruise to the most southerly latitude reached by the *Cotten* during the war provided an opportunity to see the nighttime southern sky at its clearest. During wartime, vessels at sea at night (except for hospital ships) are always fully darkened. On the bridge, anything that had to be read was illuminated with a low-powered, red-filtered flashlight. Inside all doors through which compartments could be entered from outside, curtains blocked the interior light, so that there was the equivalent of a light chamber between the outside and the inside. Our passageways were illuminated by dim, red night-lights. Those going on watch were careful to expose their eyes only to red light before reporting to the bridge, to ensure that their eyes were fully dilated for night vision.

All of this, coupled with the fact that the nearest land-based source of light was many hundreds of miles away, permitted the stars to be seen as

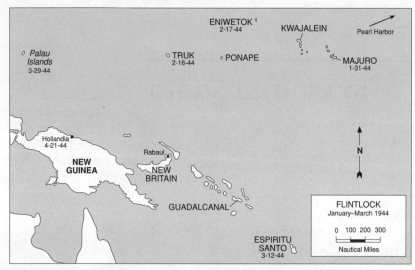

Date and location of each of the islands involved with the operations of Task Force 58 between January 31 and March 29, 1944. (See Appendix C.)

they had been by our pre-electrical forebears. The sky in such circumstances can create a powerful effect, and it becomes clear why the stars and the constellations were such major cultural factors in earlier times. When it comes to viewing the nighttime glories of the heavens, our own generations are, in the main, sadly deprived.

We on the *Cotten* had never been as far south as fifteen degrees south latitude, so our view of the southern constellations had not been complete; many of the stars had still been low on the horizon and dulled by the refractions caused by oceanic humidity. By the time we arrived near Espiritu Santo, however, the southern sky was viewable in its majesty. Compared with the northern sky, the southern sky has many more very bright stars of first or second magnitude, almost the equal of Sirius, the dog star, which can still be seen above the horizon. Stars not seen in the United States but now visible to us included those of the Southern Cross, which, while much smaller than the Big Bear, contains two very bright stars. The constellation is located very close to two more such stars, one of which is our nearest neighbor, Centaurus. Nowhere in the northern sky can one see four first-magnitude stars so close together.

Canopus, another first-magnitude star, is about ninety degrees away from the Southern Cross at the same elevation. Antares is visible in the same sky, as are Arcturus, Achernar, Betelgeuse, and Aldebaran. Betelgeuse and Antares are giant red stars, their color very noticeable in a clear sky. Celestial navigation is much more dependable here, because so many bright stars are easily visible while there is still a distinct horizon, something not accorded to voyagers in the Atlantic at forty degrees north latitude.

On the afternoon of March 12, our task group entered the harbor of Espiritu Santo, a volcanic island seventy-five miles long from north to south and thirty-five miles wide. The north end of the island consists of two long peninsulas that define a shallow, narrow bay, the western arm extending thirty-five miles and the eastern arm extending twenty miles, both directly to the north. The south shore of this bay rises abruptly from the water to the peak of the highest mountain on the island, some six thousand feet above sea level. The first view of Espiritu Santo from the sea is impressive to anyone just arriving from the atolls of the Central Pacific.

The task group anchored in the harbor next to the city of Santo, on the southeast coast of the island. The harbor is fully protected by small islands lying off the coast, which block the prevailing southeasterly trade winds. The harbor itself is deep and commodious. Early the next day the *Cotten* moored to a dock to receive fuel and stores, including fresh provisions.

The navy yard was close to the dock. As he had done each time we went near a naval base, the supply officer, Fred Butler, went to the officer in charge, armed with requisitions. For months, whenever he had submitted the normal requisitions for supplies, stores, and materiel, he had added one for a sixteen-inch bronze porthole for the wardroom. The ventilating system of the wardroom was poor, and during the weeks that we had spent cruising just above and below the equator, we had formed a universal desire, prompted by the captain, to have a porthole installed in the port bulkhead to give us sea breezes. The basic hang-up was that since the 1942–43 surface battles around Guadalcanal, portholes had not been fitted on new destroyers, as in those battles they had tended to send shards of glass flying about whenever a ship was hit. This did not seem to Captain Sloat to be the portholes' fault, however, as they were equipped with a solid bronze cover, or deadlight, that could be dogged securely shut over the glass in about fifteen seconds' time. With the solid hatch closed, the glass would be safely contained even if it completely shattered.

Once again, Butler carried his requisitions, including the one for the porthole, ashore to the supply office of the navy yard. When he returned to the ship some time later, he was accompanied by a sailor from the navy yard carrying a beautiful sixteen-inch, bronze porthole with a solid bronze deadlight. It was brought aboard and deposited in Fred's stateroom, on the deck right beside his bunk. We were all impressed, and Captain Sloat was delighted. He had seldom seemed so happy, even when he had won a superior pot at poker. At supper that night, he told us that destroyers built before the war had been known as "gold platers," for their luxurious details. Included among these luxuries were portholes in the wardroom for ventilation when under way in the tropics, which even made the food taste better. He told us that we would have the porthole installed by the next tender we went alongside, if he had to negotiate the transaction personally. For the interim, he told Butler to keep his treasure safely in his stateroom, which he did, right where it had been deposited by the sailor from the navy yard.

The captain was so elated by Fred's success that he went ashore and called the local naval officers' club. As executive officer of the destroyer *Benham*, he had visited Espiritu Santo several times, using the officers' club enough to have made some friends there among the staff. He talked them into inviting the off-duty officers of the *Cotten* to the party for the local officers being held the next evening; the only stipulation for these weekly affairs was that those attending had to wear dress white uniforms. It was my good luck to be included with the group, as was Fred Butler. At 1730 on the next afternoon, cleaned up in our dress whites and anticipating some fun, the off-duty officers of the *Cotten* boarded the gig and were conveyed across the harbor to the dock of the officers' club, which lay on the harbor.

The clubhouse was not luxurious, but the already assembled officers and navy nurses, the latter being a welcome surprise, were all resplendent in their dress uniforms and seemingly completely at ease with each other's company. The party was in full swing. We of the *Cotten* were equally elegant, but we felt somewhat like trespassers, out of place, and we were far from being at ease. This situation seemed to call for remedial action in the form of an attack on the bar, which proceeded forthwith. About two hours later, it was becoming evident that no matter how much liquor we consumed to enhance our repartee, we were going to get nowhere with the nurses, each of whom seemed to be a good friend of one or another of the shore-based officers. Rather than causing a pause in our drinking, this realization only led to more, this time to compensate for frustration.

Some time later, two of us needed to get rid of some excess bodily liquids and headed out to the garden for the purpose, as the club's facilities were by now crowded to overflowing. Finding a secluded spot behind a large tree, we proceeded to relieve ourselves, feeling that we were carefully shielded from observation. However, unbeknownst to us, a full commander and a pretty young nurse had chosen the other side of the same secluded tree for a romantic interlude.

Taken completely by surprise by the warm stream ricocheting off the tree onto her white shoes, the nurse jumped a foot in the air and let out a screech. The commander was infuriated by the gross interruption and immediately determined to exact revenge. He ordered the two of us to follow him into the clubhouse, hauling us both over to the senior officer present, to whom he reported our behavior in graphic detail. The senior officer was devoid of a sense of humor and, without discussion, expelled the two of us from the party with the added request that we not return to the club in the future. In parting I politely advised the officer who had issued the expulsion that I had been thrown out of much better places than his, adding that this would not have been difficult.

The return to the *Cotten* in the gig was something of a letdown. It was depressing to contemplate our inability to share the society of the females present, especially considering that not all of them were young or attractive. The logical conclusion was that when one had but a single night ashore in a foreign port, female companionship was going to cost money, perhaps more than we were likely to have.

At breakfast the next morning, the partygoers did not have much to say about the previous evening, and those who had stayed on board were not curious, beyond perfunctory questions about the quality of the whiskey. It evidently did not occur to any of the latter that there had been ladies present. Some even thanked the captain for arranging the opportunity, and that ended that . . . except for one small detail.

Descending to our cabins after breakfast, we were greeted by an unmistakable odor of vomit. Each cabin was thoroughly searched without locating anything out of order, but the smell was inescapably present. Several minutes later, Fred Butler went below to his cabin and noticed that the smell was worse there than anywhere else; in fact, it was disgusting. He now began a careful search of his cabin, expecting the worst. After a fruitless initial go-around, he sat disconsolately on his bunk and stared down at the porthole lying on the deck. His face paled as he slowly raised the bronze deadlight; he slammed it shut, too ill to face the evidence.

Later, Fred reconstructed the scene for us. He had gone down to his cabin after the return from the party and had fallen into his bunk. After a moment he had begun to get the spins and then had become violently sick. He had leaned out from his bunk, and seeing a porthole in front of him, had raised the deadlight and retched. He closed it again over his malodorous deposit, and collapsed back into his bunk to sleep for the night. The next morning, he had had no immediate recollection of his return to the ship or his bunk, and later he was as surprised as any of us at the solution of the mystery.

Ultimately the mess was cleaned up and the porthole restored to its pristine condition. Later, when it was finally welded into the port bulkhead of the wardroom, it became a long-lasting tribute to the captain's inspiration and the determination of our supply officer, as well as a reminder of the memorable events that had flowed from the invitation to the dress party at the officers' club in Espiritu Santo.

8

Fifth Fleet Operations in the Southwest Pacific

On March 15, two days after the party at the officers' club, our task group left Espiritu Santo and, once clear of the headland, proceeded on a north-westerly course north of and parallel to the Solomon Islands. This marked the beginning of a series of operations that lasted until May 5, during which Task Force 58 was occupied in the support of MacArthur's forces in the southwest Pacific. These operations consisted of sequential amphibious landings, first on Manus Island, which was six hundred nautical miles west of Bougainville, the furthermost American position in the Solomon Islands, and four hundred miles west of the major Japanese base on Rabaul. The landing on Manus took place on February 29, and the forces were stalled when our task group arrived in the area on March 17. The second landing was scheduled for Hollandia, on the north coast of New Guinea, some five hundred nautical miles farther west from Manus Island. D day for Hollandia was set for April 22, five weeks in the future. The use of Task Force 58 in support of these landings had been decided upon at the level of the Joint Chiefs of Staff, in Washington.

Admiral Nimitz and the navy promoted the Central Pacific invasion route as a naval-controlled operation, with the objective of seizing the Marianas and then Formosa, in order to blockade Japan and prevent any outside supplies or raw materials from reaching the home islands. The basic argument was that the Pacific War was obviously a naval war and that the campaigns of MacArthur were, at best, strategic diversions that provided minimal and peripheral benefits to the main advance, insofar as they drew enemy air power away from the Central Pacific.

To MacArthur, the war was evidently a personal—one might even say a family—affair and the liberation of the Philippines the necessary fulfillment of his pledge of honor. He refused to compromise in his demands for carrier support from the Pacific Fleet, and because he had established some potentially damaging political power, President Roosevelt, whose stamina had been diminished by deteriorating health, did not wish to cross him directly.

One careful look at the globe is enough to show that attacking the Japanese along the New Guinea/Mindanao axis is a roundabout, wasteful, time-consuming, and dangerous route compared with a Central Pacific thrust via the Marianas and Formosa. But the latter involves bypassing the Philippines, politically very difficult. The president's compromise solution was to authorize the navy to pursue its Central Pacific strategy but at the same time to allow MacArthur to continue up the New Guinea coast, and ultimately to the Philippines, with naval cover to be provided by the Pacific Fleet only during actual amphibious landings.

In order to comply with the orders of the Joint Chiefs, Admiral Spruance was directed to employ Task Force 58 for the accomplishment of two tasks: to neutralize Japanese air power on Rabaul; and to ensure that the Japanese fleet, still a powerful force, could not interfere with the landings on Manus and Hollandia. Because the nearest U.S. naval base, Majuro Atoll, was 1,700 miles north-northeast of Manus and 1,850 miles northeast of Hollandia, it would be necessary for Task Force 58 to return to Majuro once during the six-week period of the two operations for upkeep.

After our task group arrived in the area north of New Britain Island, Rabaul was quickly rendered impotent by our air groups; it was to remain so throughout these operations. In order to protect the landings both on Manus and Hollandia from the sea, Admiral Spruance now decided to seek out and attack the Japanese fleet, thought to be based at Palau, which lies thirteen hundred nautical miles to the west of Manus Island and five hundred miles off the east coast of Mindanao. Accordingly, when Task Force 58 was back in tactical concentration, our task group having been rejoined by the others on March 27, Admiral Spruance set a course for Palau, almost a thousand nautical miles to the west.

By the evening of March 29, when Task Force 58 had closed to within 250 miles of Palau, it came under persistent attack by Bettys. Our own task group was under attack almost continuously between late twilight and nightfall. In these attacks, the Japanese attempted to approach one of the three task groups simultaneously from about forty-five degrees on either bow of the formation, with at least two, optimally three or four, planes in each attacking force. The planes would fly in at high speed, low over the water, the location of the task group having been radioed to them by a spotting plane flying high overhead. As soon as the enemy planes had committed themselves to an attack run on our group, Admiral Reeves would order an emergency change in course, all ships of the formation turning to the new heading simultaneously. The new course would put the nearest attackers on the beam, where they would be subjected to the maximum radar-directed, 5-inch antiaircraft fire from the screening destroyers. If the attack survived this fire and penetrated the screen, the formation would turn again to present the stern of the carriers. The planes would then have to survive the fire of the cruisers and carriers themselves before getting close enough to launch torpedoes, which would have to chase their targets from astern.

During the hour that our task group was under attack, the Japanese made many attempts to attack according to their doctrine, but Admiral Reeves's maneuvers prevented them from ever penetrating the screening destroyers to the interior of the formation.

My general quarters station was still Sky 2, in charge of the after 40-mm and 20-mm machine guns. Because these air attacks were being made just before dark, there was no opportunity for the machine guns to be used; they could only be aimed visually, not by radar, as was the case with the 5-inch guns. At best our gunners would occasionally catch sight of the engine exhaust of Bettys that came within a thousand yards, but aiming at an engine exhaust was an exercise in futility, much like shooting at the white tail of a deer running at full speed—you could never build in a lead that would give you a chance of registering a hit. As a result, this nighttime air attack was frustrating for me and the gun crews, to say nothing of being very disorienting, due to all the course changes.

The *Cotten* kept one group of these attacking Bettys under intermittent 5-inch fire for five minutes, during which time two planes that persisted in their attack course were shot down when they closed within less than one thousand yards. Two other ships of the screen were firing at the same planes, and all three destroyers claimed that it had been their fire that had shot them down. Because the 5-inch guns were aimed in the dark by radar, no one could really tell which ship had fired the lethal shots, permitting everyone who had fired to claim the hits. By 2300 the enemy had called off the attack, and the task groups all secured from battle stations. Several planes were shot down, with no damage done to our ships.

This five-minute engagement by the *Cotten*'s 5-inch battery seemed to energize the entire crew, which had been eagerly anticipating combat ever since the duel with the submarine off Tarawa. The sound of gunfire, along with the high-speed evasive maneuvers and the sight of enemy planes plunging in flames, was a tonic to the spirits.

By daylight of March 30, all three groups of Task Force 58 were maneuvering within 150 miles of the Palau anchorage, and a full multi-air-group attack was launched. The attacking planes reported shooting down or destroying on the ground over a hundred enemy aircraft, and in later attacks they claimed that seventeen ships, mainly of auxiliary types, had been sunk in the lagoon. However, the Japanese First Mobile Fleet was nowhere to be seen, and it was apparent that it had been pulled back well out of range of Task Force 58, to be saved for another day. This was a considerable disappointment.

At nightfall of March 30, our task group was subjected to another series of airborne torpedo attacks, similar in tactics to those of the previous night. This time the attacks persisted for about an hour and a half. Admiral Reeves ordered twenty-four emergency turns during the action, with the formation steaming through the black night at twenty-five knots. Twice the *Cotten* was able to find the enemy within extreme range of its 5-inch guns; it fired under radar control for approximately two minutes each time, but without obtaining any hits.

The strikes by the air groups of Task Force 58 on the Japanese shipping and airfields of Palau ended during the evening of March 30, and after beating back the last Japanese counterattack, the task force began the two-thousand-mile voyage back to Majuro for replenishment. After one week in Majuro, the full task force then returned west eighteen hundred miles to the area north of Hollandia, arriving on April 21, the landings themselves commencing on the next day.

Task Force 58 now had fifteen carriers on station, collectively capable of putting nine hundred aircraft in the air. This overwhelming force remained in the area for five days, with no enemy aircraft or shipping left as opposition. Needless to say, the landing at Hollandia, where seventy thousand American troops made it ashore, and the outnumbered and outgunned Japanese defenders took themselves to the mountains in the interior, was a smashing success, and it was so proclaimed by MacArthur.

On April 26, Task Force 58 was relieved of its duty for the southwest Pacific command and set sail once again for Majuro, arriving there on

May 4. Aboard the *Cotten* there was relief to be free of our obligations to MacArthur and considerable satisfaction at seeing two Japanese flags painted on the port side of the bridge screen, recording the two planes claimed by the main battery during the raid on Palau.

It was now apparent that the Japanese fleet had withdrawn to the west of the Philippine Islands. It had shown no intention of venturing to aid the Japanese troops remaining in the southwest Pacific; they evidently had been left to fight to the end without further support. The Japanese were saving their fleet for a major battle, one they believed more critical to the ultimate defense of their homeland. Such a battle could not be put off much longer.

9

Majuro

During the period that the Fifth Fleet was in the southwest Pacific, Majuro was its forward operating base. Majuro is the most beautiful atoll in the Central Pacific, an opinion shared by almost everyone who has been there. Except for the one entrance channel, in the center of the northern side, the lagoon is completely surrounded by a coral reef; on the reef are approximately sixty islands and islets, on the larger of which are good stands of coconut palm trees. The shape of the lagoon is roughly elliptical, with an east-west dimension of approximately twenty-one nautical miles and a varying north-south width of from two to five nautical miles.

Task Force 58, with all its support ships, could anchor with room to spare in the eastern part of the lagoon, which was without navigational obstruction except for one small shoal in the center. The water depth was uniformly in excess of one hundred feet, right up to within two hundred yards of the sand beach. The destroyer and destroyer tender anchorage was at the very eastern end of the lagoon, a circular area about two nautical miles in diameter.

The islets of the northern reef surrounding the destroyer anchorage were set aside for recreation for groups of officers and men. There are fine coral sand beaches on the lagoon sides of these islets, perfect for swimming and sunning. To seaward lies a great coral reef, extending outward an average of six hundred yards, just below the level of the ocean; depending on the tide, there is from six inches to two feet of water above the coral. Beyond the edge of the reef, as a chart shows, the ancient volcano on which the reef rests plunges toward the ocean bottom so steeply that the one-thousand-fathom curve—where the bottom of the ocean first reaches a depth of six thousand feet—lies a scant two miles offshore.

The first time I had gone ashore had been on March 2, when we were alongside the *Prairie* for repairs. On that occasion Bob Drake, the assistant engineering officer, and I were sent ashore with two chief petty officers, one hundred enlisted men (about a third of the crew), and twenty-seven cases of beer furnished us by the *Prairie*, courtesy of Commander Destroyers, Pacific Fleet. We were ferried in the motor whaleboat and captain's gig to the small island set aside for destroyer crews on the northern reef, and we picked a section of the beach clear of other liberty parties. The beer was quickly allocated, coming to three per customer; the crew members lined up with exceptional docility to receive their rations. Unfortunately we all, Drake and I included, drank the beer so quickly that this part of the holiday seemed over before it began.

Because Majuro had not been occupied by the Japanese in force, none of the islands had been visited by the ravages of shell, bomb, or flamethrower. The palm trees were things of beauty, and the sand beach on the lagoon side was perfect. After a swim, Drake and I walked across the island to look at the coral reef on the seaward side. From the island the reef looked as though it might extend for about half a mile, the water at that state of the tide being not more than a foot above the reef. We did not go out on the coral on this first visit.

When we returned to the ship, we reported with great enthusiasm that the Pacific Fleet had finally gotten lucky regarding an advance operating base. Everyone perked up, and no one missed a chance to go ashore when his turn came afterward.

My second visit ashore came six weeks later, on April 10, after our return to Majuro from the first trip south. This time all of our officers, except for a two-man duty section, went ashore as a unit to a small section of another islet set aside for destroyer officers. We were again allotted three beers apiece, augmented this time by cigars and lunch.

Wayne Dorman, one of the assistant gunnery officers, and I decided to explore the reef after we had consumed our share of the refreshments. We waded out about a quarter of a mile from the island. There the reef took on an appearance quite unlike anything we had ever seen before or had even heard existed. While the top of the reef generally remained about knee deep, there were many gullies and crevices extending below, some to a depth of several yards. These gullies were alive with all sorts of highly colored fish, coral that looked like some sort of ocean plant life, and clams and mollusks (some of which were three feet in diameter and looked as if they could cut off your leg if you stepped into the shells). Every crevice looked different. We kept our shoes and khaki trousers on to keep from getting sliced up by the coral, which we had been warned could be poisonous.

Upon returning to rejoin the rest of our party, we were astounded to discover we had been out on the reef for over two hours. I suspect that almost everyone on the *Cotten* concluded that the pleasures provided by Majuro would never be forgotten.

Of the many services we received in Majuro, most notable was the installation of the bronze porthole that Butler had acquired in Espiritu Santo. It was effected by mechanics from the destroyer tender *Markob* when we were nested alongside, with sister ships of DesRon 50. Once it had been securely welded into position in the port bulkhead of the wardroom, it was difficult to conceive how we had managed without. Captain Sloat was pleased by the result, and no less pleased by the sincere praise he received from his subordinates for his role in initiating the project in the first place.

10

Personnel Changes

The *Cotten* swung around its anchor in Majuro Lagoon until May 7, when orders were received to escort USS *Petrof Bay*, a CVE, to Pearl Harbor, along with destroyers *Dortch* and *Barnes*. Before we left on this trip, three new officers reported aboard for permanent duty, and Hadley Griffin, the gunnery officer, was detached. The new officers were Lt. (jg) Robert Howell Snowden, Ens. Ralph W. Gearhart Jr., and Ens. Thomas K. Wood.

Snowden, ten years older than I, was immediately made the ship's first lieutenant and my new administrative boss. He was from the state of Washington and had been a boatswain's mate in the naval reserve for several years prior to the war. After being called to active duty, he had rapidly risen through the ranks to boatswain's mate first class, at which point he had been made a commissioned officer. His first tour of duty as an officer had been aboard a patrol craft based in the Aleutian Islands, he being one of four officers aboard. The waters of the North Pacific surrounding the Aleutians are continuously stormy and fogbound, and they rapidly forge those unlucky enough to sail them into seamen, with strong affinities to their ships. With this background, it was no surprise that Snowden was not only mature and tough but an excellent officer, with a gift for leadership. He rapidly achieved credibility as the *Cotten*'s first lieutenant.

Ralph Gearhart was about six months junior to me. From my viewpoint, this alone was enough to make him a welcome addition to the ship. He was given a job as assistant to the communications officer, Herb Kanter. Tom Wood, the third new addition, was a quiet person, also six months junior to me, and he was assigned to the gunnery department.

Hadley Griffin's departure permitted Roger Stokey, now relieved of his temporary duty as first lieutenant, to become gunnery officer; his new battle station was in charge of the main battery director. Wayne Dorman, who had been in command of the 40-mm and 20-mm battery as Sky 1, with me as his deputy for the after part of the battery, was reassigned to take charge of the main battery computer (Stokey's former job, located in the fire control room under the director). This left to me the command, as Sky 1, of the 40-mm and 20-mm batteries, the old station I had occupied as Sky 2 being temporarily eliminated. I had always enjoyed being around the heavy machine guns, and I took to the new assignment with considerable enthusiasm.

The Sky 1 battle station was located on the small open deck area surrounding the main battery director, directly above the pilothouse. Ola Fayard, a yeoman first class, was stationed as the Sky 1 "talker," on a sound-powered telephone circuit with the bridge, CIC, and control (the main battery director). My own combat phones were connected to the gun captains and director operators of all of the 40-mm mounts, and to all the 20-mm gun captains.

Sky 1, at the highest elevation on the ship—excepting the main battery director, stacks, and masts—had full and unobstructed 360-degree surveillance. Being directly over the bridge, Sky 1 could not help overhearing the more heated conversations between the captain, executive officer, and officer of the deck during general quarters, which permitted an intermittent overview of what was going on. The duties of Sky 1 were basically to "designate" targets (assign them to weapons) and, when the gunners reported they were "on target," to issue the command to fire at the enemy when it was within range and on a bearing free of "friendlies" that might be accidentally struck. The same procedures also applied for all practice antiaircraft firing.

The disadvantages to the new job were physical in nature, though they detracted nothing from the satisfaction of the assignment. In the first place, when 5-inch mount number 2 (just forward of the bridge) fired at a target abaft either beam, Sky 1 was some twenty feet from the muzzle of the gun, where the blast was considerable. Secondly, when the wind was directly astern, the station was downwind of both smokestacks, so that for as much as half an hour at a time it would be immersed in stack gases, which was an unpleasant experience. The wind was in fact often directly astern. During

65

dawn or evening general quarters, the task group would be conducting flight operations, which necessitated a course directly into the wind for landings and takeoffs. Between flight operations, however, to compensate for long periods on these headings, the task group's course would often be downwind; hence, whenever the speed of the wind exceeded the speed of the ship, there were periods of heavy air pollution for Sky 1. Otherwise, the job was perfect.

Cotten, Dortch, and *Barnes,* escorting *Petrof Bay,* arrived at Pearl Harbor on May 13. Wayne Dorman had received the coveted assignment of permanent officer of the deck, replacing Hadley Griffin, effective as of this trip to Pearl Harbor. During the two months that the *Cotten* had been in the southwest Pacific, I had been assigned to stand Condition III (regular steaming) watches in the combat information center and in the main battery director, to familiarize me with the radarmen of the former and the gunner's mates and fire controlmen of the latter. Having completed these assignments, I was now returned to the bridge to stand Condition III watches as the junior officer of the watch, with Wayne Dorman as the OOD.

The *Cotten* remained in Pearl Harbor for eleven days, enabling repairs to be accomplished, particularly with respect to our ordnance, and giving the crew several liberties. On one liberty, Snowden and I went to the Moana for a typical evening at the bar, where socializing with officers of other services was the main source of entertainment. We found that most of these officers were under an illusion that destroyer duty was physically the toughest job of all, with all the rolling and pitching for months on end. Of course, no one except a marine was ever disabused of that opinion, as only a destroyer sailor would know that after two months at sea one hardly noticed the motion, much less felt any discomfort.

It behooved me to work with Snowden harmoniously. He had significant skills as a leader but lacked a tactical and theoretical naval education. I had received such an education, but no one would have claimed I was either tactful or understanding. By consolidation of our backgrounds, Snowden believed, we could be a mutually supportive working team. On this evening ashore we agreed on this team-play approach, to my considerable relief.

On May 20 Gus Smythe was assigned to duty in the continental United States with a destroyer shakedown command, a particularly desirable shore duty. Everyone was pleased for Gus, who was highly regarded, but there was some disappointment that Alex Early, as the senior full lieutenant aboard, had been given his old job as executive officer. Alex had been the sonar officer since the *Cotten*'s commissioning and had always been one of the four best watch officers, his performance in both capacities being entirely satisfactory. However, he had never had the responsibility of being a department head, which entailed being in charge of a number of enlisted men, and his actual naval experience was as limited as that of any of us. On one occasion at dinner in the wardroom he had put Bowman, one of the steward's mates, on report for serving him ice cream that had melted; this was typical of many of his disciplinary actions, which inclined to pettiness.

Having had Mr. Wesson as our first exec had established unusually high expectations as to the qualifications needed to fulfill the job, and these Gus Smythe had perpetuated. Therefore, to start with, Alex Early had large shoes to fill—which was certainly not his fault. Although most of us were willing to give him a fair chance by supporting him as best we could, he was going to have to prove that he was up to the job. This change, unlike the earlier ones, weakened the command structure of the *Cotten*. Captain Sloat had kept his legendary temper in good control up to this date. We wondered how this restraint would wear, with Early as his principal subordinate.

At 0600 on May 24, the *Cotten* left Pearl Harbor for Majuro once again, this time in company with the fully repaired battleship *Washington*, its sister ship *North Carolina*, the light cruisers *Miami, Houston,* and *Vincennes* (which constituted Cruiser Division, or CruDiv, 14), and eight destroyers, including *Cotten* and *Dortch* of DesRon 50.

Snowden became a new permanent officer of the deck, replacing Alex Early, who as executive officer was relieved of watch duties. The four officers of the deck were now Stokey, Kanter, Dorman, and Snowden, of whom only Stokey remained of the original group. At the start Snowden was to need a considerable amount of assistance from his junior officer of the watch, because the tactics of Task Force 58, to say nothing of the peculiar tactical characteristics of a destroyer, were completely new to him. This was not a serious handicap, as over the past ten months several of the junior officers of the watch had received intensive practical experience, and one of these was always on watch with Snowden.

The trip to Majuro was oriented toward antiaircraft gunnery and fleet tactical exercises, both of which were held every day of the six-day voyage. For antiaircraft firing, patrol planes were launched from the battleships and cruisers to tow sleeves up and down the column of destroyers and the heavy ships; thousands of rounds were expended in increasingly successful efforts at knocking the targets out of the sky. There was enough left to the individual skills of the director operators of the 5-inch guns and 40-mm batteries, and to those of the 20-mm gun pointers, that actual firing practice sessions were a vital necessity if any accuracy was to be achieved. A sleeve towed by one of our planes, even at its highest speed, was a simple target compared to an enemy plane diving at its target at twice that speed, to say nothing of the adrenaline pumped into a gunner's system when he is shooting to kill. Still, the practice was a great help—the more practice the better.

Battle-line tactics and destroyer division tactics were necessary for well-rounded fleet performance, but drill in these areas had been largely absent from the operating procedures of the fast carrier task groups. Until this time, these groups had been more concerned with protective tactics for the carriers than with offensive maneuvers by the heavy surface units.

Our group contained no carriers, so the emphasis was on the handling of the surface units in simulated fleet actions removed from the carriers. There were main battery offset-firing exercises for the battleships and cruisers, star-shell illumination in nighttime tactical exercises, simulated torpedo attacks by destroyers in close-order division formation against the battleships, and battle-line deployment exercises, all conducted as thoroughly as a full day's schedule would allow.

Because the *Cotten* had new officers in so many battle station assignments, this cruise provided an opportunity to get the team functioning properly again. In my own case, I became familiar with the gun captains and director operators who had been under Wayne Dorman's direction, and I monitored their progress as well as that of the crews in the after stations, with whom I had been drilling previously. Due to the lack of serious gunnery practice since Task Force 58 had been off Palau (almost two months), as well as natural instinct, the gunners and director operators at first tended to shoot behind the target, not building in sufficient leads. Discussing this tendency with the men involved, I reemphasized that there was absolutely no chance to hit a target if you were firing behind it. It was preferable to start a firing run well ahead of the target, letting it catch up gradually with your stream of fire. The chances of hitting an enemy plane were slim at best, and therefore, I said, we should at least try to rattle him, by making him fly into a stream of tracers; if we fired behind him, he would not even be aware that he was being shot at. The idea of scaring the enemy was particularly appealing to some of the 20-mm gun pointers.

The gun crews steadily improved their accuracy during this training, bringing down enough sleeves to encourage the entire machine gun battery. It didn't hurt to be reminded that the primary reason that we, and the *Cotten* itself, were in Task Force 58 was to aim and shoot our weapons accurately and promptly when the occasion demanded. The routine of task force duty had made it too easy to forget that our weapons were the essence of our existence, the two days of nighttime air attacks in the vicinity of Palau Island notwithstanding.

Our formation pulled into Majuro Lagoon on May 30, and the *Cotten* anchored in berth 59.

11

Operation Forager and the Battle of the Philippine Sea

Fifteen carriers and seventy-eight-odd other combat ships of Task Force 58 were anchored in Majuro Lagoon for the week of May 29–June 6, 1944. Every effort was made to bring equipment, ordnance, and provisions up to capacity for the next operation of the Fifth Fleet.

The new offensive operation was an aggressive expansion of the previous ones, and it gave hope that the progress of the war would now be accelerated. Its code name was "Forager." The plan was built around the amphibious landing of 127,000 troops, two-thirds of which were U.S. marines and one-third U.S. Army infantry, on the islands in the Marianas of Saipan—the initial objective—then Guam and Tinian. The objective was to destroy the enemy ground forces in order that the islands could be occupied and developed into the principal Central Pacific bases for the final air, sea, and amphibious campaigns against Japan.

The Fifth Fleet was separated into two main task forces, similar to the command structure for the Marshall Islands campaign. The overall commander remained Adm. Raymond A. Spruance, commander of the Fifth Fleet. The "Joint Expeditionary Force" was designated Task Force (TF) 51, under the command of Vice Adm. R. K. Turner. It was composed of the troops, transports, supply ships, and landing craft; fourteen escort carriers, with three hundred planes aboard; seven prewar, slow battleships; and twelve cruisers and ninety destroyers and destroyer escorts. The second major subdivision of the Fifth Fleet was Task Force 58, which now consisted of four fast carrier task groups (TGs), containing in the aggregate over nine hundred aircraft, seven fleet carriers, eight light carriers, seven new and fast battleships, thirteen cruisers, and fifty-eight destroyers. Vice Adm. Marc Mitscher was the commander, aboard the carrier *Lexington*.

Both Spruance and Mitscher cautioned their commands to be mentally prepared for a far different Japanese reaction than had been seen thus far. They now credited the Japanese with the capability and motivation to send the First Mobile Fleet out to battle the Fifth Fleet once it became obvious that an invasion of the Marianas was under way. Both were of the opinion that the Japanese considered the Marianas vital to the defense of their home islands and that they would expend an all-out effort to prevent their fall. In addition to the First Mobile Fleet, the Japanese possessed considerable air power and sizable land forces, which would defend the Marianas with typical determination.

Mitscher's operation plan set out in detail the command structure, described the objectives of Task Force 58, and outlined his estimate of the enemy's capabilities. The task force, as already noted, was divided into four carrier task groups. In order of time, the first objective was the destruction of land-based Japanese air power in the Marianas. The second objective was the destruction of the Japanese First Mobile Fleet, if it should threaten the battle area subsequent to D day. Should an engagement become imminent, the seven fast battleships of TF 58 along with assigned cruisers and destroyers would leave their respective carrier task groups to form a fifth task group, TG 58.7, designated the "Battle Line," under the tactical command of Vice Adm. Willis A. Lee. The objective of the Battle Line would be to seek out a surface engagement with the Japanese fleet; it would not be compromised by the presence of the task force's lightly armed carriers, which had no defense against large-caliber shells.

The specific objective of three of the four fast carrier task groups—TGs 58.1, 58.2, and 58.3—would be to seek out and destroy the Japanese carriers and their air groups. The objective of the remaining carrier task group, TG 58.4, would be to provide fighter protection over the Battle Line.

Each of the four fast carrier task groups was an operational entity, with freedom to maneuver, launch planes, and to change course, speed, or formation as its task group commander ordered. When in "tactical concentration," the two, three, or four so involved would maintain common average courses and stay within ten to twenty miles of each other, maneuvering to suit their individual tactical needs within this framework.

From the perspective of one officer aboard one ship in TF 58, the background information provided by the various operation plans and orders was important but hardly something that bore on the daily performance of duty. What would require full concentration was the performance of the individual ship within the individual task group. The highest commander that pertained to an individual ship was therefore the task group commander, and it was upon that source of command that one's attention was focused.

The ships of Task Group 58.3, to which the *Cotten* and the rest of Des-Ron 50 now were assigned, enjoyed what was to prove a remarkable perspective during Operation Forager. In addition to Admiral Reeves in *Enterprise*, this formation contained fleet carrier *Lexington*, flagship of Vice Admiral Mitscher; battleship *Washington*, flagship of Vice Admiral Lee, who was in command of the Battle Line when formed; and heavy cruiser *Indianapolis*, flagship of Admiral Spruance, commander of the entire Fifth Fleet. These senior commanders were all in one group to make it possible for them to communicate with each other directly via short-range voice radio (TBS), so that tactics could be changed in the press of battle without misinterpretation or confusion. Those serving with this particular formation would be able to hear over their TBS receivers historic conversations among these admirals as the operation developed, an opportunity largely denied to those in the other task groups because of the separation between groups.

Task Force 58 was scheduled to sortie from Majuro on June 6, at which time our group (TG 58.3) would consist of the *Enterprise* and *Lexington*, light carriers *San Jacinto* and *Princeton*, the fast battleships *Washington*, *North Carolina*, *Indiana*, *South Dakota*, and *Alabama*, the nine destroyers of Destroyer Squadron 50, and the seven destroyers of Destroyer Squadron 1. The heavy cruiser *Indianapolis* would accompany our task group, with Admiral Spruance aboard. Of the ships in this group, all five battleships and Destroyer Squadron 1 would be detached, if so ordered, to form the nucleus and screen respectively of the Battle Line (TG 58.7).

Because the Japanese air forces in the Marianas were the first objective, Admiral Mitscher had decided that the first action would be to conduct preemptive air strikes against the airfields on Saipan, Tinian, and Guam, starting on June 12, three days before D day, and continuing through D day. Following the initial strikes, which would be launched from the east side of the Marianas, Task Force 58 would reposition itself to the west of the islands to be able to block the approach of the Japanese fleet. The Battle Line would not be formed unless it was certain that a confrontation with the enemy fleet was imminent.

The estimated strength of the Japanese First Mobile Fleet was five fleet-type and four light carriers, five battleships, and an adequate supporting complement of first-line cruisers and destroyers. Assuming that the carrier air groups were at full complement, the enemy's strength at maximum would be substantially less than that available to Task Force 58, given a ratio of three to five in carriers. In the other categories, the Japanese strength was marginally weaker but sufficient to allow the enemy to risk a night surface engagement, in which the numerical advantage of our forces could be greatly offset. If the Japanese carrier air groups could be augmented by land-based aircraft from the airfields on the Marianas, there would be the possibility of a more even battle than the numbers of carrier-based aircraft alone might indicate, assuming equal quality of equipment and skills.

As Task Force 58 put to sea from the Majuro lagoon on June 6, the known factors that made up the strategic situation went to the backs of our minds, and our attention returned to the tactical requirements of operating the *Cotten* in the screen of our task group. Captain Sloat in particular had two unique things to worry about, neither of them having anything to do with the Japanese. Being a career naval officer, his first concern was that no less than the three most senior admirals of the Fifth Fleet, in addition to the task group commander, were in a position to notice at first hand if the *Cotten* should make any obvious errors. This was apparently not a situation he was happy about. Secondly, he was not pleased with having Alex Early as the *Cotten*'s executive officer, as had been made evident by the fact that he now came to the bridge whenever Early was there. The other officers felt that the captain wanted to make certain that he could second-guess the new exec before any mistakes could be made.

Early could not help but sense the captain's mood. Being a combative person, he reacted by being overly assertive himself, and there developed a confrontational relationship between the two. The fact that he would be a certain loser in this contest seemingly made no difference whatsoever to Early, so strong was his urge to defend his dignity.

Having known him since the *Cotten*'s commissioning, the other officers were well acquainted with Early's disposition. He was about five feet five inches tall and weighed approximately 130 pounds after a big meal. He always looked a person right in the eye, and the look said, "I may be small, but I am as good a man as you are, or better, any day of the week." He had related that as a youth he had taken up boxing as his sport of preference; his twisted nose, which had been broken several times, gave weight to a theory that his defense must have rated a much lower priority than his offense. Because he was, underneath the bluster, trying to do his best as he saw it, we took him with a grain of salt, even after he became executive

72

officer and part master of our destinies aboard ship. It was his relationship with the captain and the captain's increasing irritability that were matters of concern.

The gunnery department had problems of its own, resulting from Griffin's departure and Stokey and Dorman's assuming the key positions in the direction and control of the 5-inch guns. Their opportunity to gain familiarity with their new jobs had been limited to the recent cruise from Pearl Harbor, which had afforded only five days of firing exercises. Getting the main battery director onto a fast-moving air target was not an easy thing to do, and it was an art more than a science. Self-confidence in this art needed reinforcement by much practice for a man like Stokey, who was by nature cerebral and reflective rather than aggressive and instinctive. Stokey's mind was certainly equal to the job, but he needed some time and practice, which he did not yet have. Wayne Dorman, now in charge of the main battery computer, also was in a new assignment, one in which Stokey had previously become an expert. Dorman was fully capable in anything he did aboard the *Cotten*, but he also needed more experience before he could equal Stokey's facility with the computer—which was at best a slow calculator.

As far as the heavy machine guns were concerned, I was happy with my assignment as Sky 1, which was not a new one as much as an expanded one. What Sky 1 and the gun captains wanted, and in the worst way, was an opportunity for the 40s and 20s to shoot at and destroy as many enemy aircraft as possible. The machine gun crews were a naturally aggressive group, so this part of the ship's weaponry was at least not likely to suffer from buck fever in the new operation. The factor of there being too many admirals breathing down the *Cotten*'s neck, so bothersome to the captain, amounted to less than nothing to the members of the heavy machine gun battery. It was perhaps just as well that the captain was unaware of so truly cavalier an attitude toward exalted rank.

The engineering and deck departments were both in excellent shape with regard to supervision and skill; the engineering officers remained the original group. Snowden, the new head of the deck department, already appeared to be comfortable with his duties, despite having just reported aboard. The communications department was also operating smoothly, with Kanter still in charge, assisted by Beresford and the newly arrived Gearhart.

Last, but certainly not least, was the fact that two of the four regular officers of the deck when under way, Dorman and Snowden, were brand new at the job, and a third, Kanter, was relatively new although now more confident in this role. The net result of the recent personnel changes was that several key positions aboard were in need of time at sea to reach the proficiency the *Cotten* had enjoyed a month earlier. It seemed as though the luxury of that extra time, at least for the purposes of Operation Forager, would be denied to us.

On June 6 at 1110, the *Cotten* proceeded out through the entrance channel of Majuro Lagoon to take station with the other destroyers on defensive patrol lines outside of the channel while the battleships and carriers made their exits. By noon the heavy ships had completed their sorties and taken their stations in the task group cruising formation. The other three carrier task groups were soon at sea as well. Now steaming in tactical concentration, Task Force 58 headed for the Marianas, 1,650 nautical miles to the west-northwest. The cruise was scheduled to take six days to arrive on station, a hundred miles east of Saipan, on June 12.

During the early afternoon of June 11, five days after leaving Majuro, Admiral Mitscher evidently became impatient, for he accelerated his operation plan by sending a deck load of fighters from all task groups over the enemy airfields on Saipan at maximum range, to knock down as many aircraft as possible. The fighters came back aboard at 1800, at which time TF 58 headed north.

At 0045 on the morning of June 12, our task group detected enemy planes on radar and closed up into air defense formation. The first group of enemy planes could not locate us, but they were followed two hours later by a second group. The second group's scout did find us, dropping several brilliant flares right over our formation. Then followed two attacks, just before and after 0400, which the group avoided by a series of emergency turns. In both instances our destroyers on the far side of the screen opened fire on the planes, which apparently forced them to turn away before they were in position to drop their torpedoes.

At 0415 of June 12, air strikes, this time consisting of bombers as well as the fighter groups, were launched against the Marianas by all task groups of TF 58. These attacks continued all day, the reports of the returning groups indicating surprisingly weak air opposition. At midnight on June 13, the four task groups steamed west, just north of Saipan, to arrive at dawn at a planned new operating area approximately thirty miles to the west of the island, which at times was well within visual distance.

At 1100 Admiral Reeves relayed to his task group that the air groups of TG 58.4 had located a Japanese convoy at sea and had claimed to have sunk five cargo ships, one tanker, and one destroyer, leaving an additional five cargo ships and five corvettes motionless in the water. Somewhat later, destroyer *Miller* from TG 58.2 reported picking thirty-five Japanese survivors from the ocean. At 1250 one of the *Cotten*'s lookouts spotted wreckage

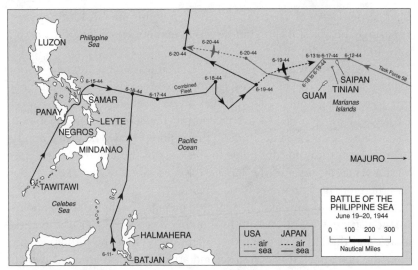

Battle of the Philippine Sea, June 1944. (See Appendix C.)

in the water, which we immediately reported to Admiral Reeves. We were ordered to leave the screen to investigate and pick up survivors. The captain maneuvered the ship toward the wreckage, and on arriving there we spotted a number of men hanging onto pieces of timber.

The captain brought the ship alongside them and stopped. After the port boarding net was lowered to the water's edge, the chief boatswain's mate directed the fire and rescue detail from the Second Division down the net to bring aboard seven uninjured individuals—six Korean laborers and one Japanese seaman. When they were up on deck, they were searched and locked up as prisoners of war. Once it became likely that everyone who had survived had been picked up, the *Cotten* returned at twenty-five knots to the task group, which by that time had left us seven miles behind. All that could be gathered from the prisoners was that their ship had been sunk in the morning and that they had been heading for Saipan when American aircraft had attacked. This abbreviated report was given to the task group commander.

During the midwatch (0000–0400) of June 14, *Indianapolis,* with Admiral Spruance aboard, left our task group to be with the assault forces and Admiral Turner on D day. Starting at sunrise, all destroyers were topped off from the heavy ships of the formation, *Cotten* again fueling from *Enterprise.* During this interval, our seven prisoners were transferred to *Enterprise* by high-line breeches buoy.

Throughout the day, aircraft of our task group continued their attacks against Saipan. At twilight *Caperton* spotted and rescued a pilot from the light carrier *Cabot* of TG 58.2; he had been on his life raft for three days. Amazingly, he was still alive, but he was in tenuous condition, due to exposure and lack of drinking water.

During the midwatch of D day, the *Cotten* was ordered to take station eight miles to the east of our task group, to act as a rendezvous point for air groups returning from predawn strikes on the beachhead areas of Saipan. At daylight we returned to our position in the screen. Flight operations against targets on Saipan continued throughout D day. The task group remained from thirty to fifty miles to the west of the landing areas, often within visual distance of the Japanese forces ashore. Our exact position was therefore now no secret to the enemy.

After sunset, enemy aircraft appeared on radar. Night fighters launched by the carriers were successful in shooting down six planes of the initial attack and thereby in keeping the enemy away from the formation. Just after the first attack was over, a second attack began. A group of two-engine torpedo planes managed to penetrate the destroyer screen, flying just above the water toward the battleships *Washington* and *North Carolina*, both of which opened up with murderous volleys of 5-inch fire at close range. Other heavy ships in the formation center joined in on the Japanese planes, now closing the carriers for their torpedo drops. Four of the enemy were shot down by the massive gunfire, but not before several torpedoes had been launched at the carriers. At this point Admiral Reeves increased the formation speed, but the sudden attack was over, and no torpedoes caught the fleeing carriers.

Admiral Mitscher's chief of staff was profoundly displeased with the screening destroyers' performances during this last attack. He was Capt. Arleigh Burke, an ex–destroyer squadron commander (DesRon 23) who had achieved considerable fame for his squadron's exploits in early 1943 in the Solomon Islands. He was known throughout the fleet as "Thirty-one-knot Burke," because of the nighttime surface battles he had fought at that speed, a most difficult undertaking. Captain Burke felt that the destroyers had let the carriers down by not getting their guns on these low-flying planes before they had passed the screen and were making their runs on the carriers. This could have resulted in a disaster if the torpedoes had struck the carriers. Burke personally picked up a TBS microphone to let the screen and everyone know by his tone that he expected the destroyers to be the first to fire on attacking torpedo planes. Assuming that his purpose had been to anger the destroyer captains, he achieved success.

By the next morning, a review of this incident by Burke's staff had revealed that the planes making the attack had been so close to the water that they were underneath the destroyers' air search radar coverage; thus, the destroyers had been unable to pick them up until they were right on us. Of course there was no moon, this being an invasion night, so no look-out had visually picked the planes up either. Having been at battle stations at the time, I for one never saw any planes until they started getting shot down by the battlewagons inside the screen. The battleships and carriers had much-improved low-level air search radars not yet available to the destroyers, so they had become aware of the attackers in time to track them with their directors and eventually to shoot most of them down.

Still, Burke's harsh critique of the destroyers' performances had a benefi-cial effect. Captain Sloat gave those of us who were in charge of the vari-ous gun batteries an irascible lecture that might pass as encouragement, the general sense of which was that we had better damn well shoot at something the next time targets were about, or else. I certainly thought he was right and sincerely hoped I would be able to see something for the machine gun batteries to shoot at.

Captain Sloat reserved some especially pointed commentary for the combat information center. He demanded to know how in hell ten Bettys (in fact, the aircraft had been only six in number and of a new twin-engine torpedo-bomber type known as "Frances") could go right down our beam at a range of four thousand yards without anyone picking them up on the air search radar. There was no satisfactory answer. While the planes had ultimately been picked up, their bearing had been given to Stokey too late for him to get the main battery director locked onto them.

In analysis of this attack, grudging credit is due the Japanese for a very effective tactic. Several planes had been sent in at a high altitude, those that were reported early in the attack, with the torpedo bombers below them, just over the water. The high planes attracted all the attention, and the American night fighters and search radars concentrated on them, while the torpedo planes raced in undetected. On our side, any credit that was due was re-served for the 5-inch batteries of the *Washington* and *North Carolina*. How-ever, even more critical was the large measure of good luck we had enjoyed, which had enabled the carriers to avoid being hit by the torpedoes.

Admiral Spruance now detached Task Groups 58.1 and 58.4 to attack the enemy airfields in the Bonin Islands, six hundred miles north of Saipan. His purpose was to prevent replacement aircraft from being sent down from Japan. In particular, he had been warned by Admiral Nimitz on June 14 that the Japanese fleet, including carriers, had been sighted at sea west of the Philippines heading eastward. This was enough notice to begin prepa-rations for an attack from the Japanese First Mobile Fleet, which could reach the Marianas area sometime within the next three to four days. The two task groups that had been sent north to the Bonins were ordered to return by June 17, at which time a rejoined and tactically concentrated Task Force 58 would be ready for a battle.

Admiral Reeves passed on to us on TBS that twenty thousand marines had successfully reached the Saipan beachhead on D day. No word was available as to their progress at this early stage of the campaign, other than that the fighting was very heavy.

An expanded contact report concerning the Japanese fleet was received from our scouting submarines to the effect that two large groups, including carriers and battleships, had been spotted heading toward the Philippine Sea. Admiral Spruance, in advising Task Force 58 of this report, estimated that the Japanese, if they proceeded toward Saipan, would be in position to attack by June 18 or 19.

At 0335 of the midwatch on June 17, *Cotten* was ordered by Admiral Reeves to investigate a radar surface target located sixty-seven hundred yards south of the screen. The ship went to battle stations, the captain took the conn, and the ship headed at flank speed directly for the target. The captain, Early, the officer of the deck (Herb Kanter), the bridge lookouts, and Sky 1 all had their glasses to their eyes, glued to the bearing of the target as given by our CIC. When CIC reported the target was within one thousand yards, the captain slowed the *Cotten* to ten knots and changed course to port, so that the target was brought broad on the starboard beam. When we were in what he deemed optimum position with respect to the target—a half-sunk, two-masted sampan barely visible in our binoculars— Captain Sloat rared back and bellowed, "All guns commence firing!"

Sky 1 gave the order "Commence firing" to the starboard 40-mm and 20-mm batteries. The director operator of 40-mm number 1, located on the forwardmost part of the starboard wing of the bridge, was standing next to the captain; even so, following the captain's line of sight to the target, he was barely able to make it out without the benefit of binoculars. Still, when he received the order to commence firing, this director operator did so immediately. As his tracers streamed toward the wreck, every other gunner or director operator of the starboard machine gun battery also opened up, firing along the stream of tracers, though some of them never actually saw their target.

Simultaneously, the 5-inch battery had fired a salvo; but unlike the machine guns, it was pointed directly away from the target, to port. Caught as completely by surprise as everyone else, the captain straightened up and shouted, "All guns, cease firing," and in the same breath, "Send Stokey to the bridge." Stokey climbed out of the main battery director, passed by Sky 1, and went down the ladder to the bridge toward a now fuming commanding officer.

For the next two minutes the combat efficiency of the *Cotten* ground to a halt as the captain relieved himself of a classic Sloat diatribe at Stokey's expense. He concluded with a wave of his arm to starboard at the low-lying hulk and a scream of, "There is your goddamn target, Stokey! I am going to light the son of a bitch up for you so any idiot can see it!" Stokey returned to the director while the 36-inch searchlight on the starboard side of the number 1 (forward) smokestack was turned on, illuminating our already pitiful-looking, waterlogged target. This time all guns, including the 5-inch, were leveled at the wreck and opened fire on command, expending a total of eight rounds of 5-inch star shell for illumination (needless, considering the use of the searchlight), eighty-eight rounds of 5-inch "common," 196 rounds of 40-mm ammunition, and ninety rounds of 20-mm. Perhaps several shots found their mark, but the sampan was already so low in the water it made a very elusive target at best.

At this point, Admiral Reeves called us on TBS asking for a report. The captain, believing correctly that the admiral wanted to move on, told Early to report back that we were leaving the target in a sinking condition with no apparent life and were returning to the formation. Early duly reported as instructed, and the *Cotten* got back to the screen as quickly as twenty-five knots would get it there. Because at this time the captain had not thought it necessary to ask Stokey what he thought he had been shooting at, none of the rest of us had the heart to bring the issue up after the fact. As a result, the reason for his action remains a mystery.

During the ensuing daylight hours, Task Force 58 was reunited and reorganized in preparation for an engagement with the Japanese fleet. The two task groups that had gone north to attack the Bonin Islands had returned, and Admiral Spruance now directed the formation of the Battle Line, Task Group 58.7. At sunset Admiral Lee in *Washington* left our formation, followed by the remaining battleships, to form up with DesRon 1 as the screen. Immediately after their departure, Cruiser Division 12— *Cleveland, Birmingham,* and *Montpelier*—joined us to replace the now-missing antiaircraft firepower of the formation nucleus, and Destroyer Division 90, consisting of four destroyers, joined the screen to replace DesRon 1. These new ships had come from Admiral Turner's Task Force 51, on loan for the coming battle.

Task Force 58 was now reoriented to position the Battle Line fifteen miles due west of our TG 58.3, with TG 58.4 twelve miles north of the Battle Line to provide it air support. TG 58.1 was stationed twelve miles north of our task group, and TG 58.2 twelve miles to the south of us. Admiral Spruance had rejoined our task group at 1600, after which he set forth by TBS his guiding principles for the coming battle. The main objective was the destruction of the Japanese carriers if they offered battle, and if this were accomplished, the destruction of the enemy's battleships. Patrols were subsequently launched to the west to search for the oncoming Japanese fleet, but without success.

During the midwatch of June 18, a patrolling submarine reported that a large enemy combat force had proceeded through the San Bernardino Strait, headed for the Marianas. The report also appeared to confirm that the Japanese were coming for us but that they would not arrive in the area west of Saipan, where TF 58 was now concentrated, until June 19 at the earliest. The other half of the First Mobile Fleet was as yet undetected. During the daylight hours of June 18, all five groups of TF 58 headed to the southwest toward the oncoming enemy fleet, with the search aircraft out in advance, looking in vain for the Japanese.

At 1825, Admiral Spruance ordered Admiral Mitscher to reverse course and to return to a position from where the heavily engaged troops on Saipan and their supporting shipping could be defended if the Japanese fleet were to slip by TF 58 during the night. In response Mitscher asked Spruance to reconsider this order and to continue to the southwest, as he believed that this course would place TF 58 close enough to the Japanese by daylight to permit a decisive air attack against the enemy carriers. Spruance replied that he would think it over, but sometime later he confirmed his first order, to return Task Force 58 to a position fifty miles west of Saipan at dawn to protect the amphibious forces against a possible "end run" by the enemy. Continuing to the southwest would leave the beachhead defenseless. Admiral Mitscher then without further discussion gave the order to TF 58 to reverse course.

Later a story was heard to the effect that prior to Forager, when tactics were being discussed between Admirals Spruance and Lee, Lee had said that he was not confident of the Battle Line's ability to conduct a night surface action with assured success, due to its insufficient nighttime training. If true, this conversation could have been a factor in Spruance's decision to return to Saipan during the night of June 18, rather than risk running into the enemy fleet in the dark. For while we enjoyed radar superiority, the Japanese optics were markedly superior during nighttime, as were their torpedoes and torpedo tactics.

During the midwatch, *Lexington* launched a night air attack and search group westward in a renewed attempt to locate the Japanese fleet, which continued to be elusive. An important tactical factor at this point was the direction of the wind, which was blowing steadily from the northeast to the southwest. This dictated that Task Force 58 would have to turn toward the wind—away from the oncoming Japanese—whenever the carriers conducted flight operations. The Japanese fleet, on the other hand, would be heading toward us whenever it conducted flight operations, and it would not have to change course at all as long as it wished to press forward to an attack. Because Japanese carrier planes enjoyed a combat range of three hundred nautical miles, seventy-five miles more than the maximum range of our planes, in theory the Japanese carriers could attack us all day long from such a range and remain beyond our ability to get to them as long as they stayed downwind from our own carriers. Therefore, because of our upwind position and the fact we still had not located the enemy fleet, our tactics would probably have to be wholly defensive throughout the day.

From 0500 to 0600, all ships went to battle stations for morning alert, passing an uneventful hour of anticipation. The new day was unusually beautiful, with a brisk northeast trade wind that brought a few widely separated high cumulus clouds and a sea covered with whitecaps. It was a perfect day for air-to-air combat. A search plane from *Enterprise* shot down a Japanese search plane at 0545, the first enemy contact of the day. At 0710 *Enterprise* launched a fighter sweep to the southeast against Japanese airfields on Guam to make certain we would not be attacked from two directions at the same time.

Alabama in the Battle Line reported that at 1007 its search radar had picked up a large group of unidentified planes 125 miles due west. Fifteen minutes later, Mitscher ordered all task groups to return to battle stations and air defense formations. All ships were directed to light off all boilers, which for the *Cotten* would permit a maximum speed of thirty-one knots. As quickly as they could, our carriers launched fighters to repel what was obviously a large force of Japanese carrier planes coming at us from the west. After forming up, our fighters were vectored out to meet the enemy by the controllers aboard the carriers. Our planes made visual contact with the Japanese at 1045, and air-to-air combat was waged thereafter on a continuous basis. The first enemy planes to reach us attacked the task group from the opposite side of the formation at 1115. A tremendous volume of antiaircraft fire went up, and apparently all of the attackers, torpedo bombers, were shot down.

At 1155 I saw a single dive bomber plunge down on *Enterprise* while the carrier was in the process of landing a group of fighters. The enemy pilot released his bomb, which exploded in the water close aboard the bow, then pulled out of his dive and came on toward *Cotten* in a high-speed attempt to escape. A moment later he came within range, and Sky 1 ordered, "Enemy plane approaching from port quarter. Commence firing when on target!" Our gunners opened up, firing seventy-six 40-mm rounds and three hundred 20-mm projectiles as the plane screamed close by on our port side. When he was abeam to port, some thousand yards away, a shell hit his right wing; it immediately came off, and he commenced a rolling, burning dive over us, hitting the water and exploding about two thousand yards off our starboard bow.

After the plane crashed, and after complimenting the gunners, I asked for the required casualty report. The port 20-mm battery reported that six men had been wounded during the brief action, all in the ankles or lower parts of their legs. Apparently a number of 20-mm guns of the heavy ships in the center of our formation around the *Enterprise* had also shot at our dive bomber, and in the process they had directed a large volume of fire in the general direction of the *Cotten,* toward which the plane was flying. Some of these projectiles had hit the deck around our port 20-mm gun station and exploded on impact; the fragments, flying out close to the deck, had cut up our six gunners.

The wounded men were immediately released from their stations, reserves from damage control taking their places. They were taken to the wardroom, where Dr. Spindler deftly removed the splinters, packed the wounds with sulfa powder, and sewed them back up. Describing the wounds as "punctures," he concluded that they were not debilitating enough to release the men from their duties. There were grumbles of dissatisfaction from several of the wounded, which included two of the steward's mates, concerning the doctor's mild assessment of their ordeal, but they all went back to their stations.

At the same time our gunners were wounded, another 20-mm shell came down on our bridge, directly below Sky 1. This shell grazed the chest of a signalman, A. J. Gifford, and went on to lodge in the left buttock of a second signalman, J. L. Cornatzer, half the shell in him and half sticking out. The last wound was most painful, but very lucky. The shell was explosive, and it could have detonated when it hit a bone but fortunately had not. Dr. Spindler later confessed that he was extremely careful when he extracted the shell from Cornatzer. After it had been removed, Cornatzer requested that he be permitted to keep it as a souvenir, but instead it was thrown over the side. The victim was told that his souvenir was the hole in his buttock, which, if he wanted to, he could show to posterity.

Later in the day we discovered that the 5-inch battery again had failed to get on the target during this action. They were having a tough time. At 1323 there was one further enemy attack on our task group, on the side away from the *Cotten,* no damage resulting.

Throughout the day, radio conversations between the carriers and their air group leaders came in over the voice circuits, assessing the battle. As nearly as could be ascertained, there had been a total of several hundred

Japanese aircraft in the attacking waves, but they had been woefully ineffective, due to apparent lack of training on the part of their pilots and to the very effective vectoring of our fighter groups by the flight controllers. Most of the enemy planes had been intercepted and destroyed far from our carriers. So few planes had actually made it in that the ships' antiaircraft fire had been able to prevent any damage from being inflicted. Of course there were losses among our aircraft, but they were light compared to the losses of the enemy. The last enemy planes disappeared from the radar screens at 1605, and Task Force 58 accordingly stood down from battle stations.

At 2208, Admiral Mitscher ordered Task Force 58 to turn to the west at flank speed, twenty-three knots, in an attempt to get close enough to the now aircraft-depleted First Mobile Fleet to launch our own air groups against its carriers. The high-speed pursuit of the enemy continued throughout the night of June 19–20, with long-range scouting planes out in front. In the morning the admiral informed us that only twenty-nine of our planes from all four carrier task groups had been lost during the preceding day's action, against Japanese losses of an estimated three hundred. If we could catch up with the enemy ships, their own air defense would be critically diminished as a result of their losses.

Our pursuit continued through the morning and early afternoon, with still no contact. Finally, at 1615, a search plane located the Japanese fleet heading for home at twenty knots, 370 miles to our west, well beyond the maximum combat range of our air groups. Despite this, and with certain knowledge that most of the planes would be out of fuel before they could get back to their carriers, Admiral Mitscher immediately headed the task force back into the wind and ordered a deck load attack launched—some 216 planes in all. Once the attack was in the air, TF 58 turned back to the west at twenty-four knots to minimize the return flight. Admiral Mitscher's devotion to the pilots under his command was known throughout the fleet. His misgivings in launching this attack were well understood by all.

Our planes arrived over the Japanese carriers at twilight with only twenty minutes of daylight remaining for their attack. As predicted, the Japanese defense was confined to antiaircraft fire, high-speed evasive maneuvers, and a limited number of fighters. Radio reports from our pilots back to the carriers indicated that one enemy carrier had been sunk and four more hit and damaged before it became too dark to continue. The flight commanders immediately rounded up their planes and headed back for their carriers in the gathering dusk.

Soon the voice circuits used by the returning pilots were filled with reports of rapidly emptying fuel tanks and requests for the position of their carriers. At twilight our task group turned to the east into the wind, still at twenty-four knots, to start landing the returning air strike. Soon, many of those waiting their turn to land were forced to ditch their planes in the water, their fuel completely used up. At 2100 Admiral Mitscher ordered all ships in Task Force 58 to turn on their 36-inch searchlights, aimed straight up in the air, so that the rest of the returning airmen could home directly in on the formation. At the same time, all destroyers in our task group except *Cotten* and *Caperton* were ordered to take stations behind the formation, so that they could stop and pick up the downed pilots without interfering with the heavy ships in the formation center. *Cotten* and *Caperton* remained ahead of the heavy ships, the sole remnants of the protective antisubmarine screen.

About thirty minutes before this spectacular effort to land or rescue the returning pilots ended, a disoriented Japanese carrier fighter pilot tried to land on the light carrier *San Jacinto* but was waved off by the landing officer. He circled the center of the formation at least two times, then proceeded slowly toward the *Cotten* about a hundred feet off the water. The plane flew right over us through the beams of our 36-inch searchlights, which lighted up the red-orange circles on the wings like a pair of small suns. It continued to fly on, away from our formation, disappearing into the night. This plane had been seen by many of the gun crews of our task group, none of which, including those of the *Cotten*, had fired on it. There must have been an overwhelming sense by everyone that this particular battle was over.

One-half hour later, with the task group still on its easterly course into the wind at flank speed, one of the last of the returning U.S. carrier pilots made a water landing alongside the *Cotten*. Early had the conn at the time, and despite the fact that our orders were to remain directly in front of the oncoming cruisers, carriers, and two remaining admirals, he ordered all engines stopped, intending to go to the rescue of the pilot in the water. The captain's temper got the best of him. He countermanded Early's order, shouting, "Belay that! All ahead flank!" Turning to Early, he bellowed, "Jesus Christ, Early, do you want the whole goddamn fleet up my asshole?" An unchastened Early then called the task group commander to report the location of the downed plane; the pilot was subsequently rescued by one of the destroyers steaming behind the heavy ships.

That brief confrontation was unavoidably overheard at Sky 1's station directly above the pilothouse. Early had committed a serious error of judgment, and it was my feeling afterward that it might have been then that the captain decided Early's experience was inadequate to the demands placed on an executive officer. After this he treated Early more courteously, but he definitely kept an eye on him.

Within fifteen minutes of the incident involving the downed plane, Admiral Reeves advised Mitscher that there were no more of our planes in the air, all having landed either aboard a carrier or in the ocean. Mitscher consented to end the landing operations and ordered the searchlights turned off at 2250. The course of Task Force 58 was reversed again to the west in hopes of catching up to any ships of the Mobile Fleet that had been damaged and slowed during our air attacks. Left behind were the four destroyers of Destroyer Division 90, which were ordered to remain in the area for the next twenty hours to search for downed pilots.

During the early morning of June 21, search planes were sent out ahead to look for enemy stragglers. One of the planes from a second search group reported sighting a group of the enemy at 0745 in a position 380 miles to the northwest of the task force. Admiral Mitscher decided that was too far to continue the pursuit without providing the destroyers with some additional fuel. The formation was slowed to permit the destroyers to fuel from the heavy ships. This operation took a full four-hour watch at twelve knots, allowing the fleeing Japanese to put additional distance between them and us. Finally, at 2030, Admiral Mitscher gave up the chase and gave the order to reverse course back toward the Marianas.

12

Task Force 58 Returns to Saipan

The pursuit of the Japanese fleet had taken TF 58 six hundred miles to the west of Saipan. On the way back, we met the destroyers of Destroyer Division (DesDiv) 90, which in the interim had picked up the pilots who had been left in the sea when the main body of TF 58 had chased the Japanese. A preliminary survey of our losses indicated that twenty of the 216 planes that had attacked the Japanese fleet had been shot down during the attack itself, and that eighty more had been forced to land at sea because they ran out of fuel. Of the crews of the latter planes, fifty-nine men had been rescued by our destroyers. The crews of the twenty planes shot down over the Japanese fleet had been lost.

At this time the extent of the carrier losses sustained by the Japanese was not known. The first estimate was that they had suffered the loss of several combat ships, including at least one carrier, but that most of their ships were now headed for safety in their home waters. It was further believed that the Japanese would be able to replace the three-hundred-odd pilots and planes they had lost, further diminishing the effect of the American victory. For these reasons there was a general feeling of frustration, a sense that a great opportunity to destroy the First Mobile Fleet had been within our grasp, but that we had let it slip by.

Because of the widely monitored debate between Admirals Spruance and Mitscher on the night before the battle opened, some thought that if Mitscher's advice had been taken, there would have been an encounter on the morning of June 19, with the planes of Task Force 58 within combat range of the Japanese fleet. Of course, no one knew what would have happened then, but it was generally believed that the Japanese ships would have suffered crippling losses and that the battle would have been decisive. A factor influencing this feeling was that the officers and men of Task Force 58 admired Admiral Mitscher and were inclined to believe in his judgment.

Being skeptical by nature, I felt that this implied criticism of Admiral Spruance's decision to return to cover Saipan on June 18 was inappropriate. What we knew, as opposed to what we could only speculate, was that the Japanese fleet had come out to oppose the landings on Saipan; had attacked our fleet with over four hundred carrier-based aircraft; had done no damage to our fleet; had not interfered with our troops ashore; and had lost most of their planes in the process. After this futile effort they had fled for their homeland, abandoning the Marianas and the Philippine Sea to our forces—not from lack of courage or fighting spirit but in the certainty that they would have lost everything had they not done so.

Had we followed Admiral Mitscher's advice, we might have achieved equal or greater success, or we might have been fooled: the Japanese might have swung wide to the north to hit our support forces near the Saipan beaches in our absence. It was therefore arguable that the safe course of action, successful as it ultimately proved, was preferable to one that was by its nature far less certain. If we accept the premise that control of the seas was the primary function of the fleet, then the Battle of the Philippine Sea, which resulted in unquestioned control of the western Pacific Ocean by the U.S. Navy, would have to be judged a major victory.

From the Japanese point of view, there was no doubt as to the result of the battle, although their propaganda cloaked their dismay. First, there was no further attempt to aid their forces in the Marianas. Their troops were expected to fight until they perished, which they did. Among those to die was Adm. Chuichi Nagumo, who had been the commander of the carrier strike force that had attacked Pearl Harbor; he committed suicide on Saipan. Secondly, Adm. Jisaburo Ozawa, who had commanded the First Mobile Fleet in the battle just ended, submitted his resignation when the fleet returned to Okinawa. Although his resignation was not accepted, no one in the Japanese government thought the battle had been anything except a victory for the United States. Third, Gen. Hideki Tojo would be forced to resign as premier after the fall of Saipan, in recognition of the fact that the war, which he had instigated, was now beyond winning.

There was an unfortunate result of the American misconceptions concerning the success of this battle. With the exception of the chief of Naval Operations, Adm. Ernest J. King, our top strategic planners did not appreciate that the extent of this victory should have required a thorough and careful reevaluation of the strategic plan for the balance of the war against Japan. Admiral Nimitz had originally recommended, during the summer of 1943, that Formosa should be the objective after the Marianas. He had repeated this recommendation in December 1943 and had followed it up every time the opportunity arose. It was apparent to him that retaking the Philippines after we had gained the Marianas was unnecessary, as they would be liberated without loss of life or property once Japan had surrendered. He and King stood together after the Battle of the Philippine Sea in pressing for this line of attack once more. Despite the navy's strategic recommendations, when President Roosevelt met with MacArthur, Nimitz, and King following the battle, MacArthur's persistent view that the Philippines must now be liberated again prevailed. The events of the next six months would be the result of MacArthur's continuing dominance at the planning table.

While the officers of Task Force 58 knew that the Japanese carrier air groups had been decisively defeated, they had no conception as to how the war should be prosecuted in the future. We were not in a position to judge the relative importance of the many islands, large or small, still under Japanese control. For us, an enemy-held island was an enemy-held island, no more, no less. Doubtless Admiral Spruance understood the well-thought-out reasoning behind the navy's plans to bypass the Philippines, but like Admiral Nimitz, he also knew when he had lost an argument.

Our task group, filled as it was with armchair analysts, returned to within sight of Saipan at 0930 on June 24. At this time TG 58.7, the Battle Line, was dissolved back into the carrier groups, the five battleships and DesRon 1 rejoining our group. Cruiser Division 12 and DesDiv 90 were then released from our formation to return to Admiral Turner's assault forces.

We were brought up to date on the progress being made by the forces ashore on Saipan. There were hints that the 27th Infantry Division was lacking in aggressiveness, at least as compared to that of the 2d and 4th Marine Divisions. This difference in attitude had resulted in an uneven offensive and a considerable extension of the time it was taking to secure the island. Because of the delay in the land offensive, Admiral Mitscher was directed to maintain elements of Task Force 58 in the Saipan-Guam area to provide additional fire support and intercept Japanese aircraft from other bases. He selected our task group for this duty, and we alone remained on station in the Marianas archipelago.

13

The *Cotten* and Destroyer Squadron 50 Screen the Battle Line

Between June 25 and July 6, our task group remained in the Marianas. Because the demands of this duty were considerably more relaxed than those of the period that had immediately preceded it, Alex Early, with the captain's approval, decided to permit Norman Campbell, Walter Walborn, and myself to stand a series of officer of the deck watches in order to qualify us as regular watch standers. During the next five weeks we took turns standing these watches, replacing the regular watch standers in succession. This did not mean that we would immediately get to stand OOD watches on a regular basis, but becoming fully qualified to do so would put us in line to replace the current watch standers when they left the ship.

The task group left the Marianas on July 6 and set sail for Eniwetok for replenishment, arriving on July 9. On the way back we learned that Admiral Nimitz had announced that Saipan had been declared secured by the assault forces of the Fifth Fleet. This announcement was technically correct, but there were still hundreds of Japanese on the island who were in no mood to give up. Mopping up these diehards would continue for many months after the announcement.

The *Cotten* and its fellow members of the task group entered the harbor at Eniwetok during the morning watch and anchored. We remained for only five days, the minimum time for basic replenishment. At Eniwetok, Fred Butler organized "moonlight requisition" forays to obtain supplies, such as paint and manila cordage, that regular requisitions were failing to obtain on a timely basis. Imagination and entrepreneurial ingenuity, backed up as needed by gifts of bourbon whiskey that had been donated to the *Cotten*'s officers' mess by Commander Destroyers Pacific, were necessary for a successful supply officer doing business in an advance naval operating base.

Eniwetok was not the natural island paradise that Majuro was, and the desirability of the place for recreation was lessened further by two circumstances. In the first place, prior to the marines' landing in mid-February, the principal islands had been subjected to an intense naval bombardment, which had destroyed all the trees. Secondly, the *Cotten*'s crew was under pressure to get the ship ready and supplied for another extended period at sea, so time for relaxed afternoons on the beach was not available. As a result, the crew had to be content with recognition of their downing the Japanese dive-bomber on June 19 by the painting of another enemy flag on the port side of the bridge screen. While these flags were a source of pride generally, the last one was particularly important to the crews of the port side heavy machine guns.

Cornatzer and Gifford, the two signalmen wounded on June 19, were transferred to the destroyer tender *Piedmont* for treatment, as their injuries were not healing properly. The six others wounded the same day had long since gone back to duty. Their wounds had healed quickly; scars and their Purple Heart medals had been the reward for their troubles.

On July 14, our departure date, Chief Boatswain's Mate Albert C. McCullough came aboard to replace CBM Alessy, who had been in charge of the deck forces since commissioning. By naval custom the chief boatswain's mate was the ranking enlisted man aboard ship and usually the most able seaman by training and experience. Alessy had been in the navy for twenty-three years, two years longer than I had been alive. He had forgotten more about seamanship than most of us were likely to know, but he also possessed most of a sailor's vices, especially when it came to heavy drinking. McCullough was about ten years younger than Alessy and seemed as genuinely happy to join the *Cotten* as Alessy obviously was to leave.

Just after noon on the same day, our task group (58.3) put back to sea. Rear Adm. A. E. Montgomery had replaced Admiral Reeves as task group commander, the carrier *Bunker Hill* becoming his flagship. *Lexington*, with Admiral Mitscher still aboard as CTF 58, and *San Jacinto* rounded out our carrier force. Battleship *Alabama* and light cruiser *Reno*, along with DesRon 50, completed the formation.

During the afternoon, the destroyers formed into column on either side of the carriers for two hours to fire antiaircraft guns at towed sleeves. At 1900 the formation resumed the normal circular cruising formation and headed west to return to the Marianas. This time the objective for our task group was to support the landing forces scheduled to hit Guam on July 21 and Tinian on July 24. It was now all but certain that there would be no further intervention by Japanese naval forces in the Marianas area. The failure of their navy to assist them did not mean, however, that the Japanese forces on Guam and Tinian would not continue to fight.

By this time Americans were not surprised at the suicidal determination of the Japanese military, having had the opportunity to observe it at first hand on Guadalcanal and Tarawa, and most recently on Saipan. The Japanese on Saipan had literally fought to the finish. At the end of the campaign there had been some four thousand Japanese troops left of the twenty-two thousand effectives at the start, not counting those hidden in the hills. These four thousand had made a final attack that for its ferocity was unprecedented. By the time the attack was over, every Japanese participant was dead. With this knowledge of the enemy, no one in the Pacific Fleet or the Marine Corps felt at this time that the Japanese believed they could be defeated. On the contrary, the end still seemed as distant as it had been when the *Cotten* had entered the Pacific area some ten months previously.

For an hour and a half on the afternoon of July 15 during the trip back to the Marianas area, the *Cotten* and *Reno* escorted *Lexington* out of the formation and into the northeasterly wind for flight operations, while the task group continued on its westerly course. It was a pleasure to operate in such a small and select formation. The ocean seemed larger, the ships smaller, and the relationship between the ships more fraternal. Reactions of the officers on watch quickened, and the ship's execution of its maneuvers was perfect. When the flight operations concluded, the three ships speeded up to overtake and rejoin the task group.

As our task group was approaching Guam at dawn on July 18, we met the Battle Line, Task Group 58.7, which had been re-formed during our absence. During the forenoon watch, the two task groups merged, the Battle Line becoming a part of our task group, 58.3. Battleships *Iowa*, *New Jersey*, *Washington*, and *Indiana* took positions with the carriers and *Alabama* in the interior of the formation, and DesDiv 4 joined the screen.

On July 19 we reached the Marianas, and the carrier air groups spent the day striking targets on Guam that had been pinpointed by aerial reconnaissance. At 1400 *Iowa, New Jersey, Alabama,* and DesDiv 100 left the formation for a two-day shore bombardment against targets on Guam immediately prior to the landing of our troops, which took place in the forenoon of July 21.

On July 24, TG 58.4 joined our group in tactical concentration, and both groups then joined with elements of the fueling group. Fueling was completed on July 25, and our two groups, TG 58.3 and TG 58.4, joined in tactical concentration with TG 58.1 and TG 58.2. That brought Task Force 58 to full force, with four fast carrier task groups, for the first time since the June battle with the Japanese fleet. Marines from the Saipan invasion force landed on the island of Tinian, only four miles away from Saipan and well within range of the Saipan-based marine artillery. On this day the air groups of Task Force 58 were active in direct support of these marines as well as the ones now progressing quickly against the Japanese troops on Guam.

The landings on both Guam and Tinian were proceeding as planned, which permitted the release of our task group at nightfall of July 26 for a high-speed run to the Palau area of the Caroline Islands. The group's mission was to make detailed aerial photographic reconnaissance flights over the island of Peleliu (which had been designated as an objective for capture by the marines in September) and on the next day the atoll of Ulithi (another future objective for the marines, to be used by the fleet as an advance naval base). This task was accomplished without difficulty, and we arrived back in the vicinity of Saipan at noon of July 30.

At this time Task Force 58 again split up, with TG 58.2 retiring to Eniwetok and TG 58.4 remaining in the Marianas, joined by four of our battleships and DesDiv 4. Our group, less the foregoing ships, entered the Saipan harbor so that the carriers could replace the rockets, bombs, and napalm that had been expended on Guam and Tinian.

We returned to sea on August 2, joined by five cruisers, *Vincennes, Houston, Miami, Mobile,* and *Reno.* Our carrier force now consisted of *Bunker Hill, Lexington, Franklin,* and light carrier *San Jacinto.* Early in the morning of August 3, the *Cotten* was directed by Admiral Montgomery to distribute a new operation order to the ships of the task group, after which it steamed north toward the Bonin Islands, six hundred miles distant, in tactical concentration with TG 58.1. The new operation orders called for two days of air strikes, the first day on Iwo Jima and the second day on Hahajima, with additional strikes on Chichi-jima. The two-task-group formation arrived at the launching position at dawn of August 4, to find the weather too squally for air operations, until the sky cleared up.

At 1210, TG 58.1 reported that its air groups were attacking ten enemy ships in Chichi-jima Harbor, some 120 miles north of our position. They had also indicated the presence of an enemy convoy fifteen miles north-west of the same island. Admiral Mitscher immediately detached Cruiser Division 13 and DesDiv 100, from TG 58.1 and TG 58.3 respectively, to join up and proceed at maximum speed toward this convoy, with orders to destroy it by gunfire. During the evening this destroyer-cruiser group caught up with the convoy and reported by radio that its ships were in the process of finishing it off.

It was that evening that I started standing my long-sought-after officer of the deck qualification watches, Walborn's and Campbell's having been successfully concluded. I took Snowden's place in the regular rotation, along with Stokey, Kanter, and Dorman, who were back in their former watch positions.

During the afternoon of the next day, August 5, our Destroyer Division 99 and CruDiv 14 were detached from Task Group 58.3 to join with CruDiv 13 and DesDiv 100, which had returned after destroying the Japanese convoy. The two cruiser divisions and the whole of our destroyer squadron, less *Caperton,* were then ordered south to join the Battle Line (TG 58.7), carrying out as many cruiser-destroyer exercises as possible en route. This group had formed up by 1900; it was designated Task Unit 58.1.7, with Commander Cruiser Division 14 (ComCruDiv 14) as officer in tactical command. These ships then deployed, with the cruiser divisions in two parallel columns and eight destroyers of DesRon 50 in a bent-line screen five thousand yards ahead. The formation set a course to effect a rendezvous with the Battle Line on the morning of August 7, a day and a half off.

During the following thirty-six hours, this group of cruisers and destroyers entered into a series of search and attack exercises, consisting of maneuvers designed to protect a line of battleships in an engagement with an enemy battle line. These maneuvers included torpedo attacks by the destroyers on the cruisers, and protective maneuvers by the destroyers and cruisers against enemy torpedo attacks. These exercises took place during the night as well as by day, and they included main battery live offset firing by the cruisers against destroyer targets.

On the morning of August 7, our cruiser-destroyer group met and joined the Battle Line, TG 58.7, which was in the process of fueling from the oiler group. All ships fueled to capacity by 1335; the oilers then departed.

The cruiser-destroyer task unit of which the *Cotten* had been a part was dissolved, and our ships officially became attached to the Battle Line. This newly constituted group's orders were now to return to Eniwetok, a thousand miles to the east, for logistical preparations for the next operation. On the trip back we were to engage in extensive maneuvers, both daytime and nighttime, in order to bring all the units to a level of proficiency acceptable to Admiral Lee in the very specialized tactical requirements of the Battle Line.

The inclusion of Destroyer Squadron 50 with the Battle Line was an important event for us. Task Force 58 was the unquestioned cutting edge of the Pacific Fleet and its dominant weapon, but TG 58.7, the Battle Line, remained the critical fallback weapon to counter the as-yet-undiminished capability of the heavily gunned surface ships of the Japanese navy. The once-powerful Japanese carrier task force had been reduced to impotence in the Battle of the Philippine Sea, at least until its air groups could be reconstituted as effective offensive forces. Because the most likely adversary in any major fleet engagement would certainly be the undamaged heavy surface striking force, our own battle line could well play a critical role. The setting for such an engagement between the two battle lines would probably be darkness, when the lack of air cover would be a minimal disadvantage for the Japanese, who were known for their proficiency in nighttime surface tactics, resulting from decades of training in this specific art.

Therefore, to be one of the two destroyer squadrons assigned to screen our battle line not only was a great honor but carried a responsibility that under the right circumstances could be of historic importance. Because our experience in destroyer-squadron fleet tactics was minimal, it behooved us to make the most of the coming exercises and to gain confidence in conning the ship during the high-speed and intricate nighttime maneuvers.

To date, night battles between surface units of the two navies had been fought only between relatively small cruiser-destroyer groups, seldom battleships—never more than two. The last time two large fleets had fought at night had been during the final stages of the Battle of Jutland in 1916. Even a most careful reconstruction of that action shows that no one was in control by the end of the battle and that confusion was pervasive on both sides. At that time the conning officers of the ships of a squadron or division at night had to concentrate their attention on maintaining their ship's proper station in either the column or, what is more difficult and more likely, *en echelon* on a line of bearing, with no time for the contemplation of the battle as a whole. In the Battle of Jutland the commanders of both fleets lost effective control of their squadrons after a small number of maneuvers, and the battle became a melee.

With the recent development of surface search radar, now on all American ships, and the perfection of the night optics on all Japanese ships, the admirals on both sides could keep track of their squadrons at night in a way that the Germans and British could not in 1916. It was now possible to keep control of a nighttime battle, even if the officers conning the individual ships might still have little feel for the overall tactical situation.

For destroyer divisions, maintenance of station in a line of bearing was critical when delivering or repelling a torpedo attack. During a battle, this line of bearing would have to be changed many times to maintain the proper alignment against the enemy, each change demanding precise maneuvering by the individual conning officers. Station was taken on the ship designated the division guide, but often the ships at the far end of the line would have to modify their positions, because the distance between the intervening ships could expand and contract like an accordion during the action. At the standard distance between ships of three hundred yards, a stadimeter—an optical range-finding device—was more useful than radar in keeping station; the junior officer of the watch was responsible for keeping the conning officer constantly advised. A ship out of position was both obvious and distracting to everyone else in the division, and very difficult for its conning officer to get back into station. Knowledge of the difficulty of nighttime battle maneuvers keyed up those who were to be responsible for the ship's performance, imparting something akin to the apprehensive feelings an athlete has before a contest.

Our formal fleet exercises began during the morning of August 8, when the various units maneuvered to take their assigned initial positions. CruDiv 13 and DesDiv 99 (including *Cotten*) were assigned to an initial station seventy-five miles ahead, and to the left, of the main body; there they were to separate into two sections, with fifteen miles between them. These positions were finally reached in the evening after dusk, at which time the battle problem commenced. Our two sections now reversed course to head back separately toward the main body. When radar contact was made, they increased speed to twenty-five knots to make gunfire and destroyer torpedo attacks on the battle line. After this exercise was completed, our cruiser-destroyer force re-formed behind the battle line until the next morning, when we returned to our original cruising positions, cruisers in column alongside the battleships, and the destroyers in a bent line ahead of the columns of heavy ships.

During the next day the entire Battle Line split into two equal groups for a new exercise. One group consisted of battleships *Washington* and *Alabama*, cruisers *Vincennes*, *Houston*, and *Miami*, and DesRon 50 (less *Cotten*); the other consisted of battleships *Iowa* and *Indiana*, cruisers *Santa Fe*, *Mobile*, and *Birmingham*, and DesRon 52, plus *Cotten*. Continuing on their general course to the east, the two groups gradually separated in order to put a distance of eighty miles between them by the following morning, at which time a simulated battle-line surface battle would be fought.

The exercise started early the next morning, August 10, when the two groups each launched scouting planes to search ahead on an arc one hundred miles in radius. At 0950 the search planes of *Cotten's* force returned, reporting the position of the "enemy." Our admiral then formed his group on a course and axis designed to close the range on the enemy, bearing to our right. Our main body consisted of battleships *Iowa* and *Indiana,* with destroyers *Stephen Potter* and *Miller* in column astern simulating additional battleships. There were three flanking columns, the left consisting of *Vincennes* and *Owen,* the right *Houston, The Sullivans,* and *Tingey,* and the center *Miami, Marshall,* and *Cotten.*

Cotten was directed to take station as a picket in the direction of the "enemy," in a position ten miles due south of our main body. While the *Cotten* was speeding at twenty-five knots to its new station, the heavy ships launched six float planes as spotters for the exercise. At 0924 we picked up the main body of the "enemy" on our radar, bearing due south at a range of forty-seven thousand yards, and the "battle" commenced. During the next hour the battleships simulated a long-range, main-battery gunfire engagement, while the cruisers and destroyers simulated simultaneous gunfire and torpedo runs on the opposing battle line.

Cotten was ordered to return from its picket station at maximum speed to join the left-flank destroyers, who were preparing their torpedo attack under the command of Commander Destroyer Squadron 52. We joined up at 1107, taking position at the end of the four-ship column for a high-speed run on the "enemy" main body. At noon both our torpedo attack and the "battle" were over, and the two recent "enemy" forces regrouped in their original formation, *Cotten* rejoining DesDiv 99.

Because each side may take evasive action in the face of torpedo or gunfire attack, such exercises became confusing. They were nonetheless stimulating and usually welcomed by the participants. For my part, I was grateful that my qualification watches happened to occur during this period, when high-speed maneuvering in close order occurred on a daily basis.

At 0600 on August 11, all of the cruisers and DesRon 50 were detached from the Battle Line with orders to proceed into the Eniwetok lagoon. The cruiser column subsequently entered the channel, with the divisions of Destroyer Squadron 50 patrolling a line on either side of the column. Once the cruisers were in the lagoon, DesRon 50 followed closely behind, the *Cotten* proceeding to berth 535, where it anchored at 1200.

With our return to Eniwetok, my OOD qualification watches were approved by Captain Sloat and were successfully concluded. While qualification had been a major ambition and foremost objective for many months, now that it was achieved my spirits became subdued at the prospect of waiting for enough vacancies to occur among the current watch standers to push me up to a permanent spot. Of course, Walborn and Campbell were just as eager as I for the first available assignment, making for a highly competitive situation, which was something of a novelty for the three of us.

Standing the OOD watch while under way with the fleet in wartime circumstances is more challenging than any other assignment, in my opinion. Officers of the deck on the larger ships were customarily experienced commanders or lieutenant commanders, yet their responsibilities and challenges were little different from those of the destroyer OODs, except that the former had considerably less opportunity to guide their ships in complicated maneuvers. Because in a little over a year I, as a twenty-two-year-old ensign, had become a fully qualified OOD on a destroyer of the Pacific Fleet, there was no question in my mind concerning my own good fortune. The events of Forager and the assignment to the Battle Line were a turning point for the *Cotten*, and no less for me.

14

Command
Changes

Back at anchor, there was opportunity for relaxation and reflection. It now seemed as though the strains of command were getting the best of Captain Sloat. He was often tired, to the degree that his characteristic quickness of temper seemed to have lost its sting. When he was on the bridge during the day, he sat in his chair and dozed away the hours, even with his most youthful OODs on watch. Having observed the total inexperience of Walborn, Campbell, and myself when we had first reported to him for duty, and considering how recently we had been qualified to stand OOD watches, one would have thought that he would have watched us more closely. He must have known his time as captain was coming to its conclusion—all the more reason for him to hope to finish up with the *Cotten* doing him credit. However, he acted as though he thought I was as qualified as I did myself, for which I was grateful.

With respect to Early, during the latest cruise the captain had been as courteous as he had ever been with us, avoiding any scenes and letting the exec go about his business, setting the ship's routine without interference or comment. What appeared to be a relaxation of the conflict between the two lightened our environment.

Shortly after the *Cotten* anchored, the squadron flagship, *C. K. Bronson*, moored alongside, to remain for one day. Captain Sloat had two visits with the squadron commander during this time, presumably giving each the opportunity to review the operations since the first of the year and to make suggestions that might have been reserved for this opportunity. Whatever was discussed was privileged, in any case.

As far as the rest of us were concerned, officers and men alike, the ten days spent anchored in berth 535 provided a generous amount of time for replenishment of provisions and ammunition, for repairs, and for upkeep that could be done by the ship's personnel. An opportunity was given to everyone for an afternoon on the beach with beer and swimming. For those who were so inclined, there was also the possibility of joining a crap game with officers of the other destroyers, perhaps thirty avid gamblers arranged in a large ring. Back on the ship, free hours were spent writing letters and reading those from home. There was ice cream for all hands at supper, and every evening after sunset a different movie was shown on the forecastle.

On August 20 the *Cotten* got under way from the destroyer anchorage and entered a floating dry dock, ARD 13. The center of the dry dock was an open well, closed at one end and with two huge watertight doors at the other. When the doors were opened, the well contained water deep enough to allow the *Cotten* to enter and moor securely in the center. The outer doors were then closed, and the water in the well was pumped out; the *Cotten* came to rest securely on blocks. The pumping-out process took the better part of the day, after which a complete inspection was made by the dock personnel of the hull, rudder, propellers, shafts, sea-injection valves, and zincs (which protected the metal hull and fittings against corrosion by electrolysis). The inspectors decided that the bottom was badly in need of scraping and painting—a full coat of antifouling paint, one coat of black boot-topping at the waterline, and one coat of camouflage paint on the hull.

Starting after supper, all hands turned to on the scraping and painting, which was accomplished and approved by sunrise of the next morning. Shortly thereafter the flooding of the dry dock was begun, a process that took about two hours. The doors were then opened, and we backed out of the dry dock and steamed over to the oiler *Manileno* to take on fuel. This completed, we got under way and returned alongside *C. K. Bronson* once again. It was hard to believe what had been accomplished in a little less than one day.

On August 23 we got under way to moor alongside the destroyer tender *Piedmont* for a five-day tender "availability," during which the repair crews of the tender performed the work orders we had submitted and that had been approved by the squadron commander. On August 24 we were advised that

Rear Adm. Frederic C. Sherman had assumed command of our task group, his flagship the fleet carrier *Essex*. On August 26 all ships of the Fifth Fleet were advised that they were being transferred to the Third Fleet, Adm. William F. Halsey commanding. Task Force 58 became Task Force 38, Admiral Mitscher still commanding in flagship *Lexington;* our task group, 58.3, became TG 38.3, Admiral Sherman in command. On August 27, our squadron commander, Capt. C. F. Chillingworth Jr., was replaced by Capt. E. R. Wilkinson. Also that day Alex Early was relieved as executive officer and detached from the *Cotten*. After packing up and making his farewells, he left the ship in the early forenoon.

During the afternoon of the following day, Lt. Cdr. Philip W. Winston came aboard the *Cotten* to relieve Cdr. Frank T. Sloat as commanding officer; Commander Sloat, in turn, was ordered to report to the Bureau of Ships in Washington, D.C. The ship went to general quarters for drill as part of the change-of-command ceremony, which was brought to a close by the reading of the new captain's orders before the entire crew, assembled "at quarters" for the purpose.

Later in the day, Lt. Robert I. Rothschild, formerly the first lieutenant of our sister ship *Dortch,* reported aboard the *Cotten* to become the new executive officer. Bob Rothschild chose to share the stateroom where I had lived since commissioning, which would give me the chance to become acquainted with the new exec somewhat sooner than the other officers.

These changes affected us directly, with respect to our commanding and executive officers, and indirectly, with respect to the higher echelons. The replacement of Admiral Spruance by Admiral Halsey created mixed emotions. I had grown to have great confidence in the judgment and tactical skill of Admiral Spruance, to the point that I cannot recall a time when I thought he should have done something other than what he actually did. This is as unusual in military life as it is in any other human endeavor, where second-guessing one's superior is considered a cultural pastime. There were those who did second-guess Admiral Spruance, but I was not one of them.

Admiral Halsey, at this time known to us mainly by his well-publicized reputation, was quite another proposition. He had enjoyed extensive press coverage and had been directly quoted as denigrating the character of our enemy. I felt that this was unnecessary, and I could not see how this conduct in a commander was going to elevate the performance of his subordinates. Our brief assignment to his Third Fleet en route to Espiritu Santo had entailed no direct contact with Halsey or his staff, so we had no feel for what his style of leadership would be or any knowledge of his tactical ability. Finally, I believed that his association with General MacArthur in the southwest Pacific over a protracted period had to have adversely affected him, so deep was my personal antipathy for the egocentric general. To sum up my own feelings, the substitution of Halsey for Spruance was not likely to be an improvement.

The replacement of Admiral Montgomery by Admiral Sherman as CTG 38.3 was not important to the personnel of a screen destroyer. Admiral Montgomery had seemed a fine commander to us, but there was no reason to believe that Admiral Sherman, an officer experienced in carrier tactics, should not do very well in his new command. For my own part, the appointment of a new squadron commander was a minor event, as we had contact with him only when the squadron was operating as a tactical unit, such as during exercises of torpedo tactics or of cruiser-destroyer search and attack tactics. These occasions were rare, although they had been somewhat more frequent of late, since our assignment to the screen of the Battle Line.

The more important changes were those on the *Cotten* itself. Without question, for the officers and men serving on a naval ship, the captain is a person of vital importance. For an officer serving under him, the captain is the source of all authority, of one's assignment to duty, and most important, of the evaluations of one's ability summarized in the "fitness reports" sent on a regular basis to the officer's personal file located in the Bureau of Personnel. The fitness report is the commanding officer's official assessment of an officer's progress and his qualifications to perform various duties. Comments pro and con as to his character, leadership abilities, quickness to learn, and ability to understand and execute orders are also appropriate in a fitness report.

Captain Sloat's fitness reports on the officers of the *Cotten* were available to Captain Winston and formed the latter's initial opinion of our wardroom. Of course, he was soon to form his own opinion, which could be considerably at odds with that of the officer he replaced. This fact of life tended to focus one's attention on endeavoring to make a solid impression on the new captain. This also required attempting to understand his personality, which in Captain Winston's case was quite different from Captain Sloat's.

Captain Winston was a Naval Academy graduate, class of 1933. He had been released from active duty due to a reduction in the size of the navy, to be recalled when the naval buildup prior to the war began. Although he had experience at sea, his most recent duty had been as an instructor at the Naval Academy. The obvious professional difference between Sloat and Winston concerned their comparative time in destroyers. Because the *Cotten* now enjoyed an experienced cadre of officers, most of whom had been to sea for at least a year in almost continuous combat, Captain Winston did not have the initial responsibility of teaching us our jobs; he could concentrate on learning his own. He was a man of quick intelligence and intellectual depth, so he did not have any difficulty fitting into his new and highly demanding job as our commanding officer.

A noticeable difference between the two captains was in their personal styles and mannerisms. Sloat had been my idea of a sea dog, with the volatile reactions and colorful vocabulary that years of sea duty will impart to almost anyone. Winston was the epitome of a Virginia gentleman, with what bordered on drawing-room manners, and for a while this characteristic kept us more than a little off balance.

The new exec, Bob Rothschild, who preferred to be called "Rocky," knew how his job should be done. The executive officer is the one who directs the officers in their duties and passes out their assignments, with the proper clearance from the captain. The ideal captain rules the ship through his exec, so that the captain is shielded from direct contact with the officers except when they are on duty as OOD. It was fortunate for us all that Rothschild was somewhat informal when it came to military etiquette, as Captain Winston was definitely a stickler in this respect.

Rothschild had a good grasp of the operation of a *Fletcher*-class destroyer, having been first lieutenant of the *Dortch* since it was commissioned. He had grown up in Winnetka, Illinois, a suburb of Chicago, and was a graduate of Williams. He was practical and tough, and he had enough self-confidence to do his job as an individual, without appeal to his superior military rank. This was a desirable approach, because a destroyer is so cramped, mechanical, and physically close to the sea that the military pomp associated with the battle line is conspicuous by its absence.

We were to find that the change of command, which can easily change the personality of a ship, affected the *Cotten* very little, despite the wide differences in the characters of our new and former commanding officers.

15

Admiral Halsey Trains the Battle Line

On August 29 we received "Commander Task Force 34 Operation Plan 10-44" from Vice Admiral Lee. Task Force 34 was the same organization that had been designated Task Group 58.7 in the Fifth Fleet, namely the Battle Line. Under the new Third Fleet table of organization, DesRon 50 was now permanently assigned to the Battle Line, as well as a member of Carrier Task Group 38.3.

The upgrading of the Battle Line from a task group to a task force was a change in emphasis as well as of organization. Admiral Halsey intended to continue to have the heavy ships of the Battle Line remain in the nucleuses of the various carrier task groups, but upgrading the Battle Line's status indicated that he meant to use it more aggressively than had Admiral Spruance. Because the Battle Line was now of equal status to the Fast Carrier Task Force of Vice Admiral Mitscher, it would fall directly under Admiral Halsey whenever it was formed, eliminating Mitscher from the chain of command.

The operation plan covered the activity of Task Force 34 for the period between the sortie from Eniwetok, scheduled for August 30, until a rendezvous could be made with Admiral Mitscher's Task Force 38 (the new designation of the Fast Carrier Task Force) in the vicinity of the Palau Islands on or about September 11.

Admiral Lee stated that the cruise of Task Force 34 would be an occasion for further training in the tactics of the battle line, in cruiser-destroyer night search and attack tactics, and in destroyer torpedo-attack tactics. The objective of Task Force 34 was to "destroy enemy naval forces in opposition to our occupation and defense of Palau Islands, Yap and Ulithi, and Philippine Island strikes." The tone of the directive reflected the aggressiveness of the Third Fleet commander, Admiral Halsey.

At dawn on the morning of August 30, the *Cotten* got under way with the other destroyers of DesRon 50 to form the customary antisubmarine screen outside the channel during the sortie of the heavy ships of Task Force 34. On the bridge along with Herb Kanter, who was OOD for the special sea detail (set for entering and leaving port), were Captain Winston, Rocky Rothschild, and our navigator, Norman Campbell. When the nine destroyers of our squadron were on station, battleships *Washington* (Admiral Lee's flagship), *Indiana*, *Alabama*, and *Massachusetts* made their sortie in column. *Cotten* and the rest of DesDiv 99 then formed a screen ahead of the column, with DesDiv 100 similarly stationed astern. Aircraft towing target-sleeves were sent from Eniwetok for practice by the machine gun batteries, now a routine exercise to get the crews reacclimated to their weapons. At 1745 the six cruisers of CruDiv 13 and CruDiv 14 and seven destroyers of DesRon 52 joined the formation.

At noon of the next day, August 31, CruDiv 13, CruDiv 14, and DesRon 50 were ordered to leave TF 34 to form a cruiser-destroyer light attack force. During the night this cruiser force split in two, with DesDiv 99 and CruDiv 14 taking station twelve miles north of CruDiv 13 and DesDiv 100. Our ships were pulling ahead of the Battle Line, so when the exercise started at 0400 of September 1, we were twenty-five miles ahead to the west. We deployed for attack much as we had practiced during the exercises of the past month, cruisers forming in line of bearing to take the destroyers that were screening the Battle Line under simulated main battery gunfire, then our own two destroyer divisions deploying in line of bearing to deliver our torpedo attack at flank speed on the Battle Line itself. The exercise was completed by 0543, when we rejoined TF 34. A similar fleet exercise was conducted during the night of September 2–3.

During early dawn of September 3, a temporary rendezvous was made with the Fast Carrier Task Force, our position being three hundred miles northeast of a new advance naval base on Manus Island. A new task group, TG 38.5, was then formed for more exercises; it consisted of battleships *Washington*, *Iowa*, *Indiana*, *Alabama*, and *Massachusetts*, along with our

DesDiv 99; the balance of the destroyers and the two cruiser divisions of Task Force 34 had been ordered to join their previously assigned carrier task groups (TGs 38.1 and 38.2). Admiral Mitscher's four carrier task groups of TF 38 then left us behind and proceeded in tactical concentration westward, toward the Palau Islands.

From a personal point of view, one of the more important radio messages we received at this time was an "Alnav" (addressed to all naval commands) announcing the most recent promotion list for junior officers. Then naval officers were automatically raised in rank when their serial numbers reached the promotion area, which both mine and Norman Campbell's had achieved as of September 1. The effect of the message was to promote us both to the rank of lieutenant, junior grade, and to increase our monthly salary by fifteen dollars per month. Despite the fact that these changes were blanket ones, they were welcome.

At 0615 on the morning of September 6, battleship New Jersey, with Admiral Halsey aboard, along with destroyers Hunt and Hickox, joined up with our formation. The captain of Hickox was still Joe Wesson, our original executive officer.

From September 6 through 10, Task Group 38.5 continued to steam independently while the fast carrier task groups delivered air strikes against Japanese positions in the Palau Islands to the east and the central Philippines to the west. Since our formation had no carriers, we continued with exercises for the battleships, drills now mainly devoted to their antiaircraft fire control. Their float planes were launched every day to make simulated torpedo attacks on the battle line, giving the 5-inch batteries a chance to track the low-flying planes as they dodged and weaved on their runs in to their launch points. In the afternoon the planes towed sleeves for the gunners to shoot at. The fire a battleship could put up, with its five twin 5-inch turrets on either side, was not only twice the volume from our own five single mounts but was also considerably more accurate, due to the greater steadiness of the gun platform.

The fast carrier task groups returned on September 10 during the morning, and Admiral Halsey and his staff transferred, via the destroyer Hunt, from New Jersey to Admiral Mitscher's flagship Lexington in TG 38.3, for a conference. The transfer between ships could only be accomplished by breeches buoy; Admiral Halsey had four trips in that precarious mode of travel before he was safely back aboard New Jersey after the conference.

While aboard the Lexington, the two admirals reviewed the operational results of the air strikes against bases on the Philippine island of Mindanao. Admiral Mitscher reported that the level of Japanese air strength in Mindanao was extremely weak and that in his opinion, there were presently no targets in the southern Philippines worth the power of Task Force 38. The two admirals agreed to recommend to Admiral Nimitz that the timetable for offensive operations in the Philippines be accelerated by two months and that seizure of Peleliu be eliminated as unnecessary. They also agreed to head TF 38 to the north to see if there were more likely targets for its air groups on Leyte, Luzon, or Formosa. Admiral Mitscher was authorized to issue orders to his carrier task groups to get such an operation under way immediately. Certainly Admiral Halsey was not going to let his fleet stand idle while he was in command.

At noon, battleship-destroyer Task Group 38.5 was dissolved, and the battleships and DesRon 50 joined Admiral Sherman's TG 38.3. Task Group 38.3 now consisted of fleet carriers *Essex* (flagship of Admiral Sherman) and *Lexington* (flagship of Admiral Mitscher) and light carriers *Princeton* and *Langley*; battleships *Washington* (flagship of Admiral Lee), *Massachusetts, Indiana,* and *Alabama*; and Cruiser Division 13, DesRon 50, and DesRon 55.

At 1430, DesDiv 99 was directed to fuel from the oiler group, and *Cotten* went alongside *Platte* for this purpose. Because *Platte* was scheduled to head for the Manus Island naval base soon after fueling *Cotten*, we were directed to transfer one of our crew members, who had been locked up aboard the ship for the past week, to the oiler so that he could be transported to Manus for a general court-martial.

The man under arrest was a pharmacist's mate who had been operating a late-night commercial sex establishment, with himself as both proprietor and sole inmate, in the confines of mount 3 of the 5-inch gun battery. This particular gun was never manned during the regular Condition III watches, because its location (directly astern of the after smokestack and forward of a deckhouse) was such that while it could fire freely to port or starboard, it was limited to high elevations when pointed fore or aft. For this reason there was guaranteed privacy for his particular business that would have been impossible anywhere else in the crowded confines of the destroyer. He probably would never have been discovered by the *Cotten*'s command structure had he not developed a heated passion for a newly arrived seventeen-year-old replacement sailor. This sailor, who had reported aboard when we had been in Eniwetok, had rebuffed the pharmacist's mate's initial advance but, being very inexperienced, had made no report of the event to his petty officer.

The pharmacist's mate's passion had then so increased in fervor that he had attacked the young sailor one night while he was asleep in his bunk, with some sixty other sailors asleep close by. The molested sailor had awakened at once and defended himself by assaulting the pharmacist's mate with enough energy and violence to pound him into the deck. This fray had been so noisy that the sixty other sailors were awakened and witnessed the disturbance. Cooler heads had eventually taken over; the pharmacist's mate had been told to leave the compartment and advised that a report would be made to the executive officer the next day.

After Rothschild heard the story from a petty officer in the morning, he had called in the young sailor, who blurted out his feelings of disgust at what had happened to him. In subsequent questioning of others, the exec had pieced together the scenario of mount 3's usage as a bordello, which finally was verified by enough sailors to constitute what he believed was sufficient evidence for referral to a general court-martial. A detailed formal report had been made up and sent to our new squadron commander by signal light. He in turn had asked the task group commander for authority to transfer the pharmacist's mate to the nearest general court-martial. The task group commander had concurred with the request and had quickly arranged for the transfer to a court on Manus, with transportation to be furnished by the oiler *Platte*.

While the *Cotten* was alongside the oiler fueling, the breeches buoy was rigged and the prisoner sent on his way. When he emerged from the breeches buoy on the oiler, some thirty feet away, he was taken into custody by an officer and led down the deck for incarceration in another makeshift brig. The prisoner patted the officer on his posterior while waving farewell to the sailors of the *Cotten*, who had lined our lifelines to observe the transfer. A loud cheer arose from our men, which provides some indication as to what now constituted high humor among the young crew members after being cooped up on a tin can for a year. Over the ensuing weeks, many watches on the *Cotten* were enlivened by stories about mount 3, the tales competing with each other in the outrageousness of their content.

When the fueling was complete, the oiler group headed south for Manus Island, and the three carrier task groups of TF 38 headed northwest for the Philippine Islands. By noon of September 12, our formation was within forty-five miles and visual distance of Siargao Island, a mountainous outcrop of volcanic origin off the northern tip of Mindanao. The water under the *Cotten*'s keel at that moment was 34,440 feet deep, the deepest part of the Philippine Trench and one of the deepest spots on the earth's surface.

Offensive air strikes were conducted against Japanese installations on Leyte and Cebu on September 12 and 13. Enemy air reaction was not effective, and our air groups claimed to have shot down many aircraft over the airfields. One enemy plane did manage to approach our task group during the day on September 12; it was at very high altitude and was able to escape without our fighters making contact.

Starting with the dawn flight operations on September 13, the *Cotten* acted as plane-guard destroyer, which was a new development. We would leave the circular screen before the start of flight operations and take station one thousand yards astern the carrier *Lexington*, to be in position to pick up any aircrew whose plane crashed on takeoff or landing. Now that there were over nine hundred planes on the carriers of TF 38 and the air groups' personnel were younger and less experienced than they had once been, every few days some pilot would ditch near his carrier, which made necessary the precaution of having a destroyer handy to pick them up promptly. Plane-guard duty was assigned to a different destroyer each day. When a plane was forced to ditch any distance away from the task group due to damage received over a target area, a float plane from one of the cruisers or battleships would be launched to make the rescue.

Enemy air activity over Leyte on September 13 was reported as sporadic. Accordingly, Task Force 38 headed farther north during the night to be in position to launch strikes against Samar, the next island north of Leyte, on the morning of September 14; this was done, without worthwhile results. At sundown on the fourteenth, the task force turned south to be in position by the next morning to launch air attacks on the island of Peleliu in advance of the first wave of marines, who were to make their landing (upon which Admiral Nimitz had insisted) at that time.

While the carriers were occupied with air support of the marines during the next morning, Admiral Halsey ordered the re-formation of Task Force 34 for some additional exercises in battle line tactics. We conducted tactical maneuvers similar to those we had gone through previously until late in the afternoon, when all ships rejoined their carrier task groups.

On September 16, *Cotten* picked up intelligence officers from *Essex, Langley,* and *Princeton* and delivered them to *Lexington* to take part in a conference reviewing what had been learned to date about the many Japanese air bases in the Philippines. We remained in the vicinity of Peleliu until noon of September 18, when TF 38 was relieved of responsibility of supporting the marines. The latter had at least established a viable beachhead, although the Peleliu operation was to prove one of the most drawn-out and costly campaigns of the Pacific War. Going ahead with the landing on Peleliu was the only respect in which Nimitz disregarded Halsey's and Mitscher's advice concerning acceleration of the assault on Leyte and elimination of landings in the Palau Islands. This was one of Admiral Nimitz's few mistakes in judgment, but a very costly one for the marines.

Course was then set for the north, with three fast carrier task groups steaming in tactical concentration, the fourth having returned to base for resupply. Our destination was a position close to the east coast of Luzon on the same latitude as Manila, with arrival scheduled for the predawn hours of September 21. During the final approach to Luzon, TF 38 was placed under radio silence by Admiral Halsey. This even restricted the use of the task group's tactical voice radio (TBS); we would have to maneuver by signal hoist, just like Admiral Horatio Nelson in 1802, in the dawn flight operations. Our final lunge toward Luzon was made at flank speed on a course directly toward the island; all ships had enough boilers on the line to reach thirty knots if necessary.

Dawn of September 21 arrived to find TF 38 in the middle of a tropical downpour so heavy that our surprise air strike had to be delayed until 0800. This day happened to be the *Cotten's* day for plane-guard duty. That required twice maneuvering from our position in the screen to plane-guard station astern of the carriers in the center and back to the screen again before the two strikes were on their way to the Manila area. At 0920 the men in our radio shack heard a Manila radio station announce that an air raid was in progress, then cease broadcasting. At the same time, our first strike reported that it was over the target area, Manila Bay, and that there were many cargo ships present but no warships. We now presumed that radio silence had ended, at least for our aircraft.

At 1015 the planes were reporting that they were being engaged by enemy fighters over Manila Bay. They also reported that the dive bombers and torpedo planes were enjoying some successes against the cargo ships, including three torpedo hits on a floating dry dock. The last strike was launched at 1430, and all planes were back on board before nightfall. The returning pilots reported that the aggregate damage inflicted had been 284 enemy aircraft destroyed, thirty-five ships sunk and twenty-seven damaged, and extensive damage done to the many enemy airfields. Such reports were always optimistic, sometimes misleadingly so.

The *Cotten* was then sent out twelve miles to the east of TG 38.3 as a night picket, with orders to return to the formation at dawn the next day. While we were out, the weather took a turn for the worse, overcast and squally, with the wind picking up considerably. At 0530 we detected several enemy planes on the air search radar seven miles away, at which we went to general quarters. Between 0545 and 0550, Stokey fired the 5-inch battery on two occasions at Japanese planes high overhead on their way toward our carriers, which were still twelve miles to our west. At 0600 we started to return to the formation at flank speed and shortly thereafter took another plane under fire with the 5-inch battery. Stokey had fired sixty rounds of 5-inch in all at these several planes without obtaining any hits, which was not surprising, as they had been several thousand feet above us on all three occasions. At 0720, back in the screen, we stood down from battle stations.

All three of the planes that our 5-inch guns fired at had been well outside the range of our heavy machine gun battery. The 40-mm was ineffective at ranges over two thousand yards, while anything over one thousand yards was fairly safe from 20-mm fire. The maximum ranges of these weapons were considerably in excess of their effective ranges, the 40-mm projectiles self-destructing after they had traveled four thousand yards.

An air strike was now launched, despite the foul weather, directed again at the Manila area. When these planes arrived over the target, they reported that the weather was much improved, while at the same time it was steadily deteriorating at sea over the carriers. At 1000 Admiral Mitscher canceled all further strikes because of the weather. The planes from the first attack group were safely back aboard before noon, at which time the task force turned to the east to rendezvous with the oiler group.

The next objective for the air groups after returning to the Philippine coast was Japanese shipping in the Visayan Sea—a small, shallow, inland body of water about eighty miles in diameter lying between the islands of Leyte, Negros, Cebu, Panay, and Masbate—through which all shipping be-tween points in the central Philippines must pass. On the afternoon of September 24, following completion of the air sweeps of the Visayan Sea, which had ended this series of operations in the Philippines, Admiral Halsey ordered the Battle Line formed once again.

At 0800 on September 25, the full complement of TF 34 was present. Throughout the forenoon the battleships held maneuvers of the Battle Line, with the cruisers and destroyers forming into columns and executing offensive and defensive tactics. During the afternoon there were antiaircraft exercises, with the heavy machine guns firing at sleeves towed by planes from Task Group 38.2, which was accompanying the Battle Line on its way to Saipan.

At 0530 of September 28, DesDiv 99 escorted *Iowa* and *New Jersey* into the Saipan harbor to replenish the ammunition that had been expended during exercises and the operations on the Philippine coast over the past several weeks. At 1604 on September 29 we left the harbor, again escorting *Iowa* and *New Jersey*, to join up with TF 34 and TG 38.2. Each group then formed up and independently set a southwesterly course for Ulithi Lagoon, which had been occupied by marines on September 23 without enemy op-position. Ulithi was ideally located for fleet operations in and around the Philippines, and it was to be the main forward operating base of the Central Pacific fleet for the next six months. We arrived outside the entrance chan-nel by dawn of the next morning, and after forming a protective screen for the entry of *Iowa* and *New Jersey*, followed them in to anchor, in the new destroyer anchorage. We thought that our powerful companions of Task Force 34 and ourselves were now as well prepared as possible for an encounter with the Japanese navy's battle line.

16

Third Fleet Operations Prior to the Battle of Leyte Gulf

The ships of Task Force 38, Ulithi Lagoon, October 1944. Courtesy of USNI.

The Third Fleet's first layover in the Ulithi lagoon lasted from October 1 to October 6, 1944. All the destroyers were short of provisions, but only one supply ship, the USS *Aldebaran,* had as yet arrived in the new anchorage. This meant that the entire task force had to take turns, two ships at a time, mooring alongside the supply ship to load up their storage lockers and reefers. Because there were no oilers in the lagoon, the destroyers refueled from the battleships.

To complicate matters, a typhoon brought such high winds by October 3 that the entire body of Task Force 34 stood to sea to wait out the storm in the lee of the atoll. This cut the time available for what had to be accomplished. On October 5, still waiting for its turn with the supply ship, the *Cotten* was directed to the *Alabama* to pick up a rear admiral and transport him and his staff to the battleship *South Dakota.* Alongside *South Dakota* to deliver the admiral, we received 217 enlisted men with all their baggage for transfer to the troop transport USS *Barnes.* We were also ordered to pick up at the same time our allotted twenty tons of provisions from the *Aldebaran,* which was moored to the other side of *South Dakota.* This entailed putting all hands to work for two hours manhandling the provisions out of *Aldebaran;* up, over, and across *South Dakota;* back down to the *Cotten;* and into the proper storage facilities. After this job was completed, we returned to our anchorage for two hours. Then the anchor was hauled up, and we steamed over to the *Barnes* to transfer the 217 men and baggage we had aboard, which was accomplished by 2000. We remained tied up to the *Barnes* overnight.

The next morning, October 6, Norman Campbell received orders to report to the naval air station in Ottumwa, Iowa, and he too went aboard the *Barnes* for transportation to Pearl Harbor. His responsibilities as navigator were assigned to Ens. Leonard Smith, a former chief quartermaster's mate who had been with us for the past two months as an assistant communications officer. I was sorry to see Campbell go but was encouraged that there was now one less competitor for the next available deck watch position. On the day before Campbell's departure, a new Annapolis ensign, William W. Stevens, had come aboard and had been assigned as another assistant first lieutenant under Snowden. This continued the policy of having a minimum of one Annapolis junior officer aboard each front-line destroyer of the Pacific Fleet.

At 0742 we were ordered to relieve the destroyer *Gatling* on patrol outside the entrance to the lagoon; we weighed anchor and headed out to sea. To a man, the crew was incensed at what it had been required to do during the typhoon-interrupted, six-day, so-called layover in Ulithi. Admiral Halsey and his staff were now as popular as Emperor Hirohito.

We maintained the seaward patrol until 1815 in the second dog watch, when TG 38.3 made its sortie in accordance with new operation orders that had been distributed the day previously. Task Group 38.3 now consisted of fleet carriers *Essex* and *Lexington* (flagships of Rear Admiral Sherman and Vice Admiral Mitscher, respectively); light carriers *Langley* and *Princeton;* battleships *Washington* (flagship of Vice Admiral Lee), *Massachusetts, South Dakota,* and *Alabama;* and Cruiser Division 13, DesRon 55, and DesRon 50. Task Force 34 had been temporarily dissolved while we were at Ulithi, accounting for the presence now of the large number of the ships of that task force with Task Group 38.3. TG 38.2 departed from Ulithi with our task group, and the two groups headed for a rendezvous with Task Groups 38.1 and 38.4 approximately five hundred miles to the north.

Our experiences since the Fast Carrier Task Force had been turned over to Admiral Halsey and the Third Fleet were topics of quiet conversation and speculation in the *Cotten's* wardroom. We had become an integral part of the Battle Line as well as Task Force 38, and it was our consensus that Admiral Halsey and Vice Admiral Lee had agreed that the Battle Line needed to be whipped into shape to be ready for a big surface engagement with the Japanese fleet. Nothing else would adequately explain the hours we had spent conducting battle-line maneuvers during the preceding weeks. If there were truth to the story that Vice Admiral Lee had expressed reservations about the Battle Line's readiness to engage the Japanese during darkness, the recent nighttime exercises had been vital from his vantage point.

Because Halsey was a known firebrand, it was believed that if he were presented with a problem similar to the one that Admiral Spruance had faced the night before the Battle of the Philippine Sea, he would be predisposed to take aggressive action. My own feeling was that Spruance's tactical style, which required a careful analysis of the pros and cons of the several available courses of action, was superior to what we believed would be Halsey's tendency to head directly for the enemy, Nelson style, at the best available speed.

Admiral Mitscher's new operation order for Task Force 38 confirmed that the landings on the island of Leyte, which had originally been planned for December, would take place on October 20, just two weeks away. The landing force would consist of 135,000 army troops under MacArthur's command. The naval forces responsible for the transport, supply, and direct defense of these troops were to be units of the Seventh Fleet under the command of Vice Adm. Thomas C. Kinkaid, who in turn was under the command of General MacArthur.

The Third Fleet, under the direct command of Admiral Halsey and consisting of Task Force 38 as well as, when formed, Task Force 34, was under the overall organizational command of Admiral Nimitz. The Third Fleet was defined as the "Covering Force" for the Leyte Gulf landings. This command organization, with two distinct and separate naval forces operating under two distinct and separate command structures, was vastly different from the unified arrangement of our previous campaigns in the Central Pacific.

The strategic objectives outlined in the operation order were threefold. First, we were to reduce Japanese air power in the Philippines, in order to protect the landings in Leyte Gulf. Because he believed that we had already eliminated most of that air power, Admiral Mitscher decided to take Task Force 38 north to destroy the Japanese aircraft based on Okinawa and Kume-jima, Formosa, and Luzon, in that order; he would cover the area directly north of Leyte during the actual landing operations on October 20. Secondly, we were to protect the northern flank of the Leyte Gulf landings from the Japanese First Mobile Fleet. Finally, we were to seek out and destroy the First Mobile Fleet if the opportunity presented itself. The implication was that these objectives were ranked in importance according to their positions in the list, although this was not definitively expressed.

Because General MacArthur's own navy, consisting of the Seventh Fleet, was in itself a powerful force, the bifurcated naval command structure did not look risky on the face of it. It did appear to give the commander of the Third Fleet wide latitude. It also appeared to represent a compromise resulting from the split in the command structure of the Pacific theater, a split that reached all the way back to the Joint Chiefs in Washington, D.C. A careful reading of our operation order led to the conclusion that the landing on Leyte was a joint and cooperative enterprise between the forces of General MacArthur and Admiral Halsey, with no central command. The overall objective was to ensure a successful landing on Leyte, but if there were any strings attached to Admiral Halsey's freedom of action, they were not discernible.

As far as the *Cotten* was concerned, we could expect to be in the screen of our carrier Task Group 38.3 for the time it would take to travel thirteen hundred miles north to Okinawa; conduct air strikes on that and neighboring islands of the Ryukyu chain; travel six hundred miles to the southwest to the vicinity of Formosa, remaining there for two and a half days of air sweeps against the many airfields on that large island; return five hundred miles south to the latitude of Manila to sweep the island of Luzon clear of the enemy; and then be on hand to cover the northern flank of the Leyte Gulf landings. At any time during this period, the Japanese navy could put in its appearance, at which point the *Cotten* would leave the carriers to join Task Force 34 and possibly have an opportunity to take part in a surface action, with battle line pitted against battle line.

This latter possibility was greeted with some skepticism. Considering that TF 38 could put nine hundred planes in the air, it was hard to conceive of there being anything left for Task Force 34 to engage should the First Mobile Fleet come forth once more. We had no doubt that Admirals Halsey and Lee would like to have a fleet action at some time during this operation, if only to establish their positions in history. We did have some doubt that the air groups of Admiral Mitscher's TF 38 would leave them anything against which to fight that fleet action. Considering the disparity between their naval resources and ours, it was also somewhat difficult to believe that the Japanese naval commanders would accommodate Admiral Halsey to the latter's satisfaction. While these thoughts and discussions were bandied about in our wardroom, we recognized that they were essentially idle speculations, considering the limitations of our strategic expertise.

At 1700 on October 7 our task group reached the rendezvous with the other three groups of TF 38, which then steamed together on a northerly heading to join the oiler group the next morning. The four task groups spent the daylight hours of October 8 fueling from the oilers, the last ship being topped off at dusk. Task Force 38 then set a course and speed to reach a launching position off Okinawa at dawn on October 10. Radio silence was again imposed, and the task force was ordered to flank speed for the thirty-six-hour advance, with full boiler power available on all ships.

The strike against Okinawa and Kume-jima was launched as scheduled at sunrise on October 10. Several of the pilots returning from the initial strike had sighted two cargo ships some thirty miles northeast of our task group, which information was immediately passed on to our task group commander. At 0955 Admiral Sherman ordered the cruiser *Mobile*, along with *Cotten* and *Gatling*, to head for the two ships to sink them. At 1000 we were free of our task group formation and went to thirty knots on a course to intercept the enemy, with *Cotten* and *Gatling* ahead on either bow of *Mobile*.

At 1051 the two enemy ships, cargo types of about twenty-five hundred tons each, came into sight at a range of twelve thousand yards. Our three ships went to battle stations and formed into column with *Gatling* in the van, followed by *Cotten* and *Mobile*. Shortly afterward, the column made a turn to the right, which brought the cargo ships on our port beam. We slowed to fifteen knots and commenced firing when the range had decreased to sixty-one hundred yards. Within two minutes the two ships had disappeared beneath the sea.

Cotten and *Gatling* searched the area where the ships had gone down for survivors. *Gatling* was able to pick up seven men, although the rescue boat's crew reported that it had had to use force to get them aboard. As soon as the *Gatling*'s boat was hoisted back on its davits, our three-ship task unit headed back toward the task group at flank speed. When we had rejoined the formation, *Gatling* went alongside Admiral Mitscher's flagship *Lexington* to pass on the seven prisoners for interrogation.

Air groups flew strikes throughout the rest of the day against airfields and installations on both Okinawa and Kume-jima, the returning pilots reporting much damage to shipping, facilities, and enemy aircraft. At sunset the day's operations were completed, and TF 38 headed due south at twenty-five knots for a fueling rendezvous, an operation that took the daylight hours of October 11 to complete.

The task force then set course to the northwest for Formosa, again at flank speed, all boilers on the line. The launch point for the attacks on Formosa was reached at dawn on October 12, and the first strike was put in the air shortly thereafter. This time we were expected by the Japanese. At 0825 a twin-engine Betty was shot down by a fighter just fifteen hundred yards ahead of *Gatling*. During this attack several other enemy planes were shot down on the far side of the task force. Destroyer *Knapp* was directed to search the water near the downed Betty, which resulted in the recovery of two dead crewmen and also some documents, which were passed on to *Lexington* for analysis.

During the day, the air groups made five major raids over Formosa, including fighter sweeps against seven large airfields. The pilots reported the customary extensive damage inflicted on facilities, as well as a large number of enemy aircraft destroyed, but on an unusually cautionary note, they advised that as many as several hundred enemy aircraft were still in combat-ready condition.

Starting at dusk, those remaining combat-ready Japanese aircraft initiated an all-out attack on Task Force 38. Our task group was under almost continual attack from 1900 on October 12 until 0124 on October 13, and the last enemy aircraft did not disappear from the radar screens until 0310. Admiral Sherman ordered thirty-seven evasive emergency turns during the attacks, with the task group at flank speed. On two occasions the enemy was within range of the *Cotten*'s 5-inch battery, which fired forty-eight rounds, without result. Twice during the midwatch of October 13, Admiral Sherman ordered all ships to make smoke in order to hide our carriers from the enemy, adding to the confusion inherent in defending against nighttime air attack.

The net result of all this frantic activity was that there was no damage to our task group or to the enemy. For the considerable effort put forth, such an outcome was hard to comprehend. The next day we learned that the major enemy effort had been concentrated against TG 38.2, some twelve miles away from our group. That group reported six enemy aircraft shot down by the night fighters, and six more by ships' gunfire. At one time their group had been close enough to our group for us to see a plane explode when it hit the water.

The combined task groups continued the heavy volume of air strikes against airfields on Formosa throughout the daylight hours of October 13, it being apparent that the objective of eliminating Japanese air forces on that island was far from accomplished. At dusk, TG 38.4 was detached to head for Luzon to conduct air sweeps of the northern half of that island ahead of the Leyte Gulf landings, a task assigned to the Third Fleet in the current operation order. The other three task groups of TF 38 remained near Formosa.

At 1700 the enemy started to attack us once again. Just before dark, *Cotten* managed to get its 5-inch main battery director locked onto a Betty when the range closed to six thousand yards. When the Betty came inside four thousand yards on the port bow, all the 5-inch and one of the port 40-mm mounts commenced firing at it, causing the plane to turn away and retire without pressing the attack. At this time we learned that the heavy cruiser *Canberra* had been torpedoed, sustaining very extensive damage. Cruiser *Wichita* maneuvered to take *Canberra* in tow with orders to return to Ulithi; the three cruisers of CruDiv 13 and four destroyers of DesDiv 100 were designated to accompany and protect them during their nine-hundred-mile retreat.

On the early morning of October 14, a last strike, containing nothing except fighters, was sent toward Formosa with orders to go exclusively after enemy aircraft. This strike returned before noon, and TF 38 started retiring to the southeast at twenty-four knots.

At 1500 the Japanese resumed very-long-range air attacks on TF 38, notwithstanding our own returning pilots' reports that enemy air activity over Formosa had been sharply reduced from the level they had encountered on the first day. The first attack on our group consisted of three dive-bombers, which streaked out of heavy clouds to dive on *Lexington*. One bomb exploded in the carrier's wake, a very near miss; the other two bombs were not visible from the *Cotten,* which was on the far side of Admiral Mitscher's flagship. Miraculously, all three enemy pilots managed to escape unscathed.

At 1709 our task group was subjected to an attack by seven torpedo bombers coming in fast and low; five managed to penetrate the screen on the far side of the formation from *Cotten*. We had just gone to general quarters when the Japanese, having dropped their torpedoes, attempted to make their retreat over the screening stations of *Bronson, Healy,* and *Dortch*. One of the planes was shot down as it passed by. Admiral Sherman's course changes during this attack enabled his ships to evade the torpedoes that were speeding through the nucleus of the task group. The enemy pilots had displayed unusual skill and determination.

Twelve miles away TG 38.1 suffered damage again. Light cruiser *Houston* received a torpedo hit that all but sank it, at about the time the enemy planes were doing their best against us. Admiral Mitscher ordered the heavy cruiser *Boston* to take *Houston* in tow and join the group screening *Canberra* and *Wichita* for their retirement to Ulithi. At sunset it started to rain, developing into a torrential downpour. This provided enough cover to prevent the enemy from locating us again, and we were out of range by the time the weather cleared up.

During the morning of October 15, TF 38 met up with the oiler group. Before fueling, *Cotten* was ordered to go alongside flagship *Lexington* to pick up Capt. Arleigh Burke, Admiral Mitscher's chief of staff, who had given the screening destroyers the verbal lashing prior to the Battle of the Philippine Sea. Captain Winston conned the *Cotten* for the twelve miles to Admiral Halsey's flagship, *New Jersey,* where Burke was to present a detailed action report covering the air strikes on Okinawa and Formosa. The overall estimate of the number of Japanese planes destroyed during the four-day period was between four and five hundred, aircraft that would be sorely missed by the Japanese in defending against the Leyte Gulf landings, now but five days ahead.

The *Cotten* fueled from the oiler *Caliente* in TG 38.2 while waiting for the conference on the fleet flagship to conclude. During that time we also went alongside carrier *Intrepid* to take aboard Wilfred Burnett, a war correspondent from the *London Daily Express*. At 1744 we were summoned to the *New Jersey* to pick up Captain Burke. We then headed back to our Task Group 38.3 at flank speed, delivering the foreign correspondent and Captain Burke to *Lexington* at 1847. *Cotten* went back to its screening station as the task group was concluding the fueling operation, at 1931.

Task Force 38 was now 550 miles due east of the northernmost tip of Luzon and six hundred miles northeast of Leyte Gulf. During the day, while we were providing transportation for Captain Burke between task groups, Admiral Sherman had reported that naval intelligence had learned that the Japanese had wildly overestimated the damage their own air attacks had inflicted on TF 38 when it had been off Formosa during October 13 and 14, and that as a result they had dispatched naval units from the Inland Sea to sink stragglers. In an effort to trap these Japanese units, three cruisers and eight destroyers, Admiral Halsey altered his operation order. He decided to leave full responsibility for the scheduled air strikes on Luzon to TG 38.4 and to have the other three task groups of TF 38 lurk out of sight to the south of the two crippled U.S. cruisers (now being towed to Ulithi by ocean-going tugs), using the cripples and their small escort as decoys.

The Japanese having failed to appear by sunset, Admiral Halsey ordered the three carrier task groups back to the northwest at flank speed so as to search for them again in the morning. This overnight, high-speed chase was in vain. We later learned from intelligence that a Japanese long-range search plane had sighted TF 38 and reported that all the United States carriers and battleships were still undamaged and operating as usual, thus negating their Formosa-based pilots' claims. This had come as a terrible shock to the overconfident enemy, which had recalled its small attack force before it could come into range of our air groups.

We remained throughout the day in our new position, five hundred miles northeast of the northern tip of Luzon and seven hundred miles north-northeast of Leyte Gulf, still searching for the enemy surface force. Finally at 1600, one of our patrol planes sighted the enemy some five hundred miles north of our position; at such extreme range, attack was not possible. Despite the distance, Admiral Halsey picked up the TBS microphone personally to order TF 38 to attack, but his wild order was rescinded after his staff had cooled him down.

At 0230 of October 17, Admiral Halsey finally gave up what could only be called a diversion, with the invasion of Leyte scheduled for three days off and three-quarters of TF 38 some seven hundred miles north of the landing beaches. He turned his fleet around and headed directly for the proper covering position north of the Leyte Gulf landings, at a flank speed of twenty-five knots.

By the morning of October 18, we were back where we were supposed to be, three hundred miles east of central Luzon. There TF 38 met the oiler group. CruDiv 13 and DesDiv 100 rejoined the task group after safely delivering the two crippled cruisers, *Canberra* and *Houston,* to the Ulithi lagoon. Fueling was completed for all ships by 1238, and our task group headed westward toward the coast of central Luzon.

At 0800 on October 19, our group was 250 miles east of Palanan Point on the east coast of Luzon, two hundred miles north of the latitude of Manila. The purpose of occupying this particular position was to protect the far northern flank of the Leyte Gulf landings. During the daylight hours the task group stayed on station by steaming in a boxlike pattern, with several interruptions for the launch and recovery of the combat air patrols.

The objective of the earlier air sweeps against Okinawa and Formosa had been to destroy as much of the enemy's air power as possible prior to the landings in Leyte Gulf on October 20. To review this operation, of the first four days of combat there had been a full day of air strikes against Okinawa (October 10), one day of transit (October 11), and two and a half days of strikes against Formosa (October 12–14). All were conducted according to plan, and the strategic objective was largely accomplished despite vigorous Japanese opposition. The plan had then called for the task force to return southward to the Luzon area, to conduct the same sort of interdiction strikes as had been successfully flown to the north.

However, the report on October 16 of three Japanese cruisers and eight destroyers heading in our direction had been distraction enough for Admiral Halsey to withhold three of the four task groups from the Luzon strikes and head them back to the north in what proved to be a two-day exercise in futility. He then returned to his original plan, which was to shield the northern flank of the landings in Leyte Gulf. This departure from the plan cost two days of air sweeps on Luzon and Samar directly prior to the October 20 landings, two days that constituted 75 percent of the scheduled preemptive strikes. We were back where we belonged by October 18, but knowledge of the condition of the enemy air bases on Luzon and of the aircraft replacements that had been sent to them was seriously deficient. Certainly the particular assignment of our Task Group 38.3 subsequent to October 20 had been compromised by the chase after the small Japanese surface force.

The assignment for TF 38 on D day (October 20) was to conduct intensive searches of the waters north of the landing area for Japanese naval forces. The interdiction of enemy air power was temporarily put on hold, as the intervention of the Japanese fleet was now a much higher risk to the success of the landings. Throughout D day, Task Groups 38.1, 38.2, and 38.3 remained in tactical concentration within ten miles of each other, all three being occupied in this massive search effort. Though this operation was impeded by unfavorable weather, by 1700 it had been completed to Admiral Halsey's satisfaction.

At nightfall our task group and TG 38.2 were directed to move to the southwest and to arrive at a new position ninety miles north of San Bernardino Strait by dawn of October 21. Our assignment during that day was to cover southern Luzon, with respect to both enemy shipping and airfields. However, foul weather prevented our air groups from achieving the objective, so this area remained a question mark at day's end. At dusk our group was withdrawn two hundred miles to the east to rendezvous with the oilers and refuel.

On October 22, the refueling completed, Admiral Halsey repositioned our group in a temporary holding area four hundred miles northeast of the Leyte Gulf beachhead and 350 miles off the nearest point of land on the east coast of Luzon. During the day battleships *Washington* and *Alabama* were detached from our group and ordered to join TG 38.4 to our south. Our task group was now alone off southern Luzon, with orders to search the coastal waters once again for enemy ships. This assignment was again impeded by miserable flying weather. We did not know it, but the stage was now set for the controversial roles Task Force 38 and Task Force 34 were to take in the Battle of Leyte Gulf. The enemy airfields of Luzon had received no serious attention from our air groups for the preceding week, both as a result of the alteration to the operation order and the subsequent bad flying weather.

17

The Battle of Leyte Gulf

American forces having secured the Leyte beachhead, General MacArthur was now basking in a worldwide spotlight created by the fulfillment of his pledge to the Filipinos to return and begin the fight for their liberation. On D day he had waded ashore in his khakis, a gold-encrusted field marshal's cap on his head and a corncob pipe in his mouth, in full view of his press photographer.

At that time, Admiral Halsey was closeted aboard the battleship *New Jersey* with no publicity and no enemy fleet yet in sight. Having served in MacArthur's shadow for so many months in the southwest Pacific, it was galling for him to be in his present position, now free of MacArthur's command and in command of the most powerful combat fleet in history, but with no enemy to fight.

Early on the morning of October 23, a radio contact report from two submarines announced that a large contingent of the enemy fleet, including battleships, cruisers, and destroyers, had been sighted in the South China Sea west of the island of Palawan, headed northeast. The report placed this enemy force some five hundred miles by sea from San Bernardino Strait, the entry passage from the west into the Philippine Sea. This was the first contact report of a task force of the enemy fleet, but because it placed the threat so far away and lacked any mention of the enemy carriers, Halsey could not yet plan a course of action. In order to locate the rest of the enemy fleet, especially the carrier task force, he directed that intensified air searches be immediately initiated. The specific instruction for our task group was to cover the waters off southern Luzon, his northern flank, the areas to the south of us being assigned to Task Groups 38.2 and 38.4.

Unfortunately, the flying conditions on October 23 were so miserable that the air searches were of doubtful value; in any case, they were completely negative. By nightfall Halsey still had no knowledge of the location of the Japanese carrier force, but he felt that it must put in an appearance at some point. He now repositioned his task groups for the next morning, October 24. He ordered Admiral Sherman to bring our TG 38.3 close to the shore of Luzon by dawn, so that our air groups could attack the enemy airfields in the Manila area and suppress Japanese air power that might have been staged from Japan via Formosa and northern Luzon during the preceding week, the period when the area had been neglected by TF 38. The long-range search to the north for the Japanese carrier fleet would necessarily be cut back while the preemptive strikes were being conducted.

Task Group 38.2, with which Halsey was steaming in *New Jersey*, was positioned outside the eastern exit of San Bernardino Strait to await the heavy Japanese surface force, should it intend to come through that passage to enter the Philippine Sea. Task Group 38.4 was ordered to take station farther south, off the coast of Samar, to be within supporting range of the Leyte Gulf beachhead; while TG 38.1, previously ordered to reprovision in Ulithi, was now out of the combat area.

Halsey's dispositions for the morning of October 24 had so separated the four task groups of TF 38 that none was close enough to any of the others to form a tactical entity with it. We in TG 38.3 were well beyond the range where we could render support to the others, or they to us. By dawn of October 24, we were in position ninety miles off the east coast of Luzon. Overnight the weather had improved for air operations, although there were still many large cumulus clouds aloft. By 0600 every ship had all boilers on the line, ready to make thirty-one knots as the task group turned into the wind to launch a full air group toward the Manila area.

The almost leisurely pace we had enjoyed since leaving Formosa on October 15 was now altered with dramatic suddenness. Within a few minutes of 0800, search planes from TG 38.2 sighted the Japanese surface attack force in the Sibuyan Sea, steaming eastward for San Bernardino Strait. At practically the same moment, a large group of enemy planes appeared on the air search radars of our task group, heading right for us from the west. At 0758 our ships went to general quarters, increased speed to twenty-four knots, and headed into the wind to launch the largest fighter combat air patrol that could quickly be put into the air. The task group had been in air defense formation since dawn.

The fighter patrols of our task group met the oncoming enemy thirty-five miles from our formation and engaged them continuously until they were right overhead. At 0840 the *Cotten* fired at one of the enemy dive-bombers as he passed over us. This plane dropped a large bomb aimed for the *Healy*, two destroyers away from us in the screen, missing it by one hundred yards. At 0858 we fired on another dive-bomber, letting up only as one of our fighters came right over us and shot down the enemy inside the formation.

While this first series of attacks on our task group was in progress, Admiral Halsey, with TG 38.2 160 miles to the south, radioed Admiral Sherman and ordered him to recall his air groups from Manila and, as soon as they were back on board the carriers, to proceed immediately to join TG 38.2 covering the exit of San Bernardino Strait. Admiral Sherman accordingly radioed our air groups, which were now over Manila, and ordered them to disengage and return to their carriers. By 0900 these air groups were preparing to land. Unfortunately, the returning planes had been closely followed by another wave of Japanese aircraft, now making the sky a confusing melee of friend and enemy.

At 0937, while our carriers were landing aircraft, *Essex* reported that a single Japanese dive-bomber had been seen in the high cumulus cloud directly above. Before anyone could fire at it, the plane went into a steep dive on the light carrier *Princeton* and planted a five-hundred-pound bomb in the middle of the flight deck. The bomb penetrated two more decks before exploding in an area where live torpedoes were stored. Shortly afterward a large black plume of smoke erupted from the wounded carrier; it swerved and slowed, unable to keep up the formation speed of twenty-four knots.

Admiral Sherman maneuvered the task group free of the faltering *Princeton* and ordered light cruisers *Birmingham* and *Reno* and destroyers *Gatling, Irwin,* and *Morrison* to form a protective screen for it. He also ordered *Birmingham* to go alongside *Princeton*, already in flames, to render firefighting and damage control assistance. At 1006, as the *Birmingham* was directing hoses into the fires, the carrier's stored torpedoes exploded in a gigantic ball of fire. The explosion was so severe that it caused great topside damage to *Birmingham* and many casualties to its crew. Lesser damage was also inflicted on nearby *Reno, Morrison,* and *Irwin* by the explosion, which was to prove fatal to the carrier itself.

At 1015 another Japanese dive-bomber emerged from the clouds to dive on carrier *Langley*, his bomb landing in the water alongside, just a hundred feet from its target. A lull then followed, during which Admiral Sherman radioed Admiral Halsey about our altered circumstances, with enemy aircraft from Luzon still expected to attack our formation in large numbers, and with two damaged ships, one perhaps fatally, to protect. He said that he would be unable to bring TG 38.3 south as ordered until our situation had been stabilized. Admiral Mitscher aboard *Lexington* concurred with this assessment.

The enemy air attacks resumed at 1330 and continued in a series of waves for the next two hours. As each wave came in, it was attacked by the combat air patrol, consisting of as many as sixteen F6F fighters aloft to protect the formation. These fighters were vectored toward the enemy by the fighter director teams on the *Essex*, so that the first engagements typically took place twenty to thirty miles from the task group, continuing as the enemy pressed in. These interceptors broke up and depleted the attacking waves so that individual planes could be dealt with by the formation's emergency maneuvers and intense shipboard antiaircraft fire.

The Japanese aircraft were generally late-model, carrier-type, single-engine dive-bombers (Vals), escorted by carrier fighters (Zekes). Their attack doctrine, similar to ours, called for gaining a position over our ships from whence the dive-bombers could plunge down to below five hundred feet before releasing their bombs on their targets, preferably our carriers.

To counter this, our ships put up their maximum firepower each time an enemy plane was sighted over the formation. With so many guns firing, at times the sky filled with 40-mm bursts (each projectile was set, as noted previously, to self-destruct at four thousand yards if it did not hit a target first); the surface of the ocean was torn by fragments of the 5-inch antiaircraft shells, because their influence fuses detonated when they came within thirty feet of any reflecting surface, including water. As the 20-mm shells would always return to the water in bunches, their splashes looked something like schools of flying fish returning to the water after flights.

The Japanese achieved their maximum penetration of our defenses in the 1330 attack, when twenty enemy aircraft were within the screen at the same time. It seemed as if every gun in the task group were on a target at one time or another.

During one of these firing sprees, three spent 5-inch projectiles descended on the *Cotten*. One, which failed to detonate, fell a hundred feet dead ahead and covered our forecastle with spray as we sped forward. At the same moment, two more exploded thirty feet above the sea, one fifty feet to starboard and one fifty feet to port, just abeam of the bridge. When the casings of the exploded shells spattered against the *Cotten*'s hull and bulk-heads, it was like being inside an oil drum being hammered with buckshot. Fortunately, no one was injured. Despite the large size of this strike, not only did the enemy fail to score a hit, but between the combat air patrol and the ships' gunfire, almost all of their planes were destroyed.

During this particular air attack, Walter Walborn, the *Cotten*'s torpedo officer, decided he wanted to visit me to see what it was like at Sky 1's battle station, having nothing to do himself. He was not prepared for the noise, the proliferation of descending projectiles of all calibers, or the high relative wind produced by the ship's twenty-five-knot speed. At his own battle station on the wings of the bridge, the bridge screen broke the relative wind and dampened a good deal of the noise. The area, including the pilothouse behind it, seemed less exposed as a result, but the reality was that there was no place at all on a destroyer that was not exposed to projectiles of any caliber, lacking armor as a destroyer does. Walborn retired during the height of the attack and later admitted that he had not felt comfortable at my battle station, while thanking me for permitting him to visit. This reaction on his part at first surprised me; I had become convinced that Sky 1 was an admirable and privileged position on the ship, having long since discounted as irrelevant any dangers that might be attached to the exposed position. On the other hand, I knew I would have been most uncomfortable at a battle station buttoned up in one of the boiler rooms—showing that familiarity breeds complacency.

The last attacking wave arrived over our formation at 1509. One bomb was dropped on *Lexington,* again scoring a nondamaging near miss. This ended the air attacks, which had been pressed with determination, despite the failure of the enemy pilots to coordinate their efforts effectively. This was attributable to a lack of training and experience among the majority of Japanese pilots, the original experienced cadre long since having been killed, most recently during the Battle of the Philippine Sea.

At 1545 the commanding officer of the *Princeton* advised Admiral Sherman that under the existing tactical situation, salvage efforts could not succeed. The admiral then ordered *Birmingham* to sink the stricken carrier, after all its surviving crew had been rescued. The last of the crew was not off until 1700, at which time *Princeton* was sunk.

At 1553 a U.S. dive-bomber (SB2C) crashed seven hundred yards off the port bow of *Cotten,* which maneuvered over to the two men seen climbing out of the sinking plane. Cdr. J. H. Mini and his crewman, Aviation Radioman First Class R. H. Frobom, were quickly rescued and brought aboard.

At 1640 one of the search planes sent out during the afternoon by our task group radioed back that it had sighted two groups of enemy ships approximately 250 miles due north of our current position. One of these groups contained two fleet carriers and one light carrier, one cruiser, and three destroyers; the second group contained four battleships, five cruisers, and six destroyers. This information, containing the long-awaited contact sighting of the enemy carriers, was quickly passed on to Admiral Halsey.

Halsey had been busy analyzing the battle reports of the pilots of TG 38.2 and TG 38.4, which had joined him from the south and had been attacking the Japanese heavy surface fleet in the Sibuyan Sea since 0800. There had been no defensive air cover for the Japanese, who had had to rely solely on their antiaircraft gunfire and evasive ship handling. Pilots from those two groups reported that they had sunk one of the two super battleships, the *Musashi*, and had heavily damaged many of the other ships, some critically. The last air strike had observed the Japanese force turning back to the west, which some on Halsey's staff construed to indicate that it was retiring from the area.

Shortly after the last of the airplanes that had been attacking the Japanese in the Sibuyan Sea were back aboard their carriers, Halsey received the report from Admiral Mitscher of the sighting of the Japanese carrier force 250 miles north of our task group (38.3). Halsey now pondered his next move.

Because so many of the enemy planes involved in the air attacks on our group had been carrier types, it was assumed that some had come originally from the just-spotted carriers, although it had seemed at the time that they had come at us from airfields in southern Luzon. Admiral Halsey apparently felt that the enemy carriers were the main threat and that the heavy surface ships he had been attacking all day were secondary, particularly now that they had been severely damaged, or so he believed. However, he must have harbored some reservations. Why were the newest and best enemy battleships and cruisers in the Sibuyan Sea? If he, Halsey, took the other task groups of TF 38 away from the blocking position at the head of San Bernardino Strait and went north to join us (TG 38.3) to attack the enemy carriers, could the Japanese heavy surface force reverse course again and threaten the Leyte Gulf landings? Should he continue to divide his forces to guard against both enemy forces, surface and carrier? Should he again recall Task Group 38.3 to the south, as he had originally ordered, and bring all of TF 38 close to Leyte Gulf to wait for the Japanese to come to him, as Spruance had done at Saipan?

Halsey must have considered each of these options. Being determined to do battle, he first decided to reunite the three available task groups of Task Force 38, so that he could count on an overwhelming power advantage. Then his problem was reduced to that of which enemy force he would face—the badly damaged surface force, last seen departing to the west in the Sibuyan Sea, or the undamaged carrier force to the north, which had apparently attacked us all day and destroyed the *Princeton*. The loss of the *Princeton* certainly influenced his decision.

So far, the Third Fleet had sunk one enemy battleship, the *Musashi*, and had damaged several of the other ships of the surface force in the Sibuyan Sea. If he were Spruance, Halsey would probably now have taken a united TF 38 to the south, toward Leyte Gulf, and waited for the Japanese to come to him. But waiting for the enemy to come to him was contrary to the essence of Admiral Halsey's belief in the spirit of the offensive, which had always driven him to the attack. To revert to a defensive posture would mean withdrawing the fleet to the head of San Bernardino Strait (though such a move would have ensured an engagement with either or both enemy forces, heavy gun ships or carriers, should they seek to attack the beachhead in Leyte Gulf). Ultimately, he was true to his inner spirit.

He would destroy the enemy carriers, which had brought victory to the enemy early in the war, and which always remained the primary threat in his mind. He concluded that he had turned back the Japanese surface forces in the Sibuyan Sea, although this belief was based more on hope than factual knowledge.

Accordingly, at 2000, Admiral Halsey directed Task Groups 38.4 and 38.2, with whom he was sailing on the *New Jersey*, to head north for a rendezvous point, and he radioed a similar order to Admiral Sherman in TG 38.3, to join him just before midnight. By 2330 the three task groups had joined in tactical concentration, and fleet course was set for due north, directly toward the Japanese carrier group. In Admiral Halsey's words, we were "en route to engage and destroy the enemy carrier force." This decision had taken the air groups of Task Force 38 well beyond their effective combat range of the western exit of San Bernardino Strait, which thereby had been left completely unguarded.

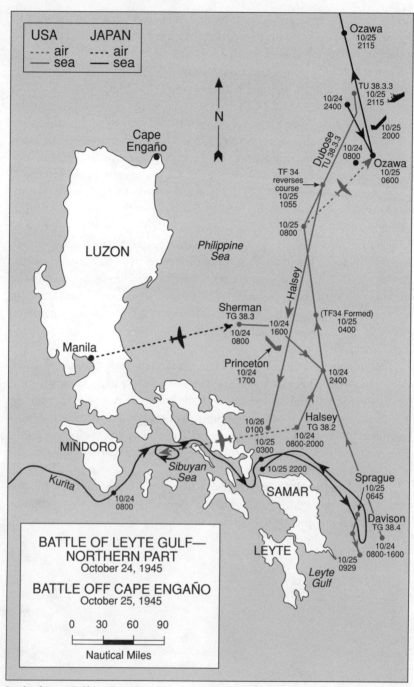

Battle of Leyte Gulf (northern part), October 24, 1945, and Battle off Cape Engaño, October 25, 1945. (See Appendix C.)

18

Action off Cape Engaño

At 0210 on October 25, night search planes from TG 38.2 reported sighting the enemy carrier force less than a hundred miles away to the north. Shortly afterward, Admiral Halsey ordered Task Force 34, the Battle Line, to take station ten miles ahead of the three carrier task groups. A complicated series of maneuvers followed, requiring the divisions of battleships, cruisers, and destroyers assigned to the Battle Line to leave their carrier groups and then re-form, with the battleship *Massachusetts* as guide. This process took an hour and a half to accomplish, inevitably slowing the pursuit of the enemy.

At 0403 Task Force 34 was properly formed up and on station ahead of the remainder of TF 38, which had also reorganized the formations of its three task groups. The battleships and cruisers were in columns of divisions in the center of the formation, and the destroyers were formed in a circular antisubmarine screen with a radius of fifty-five hundred yards from the *Massachusetts*, at the formation center. The *Cotten's* station was on the starboard beam of the guide. The course remained due north at a speed of twenty knots.

At 0530, the first break of dawn, all ships went to morning general quarters. Personnel whose battle stations were above deck were greeted by the sight of the battleships in columns, flanked by columns of cruisers, surrounded by our squadron and DesRon 52. The weather was again clear, with few of the towering cumulus clouds that had been prevalent the previous day. While everyone was tired from being at general quarters for eleven hours on October 24 (plus four or more hours of regular watches), there was an undeniable thrill at seeing those monstrous gray battleships lined up, ready and eager to put their 16-inch guns to work. At 0630, with the sun above the horizon, all ships secured from morning battle stations.

The three carrier task groups behind the Battle Line launched the first air strike at 0730. At 0830, just before the aircraft reached their objective, Admiral Halsey received a dispatch from Admiral Kinkaid, the commander of the Seventh Fleet, the essence of which was that the fast battleships of TF 34 were urgently needed at Leyte Gulf. The heavy Japanese striking force, which had last been seen retiring to the west, had reversed course after dark and was now speeding toward Leyte Gulf, and there was nothing except a group of U.S. Seventh Fleet escort carriers to stop it. Admiral Kinkaid advised Halsey that the Seventh Fleet's old battleships, which were responsible for blocking the southern flank of Leyte Gulf, had accomplished that task the night before in the successful Battle of Surigao Strait. As a result, his ships had used up most of Kinkaid's armor-piercing shells in that battle and would therefore be unable to prevent Kurita from entering Leyte Gulf from the north. At this moment, Task Force 34 was 450 miles north of the entrance to Leyte Gulf. Admiral Halsey could have turned his Battle Line back in immediate response to Kinkaid's pleas for assistance, but he continued to move toward the enemy carriers, directly away from Leyte Gulf. At 0945, an hour and a quarter after the first message from Kinkaid, a second air strike was launched.

Throughout the morning came a stream of uncoded messages from the six escort carriers off the coast of Samar, who had only a small group of destroyers and destroyer escorts in their protective screen. The ships were being fired on by Japanese battleships and heavy cruisers, and they were being hit by large-caliber shells. Each report contained another desperate request for the presence of Task Force 34.

As a result of these messages in plain language, we on the *Cotten*, along with everyone else in Task Force 34 and in Task Force 38, knew that the powerful Battle Line not only was not where it should have been but was heading away from the ships it had trained so vigorously to engage in battle. On their return from the second air strike, the pilots reported that two of the four Japanese carriers in the enemy fleet to the north were now sinking, that both of the others had been damaged, and that there was very little in the way of fighter protection remaining over the enemy task force. For Halsey to have pitted such overwhelming power against such limited opposition so far to the north of the Leyte beachhead now seemed misguided, at the very least.

At 1000 all doubts were removed by a coded message to Admiral Halsey from his direct superior, Commander in Chief, Pacific Ocean Area, Admiral Nimitz. While no one except Halsey knew what was in the message until much later, the cryptologic padding at the beginning and end of the text was not in code; combined, it formed the apparently meaningful phrase, "The world wonders." This seeming message, and the moment of its receipt in the Third Fleet, became one of those experiences that remain with everyone involved for life. Considering the stream of uncoded messages from the escort carriers, everyone surmised that Admiral Nimitz wanted to know what Admiral Halsey was doing with Task Force 34. The suspicion that Halsey had been skillfully manipulated out of position by the Japanese was disquieting, although, in deference to Halsey's rank and position, the possibility of such a thing was not discussed.

One hour after receipt of the message from Admiral Nimitz, Halsey ordered Task Force 34 to return to Leyte Gulf, five hundred miles away. Before doing so, Admiral Lee detached the four heavy cruisers *Santa Fe, Mobile, Wichita,* and *New Orleans* and also DesRon 50 with orders to continue toward the Japanese carrier force until they received further instructions from Admiral Mitscher, to whose command these ships now reverted. This done, the main body of TF 34 reversed course and headed toward San Bernardino Strait at flank speed. Admiral Mitscher then directed TG 38.3 and TG 38.4 to launch a third and final air attack toward the enemy carrier force, and at the same time he ordered TG 38.2 to accompany TF 34 on its dash back south. The final air strike was airborne by 1200.

At 1236 another message in plain language was received from the escort carriers of the Seventh Fleet. The Japanese surface fleet had just disengaged and reversed course; it was apparently heading back north to San Bernardino Strait. This action by Adm. Takeo Kurita, in command of the Japanese heavy surface ships, had resulted from his not having received a radio message sent by Adm. Jisaburo Ozawa, commander of the Japanese carrier force, advising that Halsey and the Third Fleet had been lured northward, away from Samar and Leyte. Kurita's decision to break off his attack saved the Leyte Gulf beachhead and Admiral Halsey's public reputation, but it did not alter the fact that Halsey had been taken in by a ruse. Halsey continued south at high speed with TF 34 and TG 38.2, now vainly hoping to catch Kurita before he could escape through San Bernardino Strait.

At 1400 Admiral Mitscher designated our newly constituted cruiser-destroyer group, still steaming on toward the Japanese carrier force, as

Task Unit 38.3.3 and placed it under the command of Rear Adm. Laurance T. DuBose, the commander of Cruiser Division 13. This force was to press on toward the Japanese carrier task group, some fifty miles away, and sink whatever ships were left behind when the main body retreated back toward Japan. Admiral DuBose ordered the destroyers of his force to be prepared to make night torpedo attacks on the enemy, the nearest group of which was reported to consist of one light carrier, two cruisers, and one battleship. An additional battleship, two cruisers, and three destroyers had been sighted by search aircraft somewhat farther away to the north.

Admiral DuBose continued to head his command for the nearest group of enemy ships, forming the cruisers in column preceded by the twelve destroyers in a semicircular screen. Mitscher's two remaining carrier task groups, TG 38.3 and TG 38.4, had disappeared over the horizon to the south, now also en route to San Bernardino Strait, leaving our cruiser-destroyer force to confront what was left of the Japanese carrier force.

The ten hours just past had been so eventful that it was impossible for us to sort out what had happened. The morning had seen the invincible Battle Line in impeccably correct tactical alignment, headed directly toward the Japanese carrier task force in the bright hope of ending the naval war in one mighty battle. Then, over the course of a few short hours, the realization had set in that we had been lured to the north only to allow Kurita's battle line to slip through San Bernardino Strait and drive unopposed toward the all but defenseless Leyte Gulf landing area. At the time, Admiral Halsey's unwitting personal role in this successful Japanese deception was not as clear to the officers and men of Task Force 34 as it would become sometime later, so the initial feeling was more of shock than anger.

The next blow had been Admiral Nimitz's presumed questioning of the location of Task Force 34, which had resulted in Halsey's humiliating but belated order to return that force to San Bernardino Strait when the bait— the almost defenseless Japanese carriers—was less than a hundred miles away. Those of us who were now a part of the cruiser-destroyer striking force thought we might escape some of the frustration resulting from the mispositioning of the Battle Line; at least we were now heading hell-bent for Japanese naval units that were more powerful than we were. According to aircraft search reports, they had a total of two battleships, three cruisers, and three destroyers available to protect their one remaining small, crippled carrier, which gave them considerably more firepower than Admiral DuBose had. It seemed ironic that our small force was now left to carry out an assignment that Admiral Halsey had given to the combined task forces less than half a day previously. Of course, while DuBose's orders were to sink any cripples or stragglers he could catch up with, they did not include engaging enemy battleships or getting his cruisers sunk by enemy torpedoes.

At 1457 one of the *Cotten's* lookouts spotted a yellow life raft ahead, and we were able to pick up Lt. J. R. Strane from the carrier *Essex*. Once he was aboard, the ship "rang up" thirty knots to catch up with the formation, which had continued on to the north. At 1507 we regained station, the formation having slowed to twenty knots while we were absent. Just eleven minutes later the *Cotten* actually ran over a pilot in the water, invisible to the lookouts until it was too late to turn. He passed under the hull, missing the propellers by a scant three feet, and popped up astern, his yellow life jacket flashing once in the sun. We turned to pick up Ens. Edward Denby, who was from the carrier *Enterprise;* once he was aboard, we went back to thirty knots to rejoin the formation. This time the *Cotten* had fallen far astern, and it took over an hour to catch up.

At thirty knots a destroyer becomes a different entity from a vessel passing through the water at its design hull speed or less. Hull speed for the *Cotten* was about twenty-two knots. At thirty knots, the ship would try to ride over its bow wave; the bow rose several feet, and the stern dug deep in the water. To a person standing near the stern at this speed, the surface of the ocean would be higher than eye level. In addition to the unusual fore-and-aft attitude, the ship would acquire a rigidity with respect to its rolling movement; the screws and turbines would be spinning so rapidly that they acted as gyroscopes, preventing the ship from rolling on its longitudinal axis. What motion remained would be pitch, the rise and fall of the bow. The screws would be so firmly anchored in the water that they could not be shaken loose; accordingly, all the wave action would bear on the forward part of the ship, with the screws as a pivot point. This would increase the effect of the pitching on the forward part of the ship, making it necessary to hold on tightly to avoid being tossed about like a rubber ball.

Lieutenant Strane and Ensign Denby, who had been taken to the wardroom to be examined by Dr. Spindler, were both aboard a destroyer for the first times in their lives, and as the wardroom was in the forward third of the ship, they were exposed to this unexpected up-and-down pummeling. Lieutenant Strane was in relatively good shape, but Ensign Denby had just gone through an unnerving experience. He had been shot down over the enemy carrier force, and after he bailed out, an enemy fighter had fired a burst at him while he was parachuting to the ocean surface. When he hit the water he had found that both his raft and life jacket were punctured, so he had been forced to swim to stay afloat and was therefore invisible to our lookouts, as his life jacket was under the water's surface. For two hours he had swum about, kicking away the circling sharks. Finally one shark had been able to get in a bite at one of his arms, fortunately only leaving teeth marks. Then the *Cotten* had run over him, and it was a miracle that he had not been torn asunder by the propellers. Now that he was finally safe in our wardroom, he was being nauseated by the ship's odd and rapid motion. Dr. Spindler reported later that Ensign Denby finally turned to him and said he wished that he had been left in the ocean to die in peace.

At 1615 Admiral DuBose gave the command to battle stations, the first enemy ship having appeared on radar at a range of fourteen miles, to the right of our northerly course. *Cotten* was still astern of the formation, speeding to catch up. The destroyers were ordered to leave the semicircular screen and form in two columns, one on the starboard quarter and one on the port quarter of the cruiser column. At 1624 the line of cruisers opened fire on the enemy ship, the light carrier *Chitose*, which could only return fire with its antiaircraft battery. At 1639 the formation changed course, and *Cotten* caught up with the right-flank destroyers to take a position in column astern of *C. K. Bronson*. The task unit increased speed to twenty-five knots as soon as the *Cotten* was back on station. The destroyers in the right-flank column changed course with orders to torpedo the carrier, but the latter rolled over and sank before the destroyers had gained firing position.

Our column of destroyers immediately returned to re-form on the right flank of the cruisers, passing within fifteen hundred yards of where the carrier had gone down. The water there was covered with several hundred Japanese crewmen, who had to be left to fend for themselves as we sped through. The task unit was now headed in the direction of the next Japanese ships, which were to the north of us. The formation was slowed to ten knots to allow the cruisers to recover the search planes they had sent aloft earlier to pinpoint the location of enemy ships ahead. At 1802 the task unit increased speed to twenty-five knots, the chase becoming more urgent with the coming of darkness.

At 1835 *Santa Fe* reported radar contact at a distance of thirteen miles with the enemy, believed by Admiral DuBose to be a force of one cruiser and two destroyers. The Japanese vessels had been left behind to screen the main body of the enemy—consisting of the two old battleships *Ise* and *Hyuga*, one cruiser, and five destroyers—which had been ordered to retire at maximum speed to Okinawa and safety.

At 1854 the three ships of their rear guard were within twenty thousand yards, and our four cruisers opened fire. Two of the enemy ships then reversed course, to retreat in the direction of their main body, leaving one ship, the light cruiser, to face us alone. This single remaining enemy ship opened fire on our cruiser column at 1900. It is probable that all three of the enemy ships had launched torpedoes at our formation from the twenty-thousand-yard range, well within the high-speed range of the 24-inch Japanese torpedoes when fired at an approaching target.

Our formation now changed course ninety degrees to the right to unmask our cruiser's batteries and, more importantly, to pass clear of the water in which the presumed Japanese torpedoes were likely to be. It was now twilight, and the exchange of fire between our cruisers and the enemy ship could be followed by eye through the full trajectory of each salvo, as each shell contained a tracer in its base. As the salvos were fired, the tracers arched upward toward the zenith of their trajectories, then began their descents toward their targets. The Japanese projectiles carried dye, so that when they hit the water, the towering splashes of bright purple could in this instance be easily identified by the Japanese gunnery officer, permitting him to correct the range and deflection of his next salvo. At the initial range of twenty thousand yards, each salvo took about a minute to arrive at the target. It somehow looked as if each enemy shell were coming directly for the *Cotten*, although our cruiser column was in fact the aiming point of the Japanese gunners.

At 1932, now in full darkness, Admiral DuBose ordered three of the destroyers from DesDiv 100—*Caperton, Cogswell,* and *Ingersoll*—out of the left-flank column to make a torpedo attack on the enemy ship, which had so far effectively prevented us from gaining on the retiring main body. At 1942 the cruisers checked their fire as the three destroyers closed the enemy at thirty-one knots. They reached firing position at 2020, launched five torpedoes each at the enemy ship, then turned to clear the range, permitting our cruisers to resume fire. Though the enemy ship seemed to have been damaged, it continued to maneuver at an estimated twenty-three knots and to fire on our formation until 2042, when a violent explosion occurred. Our cruisers then closed the range, firing deliberately into the now motionless, burning, and exploding ship, which rolled over and sank at 2055.

Our position was now 250 miles northeast of Cape Engaño, the northernmost tip of Luzon. At 2102 the nearest enemy ships were twenty miles ahead, and Admiral DuBose decided we could not possibly catch up with them before dawn, at which time his destroyers would be dangerously low on fuel. We would also be within air range of the enemy on Formosa, without air cover for ourselves. Accordingly, he called off the chase and ordered all of his ships to secure from battle stations. Course was then set for a rendezvous with TG 38.3 to the southeast, at a retirement speed of twenty-five knots.

By 0800 the next morning, October 26, our task unit had steamed 225 miles south from the position where the Japanese ship had sunk, and a carrier task group (TG 38.2) had appeared on radar screens. The carriers soon came into sight, fueling from oilers. Cruisers *Wichita* and *New Orleans* and destroyers *Bagley* and *Patterson* were released from our unit to rejoin TG 38.2, and *Santa Fe, Mobile,* and DesRon 50 proceeded on farther to rejoin TG 38.3. The surface attack unit was then dissolved by Admiral DuBose.

Our squadron and the two cruisers rejoined carrier Task Group 38.3 at 0945 and commenced refueling. The *Cotten's* turn came at 1139, when it went alongside the oiler *Saugatuck.* We received a total of 2,938 barrels, which represented 88 percent of a *Fletcher*-class destroyer's full storage capacity. At the beginning of this exercise, therefore, we had enough fuel for only five more hours of steaming at high speed with four boilers on the line. This factor alone had made further pursuit of the Japanese an impossibility. With the completion of refueling, we went alongside the destroyer *Patterson* to transfer a still-depressed Ensign Denby for further transport to his own carrier, *Enterprise*, in TG 38.2. At 1404 the oiler group left the formation, and the base course of Task Force 38 was changed back to the west. At 1507 the *Cotten* went alongside *Essex* to transfer the other pilots we had picked up, Cdr. J. H. Mini and his radioman, and Lt. J. R. Strane. The *Cotten* then returned to the screen.

During the afternoon watch, Admiral Mitscher conferred on Cruiser Division 13, Cruiser Division 6, and Destroyer Squadron 50 a "Well done to all hands" for the previous day's action while operating as cruiser-destroyer surface attack unit TU 38.3.3. The message from Admiral Mitscher was welcome, compensating for some of the embarrassment that had come with the realization that the Japanese had somehow managed to fool completely the Third Fleet. That the only hero in our brief nighttime engagement had been the captain of the Japanese light cruiser, who had sacrificed his command to allow his companions to retire unscathed, did not diminish the fact that the gunfire of Cruiser Divisions 13 and 6 had been accurate or that the torpedo attack by three destroyers of DesDiv 100 had been aggressively executed.

The Japanese captain's valiant effort brought down the curtain on the Battle of Leyte Gulf. His act was symbolic of the total defeat of the Combined Fleet despite a well-conceived battle plan and, in many instances, brave individual efforts. In the southern sphere of the battle, the U.S. Seventh Fleet under Kincaid had fought flawlessly in the night battle of Surigao Strait, but the effective and sacrificial delaying fight put up by the Seventh Fleet escort carriers and their screen of destroyers and destroyer escorts against Kurita's powerful striking force off Samar earned the accolades of the day. There was little left to be said for the mighty U.S. Third Fleet except that it existed, which in the end proved to be enough to control the Pacific Ocean area.

The *Cotten*'s assignment to the Battle Line had given some of us high expectations of participating in a great sea battle. The battle was in fact both immense and conclusive in scope and result, but the misdirection of Task Force 34 was a bitter disappointment to those who had harbored those too-high expectations. The truth was that the carriers and their air groups were the real power of the fleet; the heavy surface ships of both navies were anachronisms, except insofar as they provided protection for the carriers.

19

Kamikazes Enter the Pacific War

Our reassembled carrier task group steamed south down the coast of Samar during the night of October 26–27 and throughout the day of October 27, when strikes were launched against the few enemy airfields on that island. Then, at 1135 on October 28, our task group was ordered to return to Ulithi for minimal replenishment in preparation for an immediate return to sea. The *Cotten* entered the lagoon at 0705 on October 30, after the heavy units had made their separate ways to their anchorages.

Lt. (jg) Philmore H. Czarowitz reported aboard for duty for assignment as the *Cotten*'s radar officer, which was a new billet. He had specialized training in radar technology and in the latest techniques for fighter direction. He was in his mid-thirties, older than most of us, and when he first arrived, he seemed doubtful that the navy had known what it was doing when it assigned him to a destroyer with a carrier task force that was not equipped with the radios necessary to execute the requirements for fighter direction.

On October 31 the Third Fleet was advised that Vice Admiral Mitscher had been relieved as commander of Task Force 38, to be replaced by Vice Adm. J. S. McCain, formerly CTG 38.1, his flagship being carrier *Hornet*.

We also learned that on October 29 a Japanese pilot had deliberately crashed his plane, bomb and all, into the carrier *Intrepid*, in TG 38.2. On the next day the same thing had happened to the carrier *Franklin*, which had suffered such serious damage that it was now on its way back to Pearl Harbor for repairs. On the day after that, during the only day we were anchored in Ulithi, the light carrier *Belleau Wood* had received another suicide hit, taking such serious damage that it also was returning to Pearl Harbor. *Franklin* and *Belleau Wood* had both been in TG 38.4. It was beginning to look as though suicide tactics might be the enemy's new doctrine.

From the Japanese point of view, the loss of their pilots had proven to be almost certain when they encountered our carrier air groups using conventional attack doctrine, and their offensive capability had been negligible. Therefore, to ask their pilots to crash their planes into our ships did not, statistically speaking, make their collective task much more deadly, and it certainly made their efforts more effective. The Japanese high command realized that its combat ability had to be restored, and this seemed to be the only course open. From our point of view, the damage inflicted on three Third Fleet carriers in three successive days had been so serious that an immediate reassessment of defensive tactics for our carrier task groups was a necessity.

The replacement of Vice Admiral Mitscher was disturbing. Was Halsey furious that Mitscher had agreed with Admiral Sherman that TG 38.3 had been in no position to join Halsey off San Bernardino Strait on October 24, due to our being under attack by what was now estimated to have been more than two hundred Japanese aircraft? Did Halsey somehow blame this inability of our group to join him for his own ultimate decision to leave his post at the head of San Bernardino Strait to come north to join us, with its personally humiliating consequences? Perhaps no one will ever know the answers to these questions. The official reason given for Admiral Mitscher's relief was that he was exhausted from almost three-quarters of a year at his post as commander of the Fast Carrier Task Force. While this could easily have been true, the timing and circumstances of the change made it not entirely credible.

At 1525 on November 1, we exited Ulithi Lagoon with TG 38.3 to head back in haste toward the Philippines. The cause of the urgency was a deteriorating tactical situation now confronting MacArthur's command on Leyte. The Japanese were putting up a spirited resistance on the ground and continuing to send aircraft to the battlefront from Japan via Okinawa, Formosa, and Luzon. Compounding MacArthur's difficulties were heavy rains that were making it impossible for his engineers to construct runways firm enough for the land-based planes that were supposed to provide his tactical air support. Our air force planes were much heavier than their Japanese counterparts, which contained no heavy protective armor for pilots or fuel tanks. A combination of bad luck and overly optimistic assumptions by the general's staff threatened to bog down the Leyte campaign, to everyone's embarrassment.

As a result of this, Admiral Nimitz was forced to postpone the navy's planned strikes on the Japanese home islands, as well as the invasion of the island of Iwo Jima, and instead to continue to use Task Force 38 in the Philippines in tactical support of MacArthur's forces.

Our task group had been to sea for only one day when *Cotten* was ordered to accompany DesDiv 110 back to Ulithi to escort battleships *Alabama* and *Massachusetts* and a new fleet carrier, *Ticonderoga*, out for training exercises for the carrier's new air groups. *Ticonderoga* had been assigned to TG 38.3 as the replacement for *Princeton*. We left the task group with DesDiv 110 at 0045 in the morning, and by 0350 we had met up with the new carrier and two battleships as they sortied from the Ulithi entrance channel.

During the morning the *Ticonderoga* air groups practiced catapult take-offs, a new technique for launching night fighters. During the afternoon this exercise was repeated, following which the new daytime fighter pilots were allowed one more practice takeoff and landing—with the knowledge that the next time they did so, they would be going on a combat air patrol over enemy-held territory for the first time. Just before midnight we caught up with our task group; the three heavy ships we had been screening took their positions in the formation center, and *Cotten* and DesDiv 110 assumed their regular screening stations.

During the afternoon of November 4, while TF 38 was approaching the coast of Luzon, the first tactical innovation to counter the suicide, or "kami-kaze," attacks on our carriers was placed in operation. This consisted of sending out destroyers as "radar pickets"; their function was to obtain early warning of aircraft whose radar echoes did not display the signal known as IFF (identification, friend or foe). When a picket ship received a radar contact of a plane without IFF, it radioed the range and bearing to the fighter director on *Essex*, who in turn vectored out combat air patrol fighters to intercept the enemy. Picket destroyers had regularly been deployed by TF 38, but this was the first time that detecting aircraft not displaying the proper IFF signals had been made their prime purpose.

At 1140 *Ingersoll* was sent out, as radar picket number 1, to a position forty miles west of the center of TF 38. *Healy* was stationed thirteen miles from the center on the same bearing as *Ingersoll*, to act as a relay ship for the *Ingersoll*'s voice radio reports. *Gatling* was also stationed thirteen miles from the center, on a bearing sixty degrees to the right of *Ingersoll*. When these pickets were in position, the three carrier task groups sped toward Luzon at twenty-six knots.

At 0600 of November 5, the launching position was reached, and a large flight of fighters with a smaller force of bombers took off for sweeps against the enemy airfields around Manila. At 0645 the two relay destroyers, *Gatling* and *Healy*, returned to the screen; *Ingersoll* now took a lone picket station fourteen miles due west of our formation. At 0949 the first strike returned aboard the carriers, and the second strike took off at 1055.

At 1338 *Essex* reported that one enemy plane was diving on the formation center; all ships immediately went to general quarters. Despite intense antiaircraft fire, the enemy plane crashed into the after signal bridge of the *Lexington*, former flagship of Admiral Mitscher, causing some superficial damage. The plane had been hit repeatedly as it closed in, but momentum had carried it into its target, even though the pilot was probably dead before the actual crash. Within a minute another plane dove out of the clouds toward the same carrier, crashing in flames just ahead of the ship. Six minutes after this, a third plane dove at *Lexington*, again missing its target and crashing into the sea, not more than fifty feet to starboard.

These three enemy planes had managed to dive undetected on the center of our task group by making excellent use of the almost continuous cloud cover to gain attacking position. The carriers were lucky that the damage had not been much more severe.

At 1408 an enemy plane emerged from the clouds on the port beam of the *Cotten* just a hundred feet off the water, heading at high speed in our direction. I ordered the port machine gun battery to commence firing, the range being but a thousand yards and closing fast. The director operator for twin 40-mm mount number 2, just below Sky 1 on the port side, saw the plane, stared as it passed over close enough to see the enemy pilot staring back, and, apparently mesmerized by the sight, forgot to pull the trigger of his director. As the plane roared over, the director operator of 40-mm mount number 1 on the starboard side started to fire, getting off forty rounds at it as it headed away from us toward the *Ticonderoga*. The plane was quickly shot down and went into the sea well short of its intended victim. Because his original attacking position had been so close to the water and so far from the carriers, the enemy pilot could never have had much hope of getting through to them; instead, he should have been satisfied to dive into us.

No one had anything to say to the director operator of 40-mm mount number 2, who doubtless would have some trouble forgiving himself for his failure to fire. In any case, the plane had been so close when it burst forth from the clouds that had the pilot chosen to crash into us, nothing could have stopped him.

At 1740 *Essex* half-masted its colors, followed by *Cotten* and all other ships in the task group. Colors were "two blocked" (hauled back up) half an hour later, at the conclusion of funeral services for a person or persons unknown to us on the *Cotten*. At 1800 *Gatling* and *Ingersoll* were ordered out to night picket positions to the northwest and west, respectively, twelve miles from the formation center.

At 0550 on November 5, air strikes on Luzon resumed, with destroyer *Ingersoll* going out as a "strike picket" thirty-two miles to the west of the task group, to spot enemy kamikaze planes early enough to alert our gunners. The previous day's experience had shown that our daytime pickets should have been much farther away from the task group; the numbers of our own aircraft within twelve miles of the carriers had been too great to permit their radar operators to identify those not showing IFF. At 1414 enemy planes were reported twenty miles from our task group, which immediately went to general quarters and increased speed to twenty-one knots. This enemy did not get any closer, and after recovering the last returning planes from the Luzon strikes at 1523, we secured from battle stations.

This concluded the offensive air operations for the time being, and TF 38 headed eastward to refuel from the oiler group, starting the process a little before noon on November 7. Task Group 38.2, instead of fueling, departed for Ulithi for replenishment. While our own task group was refueling, *Lexington* received orders from Admiral Halsey to return to Ulithi to have the damage caused by the suicide attack of November 5 repaired. At the same time, the battleship *North Carolina* and destroyers *Stephen Potter* and the new *Benham* (named for the original *Benham*, sunk off Guadalcanal, on which Frank Sloat had been the executive officer) joined our group.

The weather then began to kick up, prolonging the fueling operation until after dark. At 1905, while *Healy*, one of the last destroyers to fuel, was alongside, its executive officer was washed overboard. Despite an extensive search for him by *Healy* and the destroyer *Porterfield*, he was never recovered.

By dawn of November 8, the weather had deteriorated further, due to the presence in the Philippine Sea of a typhoon that seemed to be heading toward us. Admiral Halsey ordered Task Force 38 to head northeast, out of the way of the typhoon center, which course was maintained throughout the day and following night. During the early morning of November 9, the storm passed by us to the west, and the weather moderated sufficiently for the resumption of flight operations. At 2130 Admiral Halsey directed TF 38 to head back west, safely behind the departing typhoon, and to close the Philippine coast to attack a Japanese convoy believed to be laden with supplies and reinforcements. Because of the delay caused by our having been pushed out of position to the eastward by the typhoon, at 0120 of November 10 our task group ceased zigzagging and increased speed to twenty-six knots in order to reach the assigned launching position. This was contrary to Pacific Fleet doctrine, which required the use of a zigzag plan while moving from one location to another.

At 0415, simultaneous but unrelated materiel casualties on battleships *North Carolina* and *Washington* caused them to slow to twenty-two and seventeen knots, respectively. *North Carolina* reported engine trouble, and *Washington* advised that it had sustained structural damage on the forecastle, which it was hard to imagine happening to a battlewagon. At 0417 *Cotten* and *Healy* were ordered to leave the formation to screen *Washington*, and *Gatling* was sent out to perform the same duty for *North Carolina*.

Washington and *North Carolina* were sister ships, the only two of their design. Built twenty years after World War I, they had been the first battleships constructed since that conflict; the later battleship classes in World War II seemed to have far fewer engineering and structural problems than they did. Despite their design problems, however, they had acquitted themselves well.

At 1024 *Washington* completed repairs to whatever had caused it to slow and increased speed to twenty-four knots, with *Cotten* and *Healy* screening ahead, to regain our task group, now many miles to the westward. Independent of us, *North Carolina* had repaired its engine room casualty and, with *Gatling*, was also speeding to rejoin. By 1230 of November 11, we had come within radar distance of our task group, then in the process of conducting strikes on the Japanese convoy, which was heading for the Japanese lines on Leyte. As soon as we had caught up to it, our small group of battleships and destroyers proceeded to their assigned positions.

The strikes against the Japanese shipping were highly successful. The ships in the destroyed convoy were later found to have had aboard an entire, fully equipped division, intended to reinforce the Leyte forces. The destruction of this convoy greatly relieved the pressure on MacArthur's command. No kamikazes were able to get close enough to the task group to dive on our ships, and with the mission concluded, we turned back to the east at 1807.

By midafternoon of the next day, three of the four task groups of TF 38 headed north for Luzon to resume offensive air operations, TG 38.2 being in Ulithi for replenishment. Launch position was reached by 0830 of November 13, when concentrated fighter sweeps directed at the enemy airfields on southern Luzon were sent out from all three groups. These sweeps continued until late afternoon; the last of our planes were back aboard their carriers by 1620. While some enemy planes had been airborne looking for us, none had approached closer than nine miles from our formation, the other two task groups faring equally well.

On November 14, the task force conducted another day-long series of fighter sweeps and air attacks against Japanese air forces in central Luzon, turning back to the east after the last plane was back aboard. On November 15, we met the oilers for refueling some four hundred miles east of Luzon, upon completion of which our task group set a course for Ulithi, leaving a just-returned TG 38.2 to continue to provide air support for MacArthur.

Our group arrived outside the entrance to Ulithi at dawn of November 17, and after the carriers, battleships, and cruisers had entered, the destroyers followed them into the anchorage. *Cotten* moored alongside destroyer tender *Cascade*. We received replacement ammunition from the tender, as well as electricity, permitting us to shut down the engineering plant for maintenance.

It had now become apparent that MacArthur's success in persuading President Roosevelt to permit the liberation of the Philippines was going to be costly for the Third Fleet. The physical nature of the Philippine Islands, with their mountains, islands and islets, reefs, passages, and bays, combined with the ease of deployment of enemy air power from Japan via Okinawa, Formosa, and Luzon, made land operations more difficult than anyone had anticipated—except perhaps the top navy admirals. The introduction of the kamikaze pilots, who had shown the vulnerability of our carriers to even one successful suicide dive, now made naval operations equally difficult.

In order to continue the forward momentum that had been achieved despite the mistakes made in the Battle of Leyte Gulf, Admiral Halsey was now obliged to keep Task Force 38 close to Luzon. That was necessary to enable our carrier fighters to cut down the Japanese buildup of their air groups, but it exposed us, in turn, to attack at any time. The adverse tropical weather at this time of the year was also a factor to contend with. The war in the Central Pacific was now on hold until the battle for the Philippines could reach the stage where MacArthur's forces would be self-sustaining.

20

Kamikazes: Midget Subs and More Planes

The *Cotten* remained alongside *Cascade* for two days and then, during the afternoon of November 19, got under way to enter a floating dry dock. In an hour and a half, all the water in the well had been pumped out, and our ship rested securely on keel blocks. Snowden and Blackburn, accompanied by their chief petty officers, gave the underwater hull an inspection. It revealed that more zincs were needed, the rope guards were missing, thirteen more feet of the starboard and two feet of the port bilge keels had broken loose, and that the protective dome for the sonar transmitter was completely missing. It took machinists seven hours to repair these defects, after which the dry dock crew started to pump the water back into the well. At 0139 on November 20, *Cotten* backed out of the dry dock and steamed over to the destroyer anchorage to moor.

The next morning, just before sunrise, the *Cotten* got under way to return to the *Cascade*. We were proceeding slowly through the anchorage when there was a tremendous explosion close aboard to port. The source of the explosion was a large oceangoing oiler, the *Mississinewa*, which had been riding at anchor fully loaded with (highly volatile) aviation gasoline and heavy fuel oil. Immediately after the initial blast, the *Mississinewa* erupted in a ball of fire as the "avgas" exploded, hurling droplets of the fuel oil high into the air along with a towering column of black smoke. The *Cotten* was close enough to the inferno to become covered with the drops of heavy oil that fell from the smoke, carried over to us by the light wind.

Captain Winston stopped the ship and ordered the gig lowered into the water. The gig's three-man crew was commanded by the coxswain, P. L. Richards; the engineer was Machinist's Mate Third Class R. L. Smith, and the "bowhook," G. A. Williams. They were to take any survivors to the hospital ship, as anyone who lived through such a conflagration would need medical attention. Richards was rugged and tough, a good man for a daunting job. When the gig was on its way to the flaming oil-covered waters surrounding the wreck, the *Cotten* headed toward the vicinity of the anchored cruisers *Biloxi* and *Mobile*, which had reported seeing a periscope nearby.

A half-hour later, Admiral Sherman ordered Winston to take temporary charge of the ships that were searching for the submarine or submarines presumed to have torpedoed the oiler from inside the lagoon. Captain Winston then organized a coordinated sonar search by destroyers *Rall* and *Halloran*, which had joined us, around *Mobile* and *Biloxi*. At 0647 *Rall* obtained a sound contact and dropped depth charges at a shallow setting off the starboard side of *Biloxi*, where the water was about 150 feet deep. At 0652 *Halloran* dropped another salvo of depth charges in the same area. Two minutes later, two dead Japanese popped to the surface near *Mobile*, after which *Halloran* dropped another barrage of depth charges near *Biloxi*. Admiral Sherman now set up a patrol inside the anchorage using the available destroyers and destroyer escorts, relieving Captain Winston of the responsibility.

At 1130 all of the destroyers of Squadron 50 were released from the patrol. *Cotten* resumed its course toward *Cascade*, and at 1220 we moored alongside the tender. At sundown our gig returned, having rescued five crewmen of the *Mississinewa* and taken them to the hospital ship for treatment. The rescued men had said to the doctor that our gig crew had risked their own lives in order to save them from the fire surrounding the *Mississinewa*. Captain Winston promptly recommended that the three be decorated, with special recognition for Coxswain Richards. Some time later, Richards was awarded the Navy and Marine Corps Medal, and both Smith and Williams were awarded the Bronze Star.

A preliminary intelligence analysis concluded that the *Mississinewa* had been torpedoed by a midget submarine, one of four that had been transported on the deck of a larger submarine and released outside the entrance of the Ulithi lagoon. One of the midgets had been destroyed outside the anchorage, two had hit reefs just inside the channel, and one had achieved the considerable success of destroying the *Mississinewa*. Its crew had been the two men killed later in the depth charge attacks.

The *Cotten* remained alongside the *Cascade* until 0415 of November 22, a day and a half later, when we got under way with DesRon 50 and TG 38.3 to sortie from Ulithi. A course was then set for the Philippines. Just after noon on November 23, we joined in tactical concentration with Task Group 38.2, Admiral McCain in command, aboard his new flagship, *Hancock*. The two task groups steamed in company for the next thirty-six hours. Just after midnight on November 24, they went to flank speed for the approach to a launching position seventy-five miles off the coast of Luzon. An enemy snooper appeared on radar during this final run, making it likely that we would encounter opposition. At 0635 we reached the launching position and turned into the northeast wind to send the first strike off to the enemy airfields of Luzon.

At 1215 two huge underwater explosions occurred just astern of the *Mobile* and close to light carrier *Langley*. These were believed to have been Japanese torpedoes dropped from clouds high above us, much too high for proper torpedo launching; they had detonated when they hit the water. The Japanese planes that dropped these torpedoes were not seen or detected as lacking IFF by anyone in the task group, as they had remained concealed in the heavy clouds. It was obvious that the pilots were not members of the kamikaze corps and, moreover, were not eager to risk a torpedo attack of the kind required by their tactical doctrine.

Fifteen minutes later, many aircraft not showing IFF appeared on the radar screens; they could not be seen, however, being well concealed in the thick cover of clouds. Task Group 38.2 reported that it was under heavy kamikaze attack, and in short order carriers *Hancock* and *Cabot* were hit glancing, and so not critical, blows. *Intrepid* was not so fortunate; it was hit by two planes and was damaged seriously enough to need naval base repairs.

Shortly after those attacks, our own formation was visited by the enemy. At 1256 a kamikaze hit the *Essex*, but the damage was not serious enough to interfere with the carrier's flight operations. Minutes later another plane dove on the *Ticonderoga*, crashing into the sea a few yards ahead of the speeding carrier. The *Cotten* fired twenty-eight rounds of 5-inch at this last plane as it passed high above us on its way in, adding to the hundreds of rounds fired by the formation. In this case the antiaircraft fire was credited with having stopped what otherwise would almost certainly have been a successful attack, as it had made the plane a flaming, uncontrolled meteor for the last thousand yards of its dive.

One of the steward's mates on *Ticonderoga* had jumped overboard, thinking the enemy plane was going to hit his 20-mm gun battery. He elected to plunge some fifty feet into the ocean as an alternative to being cremated. Seeing his life jacket bobbing in the water some minutes later, we stopped to pick him up. *Cassin Young* rescued another 20-mm gunner who had similarly preferred to take his chances in the ocean.

At 1300 planes from *Intrepid* of TG 38.2, returning from their sweeps of Luzon, were ordered to land on our carriers instead; the damage to *Intrepid*'s flight deck was too serious to land aircraft. For the two hours following nightfall, *Ticonderoga* kept two night fighters in the air as defense against further kamikaze attacks, while TF 38 returned to the east to meet oilers at dawn the next day. There were, however, no further enemy attacks. The next morning, November 26, we met up with the oilers. All our ships topped off by 1530, while TG 38.2 retired to Ulithi for repairs to its carriers, leaving our group to patrol alone off the Philippine coast.

For the next six days, our task group kept station in reserve, approximately three hundred miles off the coast of Samar, available to furnish air support for MacArthur's forces. No request for assistance materialized, so we conducted exercises against simulated kamikaze attacks. The three-hundred-mile distance placed us beyond the range of kamikazes but was close enough for us to return within range on eight hours' notice if our air groups were needed. On December 1, the task group was released from the standby station to return to Ulithi, where we arrived in the afternoon of December 2.

On December 4, Walter Walborn was detached for temporary duty at the fleet gunnery school in Pearl Harbor, which would absent him from the *Cotten* for at least two months. Coupled with the departure of Norman Campbell in September, this left me as the only remaining fully qualified officer of the deck under way, aside from the present four watch standers.

At 1400 on December 9, our last day in Ulithi, Wayne Dorman was detached from the *Cotten*, with orders to proceed to Pearl Harbor pending reassignment to new permanent duty. I was immediately advised by Rothschild that I would be standing Dorman's OOD watch rotation on a permanent basis when we next went to sea. This assignment came as a stunning surprise to me. Campbell and Walborn's departures had certainly been my good fortune, but I had never considered the possibility that Dorman would be reassigned, as he was the youngest of the four watch officers, and, of the officers on the roster when the ship had been commissioned, he had been the closest to my age. I was disappointed to lose a good friend, but elation at being selected to be one of the four watch officers at sea transcended all else. There must be outstanding moments in everyone's life, and few since have equaled this one for me. Starting on December 10, the *Cotten*'s four officers of the deck when under way would be Stokey, Kanter, Snowden, and Robinson.

21

The Great Pacific Typhoon, December 1944

While the fleet was in Ulithi, Admiral McCain distributed to Task Force 38 orders for a new operation. The objective would be to reduce Japanese air power on Luzon, particularly to neutralize the many airfields that surrounded Manila. Despite their recent setbacks, the Japanese were still able to bring replacement pilots and aircraft into the Philippines from the home islands via Formosa, and MacArthur's operations on Leyte had fallen farther behind schedule as a result.

We were also given notice that on December 15, MacArthur's forces would land on the island of Mindoro, which is at the northwestern end of the Bubuyan Sea and directly south of Manila. Mindoro would be used as a base for air force units that were to provide direct tactical air support for later landings on Luzon itself, now scheduled to take place in Lingayen Gulf in January of 1945.

This extended assignment would continue the exposure of the carriers to the new kamikaze tactics of the enemy. Because there had been such an extensive cloud cover over the waters close to Luzon, and the air had been so filled with our own aircraft during daylight hours, it had been next to impossible to prevent all kamikazes from slipping through the radar net and combat air patrols. So far, our new defensive measures had not been effective, and the damage to our carriers was a very serious matter.

As a result, additional tactics for defense against kamikazes were developed by McCain's staff. Certain destroyers in each carrier task group were provided with trained fighter-director teams capable of controlling combat air patrols of two fighters each. Because the *Cotten's* CIC (combat information center) was not equipped for the technical requirements of fighter direction, we were eliminated from this type of assignment for the time being. The plan was to position these fighter-director destroyers far from the task group, twenty-five to sixty miles away. The fighter planes assigned to them would circle high above, waiting to intercept the enemy.

The next innovation was to order that our returning planes descend as they approached the pickets to well under the cloud cover, low enough to be seen by the destroyers' lookouts. They were to circle the destroyers before proceeding to the task group and their carriers.

All ships were to take evasive action. If, for example, a kamikaze dove from astern, the ship being attacked should make a radical turn in the direction most likely to result in a miss. The hope was that the enemy pilot would be dead at his controls for the last thousand yards and that therefore his aircraft would be more like a falling shell than a guided missile.

These measures were obviously based on common sense, not some technological breakthrough. If a kamikaze pilot could get close enough to a ship to put himself well into a dive, his chances for hitting his target, even after he was killed, were reasonably good. Everyone charged with the responsibility of conning a ship was urged to plan what he should do if suddenly confronted with a diving kamikaze. Because a conning officer would have so little time to think out a proper maneuver when faced with such a problem, having a small selection of predetermined reactions in mind was the only way to react effectively.

At 0645 on December 10, the *Cotten* sortied from Ulithi with Cruiser Division 13, carrier *Ticonderoga*, and destroyers *Longshaw, Preston,* and *Ingersoll*. During the forenoon watch, my first as a regular officer of the deck, the four destroyers engaged in surface gunnery exercises with a towed sled. In the afternoon watch, there were antiaircraft exercises with towed sleeves. At 0811 on December 11, our small group joined the balance of our carrier task group, which had departed from Ulithi a day later than we had. The formation now contained a fourth carrier once again, light carrier *San Jacinto* having replaced the damaged *Lexington*. We had the same three battleships as before, as well as CruDiv 13 and a new addition, light cruiser *Oakland,* replacing *Reno*. DesRon 50 and DesRon 55 completed the roster.

During the morning the antiaircraft batteries of every ship in the task group fired at towed sleeves, following which all ships in turn were subjected to kamikaze-type dives by our own carrier aircraft, the latter drill adding a touch of reality with respect to the situation we all now faced. The drills were completed at dusk, at which time the task group headed northwest at twenty-five knots to join TG 38.1 and TG 38.2 at a rendezvous eight hundred miles east of Manila.

At noon on December 12, we met the other two task groups, with Admiral McCain, in *Hancock*, in overall command. At 1415 the task groups practiced the new countermeasures against kamikaze attacks, with picket fighter-director destroyers deployed, combat air patrols circling overhead, and other groups of our own planes aggressively simulating the enemy. When these exercises were completed, TF 38 headed northwest at twenty-three knots for a launching point fifty miles off Cape San Ildefonso, on Luzon.

The first strikes against the air bases in the Manila area were launched at 0715 on December 14. Weather conditions were very poor, both in our task group's operating area and over Manila. Our pilots reported that they were unable to see their targets in many instances. From time to time, heavy rain squalls at sea caused Admiral Sherman to maneuver our task group to clearer areas so that returning pilots could see their carriers when they came in to land.

On one of these instances, when I was on the bridge as OOD, TG 38.2 merged with our task group on a crossing course, which forced all ships to maneuver at high speed to avoid collisions. The focal point of this traffic jam was the *Cotten's* part of the screen, so that when Captain Winston reached the bridge after being advised of the situation, he was confronted with the sight of the heavy ships of the center of TG 38.2 on either side of us, steaming at twenty knots at right angles to our own course. The unusual conglomeration of task groups terminated as soon as our flight operations were concluded, at which point Admiral Sherman turned our formation to a course that promptly cleared us from our fellow task group. During this brief period of confusion, Captain Winston had maintained a dignified silence, and I was pleased that he had not seen fit to offer comment concerning my ship handling when the heavy ships were crossing ahead and astern of us.

The weather improved a bit during the afternoon, permitting the air groups to achieve better results in their fighter sweeps around the Manila area. The last returning planes were aboard their carriers at dusk, after which all three task groups turned back to the east, a course maintained until midnight of December 14. The *Cotten* was stationed as an overnight picket, twelve miles to the northwest of our task group's center. The destroyer *Pritchett* was stationed as the distant (called "Tomcat") picket, also to the northwest, sixty miles from the task group's center.

During the night of December 14–15, the task groups maintained position off the target areas of Luzon, and at 0620 *Cotten* returned to the screen. At 0800 TF 38 again launched strikes from all three task groups against air bases on Luzon. This was the day that MacArthur's forces landed on Mindoro, where they encountered no serious resistance from the few Japanese defenders. The weather was much improved over the previous day, permitting an increased number of sweeps of Luzon; reports from returning pilots indicated that enemy air activity had been reduced to ineffectiveness by the end of the day. This was the second straight day in which no enemy plane had been able to get within twenty miles of the carrier task groups, a welcome improvement.

At 0800 of December 17, *Cotten* was ordered to proceed to TG 38.2 to obtain guard mail, consisting of up-to-date intelligence reports and operating orders for Admiral Sherman from Admiral Halsey in *New Jersey* and Admiral McCain in *Hancock*. At 0945 we entered the formation of TG 38.2, at the same time as oilers joined to fuel that task group. The wind and sea were picking up, and it was soon apparent that the fueling operation would be unusually difficult for the destroyers. We had to wait until 1223 to get alongside *Hancock*, the delay being caused by flight operations and the fact that we were the third in line to approach Admiral McCain's flagship. At 1311 we proceeded to the *New Jersey*, arriving at 1354. As soon as we had received the guard mail sacks from *New Jersey*, we started on the return trip to our own task group.

While we had been inside TG 38.2, the weather had been getting steadily worse, and by the time we were ready to return home it had reached gale proportions. The fueling operation had been called off by Admiral Halsey, who instead ordered all three task groups to head toward the coast of Luzon, which his staff weather specialist believed would take us away from the storm. Halsey directed the oilers to follow the carrier task groups, so that we could all fuel the next day.

As the *Cotten* maneuvered clear of TG 38.2, Admiral Sherman changed our orders and directed us to take a position midway between TG 38.2 and TG 38.3, in order to act as a communication link. At the time we reached this linking station at 1550, Admiral Halsey revised his orders for TF 38, picking a position ninety miles north of his previous intention. The objective was to flee from the steadily increasing storm, which now was coming on with gusts of from forty to fifty knots, with seas beginning to build accordingly.

By early next morning, December 18, the weather was steadily blowing a full gale, and the few destroyers that attempted to fuel from the heavy ships of our task group parted the hoses as soon as they were brought aboard. This attempt was almost immediately put aside, and TF 38 was directed to a southerly course, which was downwind at this time, with the intention of feeling our way clear. During the forenoon watch the wind continued to accelerate, and damage to our ships was becoming a common occurrence. I had the OOD watch, and I concentrated my efforts on keeping the *Cotten*'s head downwind, which was difficult with the increasingly high seas coming from astern. Because we were a linking vessel, exact station keeping was irrelevant, a fortunate position to be in. By now the wind was blowing at a steady sixty knots, with gusts over eighty knots when we were at the tops of the seas, which were an estimated seventy feet above the troughs. This wind, measured in statute miles per hour, was now ranging between 71.5 and 95.25, defining the storm as a typhoon.

The *Cotten*'s worst moments came when seas caught up from behind, lifting the stern seventy feet higher than the bow and giving the impression that we were headed right for the ocean's floor. It felt as though each wave wanted to move our stern to port or starboard, so that it could then roll us over on our side. In order to prevent this, the rudder had to be put over to counter the wave's thrust on the stern before it could get a good start; in several exceptional cases, the outboard engine (the port engine when the stern was being pushed to port, and vice versa) had to be reversed and the inboard engine speeded up to assist the rudder. Even so, we often rolled well over forty-five degrees.

At 0923 the light carriers started to report serious damage and fires as a result of the wild rolling and pitching. *Monterey* went dead in the water, and a gasoline fire broke out in its hangar deck as planes broke loose. *San Jacinto* also had a fire in its hangar deck, for the same reason. By the time I went off watch at noon, the wind was taking off the tops of the waves as they broke, driving the water in a horizontal sheet about thirty feet above the surface, obliterating everything from sight.

During the first hour of the afternoon watch, the typhoon got steadily worse, until it was every ship for itself. The crews no longer attempted to maintain formation but hoped only to keep control of their ships as the eye of the typhoon approached, with its shifts in wind direction. On the *Cotten,* during the first hour of the 1200–1600 watch, when Herb Kanter was OOD, the bridge anemometer showed gusts of as much as ninety-three knots, or 110.75 miles per hour. The highest wind speed documented in this storm was even higher than that—one ship reported a gust of 120 miles per hour. After 1350 the storm seemed to tire, and four hours later the wind had slowed to a mere thirty knots. The storm was over. It was now time to assess the damage done to Task Force 38 and to the oiler group that had been following us.

It was standard fleet procedure, as fuel tanks were successively emptied, to fill them with saltwater. This saltwater acted as ballast, maintaining the ship's stability as it burned its fuel. Because a destroyer's stability was fragile, ballast was a vital element of good seamanship when a storm of the violence of this typhoon became a possibility. Without the weight of water in spent fuel tanks, a destroyer floated high in the water and would roll in an exaggerated manner in high wind and seas. This saltwater ballast would be pumped out prior to scheduled refuelings; unfortunately, several destroyers had just done that when they were caught by the storm and had failed to restore it when the eye approached. The sad result was the capsizing and sinking, during the worst of the storm, of three destroyers—two from the oiler group, the *Hull* and *Monaghan*, and one from TG 38.1, the *Spence*, a *Fletcher*-class destroyer like *Cotten*. All except eighty-six men, or 90 percent of the aggregate complement of these three ships, lost their lives when they sank.

What had evidently happened was that in their lightened conditions these destroyers had rolled over so far that seawater had entered air intakes to the engine rooms, shorting electrical switchboards and causing a loss of power to the steering engines. Without steering control, these ships would have almost immediately "broached," swung helplessly broadside to the oncoming seas, which would have quickly rolled them over onto their sides and held them there. Lying on their "beam ends," they would inevitably founder as successive massive seas drove ever-increasing amounts of water into their hulls or forced their open smokestacks under the surface. When each of the flooded ships sank, most of its hundreds of crew members went down as well.

As long as the *Cotten* had responded to its helm with the assistance of the engines, we had not seemed to be in immediate danger of broaching. One was conscious, however, that if steering control were lost through an engine failure or a loss of power to the rudder, the ship could be overwhelmed in an instant. Fortunately, because we had no systems failures and had maintained our ballast, we never were in danger of losing steering control. Whether or not the *Cotten* had been in serious danger, everyone aboard had been fascinated by the tremendous seas, which threw our ship about as if it were a dinghy, and by the unbelievable force of the wind, which could knock you flat if you were unlucky enough to be on deck.

The damage done to the carriers was severe. In addition to the fires on the light carriers, some two hundred aircraft had broken loose on the flight

or hangar decks and been destroyed. These losses were fairly evenly divided among the three carrier task groups. Also, I have a recollection of seeing
a fleet carrier with the forward end of its flight deck bent up nearly vertical
by the force of the sea. We later heard that a heavy cruiser had lost its bow,
up to the number 1 turret; the forecastle had broken completely loose and,
after drifting by its parent, disappeared in the storm. Many men, from
ships throughout the task force, had been washed overboard; they, when
added to the men never recovered from the three capsized destroyers,
brought the loss of life to a reported 790.

The *Cotten* remained on station as linking vessel between TG 38.2 and
our task group throughout the night of December 18–19, as the ships in the
three task groups regained their proper positions and assessed their respective storm damage. During the midwatch Admiral Halsey ordered all three
task groups south to a new rendezvous for fueling, now two days delayed.

By sunrise of December 19, the typhoon was a memory. *Cotten* was
speeding at twenty-five knots to maintain its position between the task
groups, and at 0845 we were ordered to leave the linking position and return to our task group. An hour later we had rejoined TG 38.3 and were
going alongside *Essex* to deliver the guard mail that we had picked up two
days previously. We delivered similar mail to carriers *Langley* and *San Jacinto* before being permitted to go alongside the oiler *Patuxent* to fuel.

At sunset, Halsey's staff recommended to him that a concerted effort
be made to search for men washed overboard and for any survivors from
the three lost destroyers. Accordingly, the three task groups were deployed
in a line abreast—with the destroyer screens in a bent line ahead of each
task group, a thousand yards between destroyers—to form an overall search
line covering thirty thousand yards. Because the typhoon had prevented
accurate navigation, the staff was uncertain as to where the men in the
water might be, if in fact any could be still alive. As a result, the search was
made on the basis of good intentions, guesses, and hope. During the night
many ships' lookouts reported hearing cries and whistles in the water, and
all of these hopeful reports were carefully followed up by the nearest destroyer. This search was continued throughout the day of December 20.

While we never heard of any rescues resulting from the extensive search,
we later learned that the destroyer escort USS *Tabberer*, of the oiler group,
had lost its mast and radio antenna during the worst of the storm and had
been assumed sunk with the other three screening ships. However, a day
later it was discovered that it had remained afloat and had, amazingly, picked
fifty-five men from USS *Hull* out of the water. Two days after the storm,
USS *Brown* from TG 38.3 rescued six men from one of *Monaghan*'s life
rafts, the sole survivors of that destroyer. On the same day, the destroyer

escort *Swearer,* from the screen of the oiler group, rescued six men from the *Spence,* and *Tabberer* again picked up several additional survivors, also from the *Spence.*

At 1815 Admiral Halsey called off the search and ordered TF 38 to proceed to the northwest to be in a position to launch strikes against Luzon on the morning of December 21. Nearly eight hours later, however, he changed his mind and ordered the Luzon strikes canceled. He directed TF 38 to reverse course to the east and conduct another search for possible survivors of the typhoon, probably as a result of the successful rescues that were being made by *Tabberer, Brown,* and *Swearer.* By 1000 on December 21, we were, as well as we could tell, back in the area where we had been when the storm was at its height, and all three task groups again extended their screens to make another sweep through the area. The search continued all day and throughout the night, ending the following morning.

The next day we turned to the southeast, and we arrived at the entrance to Ulithi Lagoon at 1020 on December 24. When I had quieted down enough to appreciate that on my first cruise as a permanent officer of the deck, I had encountered the awful power of a typhoon, it occurred to me that the efforts of TF 38 to prevail over the enemy, and his to keep us at bay, both seemed considerably diminished in comparison to the forces of nature.

22

In the South China Sea

The *Cotten* remained at Ulithi for five days. There the crew occupied itself with restoring the camouflage paint that had been stripped from the hull and superstructure by the force of the typhoon, as well as with performing the normal chores necessary after each period at sea.

In a critique distributed to all the units of the Pacific Fleet of the operations of the Third Fleet for December 1944, Admiral Nimitz commented that a vital part of a fleet commander's responsibility concerned the safe navigation of his command, a responsibility that applied equally to each ship's captain. By this dictum, he stated, the Third Fleet should have maneuvered to the east to clear the typhoon as a first priority, with the tactical situation secondary to the safety of the fleet. Of course, he acknowledged, each captain could not go where he thought safety lay, but he should keep his ship in ballast during violent storms, refueling schedules notwithstanding.

Admiral Halsey, setting aside the immediate past without comment, issued a plan for January that began with a return to Formosa to strike again at the Japanese air bases, followed by a thrust into the South China Sea to attack enemy airfields from French Indochina to Hong Kong. The objectives were, primarily, to batter enemy air power surrounding the northern circumference of the Philippines, and secondarily, to seek out the enemy fleet units that had fled to the northwest after the Battle of Leyte Gulf. This would prevent their opposing MacArthur's landings, scheduled for January 9, 1945, in Lingayen Gulf, on the west coast of Luzon.

Distance would be a major factor in the coming operation. It is fifteen hundred nautical miles from Ulithi to the southern tip of Formosa, and another thousand nautical miles from Formosa to the coast of French Indochina, the most remote objective. The southern coast of China (including Hong Kong) lies between the two and was another scheduled target area. Oiler groups were ordered to accompany TF 38 so that the destroyers could refuel as necessary while in the South China Sea.

There are many banks and shoals in the South China Sea, as well as a continental shelf that extends for as much as two hundred miles off the coast of China. The shallowness of the water in these areas tends to build up the seas during gales, as the waves from the deeper waters become foreshortened and heightened; ship handling is accordingly much more difficult than in the oceanic waters we were accustomed to. In deference to Admiral Nimitz's admonitions, Admiral Halsey's new operation orders called attention to these conditions and to the fact that violent storms regularly occur in the South China Sea. According to the plan, TF 38 would be at sea for four weeks, after which it would return to Ulithi.

The *Cotten* got under way at 0700 on December 30, 1944, to sortie with our task group. The carriers were *Essex, Ticonderoga, Langley,* and *San Jacinto*, with battleships *Washington* and *North Carolina*, Cruiser Division 13, and DesRons 50 and 55. By 0845 all ships were clear of the lagoon entrance.

At dawn on January 1, 1945, the Battle Line (TF 34) was formed for exercises, which led us to believe that Admiral Halsey still had not given up hope of a fight. For over twelve hours we engaged in mock battles, torpedo attacks, and cruiser-destroyer screening attacks, before returning to our carrier task groups at sunset. These battle-line exercises had a nostalgic air about them. The Japanese fleet had risked everything in the Battle of Leyte Gulf and had presented Halsey and Lee with the opportunity they had been seeking, but Halsey had allowed Task Force 34 to be taken away from the main chance by his decision to engage decoy carriers. Because the Philippines were no longer worth the exposure of the few remaining Japanese surface units, there was nothing left for Task Force 34 to fight. Halsey's great opportunity had surely passed him by.

The task groups were off Formosa at dawn of January 3 and launched air strikes, which continued for the next seven hours. Operations were then canceled, as the ceiling over the target areas had lowered to five hundred feet, effectively hiding the enemy airfields. For the same weather-related reasons, no enemy planes reached TF 38 during the day or evening.

On January 4 air attacks on Formosa were resumed, although the weather was still thoroughly overcast. The returning pilots claimed to have damaged some forty-eight enemy planes on the ground and shot down fourteen more that were airborne, but in view of the weather, the reports were taken with a grain of salt. A number of floating mines were sighted at sea on January 4, and some six of these were sunk by gunfire. There were extensive Japanese minefields around Formosa; during storms many mines would go adrift, which accounted for their presence in the area where the fleet was operating.

The attacks on Formosa were completed during the mid-afternoon of January 4, and the task force retired to the south to meet the oilers. Just after noon on January 5, with refueling concluded, the fleet headed south toward the northernmost tip of Luzon, with *Cotten* taking one of the picket stations overnight. During the morning of January 6, the task groups were able to conduct a fighter sweep of northern Luzon for three and a half hours before heavy weather canceled flight operations.

On the same morning, units of the Seventh Fleet were sweeping paths through the Japanese minefields in Lingayen Gulf, and bombardment ships were shelling the landing beaches, all in preparation for the invasion of Luzon. The landing areas were 120 miles north of Manila, to cut off from logistical support the most significant contingent of the Japanese army between the new beachhead and the southern coast of Luzon.

Reports were received of violent kamikaze attacks on ships supporting the landings, resulting in incredible damage. In two days the Seventh Fleet suffered one escort carrier sunk, one escort carrier damaged, two old battleships damaged, and three cruisers and four destroyers hit. It seemed as though the Japanese had hidden the major force of kamikazes on Luzon, as certainly we had not seen any in the Formosa area. It demonstrated that the enemy could still pack a vicious punch if given a chance to catch his breath. It also showed how difficult it was becoming to preempt the kamikaze pilots, who could effectively disperse and hide their planes until they were ready to take off on their one and only missions.

Dawn of January 7 saw TF 38 off northern Luzon, launching fighter sweeps against enemy airfields in an effort to prevent any more Japanese planes from working their way south to Lingayen Gulf. The weather was still very bad, but the carriers kept up flight operations until late in the afternoon. The destroyer *Callaghan* lost three men overboard when a freak wave covered its deck with solid water. *Callaghan* left the screen to search for the men, whom it found an hour later.

At 1600 *Cotten* was ordered to leave the task group to search for two downed pilots who had been sighted some twenty-five miles to the southwest. We headed out at flank speed and about an hour later came upon the first, Lt. R. D. Green, U.S. Marine Corps Reserve, a Corsair pilot from *Essex*. At 1743 we sighted the second, Lt. W. H. Cloward, USMCR, another *Essex* Corsair pilot. We immediately started back for our task group, arriving at a picket station twelve miles to the southwest of the formation center, where we were ordered to remain overnight. At dawn the next day, after delivering the two pilots to *Essex, Cotten* returned to the screen. At 1616 our task group headed back to the northwest at twenty-six knots, to return to Formosa.

On January 9, the day that MacArthur's forces landed at Lingayen Gulf, Task Force 38 launched fighter sweeps against the now familiar airfields on Formosa, starting at 0530. Air operations were completed by 1720, all aircraft having returned aboard the carriers. The task force then set a course for the South China Sea.

Reports from Luzon confirmed that the landings in Lingayen Gulf had been successfully accomplished and that the kamikaze attacks, which had initially been so damaging to the ships of the Seventh Fleet, had diminished to a trickle. From this it could be inferred that the operations of TF 38 against Formosa and northern Luzon had cut off air reinforcements to the Japanese defenders on Luzon, which had been their strategic objective.

At 2352 our task group passed Y'Ami Island six miles abeam to port, leaving behind the navigational obstructions that litter Luzon Strait. Our ships and our purposes were vastly different from those of the American clipper ships that had once cruised these same waters in pursuit of the China trade, but in fact that era had ended only fifty years before our time. Some of my own forebears living on the coast of Maine had earned their livelihood in the clipper ship industry, something I could not help but reflect upon as the *Cotten* entered the South China Sea.

By the morning of January 10, we were northwest of the northern tip of Luzon on a southwesterly course toward a point off Cam Ranh Bay, on the coast of French Indochina. At sunrise, three enemy search planes were shot down by night fighters from the light carrier *Independence;* it was probable that our entry into the South China Sea had been reported to the Japanese command.

At 0952 one of our planes hit the water just seven hundred yards off our bow. We maneuvered to where the plane had crashed and picked up the body of the pilot, whose skull had been fatally fractured on impact. His body was brought aboard, and while returning to the screen we reported his death to the task group commander. At 1700 a funeral service was conducted by Dr. Spindler on the fantail of the *Cotten* for Ens. C. M. McGhee, U.S. Naval Reserve, of the carrier *Ticonderoga*. He was buried at sea with military honors.

At 0730 on January 12, with the three task groups in tactical concentration, air strikes were launched against the enemy airfields in the coastal region adjacent to Cam Ranh Bay. The flying weather was good, enabling the air groups to keep up the attacks throughout the day. Completing the strikes by 1900, the returning pilots reported that many enemy aircraft had been destroyed, mostly on the ground, and that there had been no discernible Japanese air strength remaining by day's end.

At 1926, when all returning aircraft had been recovered, TF 38 turned back to the northeast to avoid the reefs and rocks around the Paracel Islands in the western half of the South China Sea. During the night of January 12–13, the wind picked up, causing the seas to mount so quickly that the twenty-one-knot fleet speed was reduced to fifteen knots to ease the heavy pounding that the destroyers were experiencing. We met the oilers an hour and a half behind schedule, at 0850, owing to the heavy weather and the reduced overnight speed.

Fueling was a slow process, due to the steepness of the seas. At 1241 *Cotten* was alongside *Neches* for fueling, and oil was pumped from 1300 until 1345, when the hose parted as we were buffeted away from the oiler. We had received a barely sufficient amount of fuel but were returned to the screen nonetheless, having used up our allotted time. At 1430, while alongside another oiler, *Gatling* lost a man overboard; just before the fueling process was canceled at twilight, another man was washed overboard, this time from *C. K. Bronson*. The task group, with the oilers remaining inside our formation, continued northeast overnight at a reduced speed of twelve knots, into the teeth of what was by now a full gale.

The morning of January 14 found us in the same area where we had been the evening before, due to the reduction in speed and radical course changes made during the night. The seas had sufficiently moderated by 0730 to resume the fueling operation, which took up most of the day. At dusk the oiler group finally left the formation, and our task group headed toward Luzon Strait. The next morning, our task group was back northnortheast of the tip of Luzon within fighter range of Formosa, but the weather had turned for the worse again, delaying flight operations until 0800. All operations were canceled at noon, as flying conditions had continued to deteriorate, finally obliterating all visibility over the target areas.

During the night of January 15–16, our task group moved back to the west, arriving 150 miles south of Hong Kong at 0800 on January 16, when strikes were put in the air to attack the airfields and "targets of opportunity" among the shipping. Our returning pilots claimed that these strikes had been effective, that many cargo ships had been sunk in the harbor and the enemy air bases largely neutralized. The air operations were concluded by 1900, at which time the task group began a retirement to the southeast, toward the western coast of Luzon.

By dawn of January 17, we were about 220 miles west of the mountains of Luzon that lie north of Lingayen Gulf. The oilers had rejoined us, and a refueling operation was scheduled. The weather had again worsened, so that the prospects did not look at all promising, the seas being big, nasty, and steep. There was some TBS conversation between Admiral Sherman on the *Essex* and his two destroyer squadron commanders as to how to go about the fueling task, considering the conditions of wind and sea. Finally it was decided that *Essex* and *Ticonderoga* as well as the two oilers would fuel the destroyers, as rigging the hoses was going to be a lengthy job at best.

At 1148 the *Cotten* was alongside the oiler *Pamansett*, with the *Essex* on the oiler's other side at the same time. We could see the gold braid of Admiral Sherman's cap on the *Essex*'s open bridge, which left no doubt that he was observing the operation. The ships were rolling badly, sometimes together and sometimes in opposite directions. It looked as if the upper deck of the oiler would come within a few feet of our masthead, a disconcerting sight. On the oiler's other side, the *Essex* was also rolling far over.

During fueling details my station had remained with the Second Division, the men of which were responsible for winching in the hoses once the heavy "messenger" lines were on board. First, the oiler would fire (with a modified shotgun) a "shot line" over to the other ship, with a heaving line attached; the receiving ship would haul it in. The heaving line was attached to the messenger, and the messenger to the fuel oil hose. Once hauled on board and connected, the end of the hose would be locked to a receptacle (from which a pipe led to the fuel tanks) and secured with lines. Both lines and hoses, however, could snap like strings if the ships surged apart or rolled sharply apart. If this occurred while the fuel oil (heated to make it less viscous) was being pumped, it would spew all over the deck and then splash into the ocean between the two ships.

The closer a destroyer was to the oiler, the more easily these evolutions could be carried out. During a storm, however, such as the one we were now in, destroyers tended to stay far from the fueling ships, in fear of a collision; this exponentially aggravated the difficulty of getting the lines and hoses aboard. The longer the lines, the greater was the likelihood of their hitting the water and being dragged. On this occasion, as a result of this exaggerated rolling, the destroyer captains, ours included, were indeed keeping their ships farther away from the oilers than usual, and the hoses and lines were being pulled out of the men's hands time and time again.

At 1205 the *Cotten's* men had the oiler's first hose connected. At 1225 the hose snapped loose. At 1324 we had the after hose connected to the forward fueling station. At 1338 this hose parted. During the ensuing ninety minutes, we were unable to get a hose back aboard; we were then ordered to give up the effort and return to the screen.

At 1659 we were ordered to go alongside flagship *Essex,* which had earlier completed fueling from the *Pamansett. Essex* was now fueling screen destroyers in the effort to speed the storm-delayed and, in our case, interrupted process. From Captain Winston's point of view, this was an intimidating assignment. The carrier loomed alongside us like a mountain. When it rolled in our direction, the flight deck seemed directly overhead; when we rolled together, our masthead seemed destined to crack into the carrier. The captain guided us in as close as he dared, which was not very close, and at 1720 our men managed to get one hose aboard. All went well for nineteen minutes, when a sudden sea parted the two ships enough to snap the hose free once more, spewing hot oil all over the *Cotten* and into the South China Sea. For our day-long exertions we had received a pitiful total of 398 barrels of fuel, about one day's consumption at fifteen knots.

This time, Admiral Sherman called our squadron commander on TBS and directed that "a more efficient Small Boy be sent alongside for fueling." The *Cotten* left the *Essex* for the screen with an uncharacteristically fuming Captain Winston on the bridge. As soon as we left the side of the *Essex,* I hurried to the bridge, as it would be my OOD watch when the refueling detail was secured and the regular steaming watch resumed. I relieved Herb Kanter as we returned to our screening station, and I did my best to avoid contact with the captain for the rest of the watch. The strain on our bridge watch was eased somewhat when the entire fueling fiasco was terminated by Admiral Sherman at 1834.

It was unusual that Admiral Sherman had voiced his displeasure at our efforts over TBS. In all the time we were under his command, I cannot recall a similar display of temper. A reasonable explanation was that Admiral Halsey in the mighty *New Jersey,* comfortable and unaffected by the storm, had probably been irritated that a simple routine like a fueling operation was delaying his ambitious schedule of operations. Halsey would have flashed a signal to Admiral McCain telling him that the fueling operation was taking too long and should be speeded up. Admiral McCain would waste no time in signaling each of his three task group commanders to speed up the fueling. It would have been then that Admiral Sherman, who did not like getting an impossible order any more than anyone else, told the screen commander to send a more efficient destroyer alongside—which was the one message in this reconstructed scenario that we actually heard. The result was that everyone got boiling mad, and the fueling operation was affected not one iota.

For the balance of the evening and through the first two watches of January 18, the task group's speed was maintained at eight knots to reduce the destroyers' pounding into the seas, which were coming from dead ahead. The wind was powerful and the seas very steep and close together, creating a difficult environment in which to maintain even a loose formation. If this blow was not quite of typhoon velocity, it certainly was a most violent storm. At noon on January 18, Halsey asked for a 1200 position from all the larger ships of TF 38. After he had received the individual ships' positions, his flag navigator came up with an averaged fleet position, which was then given out to the task force. This was a best estimate, because no "sun lines" or star sights had been possible for two days.

It was a matter of some interest that when a positive fix was finally obtained a day later, the flag navigator's dead-reckoned, best-estimate position was some sixty miles in error, due to the effect of the storm and shallow sea. This was no laughing matter in the South China Sea, where reefs and shoals abound.

Throughout the eighteenth, TF 38 struggled on to the south, not even attempting to fuel destroyers, in an effort to work clear of the storm. At 1710 another man from our squadron was washed overboard, from the *Ingersoll*, and at 1920 a man was killed on *C. K. Bronson* when green water, a solid wave, broke over the deck and crushed him against one of the 5-inch gun mounts.

The storm began to abate during the midwatch of January 19, permitting the task groups to build their speed back up to fifteen knots by 0520. At 0736 our group resumed the refueling, which had now been delayed by nearly two days. Our task group successfully completed that operation by 1841 and headed north, with the intention of leaving the South China Sea the following day.

For reasons best known to Halsey's staff, TF 38 was to leave the South China Sea via a narrow passageway called the Balintang Channel rather than the Bashi Channel, 130 miles farther north. The Balintang Channel is so narrow that our three carrier task groups would have to make the passage in succession, their screens pulled in at some points, and their maneuvering room restricted. During the approach to the straits, a number of enemy planes were shot down by combat air patrols, as the weather finally turned fair. We reached the channel entrance at 1925, and just as our task group was starting on its way through, enemy aircraft appeared directly overhead. One plane flew over the *Cotten* within range of our automatic weapons. We, along with everyone else in our task group, put up a hail of fire, causing the plane to turn away. There was now no doubt that our presence in the Balintang Channel had been reported. The rest of the five-and-a-half hour passage was uneventful, however, and we emerged unscathed at the other end at 2300.

During the first two watches of January 21, TF 38 headed to the northeast to be in position at dawn to launch fighter sweeps against the airfields of Formosa. While these fighter attacks were in progress, our task group's screening destroyers started fueling from the battleships *North Carolina* and *Washington*. The *Cotten* was alongside *North Carolina* when at 1156 an enemy air attack suddenly developed directly overhead. Fueling operations were canceled in a rush, and many ships were already firing at the enemy as the *Cotten* raced to the screen. At 1211 carriers *Ticonderoga* and *Langley* were both struck by bombs from conventional dive-bombers, not kamikazes, one of the two planes dropping the bombs being immediately shot down by gunfire.

A plume of smoke erupted from *Ticonderoga* as more Japanese planes appeared over our formation. At 1233 *Ticonderoga* reported that a group of its men had been blown overboard by the bomb blast. At 1236 a plane dove on *Essex*, its bomb narrowly missing. *Cotten* sighted another enemy plane overhead and commenced shooting with both 5-inch and machine gun batteries. This plane was shot down. Then, at 1320, we sighted life rafts in the water and picked up two of the men who had been blown overboard from *Ticonderoga*—Steward's Mate Second Class (St.M2c) Harvester Curry and Steward's Mate First Class (St.M1c) Henry Little.

At this time several mines were sighted floating inside our formation. Two were sunk by gunfire while other men from *Ticonderoga* were being picked out of the water by destroyers in the screen. A bit later *Cotten* sighted another mine, sinking it with 20-mm machine gun fire.

By 1800 all flight operations against Formosa were complete, and Task Force 38 headed to the northeast, toward Okinawa. Just after dawn on January 22, the task groups were in position to launch fighter sweeps and aerial photography missions over Okinawa, which continued throughout the day. By 1915 all planes had returned to the carriers, and TF 38 started a retirement to Ulithi, which lay 1,250 miles to the south-southeast.

During the return trip to Ulithi, the Battle Line (TF 34) was formed, this time without our squadron. This was the first time since the preceding August that we had not been a part of the Battle Line, which lent credence to a rumor we had heard when last in Ulithi that our squadron was next in line to return to the United States for a major overhaul. This prospect, unconfirmed though it was, gave a boost to morale dampened by the storm-lashed operations of the past two months. At sunrise on January 26, the task group entered Ulithi.

On the morning of January 27, DesDiv 100 received orders detaching it from the Third Fleet and instructing it to proceed to Pearl Harbor. We in DesDiv 99, however, were ordered to report to the Fifth Fleet, to be attached to Rear Adm. A. W. Radford's Task Group 58.4. Adm. Marc Mitscher was resuming command of Task Force 58, and Admiral Spruance, as commander of the Fifth Fleet, was resuming command of the ships heretofore under Halsey's command.

The fact that DesDiv 100 was being sent back to Pearl Harbor encouraged us to think that our turn should come soon. Also, there is no doubt that we were all happy to have Admirals Spruance and Mitscher back as our commanders. They both enjoyed and deserved our confidence and respect.

Admiral Halsey, despite reservations held by some as to his overall command ability, was widely admired by Americans, especially the fans of General MacArthur, for his focused aggressiveness in the prosecution of the war. Halsey had provided MacArthur's forces with vital strategic air support, and even his detractors admitted that the misdirection of Task Force 34 in the Battle of Leyte Gulf had not, as things had turned out, been a disaster. However, the navy's war was the war of the Central Pacific, not the Philippines, and Admiral Spruance could be counted on to prosecute the navy's war, first and foremost.

By noon on January 27, the wind was blowing steadily at twenty-five knots, and the nearest nest of destroyers, consisting of *C. K. Bronson* and *Gatling*, began to drag anchor and drift down on the nest containing *Caperton* and ourselves. We started to make preparations to get under way, but having only one boiler on the line and one engine room manned, we had the immediate use of only the port engine, which rendered us unable to maneuver. By 1247 *C. K. Bronson* and *Gatling*, moored together, had drifted across the bows of both *Caperton* and *Cotten*, *Bronson's* starboard side banging into us; the two ships remained in that embarrassing position until *Ingersoll* arrived an hour later to tow them away. By that time two yard tugs had also arrived on the scene, and for the next fifteen minutes there was a sequence of bizarre foul-ups involving the tugs, *C. K. Bronson*, and *Gatling*, which resulted in another collision with our nest before the two offending destroyers were finally towed away.

An investigating board, consisting of Captain Winston and Lt. Comdr. E. I. Gibson, executive officer of the *Dortch*, was ordered to prepare an official report of the circumstances of the collision, including recommendations for further action. The investigation was held on January 28 aboard the *Cotten*. From 1000 until 1600, the two-man board met in our wardroom, Captain Winston being in charge as the senior member. Despite considerable curiosity, we never heard a word as to the findings of the investigation so did not know whether or not anyone was censured. At 0800 on the next day, we went alongside the tender *Dixie* to have the damage from the collision repaired.

On February 3, Lt. Roy Blackburn and Ens. L. L. Smith were detached from the *Cotten*. Bob Drake was made chief engineering officer to replace Blackburn, and I was made navigator, replacing Smith. My new duties were added to those I already had—as officer of the deck when under way, air defense officer at general quarters, and Second Division officer. Being made navigator was unexpected, but it was a designation that I especially appreciated. This assignment required that I be on the bridge whenever we were in pilotage waters, to keep the ship's position and to advise the captain on all piloting and navigational aspects of the ship's progress.

When at sea, the navigator was required to fix the ship's position at 0800 and 2000 by observation of the stars and at 1200 by sun lines, enter these positions in the ship's log, and so advise the captain. Celestial navigation requires the use of a sextant for observations. The altitude of the body would be taken by the navigator; its bearing and the exact time of the observation would be determined by the quartermaster assisting, who would also record all the data. Observations are taken of stars at morning and evening twilight, when the brightest stars are just visible and the horizon is still discernible as a line, the clarity of which depends on the state of the weather. During the morning, sun lines would be taken and crossed with morning star lines, advanced to account for the ship's progress since then, to give a noon position. The computations of the lines of positions would be made in the chart room by the navigator, and the lines would be plotted and advanced as necessary to fix the *Cotten's* position at the designated hours.

Generally, given an opportunity to make some good observations, a navigator could fix the ship within a mile or two of its exact location. If no celestial observations were possible, the navigator would work up an estimated position based on "dead reckoning" of the ship's courses and speeds, as modified by the estimated set and drift caused by ocean currents and the wind. Such an estimated position was obviously subject to varying degrees of error, as the experience of the fleet navigator of TF 38 in the South China Sea had demonstrated.

The navigator is also responsible for the preparation and accuracy of the ship's deck logs, in which are noted all the ship's movements, courses, speeds, and combat operations, as well as major events, conditions of the wind and sea, and pertinent bearings when in pilotage waters, watch by watch, with the time of each occurrence. In a mild state of euphoria, I felt that my personal circumstances could not be improved upon, though I had some appreciation that the wide-ranging requirements of my various duties would tax to full measure my training and experience.

23

Air Strikes against Tokyo: Iwo Jima D Day

The transfer of command from Admiral Halsey (Third Fleet) to Admiral Spruance (Fifth Fleet) was accompanied by a reorientation of the Pacific Fleet toward the Central Pacific objectives. To emphasize this change, Admiral Nimitz had moved his own command headquarters from Pearl Harbor to Guam.

The Pacific Fleet would no longer have strategic ties to the Philippine campaign. By now the air force had adequate facilities in the Philippines to provide MacArthur with satisfactory air support, releasing the Fast Carrier Task Force, again designated Task Force 58, for strategic support of amphibious operations of the Fifth Fleet. The first of these objectives was Iwo Jima, where D day was now scheduled for February 19, having been delayed a month by the use of the carriers in extended support of the Luzon operation. The second objective would be the invasion of Okinawa, now scheduled for late March.

The new operation plans called for air strikes against military targets on Honshu, to reduce Japanese tactical air power in advance of the landings on Iwo Jima. The air force B-29 bombers had started strategic bombing attacks on military production facilities in the Japanese home islands, flying the

3,100-mile round-trip between Honshu and our airfields on Saipan and Tinian. The Japanese had airfields on Iwo Jima, two-fifths of the way between Saipan and Tokyo, from which they could deploy fighters against the B-29s or at least give advance warning of incoming raids. Japanese fighters had recently been able to defend against the B-29s with some success, rising to an altitude of thirty thousand feet to do so.

It therefore seemed vital to seize Iwo Jima, both to deny its use to the enemy aircraft and to provide an airstrip on which crippled B-29s could land on their return from Japan. Lacking Iwo Jima, B-29s in serious trouble would otherwise have to set down in the ocean, where their crews had small likelihood of survival. It was assumed that the Japanese on Iwo Jima would be well dug in, as the defenders would have enjoyed a six-month period between Task Force 58's first attacks during the summer of 1944 and the delayed D day in which to install well-prepared defensive positions. The marine commanders and Admiral Spruance were convinced that the coming operation would be a brutal one.

Destroyer Division 99 would be employed both in the screen of the new task group and as part of a scouting line of destroyers to be deployed thirty-six miles in advance of the five carrier task groups during the high-speed approach to Honshu. In addition, DesDiv 99 was designated as the destroyer screen for the battleships and cruisers that would be detached from Task Force 58 upon its return from Honshu to provide additional gunfire support when the marines landed on Iwo Jima. We were therefore going to serve in a wide variety of duties, wherever we could be used effectively, before being sent back to the West Coast for a navy yard overhaul.

Because the scouting line in the approach to the Tokyo area was to destroy Japanese picket boats that the high command knew were deployed across our line of advance, our squadron (and now division) commander, Capt. E. R. Wilkinson, ordered DesDiv 99 to sea for a twenty-four-hour practice session, to include salvo firing against surface targets, from dawn of February 6 until the morning of February 7.

The *Cotten* got under way from Ulithi Harbor at 0637 with the four other destroyers, in column. I was on the bridge for my first day's work as navigator, duly keeping the captain posted on the courses of the various legs of the channel, which was not a demanding initial responsibility. Once clear of the channel, the division headed to the southeast toward the exercise area.

The first exercise was calibration of the main battery fire control radars, which took the better part of an hour before everyone was satisfied that the equipment was working properly. From 0930 until 1130, each ship conducted 5-inch salvo-firing exercises at targets attached to sleds towed by a fleet tug from the Ulithi harbor command. Despite optimum conditions and the best efforts of the gun crews, neither tight salvos nor pinpoint accuracy were a foregone conclusion with the 5-inch ordnance of our *Fletcher*-class destroyers. These surface gunnery exercises were an obvious necessity if we were to achieve acceptable results against the Japanese picket boats. Later in the afternoon, the heavy machine gun batteries fired at sleeves flown out by planes from Ulithi. When the various gunnery exercises were over, each ship held individual engineering and damage control casualty drills.

After supper the five-ship division formed two sections, which separated until they were twenty-seven thousand yards apart. One at a time, each section then made simulated torpedo attacks on the other section, illuminating it with 5-inch star shells. When this exercise was completed, the division formed in a scouting line, in which configuration we cruised during the balance of the night of February 6–7.

At 0600 the next morning, the division deployed from the scouting line into column for reentry into Ulithi Harbor. Reviewing the twenty-eight hours we had been under way on this exercise, the captain and Rothschild noted that I had been on the bridge for a total of twelve hours as navigator, as officer of the deck, or taking my first evening star sights. Adding in the general quarters period of one and a half hours, I had been on the bridge for about fourteen hours out of twenty-eight. Since my various assignments would call for being on duty at least this proportion of each day and night, they decided to modify my OOD schedule to allow me six uninterrupted hours of sleep each night, between 2130 and 0330, in the expressed expectation that my disposition would immediately improve. This was accomplished by scheduling me permanently as officer of the deck for the 0400–0800 (morning watch) and the first dog watch (1600–1800), letting the other three OODs fill the remaining watches in rotation. I was more than grateful for this schedule, which was to remain in effect indefinitely.

The *Cotten* remained at anchor for the next three days, giving ample time to study the chart of Iwo Jima and the details of the operation orders covering the amphibious landings. During the early morning of February 10, we exited from Ulithi Lagoon and formed the customary destroyer screen outside the channel, awaiting the sortie of our heavy units. Once at sea, *Cotten* and *Dortch* formed a screen for cruisers *Santa Fe, Biloxi,* and *San Diego,* while the latter conducted main-battery gunnery exercises.

At 1312 our group of destroyers and cruisers was joined by battleships *Washington* and *North Carolina* and the other three destroyers of DesDiv 99 for an hour and a half of antiaircraft gunnery exercises. When these drills were completed, the entire task group regrouped and resumed cruising formation. We steamed east long enough to clear Ulithi, then formed in tactical concentration with the now five task groups of Task Force 58

(TGs 58.1, 58.2, 58.3, 58.4, and 58.5). Task Force 58 by this time consisted of seventeen carriers, an aggregate of twelve hundred aircraft, eight fast battleships, sixteen cruisers, and seventy-seven destroyers.

At 0730 the next morning, the destroyer advance scouting line was formed for practice maneuvers twelve miles astern of the assembled carrier task groups. There were four destroyer divisions in the scouting line, including DesDiv 99. We were organized into two-destroyer sections, *Cotten* and *Dortch* making one section. The sections, seven in total, were stretched out in a line with twenty thousand yards between each section, giving the scouting line a total extension of 120,000 yards, or sixty nautical miles.

During the morning of February 12, each of the destroyers in the scouting line was given an opportunity to direct the two combat air patrol planes assigned to its section in an interception of one of our aircraft, simulating a kamikaze. Mike Czarowitz, acting as the *Cotten's* fighter control officer, felt that though this was hardly sufficient practice to enable our CIC to become expert, it was at least enough to demonstrate that enemy aircraft could be intercepted, if the original identifying radar contact had been made in a timely way. After completion of the fighter direction exercises, DesDiv 99 rejoined the screen of our task group, and the scouting line was temporarily dissolved.

During the morning watch of February 13, the *Cotten* took station astern of the carrier *Randolph* in the center of our group, to act as plane guard during the nighttime flight operations. Whenever the officer of the deck knew a few moments in advance that the ship was to be a plane guard, he worked out on a maneuvering board the courses and speeds required to go from the screening station, on average six thousand yards from the task group center, to a position one thousand yards downwind of the designated carrier. The solution would take into account the *Cotten's* thousand-yard turning circle at both ends of the maneuver, and it would predict whether or not the ship would pass closer than five hundred yards to any of the heavy ships in the center while traveling between stations. When the change of station began, the ship's speed would be increased to reduce the time required for the maneuver to the minimum, twenty-seven knots being our best speed with the customary two boilers in service. When flight operations were completed, the maneuver would be reversed (in relative terms) for the return to our screening station.

When advance notice was not given, the officer of the deck would start the maneuver upon execution of the order, coming immediately to his best estimate of the proper course at the increased speed, picturing in his mind the two vectors of course and speed and the relative change in position. The junior officer of the watch and CIC hurriedly worked out maneuvering board solutions while the ship was speeding on the course initiated by the OOD. Given a great deal of experience, the OOD's first estimate of the proper course would usually be very close to the mathematical vector solution.

There were two very good reasons for a destroyer to be handled smartly and at maximum speed. First, its usefulness to the task group was minimal while it was proceeding from one station to another, so the quickest possible maneuvers maximized its ability to contribute to the group. Secondly, a destroyer's crew could sense when it was being handled decisively, as opposed to the infinite varieties of the alternative.

During morning flight operations on February 15, the *Cotten* again was in the nucleus of the formation, acting as plane guard. At 0700 we left the plane guard station to go alongside *Washington* in order to top off our tanks for the final run to Tokyo. When all destroyers that were to be in the advance scouting line had been fueled by the heavy ships, the special scouting line task group (58.8) was ordered re-formed.

DesDiv 99 joined up behind *C. K. Bronson* and went to flank speed to pull ahead of our task group, now on a base course of 340 degrees (roughly north-northwest) for the approach to Tokyo. It took the fourteen destroyers of the scouting line four hours to get on station thirty-six miles ahead of the carrier groups, which was accomplished by noon. DesDiv 99 was on the far right flank of the sixty-mile-long scouting line, and the section composed of *Cotten* and *Dortch* was the second from the extreme right. The *Cotten* at this time was 450 miles southeast of the entrance to Tokyo Bay, and the only ships visible from our bridge were our section-mate, the *Dortch*, fifteen hundred yards on our starboard beam, and those of the sections far to our right and left, represented by their mastheads.

At 1730 the fleet base course was changed forty degrees to the left, directly toward the entrance of Tokyo Bay. The scouting line was reoriented to reposition itself in advance of the five carrier task groups, and there it remained for the next twelve hours during the final run toward Honshu. By 0600 of February 16, the scouting line was within a hundred miles of the Honshu shoreline, and our starboard end of the line had still not come in contact with any Japanese picket boats.

We were within one hundred miles of the peninsula that separates Tokyo and Sagami Bays and but 170 miles southeast of the snow-capped peak of Mount Fuji. Despite being this close to the enemy's center of power, apparently alone except for the nearby *Dortch*, there was no empirical, visible evidence of how exposed we were. Because the ocean never looks the same on two occasions, at that moment our sixty-mile-long scouting line of fourteen destroyers could have been anywhere in the ocean at approximately our present latitude, as far as the senses could tell. Only the navigators knew just where we were.

The carriers, well below the horizon behind us, commenced flight operations at 0730, launching an overwhelming fighter assault on the enemy airfields on Honshu, particularly in the Tokyo-Yokohama area. The scouting line was then ordered to break up, the destroyer divisions to proceed independently at best speed to rejoin their respective carrier task groups, lying thirty-six miles to the southeast.

Several destroyers in the center of the scouting line had met Japanese picket vessels, one of which we observed being sunk by the destroyer *Haynesworth* as we were returning to our task group. At 1000 DesDiv 99 rejoined the screen of TG 58.4; air operations against the Tokyo area were still in progress. At 1800 the first day's strikes against Tokyo were completed, and the five task groups headed to the east for the first part of the night, reversing course back to the Honshu coast at midnight to be in position to resume the air attacks at dawn of February 17.

That night, when our task group resumed zigzagging after changing back to cruising formation from the air defense disposition, the destroyer *Ingraham* missed the signal and was rammed from astern by the next ship in the screen, the *Barton*. Both ships were forced to leave the formation to return to Ulithi for repairs. Accidents do occur, but this one seemed impossible to excuse, missed signal or not.

At dawn the five task groups were in position to launch the second day's strikes, which by 0730 were on the way in to their targets. Most of the day was spent steaming in defensive formation in expectation of Japanese counterattacks, which never materialized. Just after noon the weather in both our operating area and the target areas over Honshu turned foul, forcing the cancellation of the balance of the scheduled strikes. Course was then set for the southeast, toward Iwo Jima and the Bonin Islands. At 1615 Admiral Mitscher ordered DesDiv 99 to form a scouting line in advance of the southerly retirement of the five carrier task groups. An hour and a half later, we were twenty miles ahead of the fleet, spread out in a scouting line across the base course with sixteen thousand yards between each of our ships, providing a total coverage of thirty-two miles.

During the midwatch *C. K. Bronson*, in the center of our line, obtained two radar contacts ahead. These contacts were soon identified as enemy patrol craft and were taken under fire by *Gatling*, *Bronson*, and *Dortch*, the three closest ships in the scouting line. Both enemy ships were sunk, but the *Dortch* was hit by the enemy's return fire, which killed three of its men, wounded seven, and caused some minor damage to the ship. At 0815 DesDiv 99 was ordered to return to the screen of our carrier task group.

During the early afternoon of February 18, the destroyers were fueled from the heavy ships. While the fueling operation was in progress, flights from individual carriers were sent against air facilities on Chichi-jima, to make certain that there would be no enemy aircraft present to interfere with the landings on Iwo Jima, scheduled to take place during the next morning.

That afternoon the heavy cruiser *Indianapolis,* with Admiral Spruance aboard, joined our task group. At dusk DesDiv 99 was ordered to form a five-ship screen three thousand yards ahead of the task group, preparatory to leaving with the special ships for D day fire support at Iwo Jima. An hour and a half later, we were followed by the gunnery ships—battleships *Washington* and *North Carolina,* and cruisers *Biloxi, Santa Fe,* and *Indianapolis.* The ten-ship unit then set a course to the east, leaving the carrier task group behind. The destroyer screen was in the shape of a semicircle five thousand yards ahead of the guide, *Indianapolis,* the *Cotten* being on the left flank of the screen. An hour before midnight, our formation changed to a southeasterly course at twenty knots, heading for the northern tip of Iwo Jima.

The use of major ships of Task Force 58 for D day's heavy bombardment of shore positions had been made necessary by MacArthur's insistence on retaining several of the old battleships of the Seventh Fleet for his operations in the southern Philippines. While there was no military or other reason for further campaigns in the Philippines after the Japanese had retreated to the hills of Luzon, MacArthur's promise to liberate all of the islands obviously enjoyed high-level political support from Washington. The lack of those Seventh Fleet battleships for bombardment of Iwo Jima was another contentious issue for the navy.

At the end of the midwatch, the northern coast of Iwo Jima appeared on the radar screen, twenty-six thousand yards ahead on the starboard bow. The column of our heavy ships, led by *Indianapolis,* was heading ultimately for the fire support area between the transports carrying the marines and the landing beaches. The beaches, two miles long on the southeast coast of the island, started just to the right of Mount Suribachi, a volcano that constituted the island's southern tip.

At 0537, during my morning OOD watch, our tactical commander, Rear Admiral Dubose, dissolved the formation and directed each of the heavy units to proceed independently to its previously designated fire support area. At the same time, our screen commander ordered *C. K. Bronson, Gatling,* and *Healy* to screen *Indianapolis* and *North Carolina* as they moved to their positions; *Cotten* was ordered to screen *Washington,* and *Dortch* to screen *Biloxi. Washington* and *Biloxi* turned forty-five degrees to the right and increased speed to twenty knots, heading for their assigned stations, leaving it up to us to figure out how to precede them there, given that our position at the start of this maneuver had been some seven thousand yards on *Washington*'s port beam.

I worked out on the maneuvering board a solution that called for a course fifteen degrees to the right of that of the *Washington* and a speed of thirty knots, available because we had all four boilers on the line. The captain had come to the bridge when informed of our course change and the orders we had received.

Our course at high speed, through a pitch-black, moonless night, would bring us under the sterns of the four destroyers to our right—who had an easy time taking station ahead of *Indianapolis,* since that had been their position at the start of the maneuver. The captain placed himself over the rubber viewing hood of the pilothouse surface search radar repeater, which unfortunately kept me from seeing the overall picture. Because every ship was now heading for a different position, there was no way to keep track of them except to see them or observe the radar screen. In these circumstances, because the ships were changing relative position so quickly, CIC was useless to the conning officer.

The *Dortch* was ahead of us, proceeding in the same general direction as we were but at a slower speed. I had next located the *C. K. Bronson,* already sufficiently to our left to present no problem for us. I searched ahead with the binoculars and saw *Healy*, also on our port bow, and satisfied myself that on our present course and speed we would pass clear. At this moment, from his position at the radar, the captain called out, "Watch out for the *Healy!*" Out on the port bridge wing, I looked at the *Healy* again, to port; clearly, we were on a safe heading with respect to her. Instead of looking directly ahead, I turned to the open door of the pilothouse to tell the captain so. The captain now excitedly responded, "You are heading right for the *Healy!*"

This time I looked ahead as I should have done previously, and now I could make out what was in fact the *Gatling*, fine on our port bow and barely moving. I immediately ordered, "Right full rudder!" The helmsman spun the wheel all the way to the right. The *Cotten,* heeling over to port, turned to starboard quickly enough to rush past the *Gatling*, leaving it not more than two hundred feet to port and perhaps considerably less, our speed still a blistering thirty knots. From my post on the port wing of the bridge, I fancied I was looking down on the starboard depth charge racks of the other ship as we hurtled past.

I ordered the rudder back to amidships and was quickly analyzing our next move when the captain yelled out, "You are too close to the *Washington!* Don't embarrass the admiral." Of course, our maneuver to avoid the *Gatling* had brought us far to the right, and we were rapidly closing the *Washington*

Iwo Jima D Day—the first wave of marines heads for the beach on the morning of February 14, 1945. Courtesy of USNI.

as a result. I turned back to the left to compensate and then asked the captain if he would please step away from the radar so that I could reassess the situation. One glance at the repeater told me that we were now clear of the mess we had been in, and I worked out a new course to place us ahead of *Washington*, so advising the captain. He asked me if I was in control of the situation, and I reassured him that I was. I was also considerably relieved that the previous twenty minutes were now behind us.

By 0610 we were finally in position ahead of *Washington*, and at 0635 the battleship advised us that it was in its designated fire support area and that we were relieved of our escort duty. We milled about the area for forty-five more minutes until just after sunrise, when we were ordered by the screen commander to take over an antisubmarine patrol on the seaward side of the holding area for the hundreds of ships of the invasion force.

We had barely arrived at our assigned sector when the screen commander called us again, to order us to a patrol line on the right flank of the boat lanes that the landing craft were about to use to bring the first waves of marines to the beaches. We headed back into the new area, arriving at 0911, eleven minutes after the first marines had made it to the shore. The inshore point of our new patrol was about a thousand yards off the beach, from whence it ran at right angles to the beach for two miles, parallel to the right-hand boat lane. When we were close to shore it was possible to see through binoculars what was happening on the landing beaches. While the volume of gunnery from the fire support ships—which included shells from the 15-inch and 16-inch guns of the battleships, the 8-inch and 6-inch guns of the cruisers, and the 5-inch guns of destroyers, as well as

177

rockets from the special landing ships—was horrendous and continuous, whether it was resulting in any substantial damage to the defenders was open to question.

We patrolled the right-hand boat lane for approximately nine hours, during which time thirty thousand marines were landed. We were made aware by CIC, which was monitoring the voice radio circuits, that the marines were now being subjected to intense artillery and mortar fire from hidden positions, most of which seemed to be still fully operational. Unfortunately for the marines, the answer to the question on everyone's mind— had the prelanding bombardment been successful?—was now answered by a definite *no*.

Troop movement to and from the landing beaches was discontinued for the night at 1756, and the *Cotten*, in company with the *Dortch*, then headed for a rendezvous with fire support ships seven miles to the west of Mount Suribachi. This group formed up at 2130 as Task Force 54; it contained seven battleships and six cruisers in the center, and eleven destroyers, including the five ships of our division, in the screen.

At 0630 the following morning, February 20, Task Force 54 was dissolved for the day. The heavy ships proceeded independently toward their assigned fire support areas, and the destroyers were ordered to report to the Iwo Jima screen commander. The *Cotten* was to patrol in a fire-control holding (i.e., stand-by) station seven miles east of Mount Suribachi. At 1649 we rescued the crew of a torpedo plane from the *Hornet* that had been struck by enemy fire while making a napalm run, ultimately ditching in the water near our patrol lane. The pilot was Lt. (jg) C. T. Traxler, and his crewman was Aviation Radioman First Class R. E. Klunder, both of whom we brought aboard uninjured.

At 1655 we were relieved by USS *Shannon* and headed seven miles west of Suribachi again for the night rendezvous with the fire support ships, with which we steamed overnight. At 0630 on February 21, TF 54 was again broken up, and the *Cotten* was ordered to a radar picket station eleven miles northeast of the north shore of Iwo Jima. This was twenty miles away, on the opposite side of the island from the overnight cruising area, and we did not reach the assigned position until 0850.

At 1519 we were ordered alongside the transport ship *Hamlin* to transfer the *Hornet* pilot and crewman we had picked up. After making the transfer, we headed out unaccompanied for the overnight rendezvous with the fire support ships as on the previous two nights, seven miles to the west of Suribachi. While we were on our way, there was an all-ships alert to the effect that a large group of enemy planes had been spotted on radar by the

escort carrier task group that was providing direct tactical air support for
the marines. That task group was cruising some thirty-five miles northwest
of Iwo Jima, the same distance north-northwest of our rendezvous point
with Task Force 54.

At 1839 we joined the screen of TF 54, the entire formation now being
at general quarters. We received radio reports of heavy attacks on the support carriers; the attacks continued until dark. This time the enemy planes
were kamikazes, and they succeeded in hitting the old fleet carrier *Sarato-
ga* and the escort carrier *Bismarck Sea*, causing severe blast and fire damage to both. No Japanese plane came near our formation, which secured
from general quarters at 1945.

Considering that the Japanese air attack had contained an estimated
fifty aircraft, the four successful crashes on the support carriers was a small
number. These Japanese had had to fly six hundred miles south from Honshu over open water, with only the landing strip on Chichi-jima available
to them. This long, exposed flight, with the ultimate 100 percent loss of
their aircraft, made even kamikaze tactics costly for the results achieved.
The failure of the Japanese to follow up these attacks was the aspect of the
Iwo Jima operation most favorable to our forces; the battle ashore was
proving to be a charnel house for the marines.

Our own role was restricted to being available to screen our two fast
battleships and three cruisers whenever they needed us. During the day
they provided fire for the marines. The marines would dig in at night, and
each day they would advance as far as possible, with the heavy guns providing barrage fire directly ahead of their advance. Aircraft from the support carriers made day-long bombing runs over the dug-in Japanese
positions; much of the ordnance they used was napalm bombs, which were
proving more effective than the high-explosive shells, bombs, and rockets.

When the fire support ships were at their stations, the destroyers were
sent to screening lines around them and the transports, to provide protection from submarine attack. Because our seaborne forces were so close to
Japan, it was surprising that the enemy submarine forces had not put in an
appearance. Except for the one air attack of February 21, the Japanese had
apparently written off Iwo Jima—but they had called upon their troops to
battle the marines to the last man.

By now there was no doubt in anyone's mind that the Iwo Jima operation
was destined to be another landmark in the history of the U.S. Marine Corps.
The original schedule for completion of the operation had been optimistic,
calling as it had for a substantial defeat of the enemy after four days. It was
obvious that the enemy was resisting with skill and tenacity; the marines'

progress was slow and resulting in enormous casualties. Against the knowledge that the marines were encountering such desperate opposition, the *Cotten's* contribution seemed insignificant, and our inability to provide any help was depressing.

On the morning of February 22, TF 54 broke up, and the heavy ships again returned to their fire support areas. DesDiv 99 formed up in column behind *C. K. Bronson,* to mill around until we were given an assignment by the Iwo Jima screen commander. *Cotten* was ordered to fuel from the oiler *Neches,* a task that was completed at noon. We were then directed to return to radar picket station 3 to relieve the *Gatling,* arriving there a half hour later.

We remained on this station until twilight, when we received orders to join *Washington, North Carolina,* seven cruisers (including CruDiv 13), the rest of DesDiv 99, and DesDiv 106. This entire group now departed from Iwo Jima to rejoin the carrier task groups of TF 58 for another series of air strikes on the home islands of Japan. By 1800 our departing formation was on course to the east to rejoin TF 58. The marines were left with the remaining fire support units of TF 54, their own escort carrier support force, a small group of destroyers, and most important, their own courage, with which to continue the battle against their forsaken but resolute enemy.

24

A Second Strike against the Tokyo Area

The Iwo Jima fire support group steamed to the east through the night of February 22–23. By dawn it had closed with Task Groups 58.3 and 58.2, four of the cruisers joining the former and two the latter, accompanied by their destroyers. The rest of the ships continued on for another two hours to rejoin TG 58.4, the carrier task group of DesDiv 99, cruisers *Santa Fe* and *Biloxi*, and battleships *Washington* and *North Carolina*. Fueling was completed by late twilight, and Task Force 58, now consisting of four task groups, turned north toward the southern coast of Honshu.

During the night of February 24, the formation ran into heavy seas coming from ahead, forcing Admiral Mitscher to reduce speed to eighteen knots. Despite this reduction the forecastle of the destroyer *Moale* buckled, allowing the seas to enter the forward crew's berthing space when they broke over the bow. *Moale* was ordered to leave us and return south to join the fueling group.

There were now five of the nine destroyers of DesRon 60 out of service. The *Cooper* had been sunk by a torpedo in Ormoc Bay, on the western coast of Leyte in December 1944. Both *Barton* and *Sumner* had been hit by kamikazes during the Lingayen Gulf landings in early January 1945; the

Barton, back in service after being repaired, had, of course, rammed the *Ingraham* off the coast of Honshu in early February. Now the *Moale* had suffered a collapsed forecastle in a twenty-five-knot breeze. The DesRon 60 ships were of the newly designed *Sumner* class, which had joined the fleet some seven months after DesRon 50. Their structural design was evidently inferior to that of our *Fletcher* class, despite the fact that they were supposed to represent an improvement. The *Cotten's* crew was convinced that DesRon 60's high casualty rate was the major reason DesDiv 99 had not returned to the West Coast with DesDiv 100.

At 2136 the formation turned to the northwest for the final approach to the Tokyo area. During the midwatch of February 25, the seas moderated, and fleet speed was increased to twenty-two knots. At 0810, two hours later than had been planned, the first fighter sweeps were launched against the airfields of the Tokyo Bay area. Task Force 58 took antiaircraft formation at 0622 as a precaution against anticipated land-based air attacks, our location now being 170 miles from the coast of Honshu. As the planes from the last attacks against the Tokyo area were returning late that afternoon, the *Cotten* was stationed as a plane guard astern of the *Yorktown*. An F6F fighter crashed into the sea while attempting to land. We maneuvered over to pick up the pilot, Ens. Richard G. Nore, as the heavy units in the center of the task group rushed by.

At 1940 Admiral Mitscher ordered Task Force 58 to proceed to the southwest during the night to be in position to attack the heavily industrialized areas of Nagoya, Kobe, and Osaka at dawn the next day. However, the weather steadily deteriorated as the fleet cruised down the Honshu coast. By 0900 of February 26, there were head winds of twenty-five to thirty-five knots blowing directly from the designated target areas, causing Admiral Mitscher to cancel the entire operation.

The updated news from Iwo Jima was that the south end of the island, including all of Mount Suribachi, had been secured on February 25. This meant that a line had been established across the southern end from which an offensive could be launched to the north, with the seizure of the main (and southernmost) airstrip as the next objective. The marines had now established some momentum, but what had been optimistically planned as a four-day operation looked as if it would take four weeks instead.

On the evening of February 27, Admiral Mitscher detached DesDiv 99 from Task Group 58.4, which was about to return to Ulithi, and assigned us to carrier Task Group 58.3, which was headed to Okinawa to conduct air operations. We joined that task group at 1910 and reported for duty to Admiral Sherman, who commanded the task group we had belonged to for such an eventful nine months from his flagship *Essex*.

Task Force 58, reduced to the three carrier Task Groups 58.1, 58.2, and 58.3, proceeded westward toward Okinawa in order to obtain detailed photographic intelligence for use in the next planned landing operation. At twilight the photographic mission had been fulfilled, and Mitscher turned the three groups back toward Ulithi for replenishment.

On March 3, Admiral Mitscher surprised us by directing us to return immediately to Iwo Jima to report to Admiral Turner, the commander of the Iwo Jima landing force. There was no hint as to how we would be employed, but as the campaign was still grinding bloodily on, I for one was glad to be going and hoped we could be put to good use. Captain Wilkinson immediately took tactical command of our five destroyers and formed us into a scouting line heading to the northeast toward Iwo Jima.

On the morning of March 4, the dawn came in with a dead calm sea and cloudless sky. My morning star sights, on widely varying bearings, gave rare pinpoint accuracy, due to a perfect combination of the clear sky and a razor-sharp horizon. Just prior to 0800, Captain Wilkinson, alert to the ideal conditions available to the five navigators, flew a signal from the flagship's yardarm ordering all ships to report their positions by flag hoist exactly at 0800. I handed Captain Winston the customary slip of paper containing our position, and he directed the officer of the deck to have the required flags "bent on" and ready to hoist.

All five destroyers raised their hoists smartly at 0800 indicating their latitudes and longitudes. I jotted down the five positions and repaired to the chart room to record them on the chart. They plotted exactly one mile apart in latitude and on the same meridian, as close to the actual twenty-five-hundred-yard distance between ships as it was possible to compute. All five navigators had therefore come up with perfect fixes at the same time, which also happened to be the only occasion in the entire wartime career of the *Cotten* that an 0800 position was requested by the squadron commander.

At 1339 radar contact was made on Minami Iwo Jima at a distance of forty-seven miles, placing Iwo Jima itself fifteen miles farther to the north. Two hours later, Mount Suribachi was sighted, at a distance of eighteen miles. Our ships were then ordered to report individually to the Iwo Jima screen commander.

At this juncture of the battle for Iwo Jima, three categories of patrols were assigned to the destroyers and destroyer escorts serving under the screen commander. The first was an outer screen, which was the primary antisubmarine defensive shield for the many ships of the landing force armada still at anchor in the open roadstead east of the beaches. The second was an inner screen, which surrounded the inner eastern anchorage only and formed a secondary defensive line for the ships at anchor. Finally, there were a number of patrol lanes available as slots for destroyers that were on call for duty as gunfire support ships. Immediately upon reporting to the screen commander for duty, the *Cotten* was directed to a holding-area station that lay between four and five miles southwest of Mount Suribachi.

25

Iwo Jima: March 5–13, 1945

At dawn of March 5, the *Cotten* headed for the western transport area, near the southern end of Iwo Jima, to receive several tons of canned and dehydrated food and other supplies. The stores were ferried from the transport *President Jackson* and brought alongside by landing craft, then man-handled aboard by our crew. While the stores were being sent over, a fire control liaison officer of the 4th Marine Division came aboard for a consultation with Roger Stokey and Herb Kanter on the spotting and communication procedures for main battery gunfire support of the marines and for star-shell illumination of the Japanese positions.

At this point of the campaign, now exactly two weeks after D day, the front lines ran in a loop from the western shore at Hiraiwa Bay, curving north to the town of Motayama and then back in a southeasterly direction to the eastern shore, at the point where the shore turned to the west. This left the northern third of the island still securely in Japanese hands, but the balance was now held by the marines, aside from some remaining pockets of enemy troops. The marines' section of the island now included the largest airfield, on which the first crippled B-29 had made an emergency landing the previous day.

The waters directly surrounding Iwo Jima were divided on the fire control chart into areas designated as fire support sectors, and the island itself was overlaid with a grid system of hundred-yard squares. Under this grid system, fire control officers ashore designated squares, which were numbered, as gunfire targets and communicated them to assigned destroyers by voice radio. The destroyers' main battery fire control personnel and systems would then calculate how to lay the 5-inch batteries to deliver the fire to the numbered target. The first rounds were for spotting; they almost never fell where they had been requested. The aim of the battery was then corrected for range, deflection, and, for variable-time-fuse fragmentation rounds, the timing of the bursts, so that rounds detonated about thirty feet over the enemy position. Successive corrections were based on the spotter's reports of the previous rounds.

On this occasion, the marine fire control liaison officer told Stokey and Kanter that the Japanese tunnels, caves, and underground bunkers had proven to be so extensive, interlocked, and well sited and protected that the offensive had been enormously difficult. Gains were being made a few yards at a time, as the Japanese had to be burned out of their bunkers by flamethrowers, and blasted out by demolition charges.

During daylight, when the marines were making an advance, we would be called upon for fire support from our 5-inch guns. While these guns had proven useless against the enemy when he was inside his bunkers, whenever the marines advanced in the open, the enemy behind the front lines had to come out to man artillery pieces and mortars. While these gunners still had protection from fire from ahead, they were now vulnerable from directly above. The 5-inch guns of our destroyers were capable of delivering air bursts, which would shower the area directly beneath with deadly shrapnel. Provided the *Cotten*'s guns could deliver the air bursts on target, we could be of great help to the marines. Of course, this was a big *if*. During darkness we would be required to provide star-shell illumination over the Japanese-held area on a continuous basis, in order to make it difficult for the enemy to make organized attacks on our positions. Before departing, the fire control officer advised Stokey that we should be prepared for fire support duty at any time, day or night.

Because it was essential to optimize the accuracy of our daylight gunfire, Stokey and the captain concluded that whenever possible we should anchor in our designated fire control sector, and as close to shore as navigational conditions permitted. This would restrict the *Cotten*'s movement due wind and tidal currents, and it would fix the location from which our guns were fired. The closer we were to the target, the more likely we would be to place our projectiles over the assigned target area, since, as we knew, the main battery could not be counted on for pinpoint accuracy when the range was in excess of a few thousand yards. While this approach would put the *Cotten* well within range of Japanese artillery, it was unlikely that it would risk revealing its position by firing on us.

Almost immediately, we received radio orders to relieve the *Howerworth* as a fire support ship off the enemy lines on the northwest shore of the island. At 1445 we relieved *Howerworth* and stood by, lying to about fifteen hundred yards off the enemy-held beach, awaiting a radio call from the shore for a gunfire assignment. We stood at modified battle stations for almost three hours, and the crew's patience began to wear thin. Finally our fire control officer ashore called for spotting shots on one of the sectors of the Japanese lines.

The first round detonated several hundred yards short of where it was desired. Thirteen more rounds were fired over the next thirty-five minutes, with continuous adjustments by our own fire control team. At this point the marines were satisfied that we could get onto a target, which evidently had not been a foregone conclusion; we were ordered to cease firing and stand by for further orders. Having received no further orders by dark, we secured from battle stations. Because the *Cotten* had been at battle stations for five hours, apparently without necessity, the crew engaged in profane inquiry as to whether or not anyone in charge had the slightest idea of what we were supposed to be doing. The fact was that we were not yet sure what was required; we were learning the procedures as we went along.

Six hours later, at 0100, during the midwatch on March 6, we received a request that we fire a star shell every six minutes over a central point above the Japanese positions. The first shot went out at 0108, followed by fifty-nine more over the next five hours, approximately the requested one round every six minutes. Occasional shells failed to burst properly, requiring that a second be fired immediately to keep the enemy lines illuminated.

At sunrise we were ordered to a sector north of the island, again off a Japanese-held shoreline. The water in this sector was clear of rocks and shoals, the ten-fathom curve coming within seven hundred yards of the beach at the northern tip. We were lying to by 0647. An hour and a half later, the crew was summoned to general quarters, and after a short delay, a call was received from the marines to fire air bursts approximately thirty feet above an area of the Japanese lines believed to be a source of mortar fire. It required a dozen spotting rounds before our shells were over the desired sector, but then we delivered a steady fire for the ensuing four hours, before we were called off. The ship secured from general quarters, and the crew turned to gathering up the 5-inch brass shell cases that were rattling around on the main deck. During the bombardment our shells had fallen above the north slope of a ridge of the northern volcano, bursting over enemy mortar positions that were set, from the vantage point of the marine artillery, in a reverse slope.

Two hours after we had ceased firing, the *Gatling* relieved the *Cotten*, and we headed for the southeast holding area to *LST 642*, to pick up U.S. mail that it had reported it had on hand for our crew. When the *LST* was hailed, a crew member replied from their bridge that they were sorry, but they had made a mistake and actually had nothing for us. This provoked a new round of expletives from our now irascible crew, loud enough to be clearly heard aboard the *LST*.

We were next ordered to a holding station ten miles south of Mount Suribachi, where we arrived at dusk and spent a quiet night. At dawn on March 7, *Cotten* went alongside the prewar battleship *Idaho* to replenish our 5-inch ammunition supply and to turn in the used brass casings (which were reusable) from the rounds fired in interdiction bombardment and illumination. We were also given fifty rounds of white phosphorus shells; designed for spotting, these rounds had been found to be effective antipersonnel weapons.

Just after noon on March 8, we received orders to return to the fire support area, this time to the sector just off the enemy lines on the east coast. We arrived on station at 1455, and at 1518 the anchor was dropped twelve hundred yards off the center of the southern shore, just where the shoreline bends ninety degrees directly back to the west. At 1635 a request from the marines was received to fire air bursts over designated Japanese mortar positions. Our spotting rounds quickly found the proper target, and the controller called for one round a minute over the enemy position for the next hour and a half, until sunset.

With this assignment concluded, we pulled up anchor, steamed around the south end of the island to a fire support sector adjacent to the southwestern shore, and lay to as dusk turned into darkness. As soon as the light had faded, we received orders to fire one star shell every six minutes over the Japanese lines, which we continued to do until daybreak of March 9.

We remained where we were, on duty for counterbattery fire (that is, alert to fire on enemy artillery that shot at us or the marines), throughout the daylight hours of March 9, with a time-out to replace the ammunition that had been fired. That night we returned to the outer defensive screen. On March 10, we returned for the heaviest counterbattery fire duty we had engaged in to date, delivering 349 rounds of 5-inch shells, one shell every forty-five seconds, over a four-hour period. During this time the marines were able to push through the center of the enemy's line across the island to split the remaining Japanese-held area into two segments, one on the east coast and one on the northwest corner. When our controller gave the cease-fire order at noon, the *Cotten*'s deck was covered with 5-inch brass shell cases.

On the same day, after being relieved of gunfire support duty, the *Cotten* was called by heavy cruiser *Salt Lake City* to come by for seven weeks' worth of mail from stateside. The cruiser allowed us to stay moored alongside for an hour, while our cheering crew received their letters. A rare period of silence followed as every man aboard, from the captain to the newest recruit, avidly read his letters.

This interlude passed, and the *Cotten* returned to the fire control sector on the southeast side of the island. We anchored in thirty fathoms of water some fifteen hundred yards from the nearest Japanese-held position, which was the remaining pocket of resistance on the eastern bulge of the northern volcano. Star-shell illumination of this enemy pocket began after dark, at a prescribed rate of ten rounds per hour.

When anchored close to Japanese positions, the standard nighttime security procedure was to maintain the regular sea watch for engine rooms and the bridge, a readiness watch for the guns, armed sentries posted at both bow and stern, and a roving main deck security patrol covering the rest of the perimeter. With the regular OODs standing on the bridge, we were always ready to leave the area on a few minutes' notice should the enemy decide to take us under fire. Three destroyers had been hit previously by enemy artillery, and while we did not expect to be shot at, there was ample reason to be prepared.

During my morning OOD watch of March 11, the bow sentry called the bridge just before dawn to report that he had sighted a life jacket in the water. When questioned, he said he could not see a swimmer but that the life jacket was moving across, not with, the tidal current, indicating that a swimmer was providing the suspicious motion. I sent the quartermaster of the watch to the bow, along with the roving patrol, to strengthen the bow sentry's surveillance of this unusually mobile life jacket.

The life jacket then proceeded, under the watchful eyes of the stern sentry, the quartermaster, and the roving patrol, down the *Cotten*'s port side about forty feet away until it was parallel to the stern, when it turned and headed directly for the ship. When the quartermaster reported to the bridge that the life jacket was only twenty feet from the stern, I ordered the sentries to open fire at it with their rifles, which they did with accuracy, thanks to the now very short range. The life jacket immediately started to drift away, moving with the current, no longer having a motion of its own. The men at the *Cotten*'s stern were certain they had seen the head of a swimmer under the life jacket, and they believed they had hit it several times with their rifle fire.

What had actually transpired was, of course, never known. The most plausible interpretation was that a young Japanese soldier had swum the fifteen hundred yards to the *Cotten* towing an explosive charge and using a life jacket for buoyancy, determined to cripple our propellers or our rudder. If the rifle fire did not kill or severely wound him, at the least it made him drop his explosive and his hold on the life jacket and return to shore.

The watch returned to its routine as the dawn showed its first light. At 0635 we completed our firing of star shells, ninety rounds having been required for the continuous nighttime illumination of the steadily diminishing enemy-held area. At noon of March 11, *Cotten* retired to the outer defensive perimeter for a twelve-hour respite. At midnight of March 12, we returned to the fire control areas for another thirty-hour period of various daytime counterbattery and nighttime illumination assignments, which ended at dawn on March 13.

During the morning of March 13, *Cotten* was refueled, and its ammunition lockers were restocked. Fully resupplied, we headed for the outer defensive screen and relieved sister ship *Dortch* at noon. The *Dortch* returned in midafternoon, taking the screening station adjacent to the *Cotten*. The *Dortch's* signalman then passed the word to our signalman of the watch that during its absence the *Dortch* had been ordered alongside *C. K. Bronson* and that its captain, Comdr. Richard E. Myers, had conferred with Captain Wilkinson, who now was also the Iwo Jima screen commander. The reason for the meeting was that Captain Wilkinson had been ordered to send two of the destroyers of his command to an area halfway between Iwo Jima and Tokyo, some 420 miles north-northeast of Iwo Jima, to search for and destroy two Japanese patrol craft that were acting as advance radar pickets against the long-range B-29 raids from Saipan. These patrol craft were giving the Japanese home island fighter command exact information on incoming flights of B-29s, which had resulted in an increase in the number of interceptions at high altitude and steadily increasing losses of our aircraft.

Captain Wilkinson had selected the *Dortch* and *Cotten* for this mission, with the captain of the *Dortch* in tactical command. At 1625 the two destroyers left their screening stations to form a scouting line, with *Cotten* three thousand yards on the port beam of *Dortch*, on a base course to the northeast and at a speed of seventeen knots. At evening general quarters I went over the coming assignment with the gun crews of Sky 1, each man of which was as excited as I by the prospect of a long-sought-after surface action, perhaps the last such opportunity we would be afforded.

26

Encounter with Japanese Patrol Vessels

At 0800 on March 14, the *Cotten* closed to within fifteen hundred yards of the *Dortch* to permit both gunnery officers to calibrate their fire control radars. An hour later the *Cotten* began a maneuver to take a position ten miles on the port beam of *Dortch*, arriving at 0959. At 1410 the base course was slightly altered to compensate for the westerly drift, and both destroyers put all four boilers on the line.

At sunset *Cotten* was designated as the guide and was ordered to the east. *Dortch* continued to the north to a station seven and a half miles to the north of *Cotten*, while the latter increased speed to twenty knots on the base course of 090°. The *Dortch* was on station at 1900, with the arrival of darkness, at which time the two-ship scouting line began a nighttime radar search for the enemy ships, the last reported position of which lay dead ahead.

At 2031 *Dortch* gained contact with its surface search radar, the range being seven and seven-tenths miles from *Dortch*. As this placed the contact some fifteen miles from *Cotten*, we increased speed to thirty knots to close with the *Dortch* and went to battle stations. At 2057 *Cotten*'s surface search radar also made contact with the enemy, now identified as two surface ships at a range of seven and three-quarters miles. The *Cotten* steamed toward the

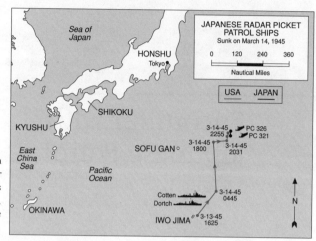

Cotten and Dortch sink Japanese radar picket patrol ships PC 321 and PC 326, March 14, 1945 (See Appendix C.).

southern target at maximum speed. Meanwhile the other target, which had separated from the first and was heading at its best speed to the north, was pursued by *Dortch*. Since our orders were to destroy both enemy ships, the only course of action available was for each destroyer to engage the closest one.

At 2109, at a range of ten thousand yards, Captain Winston ordered the *Cotten*'s main battery to fire the first five-gun salvo. The main battery continued to fire five-gun salvoes approximately every half-minute for the next hour and ten minutes, as the range to our own target gradually decreased to five thousand yards. In all this time no hits on the enemy ship were observed; Stokey in main battery control concluded that the target was steaming in circles, effectively confusing the fire control solution. The men on the 40s and 20s were caustic in their comments to Sky 1 as to the futility of the efforts of the main battery.

On the bridge, Rothschild and Winston were equally frustrated. Finally, after 850 rounds had been fired without effect, they decided to alter the style of attack radically. Stokey was ordered to cease fire. All battle stations were notified that the *Cotten* would close the enemy at high speed without firing and would slow down when the range was reduced to one thousand yards. At that range we would turn to port to unmask the starboard battery, and on command, illuminate the enemy with the starboard 36-inch searchlight and open fire simultaneously with all guns.

When I relayed this plan to the gun captains and director operators of the starboard 40- and 20-mm guns, they let out a cheer, anticipating that they would be able to accomplish what the main battery had so far failed to achieve. When the cheering subsided, I assigned specific responsibilities to the directors of the three starboard 40-mm mounts and to the starboard 20-mm gunners respectively. The targets of the 40-mm guns would be the enemy's 3-inch gun mount and 40-mm gun mounts, from left to right, our forward guns targeting the bow and midships mounts and our stern mount the right-hand ones. The objective of our starboard 40-mm fire would be to destroy the enemy guns as quickly as possible, to prevent them from doing our ship serious damage. The 20-mm gunners were to target the enemy personnel, again from left to right, to prevent their damaging us with small arms fire. Since the range would be one thousand yards, even a small-bore machine gun would be capable of inflicting serious injury or worse on the men topside on our ship.

I received acknowledgments from the director operators and gun captains of the 40-mm mounts and the talkers for the 20-mm gunners. I then told them that they knew they were good shots and that they should not have any trouble destroying their assigned targets, which would make the battle a short one.

Captain Winston was as good as his word, bringing the *Cotten* alongside the enemy at what amounted to point-blank range. As he turned to port to free up the starboard guns, he gave the order to the starboard searchlight to illuminate, and to main battery control and Sky 1, "All guns, commence firing." The beam of the searchlight found the enemy, a gunboat approximately 130 feet long, lighting it up in complete detail. All guns immediately opened up in a continuous fusillade, the tracers in the shells of all calibers screaming toward the enemy vessel.

The enemy guns our 40-mms were firing at were a 3-inch mount on the forecastle and at least three other guns mounted elsewhere, which looked something like our own 40-mms. Initially the Japanese fired back, but so sudden and overpowering was our fire that within less than a minute, all their guns were hit and out of action. The 20-mm machine gunners concentrated their fire on the enemy personnel, and within an equally short period the decks were bare, the Japanese sailors either being swept away by the hail of fire or diving overboard when their weapons had been destroyed. The 5-inch guns fired into the wooden hull of the enemy, finally hitting the target with rapid continuous fire, a 5-inch shell going out approximately every three seconds.

At 2255 the enemy, which had the number "326" on the bow, was a battered shambles. It had filled with water, and its main deck was awash, preparatory to heading for the bottom. The captain then ordered the searchlight turned off and gave the order, "Cease fire."

Captain Winston reported our target's destruction to Captain Myers of the *Dortch* at 2256. Captain Myers, now fourteen miles to the north, requested the *Cotten*'s assistance. The *Dortch*'s fire control radar had been hit by enemy fire and put out of action, with the result that *Dortch* had been unable to destroy its target. Captain Winston set the *Cotten* in motion toward the *Dortch* at thirty knots, bringing us close aboard by 2334. The *Dortch* then withdrew, turning the second enemy over to *Cotten*.

This time the *Cotten* commenced firing at a range of four thousand yards. Stokey fired five-gun salvos as before but set the shells' fuses to explode over the target instead of on impact, in the hope that the enemy's guns would be put out of action before we closed to point-blank range.

At 0011 on March 15, Captain Winston ordered the main battery to cease fire and headed the *Cotten* in to bring it alongside the second enemy ship. At 0027 the order to illuminate with the 36-inch searchlight was given, and with the enemy, *PC 321,* in the full glare of the light, all guns commenced firing. Unlike the *Cotten*'s first target, the 321 had suffered considerable damage, caused either by the *Dortch* at long range or by our recent long-range air bursts, before receiving the short-range all-caliber shelling. By 0035 the enemy ship was awash and rapidly sinking, all personnel having abandoned ship. Captain Winston gave the order to cease firing and extinguish the searchlight. The crew was then secured from battle stations, and the regular Condition III watch was resumed.

During the engagement with the Japanese patrol craft, *Cotten* had fired 1,040 rounds of 5-inch AA (antiaircraft) "common," 187 star shells, 511 rounds of 40-mm, and 630 rounds of 20-mm—the 40-mm and 20-mm rounds having been expended over the course of a few minutes. Winston's decision to take his destroyer within a thousand yards of the enemy's guns in order to accomplish the ships' destruction was obviously the reason the mission was ultimately successful, in sharp contrast to the very ineffectual early stages of the engagement. The two enemy ships were sunk in the waters above the Izu Trench, four hundred miles south-southeast of Tokyo. The ocean depth in this location is 5,673 fathoms, or 34,038 feet deep. The nearest land is 125 miles to the west-southwest, a black pinnacle of rock rising 328 feet above sea level, known to the Japanese as Sofu Gan and to Western sailors of past centuries as Lot's Wife, because of its most unusual appearance.

By 0054 *Cotten* and *Dortch* had re-formed in a scouting line with nine miles between ships, first steering a course to the southwest, then at 0145 to the south. Four hours later, the assigned search area had been fully covered without further contact, which completed our task. *Cotten* closed in to take a position three thousand yards from *Dortch* on its port beam. At sunrise each destroyer "pulled fires" from two of its four boilers. The two ships remained on the southerly course and in this configuration for the balance of the day and until dawn on March 16.

Once we regained radar contact with Iwo Jima, *Cotten* maneuvered astern of the *Dortch,* and the two ships headed for the eastern anchorage to report to Captain Wilkinson and to refuel.

27

Iwo Jima
Secured

On completion of fueling, we were sent to the outer antisubmarine screen. At noon we were dispatched to an outer radar picket station fourteen and a half miles north-northwest of Mount Suribachi, remaining there through the afternoon watch. At this stage of the Iwo Jima campaign, the main airstrip was considered secure enough to move in a group of air force P-51 fighters, the first of this type we had encountered. When the P-51 pilots returned to Iwo Jima from escorting B-29s to Japan, they would come in low over the water at very high speed, heading right for one of the destroyers, then pull up in a nearly vertical climb for several thousand feet before rolling out to circle Iwo Jima for their final approach to the airstrip. Because carrier fighter pilots were subject to rigid procedures in their landing operations, we had never seen a hotshot pilot show off before. This was a new experience for us, and the P-51s and their pilots put on a first-class exhibition.

At 1650 we were ordered to the fire support area a mile off the eastern shore, where the Japanese were stubbornly holding out on the slope of the northern volcano. We fired star shells over these tenacious Japanese from

1930 until midnight, when we were relieved by *Healy*. We remained where we were for the balance of the night, and early the next morning returned to the outer antisubmarine screen.

At midmorning, with Stokey as OOD, a sound contact was made on a possible submarine at a range of eight hundred yards and bearing due west, which was in the direction of the eastern anchorage. The screen commander was notified of the contact while Stokey changed course toward it. Five minutes later the sound contact was lost; the captain presumed that the target had turned inside our own turning circle. Winston took the conn, beginning a series of course changes at ten knots to attempt to regain contact as the ship went to battle stations. At 1059 the sonar operator regained contact at a range of seventeen hundred yards, now on a bearing to the southeast of *Cotten* and still between us and the many ships in the eastern anchorage.

Captain Winston increased speed to fifteen knots, headed for the contact, and three minutes later ordered a full pattern of eleven depth charges dropped at medium depth setting, along with a dye marker over the center of the pattern. The screen commander ordered destroyer *Dionne* to assist, and it headed for the area where the *Cotten* had dropped the dye marker. The *Cotten,* having lost sound contact just prior to dropping the depth charges, now circled at ten knots in an attempt to regain contact.

Sound contact was again regained at a range of 350 yards, too close for the captain to initiate a depth charge attack. He maneuvered to open the range to prepare for a second attack, but sonar contact was again lost, this time for good. We continued to search, along with destroyers *Dionne* and *Elden,* for a little over three hours, when the effort was discontinued by the screen commander. Everyone involved, including the screen commander and the three destroyer captains, had by now concluded that our sound contact had not been a Japanese submarine after all. The inability of the destroyers to regain contact after a coordinated, three-hour search, and the fact that no torpedoes had been fired at the anchored ships that lay only fourteen thousand yards to the west of the initial contact, made this assessment seem a reasonable one, although it did not explain the nature of the contact. The *Cotten* secured from general quarters and returned to the outer screen, where it remained overnight.

That evening, Commander Task Force 51 declared that Iwo Jima was secure. This was technically correct, although hundreds of Japanese remained in bunkers, and all of them the marines would have to kill or take prisoner.

On the morning of March 19, we were ordered fifty miles north of Mount Suribachi, to a radar picket station twenty-four miles west of Kito Iwo Jima. This was the northernmost picket station in the Iwo Jima area, and it was positioned to give early warning of approaching enemy aircraft. However, there had been no sign of enemy aircraft since a nighttime alert on March 9.

We had only been on station for an hour when instructions were received to head to where a B-29 had reportedly crashed into the sea, crippled by a fighter interceptor over Japan. When we arrived at the designated position at 1000, we were unable to find any evidence of wreckage of the B-29 or any sign of the crew. We started a box search, steering ever-expanding legs on the cardinal headings, continuing throughout the day and the night of March 19–20.

During the twenty-three-hour search, Rothschild called the officers to the wardroom to announce that our ship would be returning to the West Coast in about one week for the awaited major overhaul. He instructed us to prepare work orders for our departments to cover all needed repairs; he emphasized that we should be thorough, as this would be the only major navy yard availability the *Cotten* was likely to enjoy until the war was over. He also advised that each of us was eligible for a twenty-day leave, for which we should submit formal requests. We were also responsible for organizing a leave schedule for the men in our divisions. On the basis of this announcement, I drafted a letter to my parents to let them know I would be calling them on the phone in the not-too-distant future and that I would soon be able to pay them a visit.

At 0848 on the morning of March 20, we received orders to discontinue the search for the downed B-29 and return to Iwo Jima. We arrived at the outer screen at sunset and stayed until the next morning, when we returned to the eastern anchorage. Finally, at 0900 on March 28, Captain Wilkinson detached the *Cotten* from the Iwo Jima screen with orders to escort, together with the destroyer *Loeser,* the transport *Auburn* and the supply ships *Britain Victory* and *Legion Victory* to Eniwetok. From Eniwetok the *Cotten* would proceed in company with the *Auburn* to Pearl Harbor, to report to Commander Destroyers, Pacific Fleet, for routing to San Francisco.

The receipt of this order, even though it had been expected, thrilled every man aboard. Each one now focused his private reveries beyond the trip across the Pacific Ocean to building his individual plans for leave. The events of the past month were brushed aside, and even the war with Japan was on hold as far as the crew of the *Cotten* was concerned. Shared thoughts were directed toward the first night ashore, notwithstanding that sixty-three hundred miles of Pacific Ocean lay between Iwo Jima and San Francisco. Friends gathered in twos and threes to discuss plans of action, inevitably focused on the consumption of alcohol and pursuit of women. Strangely, there was little or no discussion devoted to the subject of a well-balanced meal, despite the recent diet of dehydrated and canned provisions. Everyone was looking forward to the first meal of fresh vegetables, fruit, and red meat, but since our basic needs for food were being met, this urge was not as interesting as the others.

The distance from Iwo Jima to Eniwetok is almost fifteen hundred nautical miles, and our motley formation took five days to cover it. The large vessels we were escorting managed to break down on no less than four separate occasions, in itself the subject of disparaging humor on the bridge; we would have to circle around the motionless larger ship, which would be wallowing in the swell while attempting to get its engine room functioning again.

On April 2 we reached Eniwetok, refueled, and departed again with *Auburn* at 1709, thence setting our course for Pearl Harbor, twenty-four hundred miles to the east. This trip took eight days, our scheduled arrival date being the morning of April 10. The *Auburn* broke down on only two occasions during the eight days, a noticeable improvement over the first leg of the voyage.

Starting on April 6, the OOD watches were taken over by Ralph Gearhart, Bob Drake, Tom Wood, Spencer Beresford, Bob McCracken, Carl Holthausen, Bill Stevens, and Mike Czarowitz, allowing those of us who had been standing the regular OOD watches for the preceding seven weeks a respite. During the morning watch on April 10, the *Auburn* and *Cotten* entered Pearl Harbor. There, Lt. (jg) Walter Walborn, our original torpedo officer, returned aboard after having spent three months at the fleet gunnery and torpedo school. Ens. John J. Bock, a recent Annapolis graduate, reported aboard as an understudy for Fred Butler, with the prospect of relieving Butler as the *Cotten's* supply officer when we arrived at San Francisco.

Having spent all of three hours and a few minutes in Pearl Harbor, the *Cotten* received orders to meet the former civilian cruise ship, now fast troop transport, SS *Lurline* outside of Honolulu Harbor and to escort it for the first five hours of its trip to San Francisco. After that, the *Lurline* would speed up, and *Cotten* was to proceed independently to San Francisco at 17.5 knots and report to the U.S. Naval Dry Docks at Hunters Point for overhaul.

We got under way immediately, with not a tear shed at the prospect of leaving Pearl Harbor, and met the *Lurline* at 1645 as it emerged from the Honolulu harbor at a crisp 19.5 knots. Course was set for the northeast at that speed, *Cotten* patrolling three thousand yards ahead.

At 2200 the *Cotten* slowed to 17.5 knots, allowing *Lurline* to press on independently. We started to zigzag according to the standard zigzag plan of Task Force 58, to remind everyone that there was still a war going on, despite the fact that we were headed for "Frisco," now only twenty-four hundred miles to the northeast. This distance is enough that a great circle route saves many miles compared with a straight-line course on a Mercator chart. With

USS Cotten *off Farallon Islands, April 15, 1945.*

the exception of the morning watch—which I resumed standing, inasmuch as I had to be up before dawn in any event to shoot the morning stars—the OOD watch standers were Gearhart, Stevens, Wood, Walborn, and Czarowitz, pampering the other regular OODs so they would be sufficiently rested to go on leave.

Rothschild had told me I would go on leave as soon as we were docked at Hunters Point, so I hurried to get the navigator's work orders prepared, with the prodding and help of Ivo Duvall, the chief quartermaster. I proofread the deck logs, which had been typed up and were now on a current basis. The supply office ordered transportation by radio, in advance of our arrival, for those of us who planned to go home. In my case this involved a Pullman reservation on the train from San Francisco to Chicago, where my parents lived.

On April 12, the United States was notified that President Franklin D. Roosevelt had died and that the vice president, Harry S. Truman, had been sworn in as the new president of the United States. Roosevelt had been revered by most of the *Cotten*'s crew, and there were many misgivings as to how the country would fare under the leadership of the unknown Mr. Truman. Whatever any of us had thought about his leadership or his presidency, Roosevelt's death represented the end of a watershed historical era, one that had covered the great world economic depression of the 1930s as well as World War II.

Although it took five and a half days, this particular voyage passed in a blur. At 1816 on April 15, CIC picked up the Farallon Islands at the incredible distance of 146 miles on the air search radar. At 2100 we changed our course to head for the entrance to San Francisco Bay, now directly to the east. At 0500 on April 16, we passed the Farallon Islands seven thousand yards abeam to port and increased our speed to twenty knots.

Both the captain and exec were on the bridge, as excited as anyone by the prospect of coming home. They had each managed to have their wives notified of the estimated date of our arrival, so they expected to receive warm greetings in a few scant hours. We proceeded without incident for the next hour, except that the *Cotten* was photographed, with the Farallon Islands in the background, by an enterprising waterborne entrepreneur. Midchannel buoy "King" was passed abeam to port at 0603. Suddenly we were encased in a wall of fog, the first experienced by the *Cotten*, and I recommended that the speed be reduced to fifteen knots, as our visibility was less than one thousand yards. Our speed was immediately reduced, but one minute later I was sufficiently apprehensive to recommend that we slow to ten knots. We started to sound fog signals, using our whistle. One minute more and we saw a fishing smack emerge from the still-thickening fog, dead ahead. The captain ordered, "All back emergency full! Right full rudder!" We passed the other vessel abeam to port, with about two hundred feet to spare. The captain ordered the engines stopped and turned to me to inquire, in an irritated manner, whether I wanted him to engage a pilot to take us through the fog bank. To do so would have delayed our arrival until late afternoon, and I had no intention of being the highly visible cause of such a disaster. My response was, "Captain, a pilot is not necessary."

I checked the radar repeater and decided that because the fog was getting steadily thicker and several other ships appeared to be exiting the narrow channel over the bar that had to be crossed on the seaward side of the antisubmarine net tenders, we should lie to until the traffic had passed. I advised the captain of the traffic, showing him the channel through the outer bank that lies in a semicircle seven miles to seaward of Golden Gate Bridge, and he reluctantly agreed that we should continue to lie to. We then contacted the submarine net tenders on TBS to inquire about the traffic, and they replied that there was a large number of ships waiting to cross the bar from San Francisco Bay to the Pacific. They requested that we lie to on the seaward side of the bar until the channel had cleared, which would take several hours—confirming our own conclusion.

We lay to for the next five hours, a steady stream of traffic passing us out to sea; we continued to sound our fog signals as we hovered impatiently. Finally at 1255 the channel, eight hundred yards wide and marked on either side by a string of four channel buoys, was clear of traffic. I told the captain we could proceed and gave him the course. We started in through the channel, the visibility still so restricted that the jackstaff on the bow could hardly be seen. Our speed was ten knots, and an offshore tidal current heading north began to set us to the left of the channel into the westbound traffic lane. I advised the captain to increase speed to fifteen knots and come ten degrees to the right to compensate for the force of the northerly set, the strength of which had come as a surprise to me.

At the next buoy, our northerly set was still marked, and I advised the captain to increase speed to twenty knots, the path ahead remaining clear of shipping on our radar. I advised one more ten-degree course change to the right, and finally I recommended increasing speed to twenty-five knots. These last adjustments fully countered the set of the current, and as we picked up speed, the Cotten threw its splendid bow waves, and its long flank-speed wake trailed far astern. The ship passed clear of the buoys marking the bar, passed buoy "4" abeam to port, and emerged clear of the fog bank at 1330, the long "homeward bound" pennant streaming aft from the masthead and a bone in her teeth. The captain slowed the engines as we passed through the net tenders and under Golden Gate Bridge, but we retained enough of our flank speed to make a memorable entrance into beautiful San Francisco Bay. We gradually slowed to ten knots, the maximum legal speed for those waters, and at 1453 dropped the hook off Treasure Island.

While we were at anchor, two of Cotten's former chief petty officers who had received promotions to warrant officer, Machinist Novie L. Perry and Torpedoman John E. Cunningham, were transferred to the commandant of the Twelfth Naval District, for further assignment to duties ashore. Three other enlisted men, including the director operator of 40-mm mount number 2, Leonard Winkel, Fire Controlman Third Class, were transferred to shore for advanced technical schooling. Winkel was sent to the fire control school in San Diego to learn how to maintain a new-type radar for use with the two quad 40-mm mounts we were to receive during the Hunters Point overhaul. These men hitched a ride ashore to Treasure Island in the boat that had delivered official orders for an overhaul, and they went with the best wishes of all hands. Especially regarded was Torpedoman Cunningham, who possessed a magnificent multicolored tattoo of an American eagle emblazoned on his chest, extending from his shoulders to his groin.

An hour after anchoring, the Cotten was under way to the Mare Island Naval Ammunition Depot, following the channel governing the twenty-five-mile trip north through San Francisco and San Pablo Bays. We arrived outside Mare Island at 1722, when pilot F. J. Summers came aboard, with two tugs at his disposal, to maneuver the Cotten alongside Dock 35. All hands were immediately turned to, removing the ammunition, depth charges, and torpedoes, which was completed by 2000. Although it had been a long day for everyone, the entire crew of the Cotten went to sleep that night in a state of euphoric contentment.

Early the next morning, the *Cotten* got under way from the dock at Mare Island and at 0600 started back toward San Francisco Bay. We steamed past San Francisco toward Hunters Point at the south end of the city limits, where we hove to at 0845 to take aboard pilot E. T. Peterson, who took the conn to moor us to Pier 11, U.S. Naval Dry Docks, Hunters Point, San Francisco, California.

At 1600 six officers, including myself, left on leave. It had been sixty-six days since we had departed from Ulithi and fifty-six days since we had consumed the last of our fresh provisions. It had also been seven days short of twenty-one months since I had moved aboard the *Cotten* the day it was commissioned, July 24, 1943.

28

Shore Leave

An hour after docking at Hunters Point, I had packed a suitcase, picked up my leave papers, and left the ship. Taking a taxi to the railroad station, I collected my tickets and Pullman reservations and headed for the nearest bar for the first drink in many months. I left the saloon for a nearby restaurant, my thirst for alcohol far from quenched, to eat a huge tomato salad and drink two glasses of milk; I had felt a bodily craving for both items that surprised me and demanded satisfaction.

Having advised my mother and father when my train was due to arrive in Chicago, I boarded the train to locate my accommodations, stored my suitcase under the seat, and greeted a fellow naval officer who had the bunk above me. Together we immediately headed for the lounge car. It was fortunate we were among the first arrivals, as it soon became apparent that 95 percent of the passengers were in our circumstances—navy and marine officers from the Pacific going home on leave. This being the case, there were about 150 thirsty men for about half as many seats, ensuring that once seated, no one was likely to leave.

Every one of the military passengers was eager for female companionship, but the odds against success on this train, even though it was going to take almost two full days to get to Chicago, seemed overwhelming. Of the fifteen passengers who were not naval or marine officers on leave, four were women who were too old to be prospects for even this female-starved group, and eight were businessmen, which left only three young women for the 150 young men. The net result of the demographics of this train trip was that the atmosphere was more reminiscent of a crap game and beer party on Mog Mog Island of Ulithi Atoll than the civilian frolic I had looked forward to.

Two of the three young ladies on the train turned out to be newlyweds returning home to their families after seeing their husbands off to the war. Because of their recently acquired marital status, as well as the fifty-to-one ratio of men to women, the odds against success were even worse than they had first appeared. Of course, this did not stop most of us from trying to line up some sort of relationship with one of the three women. While there was plenty of time, considering the length of the trip, getting a free moment alone with the quarry was definitely a matter of luck.

In the few minutes I had for a private discourse with one of them, I learned that having seen her new husband off to the Pacific, she was returning to her parents' home in Chicago to wait for his return, sometime in the distant future. I had wit enough to invite her out to dinner the night following our arrival in Chicago, and I was delighted when she readily accepted—the prospect of staying home alone with her parents was not at all appealing to her. This arrangement made, she was happy to pick me as her particular friend on the train, to the confusion of most of the others, who never found a way to beat the odds.

Arriving in Chicago two days later, I said good-bye to my young lady friend, having arranged a meeting place for the next evening, and took a cab to my parents' residence on Chicago's Near North side. The homecoming was a sentimental one. I was touched to see how happy they were to see me, and also that they had obviously worried a great deal more about my safety than I had. They were an attentive audience, and because the navy had given us permission to talk about events that had happened at least thirty days in the past, I had a backlog of stories to tell, and I enjoyed telling them. While the twenty-one months that had elapsed since we had last been together seemed a lifetime to me, it was but a wink of the eye to them. In their memories I was still a college student, and my twenty-two-year-old physical presence did nothing to dispel the memory. On the other hand, I was so relieved to be home again, however brief the interlude, that I had no inclination to prove how much I had changed. In fact, the only change I was aware of was entirely due to the specialized experience I had enjoyed aboard the *Cotten*, and the mere chance to tell stories of the events themselves seemed to satisfy the urge for individual recognition.

My parents had arranged a busy schedule that included dates with a young lady with whom I had gone to school and evenings with some of their friends I had known while growing up. They had planned a trip for me to the East Coast and had acquired the hard-to-obtain train reservations. I would see my younger brother Keith at Quantico, Virginia, preparing for his marine commission, and his wife in Washington, D.C., then go by train to Boston to see my youngest brother Ralph, a student at Milton Academy. At the end of the trip I would return to Chicago for a few final days with my mother and father. While this schedule meant that travel time would take up over five days of my twenty-day leave, it was well worth it to have the chance to see my brothers. Because I would use up so much time in this trip to the East Coast, my father had obtained a plane reservation from Chicago to San Francisco that would get me back before my leave expired.

On the evening of the second day home, the young lady of the train and I met as planned. We spent the evening trying to enjoy ourselves, without much success. I was uncomfortable, because I had been forced to cancel one of the dates my parents had arranged; the girl's parents were among my parents' closer friends. My date seemed equally constrained by second thoughts, perhaps prompted by disapproval on the part of her parents.

At breakfast the next morning, seeing that I had already caused my mother and father some embarrassment, I resolved to try to make them happy while I was with them and to save my carousing for San Francisco when the leave was over. During the remainder of the week at home, I had two dates with the longtime acquaintance whom I had stood up. We got along well enough, and I managed not to get into any serious trouble as far as personal conduct was concerned.

The war was the principal subject matter of my conversations with everyone, as my small talk on any other topic was woefully lacking. It did not take long to realize that life on the home front had greatly changed in two short years. Food and gasoline were scarce and rationed by the government; ration cards were required for everyone. Meat, butter, and eggs, for which I had an insatiable craving, were particularly scarce. Prices were universally regulated by the government, and that had produced a thriving black market controlled by the laws of supply, demand, and greed. Because the money supply had been exponentially expanded to pay for war production, and because for the first time in fifteen years there was no unemployment, there was much more money in circulation than available goods on which to spend it. Unhappiness at the inability to consume made a fertile ground for an underground and illegal cash economy.

I could not participate in the talk about the inconvenience of wartime living, as even with all the deprivations, it seemed opulent to me. Certainly it was not that I resented the fact that people complained about things that seemed luxurious to me; it just did not make sense.

My few dates, while exciting and pleasant, somehow made me feel a bit ill at ease, though I enjoyed myself fully at the same time. I had no intention of getting married, having no idea how I would support myself after the war was over. I certainly did not want the responsibility of a wife, especially one whom I would leave behind when I returned to the *Cotten*. On the other hand, the young women on the home front managed to project the impression that marriage was highly desirable, both as a matter of principle and particularly as it related to them individually. Since the question of whether my relationship with the young women I dated was that of a friend or a potential mate was itself off limits, it was not surprising that no extended relationship developed at all. From that point of view, my leave was a non-event.

Another aspect of life at home that surprised me concerned the public's impression of the conduct and prosecution of the war, which had apparently developed as a result of propaganda by President Roosevelt's administration. The objective of the propaganda had been to convince the American people that our war aims, which called for the unconditional surrender of Germany and Japan, were based on the idealistic terms of the Atlantic Charter. This charter, put together by Churchill and Roosevelt four months before Pearl Harbor, had been based on the novel principle that the people of every nation had the right to determine its own form of government. The implication was that there had to be some sort of world organization to see this ideal realized once the war was over.

When the United States had become involved in the war and the unconditional surrender of Germany and Japan had become a national objective, one would have thought that the Atlantic Charter might have been superseded by current realities. Despite the facts that one of our allies, the Soviet Union, was controlled by the most centralized of dictatorships, with internal spy and police organizations, and that Great Britain was still a great colonial power, American propaganda had persisted in the claim that the idealistic Atlantic Charter was the cornerstone of our postwar aims.

A constructive discussion of these matters, however, was beyond me. I had no ambition for our country to improve the political lot of billions of foreigners, so to me the Atlantic Charter represented an incomprehensible and futile doctrine. I certainly went along with the objective of defeating our enemies; in the case of Japan, however, I felt that unconditional surrender might be an unbelievably difficult thing to bring about.

There were mixed feelings about Mr. Roosevelt's recent death. On the one hand, he had evidently been very ill for many months, well prior to the 1944 election, so the country's loss, if his absence at the helm of government was a loss, had actually occurred much earlier than his death. On the other hand, Harry Truman was an unknown. Considered a political hack by my father, and thought by the American public to be incapable of filling Mr. Roosevelt's shoes, he was going to have to prove himself from scratch. In either case, how the country was run was not a subject in which I had any knowledge—or, as a result, much interest.

Fortunately for me, everyone was understanding concerning my interests, so conversations stayed by and large on the few subjects that held the center of my own intellectual horizon, if not theirs. For example, because the Iwo Jima campaign was so recent and its details so filled my mind, it was natural that I would voice a strong opinion that the Japanese would never unconditionally surrender their home islands, that on the contrary they would defend them to the last man.

Now that the Okinawa campaign had started, D day there having been on April 1, while the *Cotten* was en route to Hunters Point, we knew why the Japanese had not used any of their remaining air groups against us at Iwo Jima after the one attempt on February 21. They had saved them all, several thousand planes, for Okinawa. While I was on leave, they were scoring great successes with kamikaze attacks on the ships supporting the Okinawa landing forces, including the carriers of Task Force 58 and especially the destroyers on radar picket stations around Okinawa (similar in purpose to those we had patrolled late in the Iwo Jima campaign). By April 10, when I boarded the train in San Francisco, no less than eight destroyers had already been sunk by kamikazes around Okinawa, with no letup in sight.

I expressed my feeling that the *Cotten* was indeed lucky to be out of the Okinawa campaign, but I would conclude that because the Japanese defense was becoming more determined, not less so, the enemy's ultimate willingness to surrender was open to doubt, notwithstanding what seemed to be the current impression of the American public. I was firmly convinced that when the *Cotten* returned to the Pacific after overhaul, the war would still be far from over.

One evening, my date made a statement to the effect that the war was going to be over before I thought, because of a powerful new weapon that was being developed. I ridiculed the idea that any possible new weapon could have any effect on the Japanese, who had proven to be able to stand up to the most incredible bombardment without giving an inch, and who would die to a man in their defensive positions. In fact her optimism, resulting from some foreknowledge of a true super-weapon, was closer to the mark than my own evaluation, based though it was on personal experience. At the time, however, I was irritated, as it seemed to trivialize the efforts currently being expended by our naval and marine forces.

One night my mother and father invited for dinner a well-regarded Chicago radio news commentator, Clifton Utley, and his wife. I declaimed at some length on the subject of General MacArthur, who evidently was considered to be a great military genius by the home front; I gave vent to the considerable antipathy some of us in the navy had for the "pompous poseur." I hope I was able to articulate the reasons why I believed that MacArthur's southern strategy, culminating in the liberation of the Philippine Islands, had been a needless diversion, only prolonging the war and giving the Japanese opportunities to engage us on terms that required huge logistical resources and manpower on our part.

I also explained, in like mode, my opinion that the widely held admiration for Admiral Halsey was misplaced, that the admiral who won battles was Raymond Spruance, not Halsey. Whether anyone paid any attention to my novel opinions is doubtful, but I felt better for having expressed them.

The midleave excursion to the East Coast to see my young brother and his new bride in Washington, and my friends and youngest brother in the greater Boston area, was a whirlwind affair, more than half of it spent aboard trains. When I returned to Chicago for the final three days with my mother and father, we faced up to the fact that a wartime leave was all too short and that many of the things we wanted to say would remain unspoken, at least for this chapter of our lives.

The flight back to San Francisco from Chicago, aboard a United Airlines DC-3, lasted from the afternoon of May 6 until the morning of May 7. At 0800 I returned to the ship, which now rested on blocks in Dry Dock 2, Hunters Point, reporting back for duty to the officer of the deck, Lt. (jg) Bob McCracken.

29

Hunters Point

No crew ever appreciated a wartime navy yard overhaul more than did the officers and men of the *Cotten*. The time at Hunters Point covered the sixty-seven days between April 17 and June 23, 1945, during which every man who had been aboard since commissioning enjoyed a twenty-day home leave, with shorter periods for newer crewmen.

Those of us who had gone on leave first returned on May 7 and could look forward to six more weeks of shore duty, for the first part of which we were housed ashore. The crew members were assigned to barracks and the officers to quarters in the Hunters Point complex: single officers were in the bachelor officers' quarters (known as the "BOQ"), and Captain Winston, Rothschild, Stokey, and Walborn were in apartments that were available for the married officers.

Rothschild brought us up to date. Our watch duties were going to be light, consisting of a twenty-four-hour deck watch once every four days. During that watch we had to be available to the navy yard and would be required to prepare a deck log covering any events of note. He summarized the latest combat news from the Pacific, emphasizing the beating the ships of the Fifth Fleet, especially the destroyers, were taking from kamikazes around Okinawa. Because of this, in fact, the *Cotten* was being fitted out as a radar picket destroyer for the next operation. To this end it was receiving advanced communications equipment, a larger 40-mm battery, and an alternative method of fire control that would permit controlling individual 5-inch guns with 40-mm gun directors. These changes would give us added firepower against the kamikazes, especially in the likely event we were attacked by more than one. Rocky's review was not entirely reassuring, but the combat zone seemed far away, and I, for one, was unable to get too worried about what lay ahead.

Rocky told me about a new radio navigation technique called "Loran" that was being installed on the *Cotten;* I had been enrolled in the four-day Loran school on Treasure Island. The new communication equipment being fitted would give us much better control of combat air patrols assigned to protect us when we were on radar picket duty.

We would each have to keep up the paperwork for our departments, which would take perhaps an hour or two a day, but otherwise there would be little to interfere with whatever forms of self-indulgence we could come up with. Rocky invited us to an officers' party at his quarters for the night of May 15 to meet his wife and Philip Winston's. We would also meet Lt. Cdr. Joseph D. Linehan, who was to become our new commanding officer, and his wife. Other officers reporting aboard would also be at Rocky's party, including a new doctor and three new ensigns.

That evening Gearhart and I had supper at the officers' club, and then we took a taxi to the St. Francis—an old-time, stately, beautifully maintained and popular hotel that was a perfect place to start a night on the town. The paneled bar made drinking respectable, and since drinking was an avocation for single naval officers, it was well to start out, at least, in a dignified environment. On that first evening we learned that there were three thousand bars in San Francisco, and it seemed that it would be a worthwhile achievement to visit them all while we were living at Hunters Point. We made a good start that night before returning to the safety of our rooms at the BOQ.

The next day, a quartermaster and I requisitioned a truck at the navy yard to drive the ship's chronometers to Mare Island to get them cleaned and to have new rate-of-change cards prepared for each of them. The drive took about an hour each way, through downtown San Francisco, across the Golden Gate Bridge to the west shore of the northern part of San Francisco Bay, and on to Mare Island. We had four chronometers, three regularly used for navigation and the fourth a spare, in case one of the regular three changed its rate of gain or loss.

While the care and use of chronometers was an obligation of the navigator, from a practical point of view it was a fallback technology, as we regularly obtained the exact time from a radio signal sent out from Pearl Harbor. However, I considered the chronometers symbolic of naval tradition, and I had used them at least once a week in computing the lines of position from the celestial sights. They had always proved correct to the second, showing that in this instance the traditional way was as accurate as the electronic way.

The drive to and from Mare Island was practically free of traffic, except in the heart of downtown San Francisco, where there were occasional pauses at red lights. This drive brought home the effect of the wartime shortage of gasoline, tires, and new cars; the area had a peaceful and archaic aura, and the beauty of the scenes became etched in memory. Over the following few days, I accustomed myself to the luxury of our situation, a nontaxing work schedule combined with freedom to dissipate on a nightly basis, save only the one day in four when I had the deck watch.

On the night of May 10, Gearhart had a date with a girl from Cedar Rapids who was in her senior year at Mills College and who was the daughter of one of his mother's closest friends. His mother had extracted a promise that he would do this for her sake; to give him credit, he did it without complaint. In fact, he was so pleased with the young lady that he asked her for a second date, which she agreed to for the third night following. However, as a condition, she made Gearhart promise that he would get one of his fellow officers as a blind date for one of her best friends. Her friend had been married to a young naval officer who had served aboard a submarine that had been sunk by the Japanese in the Pacific; after being married less than half a year, she had found herself widowed at the age of twenty-one. According to Gearhart's date, she had been so distraught at her husband's death that she had resolutely refused to have anything to do with men since that time. Only the Mills College graduation ball, coming up on May 26, had reconciled her to the necessity of having an escort, especially since she had been elected president of the graduating class of 1946.

Gearhart and I had another night on the town on May 12, during which, at a moment when he thought I might agree to anything having to do with women, he asked me to go out with him, his new girl, and her friend. I told him absolutely no, that I was not going out on a blind date, and that he would have to get someone else. My refusal reflected a long-standing aversion to blind dates, and I put the matter out of mind.

The next day, I made an appointment to see a navy dentist on the base for a checkup. At two in the afternoon I arrived at his office, a dingy little cubicle that contained typical dental equipment and one dentist's chair. I immediately found myself reclining in the chair, mouth wide open. After checking me over, he said that my teeth were being squeezed by the four emerging wisdom teeth, the lower two not having broken through the gums. The pressure exerted by these large teeth was jamming the others tightly together, which would shortly result in cavities in all the molars where they were touching each other.

This news was distressing, as it sounded as if I were going to spend the rest of my period ashore sitting in his chair. I asked him to outline the minimum treatment needed for the future benefit of my teeth, to which he immediately replied, "Let me extract your four wisdom teeth. I can pull out both the upper and lower ones on one side today, and in about two weeks you can come back and I will remove the other two. That will be all that you really need have done at this time." This sounded almost too good to be true, but I grabbed the bait and told him to go ahead.

He put novocaine on the left side of both upper and lower jaws, waited a minute to let the shots take hold, told me to open my mouth, grabbed his pliers, and attacked an upper wisdom tooth, which had broken through the gum. In about ten seconds he had it out without much effort on his part or pain on mine. I definitely breathed more easily.

After mopping up the upper jaw and gauzing the empty socket, he started in on the lower tooth, which still remained imbedded under the gum. After some shoving to and fro to break the gum and the tissues holding the tooth, he started to pull. After five minutes or so of strained tugging that I felt down to my toes, he paused for a rest and told me that the roots of the tooth had evidently wrapped themselves around the jawbone. Fortunately, he said, the bone involved was a small one and would break without permanent injury to my mouth, but he was going to have to exert considerable pressure to accomplish the extraction. I was numbed enough to make no comment, and as soon as he had regained his strength he resumed the onslaught.

Finally the tooth came out, along with some bone and a lot of blood. The abuse to my body had been enough to leave me speechless while he was mopping up the carnage and bandaging the hole in my jaw with gauze. He then told me that everything was fine and that I would recover in a day or so. He said that chips of the broken bone would work themselves through to the surface of the gum for the next few months but that the wound would eventually heal and I had nothing to worry about. He scheduled me for a return visit on May 26, and I left his office.

I headed for my room, went to bed, and remained there until supper time, when I roused myself enough to go to the officers' club for a solitary supper, not feeling in any way sociable. Two scotches improved the out-look, numbing the pain enough for me to get down a bowl of soup and some spaghetti, after which I returned to my room and bed for a welcome night's rest.

I was fully recovered from the experience by the next morning, feeling good enough to join Gearhart for a hearty breakfast. The only thing re-minding me of the dentist was the necessity of chewing everything on the right side of the mouth. The dentist had asked me to keep the gauze in the wounded side for three days, rendering that side useless for anything more solid than whiskey.

Gearhart had no time to hear about my dental history but got right into his own subject of interest, his date of the previous night. He had told his girl that I would not go out with her best friend, expecting that to end the matter. However, she had taken great exception to his failure to accom-plish a simple request that had obviously been very important to her. In fact, she was in a bit of a temper. I told Gearhart that friendship was more important to me than the strain of going out with a college girl—he could count on me. He then advised me that my future blind date also had mis-givings; she wanted a trial date to see whether or not I would be satisfacto-ry as her escort for the graduation ball. The shoe was now on the other foot, and the trial date was set for the evening of May 16, the fifteenth being set aside for Rocky's party.

Though I was the watch officer that evening, I attended Rocky's party, which was held in his apartment on the base, merely abstaining from drink in deference to my duty status. There were no surprises at the party, with the possible exception of meeting Rocky's wife. She was a tiny Irish lassie, looking about five years younger than she could possibly have been. She and Rocky made quite a pair, disparate in appearance and background but obviously a devoted couple. You could not help wishing them the best of luck. Captain Winston's wife seemed well matched to our sometimes fas-tidious commanding officer, and the presence of the two of them was definitely a restraining influence on the amount of alcohol consumed.

Lieutenant Commander Linehan had reported in at 1300. He and his wife had just arrived from San Diego, where he had been attending the West Coast sound school and where they owned a home. They were a nice-looking young couple, and from his athletic appearance and demean-or, Joe Linehan looked as though the *Cotten* would have another capable commander, however different in personality he might prove to be from his two predecessors. He was obviously more easygoing by nature than Captain Winston, but considering the fact that the *Cotten*'s officers and crew were now fully trained and experienced, his worries, if he had them, probably concerned more his own performance than the possibility that his crew would cause him grief.

The other new officers in attendance were Lt. (jg) Paul R. Patterson, Dr. Howard Spindler's relief; Ens. Glynn Cremer, another assistant communications officer; Ens. David Kilmer, a new sound officer; and Ens. John Bock, Fred Butler's relief as our supply officer, appearing with his newly acquired wife. Fred also came to Rocky's party, despite having been detached from the *Cotten* at noon of the same day, to say farewell to his shipmates of the past twenty-three months.

The story that was told at the party about John Bock and his wife was one of the more unusual tales of wartime romance, of which there were many. John, who had reported aboard in April when we had stopped at Pearl Harbor, had gone on a short leave when we had first arrived in San Francisco to visit his fiancee on the East Coast. Fred Butler had agreed to remain on the *Cotten*'s roster while John was gone, to keep the ship's supply department functioning when we were at the navy yard. Something had happened to John's relationship with his East Coast love, whom he had known and courted while he was at the Naval Academy. Why they broke up was not common knowledge, but John had ended his visit without a new bride—in fact, without even a fiancee.

He had returned to San Francisco on a United DC-3, which, with the many stopovers, gave him twenty-four hours in which to meet, become acquainted with, fall in love with, propose to, and become betrothed to one of the better-looking stewardesses on his flight. Three days after returning to San Francisco the two had been married, so that John was now one of the few married officers on our roster. This tale brought home how easy it was to act in an irrational manner because of the effect our wartime lifestyle had upon romantic attachments. While I wished John and his bride a long and happy wedded life, I determined to avoid the risks involved, by remaining single as long as my economic prospects were as bleak as they were likely to be for the foreseeable future.

I stayed at the party for two hours, then went over to the *Cotten* in dry dock to check with the duty petty officer and write up the afternoon and evening deck logs. I stayed around, chatting with the men, for another hour before returning to my room for the night. My watch was over at noon of the next day, May 16.

That evening, decked out in my best dress-blue uniform, I met Gearhart at the officers' club at five o'clock for a preparatory couple of scotch-and-sodas at the bar. Sufficiently relaxed, we engaged a cab for the rendezvous with the college girls at the St. Francis, arriving there at six. We waited in the lounge for about fifteen minutes before they appeared. Gearhart's girl, an attractive blond, introduced her friend Joan, and the four of us chatted for a few minutes before shoving off for the restaurant where we had made reservations, up the hill a half mile or so away.

There had been no prior discussion between Gearhart and his girl as to what sort of person Joan was. No physical description had been forthcoming, nor references to her intelligence. Under the circumstances, he and I were both considerably shocked by the vision that materialized before our eyes.

Joan was tall and slender, and her short dress displayed spectacular legs and a beautiful figure. Her face was classic and her smile dazzling, set off by rich brunette hair that blended in with the rest of an eye-catching total effect. When we went out of the hotel for the walk up the hill, Gearhart and his girl walked behind us—so that, as he later confessed, he could feast his eyes on Joan's figure before him, especially her legs. Joan and I chatted away, which was easy, as she had a lively wit and was quite articulate and adept at putting one at ease.

We found our restaurant after a short hike and enjoyed a superior supper, reasonably good wine, and certainly first-class feminine companionship. At one point during the evening, Joan asked me in a conversational way whether or not I believed in "free love." Being a product of New England parentage, I told her, I was not well grounded in the concept. While the doctrine sounded interesting enough, I was somehow convinced that my uncomfortable response had probably ruled out a sexual dalliance. Joan was undeniably charming and lovely, and despite the fact that I was immediately attracted to her, this inadvertent revelation of my naiveté did not upset me. I knew full well that we were all living in a romantic era that intensified the natural instinct to find a mate. Under these conditions, getting involved with a beautiful woman would be a risky business and one that was not on my agenda, marriage not being an acceptable option. Even though these misgivings were my guide, I knew I had to see as much of her as I could in the short time that would be allotted to us, a conclusion reached on the basis of our first date.

I asked her for another date, just the two of us. She agreed, and we set May 18 for our second meeting. When midnight approached, Gearhart and I took the two girls back to Mills College in a cab and then returned to Hunters Point. We had a nightcap at the officers' club to chat about the evening before turning in. During the give and take, I was forced to admit that he had done me a spectacular favor in selecting me to go on this particular double date. I also admitted that if I had been allowed to pass the opportunity by, as I had first intended, it would have been a tragedy. On the other hand, if I had been lucky in the way things turned out, good luck should not be denigrated.

At eleven o'clock on May 18, Lt. Cdr. Joseph D. Linehan, USN, formally relieved Cdr. Philip W. Winston, USN, as commanding officer of the USS *Cotten*. The traditional change of command ceremony was held on the ship, still on blocks in Dry Dock 2, and was attended by the officers not on leave. Final farewells were said to Captain Winston, who had certainly acquitted himself admirably during the nine months of his command, practically all of which had been at sea with the Fast Carrier Task Force. For his service while he had been aboard, he had been awarded the Bronze Star.

Captain Linehan and Rocky were already well along in the reorganization of the *Cotten,* which entailed the assignment of duties to the new officers, evaluation of everyone's qualifications, and an update of the ship's watch, quarter, and station bill. The latter had required considerable revision, due to the changes in our armament and communications equipment being made in the overhaul. The regular officers of the deck when under way were to be Howie Snowden, Walter Walborn, Ralph Gearhart, and myself, as both Herb Kanter and Roger Stokey were scheduled to be transferred off the *Cotten* before we returned to Pearl Harbor.

In the reorganization I was assigned the same duties I had had before, plus a new one, that of tactical officer. When we went back to sea, we were going to have a large group of new ensigns aboard, none of whom had ever had prior sea duty; it would be my assignment in this new capacity to teach each of them the fundamentals of destroyer ship handling.

In the early evening of the same day, in a mood of eager anticipation, I pulled myself together in my best, freshly cleaned, blue uniform and engaged a cab for Mills College to pick up Joan. I met her at her dormitory; she introduced me to the housemistress for a brief chat, and we were soon off on our date. She was as enticing as I had pictured her, and I relaxed, vowing to enjoy the evening without a care in the world.

We had a quiet dinner, with a few appropriate glasses of wine to accompany it. In our chatter we each revealed some of the hopes and expectations we held for the future, as well as some of our past histories. After supper we went to a place where there was a small band and passed the rest of the evening in conversation and on the dance floor. It had been a long time since I had the pleasure of dancing, much less with a young lady who was both beautiful and cerebral, and the close physical contact, along with the heightened feeling of companionship, put me in a state of euphoria.

While Joan was a year younger than I, she had been married, and being in the company of a man she was comfortable with was something with which she had happy associations. I had never had a similar relationship, happy or otherwise; I had arrived at the age of twenty-two with limited social experiences with women, having been in a boys' boarding school, a men's college, and a warship long at sea. This being the case, it seemed that a sensible course would be to let her more or less be the guide for our relationship. This approach seemed to be satisfactory to each of us, and over the short term it could not possibly cause any problem.

When it came time to return Joan to Mills College, we buttoned up our act and called it a night. Back at her dorm we had a long good-night chat, which included making a date for May 24, when I would be nearby at the Loran school. Also, Joan now formally invited me to be her escort at the May 26 graduation ball. I then left her and returned to Hunters Point.

Two days later, navy yard personnel floated the *Cotten* from Dry Dock 2 and shifted it to Berth 2. Pilot Opland supervised the operation, using three navy tugs to push the ship over. Shore power and electricity were reconnected once the ship was securely moored; as yet the crew of the *Cotten* had not moved back aboard.

On May 21 I was detached for temporary duty at the Loran school at Treasure Island. I commuted to school each day, returning to the BOQ at Hunters Point each evening. The course ended with the afternoon class on May 24; Joan and I met for our date after I checked out of school. We dined, danced, and conversed the evening away, finding new areas of mutual interest. One of the subjects that had attracted each of us was English literature, which had been my major at college and was hers as well. We discussed authors and works, more to commune than to communicate. By the time this evening was over, I had the feeling that we were becoming very compatible, probably because we each wanted to be. We said good-night fondly, anticipating our next meeting two nights hence at the college ball. Joan was going to return home to Los Angeles the day after the graduation ceremonies, and though we expressed confidence that we would see each other again soon after that, I could not for the life of me generate any real confidence about it.

I checked back aboard the *Cotten* the next morning to find that the yard was scheduled to complete the heavy construction work two days later, which would permit the crew to move back aboard on May 28. There would still be plenty of confusion and shipyard work going on, but the essentials would be functioning, and it was time we all got back to our jobs.

I kept my appointment with the navy dentist at ten in the morning on May 26, the day of the Mills College graduation ball, hoping that the two events would not prove to be at cross purposes. I told the dentist that the left side of my jaw seemed to have healed nicely after the nurse had removed the gauze three days after the first extraction. I was not apprehensive, expecting the teeth on the right side to be easier to pull than the first two had been. The dentist sat me in the chair as before and gave my mouth an inspection. He affirmed that the first two wounds were healing nicely, and he administered the novocaine to the upper and lower jaw on the right side.

He went after the upper tooth first, and it came out easily, the roots as straight as spikes. The right lower tooth was impacted, as had been its companion on the left; after cutting away the gum he started in, pushing, pulling, and tugging with his pliers. Unfortunately for me, this tooth proved to have hooked its roots around the jawbone even more securely than the other one had. It took twenty minutes of heaving to break the bone to free the tooth, after which it could be wrenched loose. While the dentist cleaned and bandaged me up, it sank in that I was going to be in great shape to escort Joan at her ball, the opening scene of which would commence some seven and a half hours from that moment.

The dentist used tweezers to extract five or six splinters of bone from my gum before sterilizing the mess and gauzing up the wound. He looked apprehensive, which, considering the casual attitude toward the brutalization of his patients he had demonstrated earlier, confirmed my feeling that I had gone from perfect health to a dire state of incapacity in a mere twenty minutes. He took my temperature, which was 101.5 degrees, and advised me to go to bed for the day and take it easy. He asked me to come back in four days to have the gauze removed, and to see a doctor in the interim if I felt it advisable. He helped me out of the chair, and I left to return to my room and my bed. This time I skipped lunch and spent the rest of the day in bed.

At five o'clock I got up, showered, shaved, and started to brush my teeth, only to find that my jaw was frozen shut. I continued to prepare for the forthcoming appearance at Mills College, thinking that I could be a great conversationalist at the festivities if only I knew some sign language.

Gearhart stopped by at half past five. When he saw my pale demeanor and frozen jaw, he hustled me to the officers' club bar for some reconstructive, orally administered pain killer. He prescribed Teacher's Highland Cream, straight, administered via a straw, the dosage being four shots over a time frame of about fifteen minutes. Gearhart took the same medication, although he tempered it with ice and a splash of soda to calm his nerves at the prospect of having to get me to the ball on time in such doubtful condition.

The scotch freed up my jaw, so I could talk again, but it had entered my bloodstream without interference from anything resembling food or nonalcoholic liquid in my stomach. This resulted in a quick state of intoxication that lasted for the taxi ride to Mills, our meeting with our dates, and my introduction to the president of the college, between whom and Joan I was to sit for dinner. In fact the party was in full swing when I first achieved full consciousness and found myself dancing with Joan, holding on tightly, only partially for support. Gearhart had told her the cause of my plight, so instead of being mad at my condition, she was actually sympathetic. This restored my health sufficiently to let the rest of the party pass without embarrassment to either her or myself.

The ball appeared to be a success, the young women of the graduating class obviously radiant at the prospect of receiving their degrees the next day and of freeing themselves from the restraints of their struggles with academia. My own contribution was doubtful, although I seemed to improve in vitality as the evening wore on. When the ball ended at midnight, our dates persuaded Gearhart and me to take them out nightclubbing in San Francisco, which we did until closing time, somewhere around four in the morning. Joan and I then hiked alone to the western limits of the city to observe the ocean as night turned into day, holding hands and preparing to say good-bye.

We finally returned to Mills and took a sentimental departure, leaving me sad and a bit weary, to say the least. I then returned to Hunters Point and my bed, where I remained until half past five that evening, when I met Gearhart at the officers' club. After supper there we proceeded to the St. Francis to pick up where we had left off prior to our romantic interlude with the nice young ladies from Mills College.

At 1300 on May 28, the entire crew moved back to the *Cotten*, and I transferred my own belongings back to my cabin, the same quarters I had occupied since the ship had been commissioned.

30

Stateside Duty Comes to an End

The *Cotten* was now back in full military routine. It was a return to normalcy from all the excitement of going on leave and the subsequent novelty of spending one's evenings either in the company of a lovely young lady or with shipmates in the pursuit of the ageless preferences of sailors, whiskey and women of modest status.

I first devoted time to practicing with the newly installed Loran equipment and was soon able to obtain dockside fixes with some ease. I felt that Loran could be helpful as an offshore navigational aid, especially when the sky was overcast and celestial navigation was not possible. However, Loran was definitely in the experimental stage, and two of its characteristics were unsatisfactory as far as I was concerned. First, because daylight range was limited by the direct linear distance from the top of Loran towers to our receiving antenna, fixes of one-mile accuracy were obtainable only in the areas where signals from four such towers could be received at the same time. This meant that until towers were built worldwide, Loran would be limited to areas around major ocean ports. Secondly, at night the Loran signals bounced off the ionosphere, greatly extending their effective range but making the reception fuzzy and difficult to read. This in turn reduced the accuracy of the nighttime fixes significantly. My own practical conclusion was that while Loran was a great idea and could be helpful, at the moment it was still in the gadget phase.

Next on my agenda, and more to the point, was the study of the changes that had been made to the heavy machine gun battery under the direction of Sky 1. The seven old 20-mm single-barreled mounts had been replaced by six new two-barreled mounts, increasing the total number of barrels from seven to twelve. This was a large increase in 20-mm firepower, but a 20-mm shell, even though it would explode on contact, could not stop the momentum of a kamikaze; therefore this increase in firepower was not of great help in solving that problem.

The two midships twin 40-mm mounts had been replaced by two new four-barreled ("quad") 40-mm mounts plus a new Mark 35 radar for the directors. A 40-mm shell exploded on contact with eight times the power of the 20-mm, so this change in our armament could conceivably help us defend against the kamikaze, provided our gunfire was extraordinarily accurate. The changes in the 40-mm battery had added considerable topside weight to our destroyer, and to compensate for this, the forward torpedo mount had been removed, reducing our total torpedo battery from ten tubes to five.

Finally, a new fire control feature had been added that permitted individual 5-inch mounts to be controlled by the closest 40-mm directors. This would allow Sky 1 to take several attacking kamikazes under fire at the same time with a 40-mm mount and a 5-inch mount, both under the same 40-mm director. It was now inescapably apparent that the main battery director and fire control computer of the typical destroyer were ineffective against diving kamikazes. The director was too slow to track a rapidly moving aircraft, and the computer was too slow to develop an accurate solution whenever changes in elevation, deflection, and range were initially rapid.

On the other hand, the 40-mm director was aimed by the operator as easily as a shotgun and could be trained onto a diving plane, bringing both the 40-mm and 5-inch mounts right along to the point of aim in a matter of seconds. With the new hookup, 5-inch influence-fused shells would parallel the stream of 40-mm shells fired at a kamikaze—and one 5-inch shell detonation was sufficient to knock him out of the sky.

Since the start of the Okinawa operation, fourteen destroyers had been sunk by the time the navy yard completed our overhaul, which gave me the feeling that our reinforced antiaircraft defenses would of necessity be our principal hope for survival. Being an optimist, I felt we had a chance to be up to the job, provided we could learn to use the new hookup with the 5-inch guns.

During the next week, both the crew and the yard workmen labored day and night to clean up the mess that had built up while in dry dock, as well as to check all the moving parts of our ship. The airtightness of all hatches and doors was tested, the watertightness of compartments was proven, all the ordnance and fire control equipment was thoroughly serviced and checked, and all radio and electronic gear was reserviced, checked, and calibrated.

Roger Stokey's expected transfer off the ship came through on June 6. He made his farewells to everyone, particularly wishing Walt Walborn success for the future as the *Cotten*'s third gunnery officer.

The gyro compass was started on June 8. Early in the morning of June 9, fires were lighted under number 2 and 4 boilers. Dock power and electricity were disconnected at 0710, at which time the boilers' main steam stops were opened, and the generators assumed the ship's electrical load.

At 0749 the *Cotten* got under way from Hunters Point. At 0800 the pilot departed, and the *Cotten* headed north into San Francisco Bay, with the captain and navigator on the bridge. We arrived first at the degaussing range for a series of runs on different headings to enable technicians, adjusting electrical coils within the ship, to eliminate the ship's magnetic field. This was accomplished in an hour, and we then proceeded up the narrow San Pablo Bay channel toward Mare Island.

It felt good to be back on the bridge and under way after what seemed such a prolonged absence. It was almost like a yachting trip; it was rejuvenating to breathe the fresh air, to see the sunshine reflecting off the ripples on the water. The ship felt alive, the deck subtly sensitive to the vibrations of the machinery and the rotation of the propellers, some one hundred turns per minute at the ten knots we were making through the water. We arrived in the vicinity of the ammunition depot on Mare Island at 1030.

Once moored, the *Cotten*'s crew, in an "all hands" effort, proceeded to bring aboard and stow 2,100 rounds of 5-inch shells and powder cases, 11,936 rounds of 40-mm cartridges, 44,640 rounds of 20-mm cartridges, and seventy-three depth charges. This is not an easy undertaking, and in this instance it required seven and a half hours to accomplish. The yachting aspect of the day's cruise was definitely not in evidence at Mare Island.

We got under way at 1835 for the return trip to Hunters Point—again a pleasant interlude, especially the cruise by San Francisco at the end of the day. We arrived at 2025 and were securely moored by 2036, pulling fires from one of the two boilers that had been in use, ship's power now being furnished by one boiler "steaming auxiliary." Fresh water, flushing water, and telephone services were again furnished from the dock.

We remained for three days while the navy yard and ship's force worked to pull everything together for a full-power run at sea. At dawn of June 12, the *Cotten* went to sea, exiting San Francisco Bay by way of the submarine nets and the channel through the outer bar. Accompanying us were yard supervisors from Hunters Point, who were looking forward to the thrill of riding a destroyer. When south of the Farallon Islands, we commenced the scheduled two-hour-long full-power run at a speed of 31.5 knots, first to the west into the teeth of a stiff westerly breeze, then back east, to end in an area that was clear of shipping. We then fired all guns and dropped a full pattern of depth charges at a slow speed, to test all of our ordnance systems. By this time all the Hunters Point personnel, to a man, were suffering from acute seasickness and had retired to bunks below decks. Including the time in transit from and to Hunters Point, these exercises took the entire day. We returned to the dock at sunset, and our guests departed as soon as the gangway was in place.

Some damage had been sustained during the full-power run and ordnance testing, and it required five days in dry dock to repair, the major job involving the port propeller shaft, which had started to vibrate when the depth charge pattern was dropped. This time the crew remained aboard, concentrating on drills and their ship's work in preparation for the shakedown exercises, which lay less than a week away.

At 0800 on June 20, with all repairs completed, the *Cotten* left the dry dock to return to the area south of the Farallon Islands. There we repeated the full-power trial (this time for four hours) and again exercised all guns, but omitting the dropping of depth charges, at the express request of the navy yard. In addition we conducted one emergency crash-back exercise, going from flank speed ahead to "all engines back emergency full." This time no damages resulted, and the *Cotten* passed the test with flying colors.

We remained at Hunters Point for two days, enjoying the last evenings ashore before final departure from San Francisco. During these last days, two new ensigns reported aboard for duty, Dale S. Gronsdahl, assigned as an assistant first lieutenant, and Daniel Hrtko, assigned as an assistant engineering officer. Like the other new ensigns, neither of them had sea experience.

On June 21 three officers and a technician from the staff of the Pacific Fleet Operational Command reported aboard to supervise the exercises that were scheduled to start once the *Cotten* arrived at San Diego. June 23 arrived, and the *Cotten* departed from Hunters Point at dawn to steam alone to San Diego.

The *Cotten's* run south took from the morning of June 23 to noon of June 24, at which time we tied up alongside the *C. K. Bronson* in San Diego Harbor. That afternoon an inspection team from the Pacific Training Command came aboard to go over the *Cotten*, its crew, and equipment with a fine-toothed comb. It was a two-hour, spit-and-polish, military inspection, a reminder that we were expected to be serious about the retraining. A better inducement for taking our retraining seriously had been the sight of the destroyer *Hazelwood* coming into Hunters Point during our last week of overhaul. *Hazelwood* had been crushed by kamikazes off Okinawa; perhaps it would have been more sensible to scuttle the ship where it had been struck than to bring home such a tangle of battered and rusty metal.

After the inspection, the *Cotten's* officers gathered in the wardroom for a briefing on the drill schedule for the next ten days. The first two days, June 25 and 26, would be spent working with the escort carrier *Greenwich Bay* and the submarine *Tautog* in coordinated antisubmarine exercises. The next two days would be divided equally between antiaircraft firing and long-range main battery exercises. June 29 would be devoted to torpedo firing, with three single torpedo shots scheduled.

From June 30 to July 3, there would be a three-day cruise in company with *C. K. Bronson* and *Gatling*. First on the schedule would be main battery shore bombardment and nighttime illumination of Pyramid Cove on San Clemente Island, lasting through noon of July 1. That night, surface illumination exercises would be conducted with *C. K. Bronson*, utilizing 5-inch star shells. During the morning of July 2, *C. K. Bronson* and the *Cotten* would have an opportunity to fire at powered drone aircraft, a new training device touted as an improvement over towed sleeves. On the afternoon of July 2, *Dortch* and *Cotten* were to conduct high-speed tactical maneuvers. On July 3, destroyers *Ross* and *Cotten* were scheduled for radar spotting exercises, wherein fall of shot was to be observed by radar rather than by sight, simulating night battle conditions, followed by a long-range battle problem with offset main battery salvo fire. After this exercise, we were to return to San Diego for replenishment.

On July 4, coincidentally my twenty-third birthday, the *Cotten* would return to San Clemente Island for shore bombardment and a full-course battle problem, in which instructors on board would impose simulated materiel damage and personnel casualties that called for corrective actions by the crew. On the completion of the battle problem, we were to return to San Diego to replace our ammunition and refuel. If we were given passing grades by the Training Command, we would be cleared to leave San Diego for Pearl Harbor for further shakedown training exercises preparatory to rejoining the Pacific Fleet.

The actual shakedown exercises followed the original format in complete detail. To those who had been aboard the *Cotten* for the past two years, there was nothing new in the training agenda except for firing at the drone aircraft, which was considerably more challenging than firing at towed sleeves.

The drones were small, relatively high-speed, pilotless aircraft, about one-fifth the size of a fighter plane. They were remotely controlled by operators aboard AVR boats, large, high-speed harbor rescue boats fitted out to carry and service these targets. The drones, once launched by the controllers, buzzed by the *Cotten* at varying ranges for firing runs, including a number in which the 5-inch guns were controlled by the 40-mm director operators. When the drones were finally flown to within one thousand yards of the *Cotten,* our combined batteries were able to shoot them down; after three of them had been destroyed at that range, the exercises were concluded.

A fair assessment of the improvement in the firepower of the *Cotten's* 40-mm and 20-mm batteries would be that the likelihood of achieving a lethal hit at a range of a thousand yards had been increased by as much as 40 to 50 percent. The increase in probability of hits by the 40-mm battery was in the lower end of this range. Despite this more effective firepower, it was my feeling that the *Cotten* remained seriously undergunned vis-à-vis a diving kamikaze unless the 5-inch guns were hooked up with the 40-mm directors.

There was little doubt in anyone's mind that ten days of constant practice helped clear away the cobwebs that had built up over the long period ashore. For the new personnel, to whom the *Cotten* was a strange and intimidating environment, the shakedown was a confidence builder, especially as the older hands were helpful toward the struggling newcomers. Walter Walborn was able to practice his trade in the main battery director in the shore bombardment exercises. With Herb Kanter's transfer on June 30 from the *Cotten* to become the executive officer of an attack transport ship, the *Wadleigh*, Spencer Beresford became the communications officer, and Ralph Gearhart became the permanent officer of the deck for general quarters. The four OODs when under way were now Snowden, Robinson, Gearhart, and Walborn. Captain Linehan fitted smoothly into his new command, proving to be likable as well as highly competent.

On the morning of July 5, the Training Command gave its stamp of approval to the *Cotten's* performance, and we were ordered to report to Pearl Harbor for further training. The *Cotten's* officers were now given access to the secret combat assessment of the Okinawa operation, which had officially been declared completed on July 2. The navy's losses during the three-and-a-half-month campaign had been thirty-four ships sunk, including fifteen destroyers, and 368 vessels damaged, of which eighty-eight were destroyers. Naval personnel losses were estimated at forty-nine hundred killed or missing and forty-eight hundred wounded, almost all of these losses being caused by the estimated twenty-five hundred kamikazes expended by the Japanese. The kamikaze force had proven to be brutally effective.

Preparations for the next operation were being completed by Admiral Nimitz's and General MacArthur's staffs, who were now working together toward a common purpose, the landing of a large invasion force on the island of Kyushu, nearest of the Japanese home islands to the new advance base on Okinawa. With its augmented 40-mm and 20-mm batteries and more versatile fire control system, the *Cotten* would presumably be assigned one of the radar picket stations surrounding the landing beaches as an early line of defense against the kamikazes, which were estimated to be numbered in the thousands.

During the *Cotten's* trip to Pearl Harbor, Rothschild, Gearhart, and I happened to be alone together in the wardroom on a quiet afternoon, having a cup of coffee. Rocky took the opportunity to tell us in confidence that our new doctor, Paul Patterson, had come to him to report that he thought Gearhart and I had drunk too much while we were at Hunters Point and that he had concluded we were alcoholics.

Rocky said that he had told the doctor that he should not worry about us, as there was no liquor available aboard the ship; whatever our weaknesses were ashore, they were not a factor when we were on duty at sea. Rocky reminded us that the doctor had been a pediatrician in a children's clinic in civilian life and was obviously more accustomed to infants and their mothers than the lifestyle of sailors or of young, single naval officers. Rocky asked us to treat Dr. Patterson with courtesy, as though he were still a civilian, which of course he was, and to refrain from hazing him, which he had observed we were in the habit of doing.

Gearhart and I had only recently made a bet with the doctor, for a hundred dollars apiece, to the effect that the *Cotten* would see action against the Japanese before they surrendered. We thought the doctor was crazy to take such a bet and were looking forward to the first kamikaze attack so we could pocket our winnings. Rocky's revelation of Patterson's medical opinion of our drinking propensities only made us more eager for the sight of the red-orange meatballs on the wings of our first kamikaze. Since our pay as lieutenants, junior grade, was the grand sum of $183.33 per month, the extra hundred dollars would be a welcome bonus.

Inasmuch as the Japanese had lost the capability to use the seas, due to the all but complete destruction of their navy, their ultimate surrender, with terms, was a foregone conclusion. Their one remaining major military asset was their culturally inspired capacity to defend the homeland to the last man, expending their lives in exchange for every inch of real estate. I, and presumably Gearhart as well, projected the future of the war in terms of the recent past, concluding that the odds against an early end were prohibitive.

The difference between our present expectations and those we had held when the *Cotten* joined the Fifth Fleet in the autumn of 1943 were reflective of more than the difference between experience and inexperience. The Japanese Combined fleet had then been considered a major threat in the Central Pacific, and Japanese island-based air power had provided integral support to it. We had therefore anticipated a future in which large forces would meet in decisive battles, in which an admiral's skill and luck would be important factors. The magnitude of this prospect was beyond comprehension, which seemed to inspire each individual to do his best, despite endemic boredom and the Spartan lifestyle.

Now, in July of 1945, our perspective of the war was completely changed. The Japanese navy was destroyed, and there was no conventional land-based Japanese air power capable of competing either with the air groups of the Fast Carrier Task Force or with the air forces based in the Marianas, and now on Okinawa. The major Japanese cities were being consumed by fire, their defense industry was becoming impotent, and both food and fuel for civilian consumption were in critically short supply due to the destruction of their merchant marine. All that remained was their army, still largely intact on the home islands, and the home-based kamikazes, held back for the day when our troops would land on Kyushu. So no large-scale fleet action was possible for the United States Navy, only individual ship actions involving either shore bombardment duels with Japanese artillery or defense against kamikazes. Now the future seemed predictable, with individual pitted against individual, as opposed to fleet against fleet. Our stage had been shifted from a monumental scale to a very small one, and the hazards seemed to have grown rather than diminished as a result of our past success and the fatalistic tenacity of the enemy.

Our innate conservatism makes us yearn for the devil we are accustomed to. In this case, the old war seemed infinitely preferable to the present one, which had become a meat grinder, devoid of idealistic overtones. This is not to say that duty aboard the *Cotten* had become less challenging, or one's attitude toward his assignment less committed. On the contrary, the danger posed by the prospect of encounters with kamikazes was sufficiently real to motivate almost everyone to master the requirements of his battle station. But the climate of the war was definitely different. It was as though we had enjoyed a prolonged period of tropical weather, with sunny periods interspersed with periods of violent storms, and had now moved into a different environment in which it was always cloudy, overcast, and very depressing.

There is little question that other factors contributing to my somewhat gloomy outlook were our physical departure from the pleasures of San Francisco, the loss of a newfound lady friend so soon after she had crossed my path, and, to give Paul Patterson his due, the complete deprivation of a sailor's best friend, distilled liquid potables.

The *Cotten* made Pearl Harbor at 1308 on July 11. During the afternoon *Gatling* moored to our starboard side, *Healy* moored to port, and *C. K. Bronson* moored alongside *Healy*. On July 12 all four destroyers refueled and received enough ammunition to fill their magazines. Captain Linehan paid a call on our squadron commander, Capt. E. R. Wilkinson, aboard *C. K. Bronson*, and he was given an outline of our continuing training assignments through the end of July while the squadron remained based in Pearl Harbor.

The *Cotten* was ordered to sea on July 13 with *C. K. Bronson* and the fleet carrier *Intrepid* for a five-day cruise devoted to antiaircraft practice, including firing at drones on the final day. The firing exercises of the machine gun batteries against drones were the most useful. *Cotten* and *C. K. Bronson* were stationed in column astern of *Intrepid* to shoot at the drones, which were flown past the three of us until destroyed by the hail of 5-inch, 40-mm, and 20-mm projectiles. More than a dozen expensive targets were destroyed in this particular exercise. Just after noon on July 18, our three-ship formation entered Pearl Harbor channel, the *Cotten* mooring in a destroyer nest.

The next training cruise was of four days' duration, in company with *C. K. Bronson*, lasting from early morning of July 19 through the late afternoon of July 23. The curriculum was devoted to antiaircraft gunnery, interspersed with three separate sessions when the two destroyers practiced high-speed, evasive maneuvers against simulated kamikaze attacks by aircraft whose crews had been especially trained for this purpose. These kamikaze drills were of ninety minutes' duration, one each on three of the four days. Every officer standing bridge watches was given instruction on the recommended tactics for twisting and turning a destroyer during a kamikaze attack. After observing these tactics executed by the experienced watch standers, the other officers were given an opportunity to conn the ship during the subsequent attack runs. Although this practice was far different from the real thing, no one doubted that it would contribute to the *Cotten*'s effectiveness in the coming invasion of Kyushu.

The two destroyers returned to Pearl Harbor on July 23 for replenishment, returning to sea on the morning of July 24 for a full day of torpedo exercises. The *Cotten* fired five torpedoes in five separate runs. On the last run the torpedo ran in circles, sinking instead of popping to the surface for

228

retrieval when it ran out of fuel. Losing a torpedo was something a destroyer captain never wanted to have happen on his watch, but the changed war situation, with its lack of remaining targets for a destroyer's torpedoes, was such that Captain Linehan doubtless did not lose any sleep over this incident. After searching in vain for half an hour for the errant weapon, the *Cotten* returned to Pearl Harbor.

We headed out to sea again on the afternoon of July 25 for two days of shore bombardment against target areas on Kahoolawe Island, in company with *C. K. Bronson, Sumner, O'Brien,* and *Coghlan.* An interesting problem for Walter Walborn entailed firing on targets on the reverse (that is, the far-side) slope of one of the hills, one application of what is called "indirect firing," using reduced charges to allow the rounds to drop more steeply. The other standard exercises included call-fire bombardment (that is, in response to no-notice requests from ashore) of both day and nighttime varieties, and nighttime star-shell illumination. The 40-mm battery also exercised at direct fire in these bombardment exercises.

On the morning of July 30, Rothschild was relieved as the *Cotten's* executive officer by Howie Snowden, and Bill Stevens assumed Snowden's responsibilities as first lieutenant. Snowden's slot as OOD when under way was assigned to Tom Wood, now the senior assistant gunnery officer.

Our shakedown period was formally concluded. We were to get under way immediately and proceed in company with the carrier *Intrepid* and destroyer *Ross* to Eniwetok, in the Marshall Islands, where we were to report for duty to the Third Fleet, commanded by Admiral Halsey. When the Okinawa campaign ended, Admiral Halsey's Third Fleet had taken over the ships of Admiral Spruance and the Fifth Fleet, and the Fast Carrier Task Force had been redesignated Task Force 38. Previous misgivings concerning Halsey's leadership now seemed irrelevant: he no longer occupied a role capable of affecting our destiny, now that the war had entered its final phase. What now mattered to the fleet was its efficient organization and its replenishment on station off the enemy's coastline, both functions of a hardworking staff—not of the leadership, inspired or otherwise, of a charismatic commander. The opponents of the Pacific fleet were no longer fleets of carriers, battleships, cruisers, and destroyers manned by trained crews and maneuvered by skilled professionals. They were now teenaged youths in the cockpits of individual planes.

31

The War Ends

Our route to Eniwetok included a side trip to strike Wake Island, one of the many islands bypassed during the campaign across the Central Pacific. Japanese submarines had delivered food and ammunition to these islands to keep their troops supplied, if in a spartan fashion. The air groups aboard *Intrepid* were for the most part without combat experience, and these strikes would provide them an opportunity to attack an enemy target and experience hostile antiaircraft gunfire for the first time without the additional danger of encountering enemy aircraft.

Just before noon on July 30, the *Intrepid*, with *Cotten* and *Ross* as escorts, cleared Pearl Harbor and set a course to the west. During each of the days that followed, the *Intrepid*'s air groups were sent aloft for tactical exercises, and the antiaircraft crews of the carrier and two destroyers were given time for target practice.

We arrived within sixty miles of Wake Island at dawn on August 6. The *Intrepid*'s first air strike was launched during the next thirty minutes, and the young pilots formed up and were on their way to bomb enemy targets for the first time. By 0822 our ships had approached within sight of Wake

Island, smoke from the bombs dropped by the pilots rising into the sky above the well-entrenched Japanese positions.

At 1330 one of the returning dive-bombers, damaged by enemy antiaircraft fire, landed in the water some eight hundred yards off the *Cotten's* bow. Within minutes we had the uninjured pilot, James Davidson, and his crewman, Clinton Lake, back aboard. The *Cotten* wheeled about and, as soon as the flight operations were completed, went alongside *Intrepid* to return our passengers to the carrier. At 1734 the operations against Wake were ended, and all other planes had returned safely. Our formation then turned to the south-southwest to resume the trip to Eniwetok.

That evening, August 6, 1945, the fleet radio news announced that a "nuclear device" with the explosive power of twenty thousand tons of TNT had been detonated over Hiroshima. The report was brief, merely stating that the destruction of the city had been complete and that the loss of life was presumed to have been heavy. None of us knew what to make of this, as the term "nuclear device" was not in our vocabulary. If the assessment of the destruction it had caused was anywhere near accurate, and if the United States possessed more of these "devices," the war might well come to an earlier conclusion than most of us had believed possible.

We arrived at Eniwetok in the late afternoon of August 7. We remained at anchor through the morning watch of August 11, everyone's attention riveted to the radio reports from Pearl Harbor. On August 8 we learned that the Russians had declared war on Japan and had sent their Far Eastern divisions against the Japanese armies in Manchuria. Most of the men of the *Cotten* hailed this event as a further step toward ending the war, but I felt that it was reminiscent of Mussolini's invasion of France in 1940 after the French army had been crushed by the Germans. At that time, the American press had likened the Italian dictator to a cowardly jackal, which I had felt was a fair comparison. It was my private opinion that the Russians' only motive was a desire to grab as much territory and loot as they could while the getting was good.

The next day, August 9, the Pacific Fleet radio service reported the dropping of a second "nuclear device," now also called an "atomic bomb," on Nagasaki, producing the same crushing devastation as had been visited upon Hiroshima. This seemed to confirm that the United States was capable of producing atomic bombs in some quantity, making the end of the war now both inevitable and imminent.

The following day, August 10, the radio announced that the Japanese government had agreed to the terms of the Potsdam Agreement, which called for an "unconditional surrender," subject to the condition that the

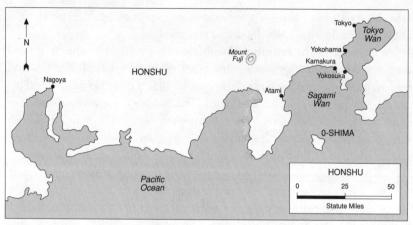

Southern coast of Honshu and Tokyo and Sagami Bays. (See Appendix C.)

emperor not be deposed. Of course, to insist upon even this one condition was hardly agreeing to an "unconditional surrender," so the war continued, and everyone held his breath. The Allies answered the Japanese government to the effect that the condition with respect to the emperor would be acceptable, provided that the emperor, along with the Japanese people at large, were subject to the directives of the supreme commander of the Allied powers. The war continued while the Japanese government debated this response of the Allies.

The rapidly developing dénouement was a stunning surprise to me. Because Gearhart and I had told everyone of our bet with Dr. Paul Patterson, we were the subject of good-natured ribbing from our fellow officers, since we were in the unique position of being the only persons aboard the *Cotten*, if not in the U.S. Navy, who had any reason at all to suffer by the ending of World War II.

On August 11, with the Japanese still debating the Allies' response to their offer to surrender, the *Cotten* and the rest of DesDiv 99—all five ships of which had now arrived at Eniwetok—received orders to get under way with the battleship *New Jersey* for Guam, which was now the home of the headquarters of Commander in Chief, Pacific Fleet. Our formation arrived off Guam by noon of August 13 and entered Apra Harbor. No response to the Allies' last message regarding the emperor's status had been forthcoming during our two-day trip from Eniwetok, which left the war in a continuing state of limbo. That evening a group of us went ashore to the large officers' club at Apra Harbor for a drink. The bar was lined five men deep with navy and marine officers, so it took fifteen minutes of strenuous elbowing to get served. The atmosphere was steamy, noisy, dirty, and fly infested, which encouraged no one to linger.

On the next day, August 14, 1945, the fleet radio announced that the Japanese government had accepted the Allies' requirement that the emperor be subject to the direction of the supreme commander of the Allied powers, as well as all other terms of the Potsdam Agreement. The moment this information was received, every ship in Apra Harbor sounded its siren and whistle in a fifteen-minute celebration of what we believed to be the end of the war, the United States having apparently achieved its war aims without significant compromise. Of course, the mood was universally euphoric.

It was during this atmosphere of happy camaraderie that Lt. (jg) Gearhart and Lt. (jg) Robinson paid a call on Lt. (jg) Paul Patterson, M.D., and paid the latter one hundred dollars each, according to the terms of our wager concerning the end of the war. With the bet lost and out of the way, my thoughts were directed to the now greatly altered future, which might well include participation of the *Cotten* in the coming occupation of Japan by American armed forces. It now seemed obvious that such a prospect was a monumental improvement over what we had been looking forward to some eight days previously, and that it was well worth the loss of a hundred dollars.

32

Transition

At 0800 on August 15 Radio Guam reported that the emperor of Japan had gone on the radio to announce to his people that Japan had agreed to cease hostilities and to accept the terms of surrender as specified by the Potsdam Conference. This news did not differ in substance from the information received on the previous evening, but now that it had come from the emperor in person, it seemed probable that the Japanese armed forces would obey the orders to surrender.

As a precaution, Admirals Nimitz and Halsey ordered all naval units in contact with Japanese forces to remain in a state of combat readiness and to destroy any Japanese military unit that approached. All commands were cautioned to be prepared to defend against isolated units that might be ready to sacrifice themselves in suicide attacks despite the emperor's order to lay down their arms.

At 1600 *C. K. Bronson*, *Cotten*, and *Dortch* got under way from Apra Harbor with units of the 4th Marine Division that were to take control of the Yokosuka naval base, the main operating base of the Japanese navy, located on Tokyo Bay south of Yokohama. Our three destroyers were to escort the six attack transports containing these marines north until we met their final escorts, after which we were to continue on to join Task Force 38, the Fast Carrier Task Force. It was now becoming evident that the initial occupation of Japan had been thoroughly planned in advance. This came as a surprise to me, although it should not have.

By 1950 the transports had formed up in two columns, with our destroyers in a screen ahead of the guide transport. We continued north for two and a half days, until sunset of August 18, when we met the escort vessels that were to accompany the transports the rest of the way to Japan.

On August 19 our three destroyers joined the screen of TG 38.3, which consisted of fleet carriers *Essex, Ticonderoga,* and *Randolph,* light carriers *Monterey* and *Bataan,* battleships *North Carolina* and *South Dakota,* CruDiv 17 plus *Oakland* and *Tucson,* and an overpopulated screen of twenty-one destroyers. Task Group 38.3 was to cruise approximately 250 miles south-southeast of Tokyo Bay while the details of the formal surrender ceremonies were being worked out. On August 21, as we steamed in this holding area, the task group was joined by the British carrier HMS *Indefatigable* and eight British destroyers. On the same day, operation orders were completed and printed covering the organization and disposition of the fleet during the surrender ceremonies. The future assignment of a soon-to-be-reunited Destroyer Squadron 50 was included: the squadron was to be a part of the support force for the marines taking control of Yokosuka Naval Base. This assignment would place the *Cotten* in the advance contingent of ships that were to steam toward the shores of Japan.

During the following five days, August 22 to 27, the huge United States and British armada continued to patrol south and southeast of Tokyo Bay, while the Japanese cleared lanes through their extensive minefields and generally prepared for the surrender of their military forces. During this waiting period all destroyers were refueled on a daily basis to maintain their full combat capability.

During one of the refuelings, with the *Cotten* alongside the oiler *Merrimack,* a pressure surge from the oiler's fuel oil pump caused hot oil to escape from an air vent of one of the *Cotten*'s fuel oil tanks and flood one of the adjacent compartments, where supplies were stored for the ship's store. Among the supplies that came in contact with the oil was a complete, unopened case of Old Gold cigarettes, fifty cartons in all, being held for resale to the crew.

John Bock, the *Cotten*'s new supply officer, decided that he should not sell these cigarettes to our crew but instead to "survey" them formally from his inventory and dump them overboard at night along with the ship's trash and garbage. During a discussion of this subject that evening at dinner, Gearhart and I asked to have the case surveyed to us rather than thrown overboard, to which Bock, with some misgivings, eventually agreed. The outside of the case was cleaned up to our satisfaction, and it was stowed for future use in my stateroom. The two of us believed that because cigarettes were sold by the ship's store on an egalitarian, rationed basis that limited the amount any individual could purchase, it was prudent to have this case in our personal inventory; cigarettes might prove of value once the *Cotten* became a part of the occupation force. We carefully inspected several of the cartons inside the surveyed case to satisfy ourselves that there was no discernible evidence of the oil that had slopped on it.

On August 22, every carrier in Task Force 38 launched full deck loads of aircraft, which then formed up to fly in formation over the ships below. There must have been at least fifteen hundred aircraft in the display, which was evidently for the purpose of providing the home front with some encouraging propaganda, or to awe the Japanese. While these fleet air displays were in progress, *South Dakota,* now with Fleet Admiral Nimitz aboard, Cruiser Division 17, and our Destroyer Division 99 were detached from TG 38.3 and directed to join TG 35.1, one of the support force task groups that had just been established by the operation order governing the initial phase of the coming occupation of Japan.

At 1412 our group of ships joined up with the light carrier *Cowpens,* Cruiser Division 10, and Destroyer Division 100, which, together with us, now constituted Task Group 35.1. Coincidentally, this also reunited the two divisions of DesRon 50, which had been separated since the end of January.

On August 26, with the lanes through the minefields reportedly cleared, the new support force left the holding area to head north toward Sagami Bay, leaving behind the Fast Carrier Task Force, which would continue to cruise off shore as protective cover. The weather now caused a further delay, as heavy seas obliged the support force to reduce speed and reverse course for part of the night. By the morning of August 27, the entire support force had finally closed to within twenty-five miles of Nojima Saki, the peninsula forming the east arm of the entrance to Tokyo Bay, and was steady on a course to enter Sagami Bay.

On the previous day the navy had announced the names of the ships that were to participate in the occupation of the Tokyo area. These ships constituted the several task groups of Task Force 35, including our group, TG 35.1. The selection of the capital ships of Task Force 35 befitted the ending of the Pacific War. The ten battleships of the support force included the *Missouri,* Admiral Halsey's flagship, named for the home state of President Truman; it would also have General MacArthur aboard, and it would be the site of the actual signing of the surrender documents. Others were the *South Dakota,* flagship of Admiral Nimitz, commander of the allied naval forces, and the *Iowa;* HMS *King George V,* flagship of the British Pacific fleet, and HMS *Duke of York;* and finally, five of the battleships crippled in the December 7, 1941, Japanese attack on Pearl Harbor—the *West Virginia, New Mexico, Idaho, Colorado,* and *Tennessee.*

Just astern of the column of old battleships steamed the attack transports carrying the 4th Marine Division, with their support vessels. Our group, TG 35.1, with our destroyer squadron fanned out in the van, brought up the rear of this parade. The assignment of DesRon 50 to the occupation force was occasioned by our recent West Coast overhaul, which made our ships the most up to date technically and their crews the most thoroughly trained in counter-kamikaze tactics. The inclusion of DesRon 50 with this victory group was a signal privilege, whatever had prompted our being selected.

To commemorate the occasion, Admiral Nimitz now ordered all ships of the support force to fly their battle flags from their foremasts in place of the regular ensigns. Battle flags are huge U.S. flags that serve the same purpose as did the eagles of the Roman legions, to inspire the officers and men with heightened patriotism at critical moments. There was no doubt that this event was such a moment.

At 0830 a lone Japanese destroyer met the battleship *Missouri* and transferred interpreters and pilots to the flagship. Once this transfer had been completed, the support force continued on its way into Sagami Bay. At 0930 all ships in the procession went to general quarters, with all boilers on the line. At 1115 the *Cotten* passed Oshima, marking the seaward extremity of the bay, two and one-half miles abeam to our port, as we entered the cleared entry lanes through the Japanese minefields. The day was crisp and bright, and the snowcapped peak of Mount Fuji was clearly visible in the distance to the west.

From 1240 until 1750, the light carrier *Cowpens,* escorted by DesDiv 99, now well inside Sagami Bay, conducted flight operations in order to maintain a combat air patrol of fighters above the main body of the support force and transports, which was now proceeding to an area adjacent to the northwest shore of the bay, designated as our fleet anchorage. During the afternoon the marines started ashore, escorted by the Japanese officials, to proceed overland to Yokosuka Naval Base. At 1430 all ships of the support force secured from general quarters, marking the end of the emotional commencement of the occupation of Japan. When the *Cowpens* completed flight operations, it proceeded to the fleet anchorage for the night. At the same time the destroyers of DesDiv 99 were individually assigned to picket stations, each of which consisted of a ten-mile patrol line along the coast of Sagami Bay and surrounding the new fleet anchorage. The *Cotten* was assigned to picket station 9, where we arrived for duty at 1845.

Picket station 9 ran in a north-south direction for the prescribed ten miles. The southern end of the line was three and a half miles east-north-east of Kawana Point, the southern arm of Ito Harbor. The northern end of the line was two and one-third miles east of Manazuru Point, the northern arm of Atami Harbor. The *Cotten* began to patrol this line, taking an hour to cover the distance in each direction. Because we were in pilot waters and had been at general quarters during the entire day, Gearhart and I had been on the bridge alternating as officer of the deck on a watch on/watch off basis. When I was relieved at 1945, just an hour after starting to patrol our picket station, I went directly to the wardroom for supper, after which I sat down with the *Encyclopaedia Britannica* to see if there was anything to be learned about Atami or the coast of Sagami Bay.

There was an article on the town of Atami itself, in some detail. It was described as a well-patronized resort area for the Japanese aristocracy and Tokyo business leaders, many of whom had built vacation homes there. Rail service from Tokyo had been in operation for about ten years. What particularly caught my attention and interest was the reference to the existence in Atami of several renowned geisha establishments. The next morning at breakfast, I reported my findings to Gearhart, Snowden, and Drake. The three of them became as interested as I, and we agreed to go to Atami for a serious visit as soon as such an exploration was possible.

At 1240 the next day, August 28, one of our lookouts reported a flashing light or mirror, pointed in our direction from south of Atami. Some time earlier we had been advised that some escaped Allied prisoners of war were thought to be in the area. We therefore reported the sighting to the squadron commander, who gave us clearance to leave the patrol line and investigate more closely, with the proviso that we keep outside the one-hundred-fathom curve.

Gearhart again had the OOD watch, and I joined him and Captain Line-han on the bridge as we headed toward the coast where the light had been seen. The hundred-fathom curve came within a mile of the beach at that point; the *Cotten* lay to while the gig was lowered with the boat crew and the fire and rescue detail, under the command of Dale Gronsdahl, one of the recently arrived ensigns, and now the new Second Division officer. The gig proceeded ashore with instructions to see if there was any sign of the escaped POWs. It was absent from sight for over an hour before returning.

Gronsdahl reported that he had gone ashore and had attempted to communicate the purpose of his inquiry to several fishermen without any success, due either to the complete inability of all concerned to speak a common language, or what was just as probable, to there being no POWs in the area. After the gig had been returned aboard the *Cotten*, we reported the negative result of the investigation to the squadron commander and headed back to our picket station.

While we had been lying to off Atami, Gearhart and I had carefully surveyed the areas closest to us with our binoculars to augment as best we could what we had learned from the encyclopedia. The town itself is located within the crater of an ancient volcano, long since brought to the level of the seacoast by geological subsidence and erosion. The eastern rim of the crater lies mostly below sea level in Sagami Bay, out of sight and, with the exception of one point, sufficiently below the surface to be no hazard to navigation. The west rim of the crater surrounds the western boundaries of the town, rising to a height of two thousand feet within two miles of the water's edge. The town itself was oriental in its architecture, with the noticeable exception of a European-type structure some distance from the water and higher in elevation. This last building appeared to be a medium-sized hotel—a logical assumption, given the resort nature of the area. The town presented an attractive appearance, with no visible war damage.

Scanning farther to the west, we could see the snowcapped peak of Mount Fuji looming majestically, rising to its maximum height of 12,170 feet, only twenty-six miles from the center of Atami. Because the base of Mount Fuji was obscured by the nearby western rim of the Atami volcano remnant, it looked to us as though Atami was nestled on the slope of Mount Fuji, although this was not the case. Three miles to the southeast was the island of Hatsu-Shima, about eight hundred yards in diameter, on which we could see numerous fishermen's shacks. This island, in the midst of water considerably more shallow than one hundred fathoms, could well have been part of the submerged crater rim of the volcano, rising sufficiently to appear above the level of the bay.

At 2100 the *Cotten* was relieved by the *Healy* so that we could steam for the fleet anchorage area, some twenty miles to the northeast, to refuel. Upon completion, we returned south to patrol a ten-mile picket line just north of our original one, continuing this new patrol for the ensuing three days without any further interruptions to the routine.

The three days of patrol enabled Gearhart and me to speculate on what we would be able to do for recreation once the occupation of Japan began in earnest. We agreed that our recent partnership in the fifty-carton case of Old Golds had created a financial element to be considered when planning how to take best advantage of a once-in-a-lifetime chance to participate in the occupation of a defeated country. We further agreed that our good luck in being aboard the first American ship assigned to patrol near Atami, to say nothing of having closed within visual distance in search of nonexistent POWs, constituted an omen that Atami was to be of importance to us, if we chose to make it so.

33

The Tokyo Bay Occupation Force

During the three days that the *Cotten* was on patrol, perceptions of both present and future prospects gradually changed, first as they related to life aboard the destroyer, and second as they related to a now-impending return to civilian life. Only three weeks earlier, the *Cotten* and its crew had been rearmed, retrained, and mentally prepared to resume their place in the fight against a bruised and battered, but still deadly and resolute, enemy. Now we were steaming serenely along that enemy's coast, in full view of Mount Fuji, with the enemy, to everyone's apparent satisfaction, having finally given up the struggle. Once one accepted that the war lay in the past, the future suddenly lost its focus, which was confusing, especially to those too young to have known any adult life except service aboard a destroyer. In my own case, the expertise gained over a five-year period of schooling, training, and active duty suddenly lost a great deal of its value, at least from the point of view of a long-term, viable vocation.

At first the wardroom conversations were biased toward eager anticipation of a return to civilian life, with its freedom and pleasures. This phase lasted but briefly, all of the younger officers having absolutely no idea what civilian life entailed, especially with respect to earning a living. The dilemma was resolved for most, certainly for Gearhart and myself, by the conclusion that it would be best to enjoy the immediate future, accepting whatever rewards might come our way, and to push into the background any concern over the individual adjustments that would be necessary later on.

At 1600 on August 31, the leisurely, contemplative routine ended. The *Cotten* was relieved on station and directed to proceed to the Sagami Bay anchorage, where we were to lie to adjacent to the cruiser *Pasadena*, flagship of Rear Adm. Cary P. Jones, commander of the support force, Task Force 35. The *Cotten* arrived at 1704, lay to, and lowered the gig to carry Captain Linehan to the flagship for a captains' conference with the admiral. He returned at 1806 with our copy of the operation order, which we all had an opportunity to review. Until further notice the *Cotten* and DesRon 50 were to be permanent parts of the Tokyo Bay occupation force, with our home port being the Yokosuka naval base. Detailed timetables covering ships' movements over the next four days, as well as charts of anchorages, locations of the minefields and the channels through those minefields, and the current Japanese chart of Yokosuka Harbor were also with the package.

On the next morning, September 1, half the ships in the Sagami Bay fleet anchorage departed to anchor in Tokyo Bay, accompanying the *Missouri*, which now carried General MacArthur as well as Admiral Halsey. At 0930 on September 2, the surrender ceremonies were held aboard the *Missouri*, following which General MacArthur made a brief radio address to the American people, which was carried worldwide. The Japanese representatives having signed the surrender agreement, the war with Japan was formally and officially at an end.

The preeminent position of General MacArthur in the surrender proceedings foreshadowed the announcement shortly thereafter of his appointment as Supreme Commander Allied Powers (SCAP), which placed him in absolute command of the Japanese nation and of the occupation forces. Because of the navy's long-held antipathy toward MacArthur, his elevation to this unprecedented post of power provided us a convenient new object for our hostility, replacing the Japanese themselves.

On the morning of September 3, it was the *Cotten*'s turn to leave Sagami Bay, along with the other destroyers of DesDiv 99, the prewar battleships *Idaho* and *New Mexico*, and heavy cruisers *Chicago*, *Boston*, *Wilkes-Barre*, and *Springfield*. All the picket stations on Sagami Bay were permanently eliminated as we brought up our anchors and got under way at 0730.

We arrived at the entrance of the approach channel to Tokyo Bay at 0927, the eleven ships of our contingent forming up in column—the battleships in the van, followed by the cruisers, then the destroyers. The trip up the cleared channel, which at several points was still hemmed in by uncleared minefields and numerous shoals, took an hour and a half; at its conclusion, we entered Tokyo Bay proper. At noon our group was dispersed, and all of the ships were assigned anchorages, the *Cotten*'s being approximately three miles northeast of Yokosuka Naval Base. While piloting the *Cotten* to the anchorage, we had our first look at Tokyo Bay, which, according to the operation order, would be our home until further notice.

Tokyo Bay extends thirty miles on a north-northeasterly axis from the Yokosuka naval base at the south to Funabashi at the north, with Tokyo and Yokohama extending along the western shore for practically the entire distance. The average width of the bay is about fourteen miles; much of the water along the eastern shore line is quite shallow, with numerous shoals. In overall area and configuration, Tokyo Bay is almost identical to the inner part of Sagami Bay, called Sagami Wan by the Japanese, except that the longer dimension of the latter is on an east-west axis.

However, the two bays resemble each other in size alone. Whereas Sagami Wan is an object of great natural beauty, comparable to Penobscot Bay in Maine, where I had spent my summers as a youth, Tokyo Bay is a shallow, mud-bottomed pond surrounded largely by lowlands. Only to the northeast of Tokyo Bay and many miles in the distance can you see mountains. Except for the channel and anchorage buoys, the only material objects we could see that were in working condition were the assembled ships of the support force of the Third Fleet and representatives of the British Pacific Fleet. The sole Japanese ship to be seen was HIJMS *Nagato*, a prewar battleship, riding at a mooring. It was a rusting, junky-looking affair, apparently still in commission, inasmuch as it continuously emitted a plume of oily smoke from a single smokestack.

Although the western shore of Tokyo Bay was too far from the *Cotten*'s berth to make out details, it seemed that both Yokohama and Tokyo had been burned to the ground. We immediately became apprehensive that it might be some time before we could enjoy the perquisites of victory that we had so recently concluded were our due.

We remained at anchor, in a growing state of boredom, from September 3 until September 7. We then got under way for some eight hours to pick up provisions from the supply ship *Lesuth* and refuel from the oiler *Patuxent*, both of those ships being anchored closer to Tokyo than to our anchorage. Included with the guard mail was a general message from the Third Fleet command to the effect that a naval officers' club was now open and operating in the Yokosuka naval base; the officers of the ships of the support force were entitled to use it and whatever other facilities might from time to time become available. With the same guard mail came specific orders from Halsey's command to the *Cotten* and *Dortch*, requiring that both ships leave Tokyo Bay in the late afternoon of September 9 to report to Task Group 38.1. The net impact of these messages was that we would have the opportunity to go ashore on the next day only, September 8, before going back to sea.

At dinner that evening, Snowden, Drake, Gearhart, and I decided to go ashore to take the opportunity to get acquainted with Yokosuka and to break what was becoming a monotonous stretch of duty. Snowden sat down with the captain and set up a boat schedule to and from Yokosuka, to start at noon on September 8. The four of us were included with the first boat trip, among the twenty-three passengers that the gig could carry in addition to the three-man boat crew.

September 8 turned out to be a nasty day, with rain and a fifteen- to twenty-knot wind. As there is a large enough unprotected expanse of water in Tokyo Bay for the wind to whip up a considerable chop, the three-mile trip to Yokosuka took about forty minutes, and the gig was under spray most of the time. There was room for eight of the passengers to sit under the canopy over the forward section of the boat, so those of us who rated the privilege could make the trip without getting a thorough soaking. The gig's crew, though out in the open, were outfitted in foul weather gear and so were protected from the elements.

We arrived at the Yokosuka small-boat dock a little before one o'clock, and the four of us were directed by the shore patrol to the base headquarters. After a short wait we were ushered into a small cubicle containing a young staff officer, who sat at a desk loaded with papers. Although he looked harassed, he was cheerful enough and asked how he could help us.

Snowden presented our case. He introduced us and said that because the *Cotten* was to be assigned to the occupation forces until further notice, we felt it necessary to familiarize ourselves with the current regulations regarding the freedom of movement of our ship's company in the civilian areas of Japan, as well as to form a general idea of the future prospects for liberty. He made a comment to the effect that we had been swinging around our anchor for the past week without a thing to do for recreation, which would shortly result in serious lowering of the crew's morale. This preamble concluded, Snowden paused to let our host respond.

The staff officer replied that everyone from Admiral Halsey on down was fully aware of the necessity to give our ships' crews plenty of opportunity to unwind. He said that just as soon as the Japanese government could assure General MacArthur that its armed forces had been brought under complete control, and the process of their demilitarization was under way—with full assurance that no zealots would be tempted to satisfy some xenophobic blood-lust—we would be given freedom of movement throughout the home islands, at our own risk. He added that General MacArthur had already determined that the administration of the Japanese empire would continue to be in the hands of the Japanese government, including the civilian police establishment—subject, however, to MacArthur's oversight.

He then advised us that the navy had been given the use of a number of army command cars, which were available to take groups of naval officers like ourselves on inspection tours of Yokohama and Tokyo. If we wanted, he would sign us up for a car. Snowden replied that we were going to sea for a week and could not go ashore again until September 17 at the earliest. That presented no problem; the staff officer reserved a command car in Snowden's name for the full day of September 18, starting at eleven in the morning. Snowden then said that the four of us wanted to take several two- or three-day trips to the town of Atami, as soon as such a trip was possible. He asked the staff officer if he could obtain a schedule of the train service to Atami, as well as information as to hotel service there.

The young officer commented that he had heard a lot of requests, but we were the first and only ones who had expressed an interest in Atami. He said he would have the information for us by the time we returned to Yokosuka. He added that from what he had been able to piece together, we probably would be able to take our trip to Atami by the end of September.

We then moved into a general conversation, asking a number of questions about the nature of our duties and the overall state of the Japanese civilian economy. The staff officer replied that he could not tell us about specific duties, but that we should expect to go to sea on occasion to relieve destroyers screening the carrier task group on patrol off Honshu. We might also be detailed as one of several naval units that were to supervise the destruction of military hardware stored in the harbors that fronted on the Pacific Ocean. Other than duties of this nature, we could expect to spend most of our time either anchored in Tokyo Bay or moored to buoys at Yokosuka Naval Base, our principal function being to serve as a highly visible military presence.

He advised us that the Japanese economy had all but shut down due to the destruction of the merchant marine and the devastation of urban factories. Because of this, no U.S. currency would be permitted in Japan; its circulation could only complete the impoverishment of the general population. Instead, the occupation forces would be paid in military currency only, denominated in yen, which would be made legal tender by the Japanese government; a military proclamation putting this arrangement into effect was expected momentarily. He had no better idea about what the yen/dollar relationship was going to be than we did, but we would all find out within a few days. He did say that he was certain that once this program became effective, it would become illegal for us to bring U.S. currency into Japan.

With respect to the question of the interrelationship between ourselves and the Japanese population, General MacArthur had made that subject one of his earliest priorities. MacArthur had been adamant that the forces under his command would at all times conduct themselves with courtesy and self-restraint, that all Japanese laws were to be respected, and that absolutely no abuses of the civilian population would be tolerated. On the other hand, he had been equally firm in demanding that the safety of the occupation forces be guaranteed by the Japanese government. We agreed that this sounded not only fair but completely sensible.

Expanding on this subject, he told us that the U.S. high command and the Japanese government agreed that the occupation forces should be able to enjoy some perquisites that perhaps fell outside a strict interpretation of certain regulations. While these perquisites would never be codified and would probably be removed at a later date, we should be prepared to enjoy them for the time being. Items that came to his mind were participation in the barter economy and the possibility of developing personal relationships with individual Japanese civilians. For the public record, however, fraternization would be discouraged.

Finally, he advised us that the possibilities for recreation, our immediate concern, were limited to the society of the officers' club and the freedom to walk about the streets of Yokosuka during daylight hours. He agreed that this was a sparse diet, but better days would surely come. We thanked our new friend as we departed for his sensible briefing, and after locating the officers' club for use later in the day, left the naval base for the streets of Yokosuka.

The buildings of Yokosuka had not been damaged by the war, except by the fact that maintenance, including painting, had certainly been neglected for several years. Everything was down at the heels, although there were numerous shops open for business that looked as though they were set up to trade with the occupation forces. Having no money on us except a few dollars to pay for drinks at the officers' club, we went into the shops as onlookers only, surveying the silks, prints, and laquerware that were on attractive display. The prices, in yen, were meaningless, as we as yet had no way of knowing what the conversion rate was.

The four of us tended to disperse from time to time as we followed up on things that were of interest on an individual basis. On one of these occasions, as I was browsing through some simple landscape prints in one of the shops, the attendant asked me, by gesturing, if I had any cigarettes.

I pulled my Camels from my pocket, noted that there were about ten cigarettes left, and handed him the pack. He carefully counted the contents,
then reached into his pocket to pull out a roll of Japanese currency. He
counted out some bills, which he handed me. I counted his money, which
came to 540 yen, said "OK," and we both smiled—thereby closing my first
experience with what was already referred to as the "black market." I had
no idea how much I had received for half a pack of cigarettes, which had
cost me five and a half cents per pack at the ship's store, but there were
enough yen now in my pocket to give the impression that the fifty cartons
that Gearhart and I owned in partnership probably represented, at the very
least, several months' salary apiece. This thought cheered me up considerably. The chap I had sold the cigarettes to managed to convey the message
that if I had more to sell, I should come back to see him, and he would pay
the highest going rate. This reinforced my impression that our stash of oil-
tainted Old Golds might well represent, if not a small fortune, at least a
plentiful source of funds.

I left the shop, wandered through others, and rejoined my companions
to return to the naval base, where we arrived in time to crash the officers'
club bar for the five o'clock opening. We noted that although it was only
one minute past opening time, the place was already doing a land-office
business. We elbowed our way in, obtained two drinks apiece, and found
one of the few remaining tables, where we sat to contemplate the scene.

We had not been ashore since August 13 at the sweltering officers' club
in Apra Harbor, some four weeks previously. The drinks relaxed us as we
chatted about our surroundings and our stroll through Yokosuka. At one
point, when Snowden and Drake were at the bar for refills, I told Gearhart
the details of the transaction I had made with my cigarettes, only to find
that he had had the same experience but had received about 10 percent
more yen than I on a per-cigarette basis. We concluded that our fifty cartons must have a considerable monetary value and that when we returned
to Tokyo Bay from our week at sea, item number one on our agenda should
be to set about converting them to cash. It seemed to us, from our limited
exposure to economic theory, that the quicker the conversion was made,
the higher the price would be. A further consideration was the possibility
that General MacArthur might well come up with the idea of making the
black market an illegal activity, which also urged a strategy of early liquida-
tion of our merchandise.

We ended our business discussion when Snowden and Drake returned
with their drinks, eager to tell us of an experience they had just had at the
bar. As usual, their approach had involved pushing and elbowing their way
through the crowd; when they had finally arrived, they found standing next

to them two towering Soviet naval officers, outfitted in wrinkled white tunics with gilded shoulder boards. Snowden, who was already in a friendly mood, had gone up to the nearest Russian and pounded him on the back as hard as he could, hollering *"Tovarishch!"* Snowden was about six foot one and 190 pounds, confident of his own strength. However, the Russian had been at least six foot four and 240 pounds, according to Snowden, who assured us that his hand had almost broken when it hit the Russian's back. According to Drake the Soviet had turned around, smiled broadly at Snowden, clapped him on the back, and returned the salutation *"Tovarishch!"* in a booming voice. So hard had been the Russian's blow that Snowden had staggered about ten feet through the crowd, barely remaining upright, his just-acquired drink knocked from his hand. Chastened, and in no mood to extend his conversation, he had returned to the bar to replace his drink. On their way back to our table, Drake had asked another officer where the Russians had come from, to be told that some "goddamn idiot in the American State Department invited them."

About an hour and several drinks later, our conversation turned to speculation about Atami and, in connection with Atami, about the true nature of geisha houses and geisha girls. On this cheerful subject the lion's share of the rest of the evening was passed. We returned to the *Cotten* on the last boat trip, at the stroke of midnight, in a much better state of mind than when we had first boarded the gig, twelve hours earlier.

34

Tokyo

At 1700 of September 9, the *Cotten* and *Dortch* got under way in accordance with the orders we had received. Although our command consisted of only the two destroyers, it was considered a tactical unit, and because Captain Linehan was senior, he had been designated as the officer in tactical command, or OTC. We signaled the *Dortch* to take station six hundred yards astern, and then we headed down the channel at fifteen knots. The captain and I remained on the bridge until 1830, when we cleared the swept channel. Before leaving the bridge, the captain left a series of course changes in the Night Order Book and sent the same orders to the *Dortch* by TBS. These courses formed a ten-mile square that would keep us within fifteen miles of the rendezvous with the carrier task group, which was to take place at dawn. We slowed to ten knots and enjoyed a good night's sleep, the familiar movement of our ship gently rocking our bunks.

At 0345 the next morning, I arrived on the bridge to relieve the OOD, as I still regularly stood the 0400–0800 watch. An hour later our surface search radar picked up the task group at a distance of sixteen miles. I notified the captain, who was asleep in his sea cabin, and he passed the word back to "join up as ordered." This would involve the *Dortch* as well as the *Cotten*, and I decided that if the captain did not want to get up at 0455 to fulfill his responsibility as a destroyer division commander, I would do the job for him.

I spent five minutes at the maneuvering board plotting a sequence of three courses that would take us toward the task group, which was moving to the east-northeast at fifteen knots. Under the plan I had selected, we would steam at twenty-five knots for the full hour required—on the first course for fifteen minutes, the second also for fifteen minutes, and the final leg for thirty minutes. We would travel a total distance of twenty-five miles and arrive on the dot of 0600, the time specified in our orders. The final half-hour leg would take our two-ship destroyer division toward the carrier task group in a simulated torpedo attack on its port bow, my private hypothetical launching point for our ten simulated torpedoes being at a range of ten thousand yards, exactly broad on the port bow of the carrier at the center of the task group. I also decided to make the *Dortch* change station each time we changed course, to give its OOD something to do.

At 0500 I called the *Dortch* on TBS and gave a signal changing the formation course and speed and reducing distance between ships to three hundred yards. After the *Dortch* acknowledged, I executed the signal and went to the new course, the *Dortch* rapidly taking its new station. Fifteen minutes later I again called the *Dortch* on TBS with a signal to change the formation course and to take a station at a distance of one thousand yards. *Dortch* acknowledged, I executed the signal, and we came to our new course at flank speed, the *Dortch* increasing its distance to the prescribed one thousand yards. At 0530 I sent the final maneuvering signal, and at 0548 we passed our torpedo launch point, of significance only to myself.

By 0600, as we were rapidly closing the task group, I called the task group commander to report our two-ship unit for duty; he called back to acknowledge, ordering *Cotten* to go alongside carrier *Bon Homme Richard* to fuel and *Dortch* to go alongside *Yorktown* for the same purpose. I acknowledged the order and raised a signal-flag hoist that *Dortch* was to proceed as directed. When this hoist was two blocked by *Dortch,* we hauled the signal down, thereby executing it, and Captain Linehan's duty as the OTC of a two-destroyer tactical unit was formally complete.

As we headed toward the *Bon Homme Richard,* the fueling details were called away and rapidly manned. The captain appeared on the bridge, and we said good morning. When the *Cotten* approached *Bon Homme Richard* from astern, on its starboard quarter, I expected the captain to relieve me at the conn, as was the custom. Instead, he never said a word, and as we came into position I slowed our speed to match that of the carrier. The fuel lines were brought aboard, and fueling commenced. I kept the *Cotten* as close to the carrier as I could without scraping its sides, and our tanks were topped off in twenty-five minutes, from the beginning of the operation to its end.

After all lines were returned, I maneuvered the *Cotten* to our assigned screening station and, when in position, turned over the conn to the junior officer of the watch. At 0745 I was relieved as OOD by Walt Walborn. Before leaving the bridge, I went over to Captain Linehan to report that I had been relieved and also to thank him for allowing me the privilege of conning the *Cotten* during the fueling from the carrier. He smiled and said it had been his pleasure.

During the following six days, the *Cotten's* duties with the carrier task group were reminiscent of those we had carried out for so many months in the Central Pacific. We passed mail, we fueled, we changed screening stations, we took plane guard station, and we fired our antiaircraft batteries at towed sleeves. The only disconcerting aspect of this exercise was nighttime steaming with the running lights of all ships burning brightly. Coming on watch, it was very unnerving to be greeted by the whole formation obscenely sparkling with red and green running lights and white masthead and stern lights.

Mike Czarowitz and Bob Drake started standing OOD watches during this short cruise, to give them a chance to add qualification as an officer of the deck to their fitness reports. Neither had stood bridge watches during the war, except during our return to San Francisco from Eniwetok, but they were now senior full lieutenants, and Captain Linehan believed they deserved to have this opportunity. Mike's regular assignment was still as our radar officer, and Bob Drake was, of course, the chief engineer.

There was a practical reason as well for these two to become qualified as OODs. They were both bachelors, as were Snowden, Gearhart, and myself, and bachelorhood meant remaining on active duty for some time to come. The navy had just released preliminary guidelines covering the planned demobilization of more than half of its wartime personnel over the coming months. The most important characteristic for the individual under these guidelines was his marital status, with the married officers and men receiving earliest priority for release from active duty. Walter Walborn and Tom Wood, the other two regular OODs beside Gearhart and myself, were married and therefore would probably soon be leaving the *Cotten*. Because so many of our other officers were now young ensigns, with very little experience, it made good sense for the captain to get Drake and Czarowitz qualified.

On the morning of September 16, the five carriers of the task group and destroyers *Hale, Heermann, Chevalier, Rodgers, Dortch,* and *Cotten* were ordered to enter Tokyo Bay and proceed to the anchorage. The cruisers and DesRon 60 had been ordered to remain at sea. At 0725 we entered the channel, carriers in the van, followed by the destroyers.

The afternoon of the next day, thirty-seven men, for the most part petty officers, were transferred off the ship for return to the United States and release from active duty. Included with this group was Ivo Duvall, the chief quartermaster, who had been with the ship since it was commissioned. In exchange for our thirty-seven experienced petty officers, we received thirteen replacements, also rated men.

On the next day, September 18, Snowden reinstated the boat schedule to and from Yokosuka; the gig departed at ten in the morning with Snowden, Drake, Gearhart, and myself aboard, along with others granted liberty. The weather had cleared up, so we had a pleasant ride ashore; the trip took the good part of an hour, as we were anchored a bit farther away from Yokosuka than previously. There had been a storm during the midwatch early that morning, and destroyers had dragged their anchors all around us. We had dropped our second anchor; it and a much longer scope (length) of chain had held us in place, despite the mud bottom, which was very poor holding ground. The *Dortch* had held as well, but the *Gatling* and *Ross* had both dragged right by us. The storm had cleared up by sunrise, bringing the clear weather behind it.

The gig arrived at the Yokosuka boat dock at about eleven. The four of us walked over to the base commander's offices, where we called upon the same staff officer who had received us the last time we had been ashore. He was glad to see us again and said that our command car was ready and waiting, but that considering the hour, perhaps we would prefer to have an early lunch at the officers' club before setting off on the tour of Tokyo. He said that we had a good, sensible driver, a marine corporal, and he handed us a printed sheet that described the highlights of the city, marked on an outline map of what had been the metropolis of Tokyo. The suggestions sounded good, so when we located our car we asked the driver to take an early lunch as well, arranging to meet him at the car pool at a quarter past twelve.

Our staff officer friend had also furnished us with train schedules and maps of Tokyo, Yokosuka, Kamakura, and the coastal areas of Sagami Wan, as far south as Atami. While we had been with the task group, the regulations concerning military currency had been issued; they mandated that all personnel would receive their pay in military scrip, at the rate of 360 yen to the dollar. He had obtained information on the location, facilities, and services of a premier, European-style hotel in Atami, reporting that it had been highly recommended by Japanese government officials. After exchanging pleasantries and proffering thanks for his efforts in our behalf, we took our leave and headed for the officers' club.

We sat down for a quick lunch. The food was several notches higher than that of the *Cotten,* if not exactly gourmet quality. Table service was by young Japanese, former sailors now employed by the U.S. Navy as waiters and busboys; they were probably appreciative of the steady employment and income, if not of the necessity of working for their recent enemies. The service we received from them was considerably better than the food. After lunch we headed for the car pool and met our driver, Corporal Schmidt, USMCR, right on schedule. He suggested we drive right into Tokyo to start, heading toward the Imperial Palace, some thirty miles away. We climbed aboard the command car and started off, leaving the safety of Yokosuka behind.

Our route was mostly through areas that had been destroyed in the great fire raids. The sight brought home as nothing else could the devastating destruction that had been measured out to the city of Tokyo. A firestorm brings everything in a city to a common denominator—piles of bricks, concrete, and piping. There was nothing to break the visual monotony except the groups of men and women working away in their attempts to start rebuilding, which required first the removal of the residue of war.

The people on the streets were a sharp contrast to the depressing physical environment. At this time the population of Japan was supposed to be about ninety million, less than half that of the United States. The area of the Japanese home islands was 145,883 square miles, according to our encyclopedia, of which 38,628 square miles were habitable. The overall density was therefore 2,330 people per habitable square mile, one of the world's higher densities, and this included the farmland, where the concentration was but a fraction of that of the urban areas.

Therefore the million or so Japanese who lived in Tokyo and Yokohama and had lost their homes in the fires had nowhere to go on a permanent basis, and as soon as the war and the bombings were over they began to rebuild. What impressed us most was the number of children in evidence. No matter where you looked, there were children, either helping their families with the cleanup or playing in the streets or climbing on top of the piles of rubble. No matter how many Japanese had been killed, their replacements were, from all appearances, ready to work with their families rebuilding their country. While it was apparent that the Japanese had been reduced to abject poverty, the people we saw working with their hands clearing up the debris looked as though their spirits were intact. They certainly did not seem to expect help from anyone.

The drive north toward the Imperial Palace grounds was slow, taking over an hour. The Imperial Palace, a compound surrounded by a moat, was off limits to both the Japanese people and the occupation forces, with the exception of General MacArthur. The emperor's quarters were apparently undamaged, the surrounding moat having been a sufficient firebreak to protect the entire compound.

Outside the Imperial Palace was a building standing above the rubble, and there we were driven for our first stop. Corporal Schmidt told us that this structure was the Imperial Hotel, or at least the skeleton of the Imperial Hotel, which had been designed by the American architect Frank Lloyd Wright. We got out of the command car and walked to the building, which looked to be about nine stories tall. All that remained were the exterior framing (lacking much of the outside wall), the supporting columns, the reinforced concrete floors (denuded of their wood coverings by the fire), and the reinforced concrete stairways. We climbed up one of the stairways to about the level of the sixth floor. There we walked out to the perimeter and walked around the circumference, pausing to look at the rubble that had once been the shopping and business sections of Tokyo.

We returned to the command car to resume our tour of Tokyo, and later the Yokohama port area, under the guidance of Corporal Schmidt. Everywhere the Japanese were hard at work cleaning up—using their hands, backs, and wheelbarrows to load trucks with debris. The truck engines were powered by wood: the wood, heated by charcoal in a boiler, gave off volatile gases that in turn were burned in an internal combustion engine, operating on the diesel principle. Refined petroleum fuels were not available to the Japanese.

This was to be our one and only trip to Tokyo, but it was sufficient to convince us that while the Japanese nation had lost a war, the Japanese people had lost nothing but their factories, their cities, and the shirts off their backs. Their leaders had led them down a blind alley, and the people had followed them without faltering, despite the murderous beating they had absorbed. Whatever we had thought of them during the war, they were an impressive people. Somehow it did not surprise us that they were now exhibiting no bitterness but on the contrary were right back at work, with considerable skill and energy. My personal reaction, which I expounded upon in letters to my parents over the following weeks, was that the Japanese somehow did not consider their defeat as final or in any way humiliating, but as one engagement in a long-term contest. While I may have been wrong in how I anticipated they would resume the contest, I had it right in principle.

35

The *Cotten* Acquires a Kamikaze Speedboat

Following the drive to Tokyo, Gearhart and I began to look forward to expanding our activities ashore. As a necessary first priority, we decided to try our hands at selling Old Golds in the shops of Yokosuka. Because we had no wish to look ridiculous walking the streets carrying a sack stuffed with packages of cigarettes, we devoted a morning to sewing compartments in the lining of our long, hooded, cotton-lined, olive-drab foul-weather coats, designed for standing bridge watches in cold weather. In an hour's time we each had fabricated slots in the lining that would comfortably accommodate three cartons without altering our appearance, except for a modest widening of girth. These alterations were completed in time to board the gig for Yokosuka after lunch on September 20.

After arriving at Yokosuka, we headed for the shopping area, separating to conduct individual attempts to bargain away the Old Golds. For my part, the fact that these cigarettes had once been in a room flooded with hot fuel oil did not seem relevant, and I certainly was not going to be called upon to warrant that their recent history was unblemished. To say that I was completely at ease in this endeavor would not, however, be wholly accurate.

I returned to the shop where the attendant had solicited my ten ciga-rettes and walked in. I thought I recognized the chap, but at this stage all Japanese looked the same to me, so I approached him with some caution. He may have been suffering from a lack of certainty for a similar reason—that all Americans still looked the same to him—as he greeted me with some hesitance as well. Of course, it could have been the jacket, which distinctly altered my appearance.

I decided to be blunt, so I opened the exchange with sign language indicating that I wondered if he was still interested in buying "American cigarettos." He beamed with recognition, said "Hai, hai," and led me to the rear of the store. Out of the prying eyes of the public, I extracted the thirty packs from the lining of my coat and laid them out on his desk, an impressive pile of "pristine" American trade goods. His eyes fairly bulged at the sight as he bowed and smiled. Out came an abacus, and after a couple of deft flips of the counters, he went to a cash box, unlocked it, and counted out what appeared to me a king's ransom in well-circulated Japanese currency.

He handed the wad to me with a bow, and I in turn counted the bills, which came to a total of 32,400 yen—the equivalent of ninety American dollars at the rate of exchange by which our navy pay was computed. With-out the abacus, I mentally reduced this to thirty dollars a carton. For my 50 percent share of the fifty cartons in our case, I could anticipate a total of $750, which represented approximately two-thirds of a full year's tuition, room, and board at Harvard University during my last year at college, and over four months' pay at my current salary. I was far from disappointed and so advised my counterpart in the deal, again primarily in sign language. He appeared as satisfied as I at the conclusion of the transaction, which led me to believe that he had bought the Old Golds for resale, doubtless at a substantial markup, and never intended to smoke them himself. I lingered in his shop long enough to buy three inexpensive watercolor sketches and to exchange pleasantries in what I hoped was an acceptably courteous manner. In due course I departed, indicating an intention to return at a later date.

Gearhart and I met at the Yokosuka officers' club bar sometime later to review our transactions over a few scotch and sodas. Again he had outbar-gained me, but this time by only a little, and because he had made more costly purchases, my net profits exceeded his; I had some thirty thousand yen in my pocket. We did not stay long, returning to the *Cotten* for supper.

When we arrived on the ship, it was to learn that the *Cotten* had been assigned duties at sea with a demilitarization unit, the job beginning the next day. We also learned that Admiral Spruance had once again traded off with Admiral Halsey, with the result that all Third Fleet units were reassigned to the Fifth Fleet. The support force was redesignated Task Force 53, from the former designation as Task Force 35.

There was a considerable amount of griping about the *Cotten*'s being sent to sea again, because further exploration into the commercial and sociological characteristics of Honshu had to be put on hold for the next four days. Another cause for complaint concerned the location and quality of our anchorage, some four miles from the dock at Yokosuka. In the first place, the holding ground was as bad as we had ever experienced, which, coupled with the open configuration of Tokyo Bay, promised a danger of dragging anchor every time the wind kicked up. The latter could be a regular occurrence during the hurricane season, which it happened to be at present. Secondly, because we were dependent upon our two, slow-moving, twenty-six-foot whaleboats for transportation to and from the dock at Yokosuka, there were limitations on the size of the liberty parties. Since every member of the crew now wanted to go ashore every other day, this transportation bottleneck was akin to rubbing salt into open wounds. Sailors enjoy complaining as a pastime in any case, but the present circumstances were adding fuel to the fire.

At 1351 on September 21, the *Cotten* joined Demilitarization Unit Able (or, as the navy would say today, Alfa), the other ships being the heavy cruiser *Boston*, the attack transports *Begor* and *Molala,* and the destroyer *Healy.* This five-ship group then proceeded down the channel, clearing the passage through the minefields and reaching open water by 1500. Early the next morning, the *Boston* and two attack transports anchored outside Onahama Ko, leaving *Cotten* and *Healy* to patrol while the marines from *Boston* proceeded to the beach in landing craft. At 0748 the two destroyers were given permission to anchor; the *Cotten* picked a spot some half mile off a sandy beach, in six fathoms of water.

Both our boats were sent ashore with volunteer working parties, which included Snowden and myself as the two officers, to assist the marines, who were now working in a storage warehouse on the harbor shore. The warehouse contained ten midget submarines, fifty live torpedoes, and twenty-eight small speedboats that had been rigged as suicide craft, with large explosive warheads in their bows. After the marines had removed the warheads, the *Cotten*'s working parties dragged eight of the suicide boats to the water, and our two whaleboats towed them in lines out of the harbor, four astern of each whaleboat.

When we had exited the harbor and were in deep enough water, we sank seven of the boats, but at the persuasive urging of Chief Boatswain's Mate McCullough, Snowden decided on the spot to save the eighth, the best looking, for our own use as a high-speed liberty boat. When we returned to the *Cotten* with the prize in tow, we were greeted with cheers from the entire crew, from Captain Linehan on down. There was no shortage of volunteers to get the prize aboard the ship and secured on the main deck at the end of the after deckhouse. The carpenter's mate carefully checked the hull, which was unfinished plywood, and made a number of structural repairs to the bow where the explosive had been removed. After he announced that the boat was safe to operate at high speed, two motor machinist mates cleaned and serviced the two Chevrolet-type six-cylinder engines that furnished power to the two screws. When their work was finished, the boat was painted our camouflage gray, which blended it right in with our deckhouse, where it was carefully secured for sea.

Other working parties had towed the midget subs and remaining suicide boats out and had destroyed them, and the warheads and other explosives had been detonated. By 1700 the assignment with respect to Onahama was completed, and an hour later the five ships got under way. Course was set to the west for two hours, then south at ten knots overnight, toward the small harbor of Chosi. Early the next morning, September 23, the *Boston* anchored outside the Chosi harbor on the river Tone and sent a contingent of marines ashore to survey the Japanese armaments, as had been done at Onahama. While this reconnaissance was in process, *Cotten* and *Healy* patrolled to seaward of the two anchored transports until 1030, when we too were given permission to anchor off the coast in open water, fifteen hundred yards from the Inubo Saki light.

Marines from *Begor* and *Molala* now joined those already ashore to begin the destruction of a reported 128 suicide craft, of several configurations. Although this job was more extensive than at Onohama, we and the *Healy* were not invited to assist, perhaps because the captain of the *Boston* was aware that we had confiscated rather than destroyed the craft now neatly secured to our deck. It required two days for the marines to get the job done without our help, and our group did not leave Chosi until 1730 the following day, September 24.

We began our return to Tokyo Bay, entertaining hopes for time to enjoy some deserved leisure. At dawn on September 25, we entered the channel to Tokyo Bay behind the *Boston*, and at 0900 the *Cotten* was released from duty with the demilitarization unit.

During the day the speedboat was given trial runs under the direction of the chief boatswain's mate, who had been first to realize the potential value of this craft to our ship. The sailors of the *Cogswell* were not able to conceal their envy at our new boat, and several members of their crew were given rides, to ensure that their envy would be long lasting. That afternoon orders came for McCullough's transfer off the *Cotten* to return to the West Coast. He was a popular and assertive chief; it was lucky that his transfer had not come through a week earlier.

Snowden incorporated the speedboat in the regular liberty boat schedule to Yokosuka beginning September 26, limiting its passengers to enlisted personnel only. Although it would only hold four passengers, its thirty-five-knot speed, compared with the five and three-quarter knots of the whaleboats, increased the ship's ability to transfer the crew to the dock for afternoon liberty by about 50 percent. This proved to be a tremendous morale booster, disproportionate to the actual benefits enjoyed ashore by the crew. Strange as it seems, the acquisition of the speedboat was seriously believed to be a harbinger of good fortune.

36

The Tokyo Bay Roadstead

Snowden and Gearhart went ashore on September 26, in order, among other things, to discover whether it would now be possible for the four of us, Drake and myself included, to take a three-day pass to Atami. While they were in Yokosuka, they learned that a geisha house had been established exclusively for American naval officers, in a building four blocks from the navy yard. Owned and operated by Japanese, the enterprise was reportedly inspected on a daily basis by U.S. Navy medical officers. They also discovered that two similar clubs had been set up, one for enlisted personnel and one for chief petty officers, so that the venture would be an egalitarian one.

Not being content to rely on the rumor alone, they proceeded immediately to check the officers' geisha house personally. They spotted the building, assuring themselves that it was the one they were looking for by the rows of black shoes lining the stairway to the entrance. They removed their own shoes and entered. In the reception room, attractive young women attired in kimonos knelt behind a low table at one end; behind them sat a decorous-looking older woman, similarly attired. She smiled at Snowden and Gearhart, beckoned them to sit on the floor, and pointed to the giggly young ladies.

Snowden and Gearhart each made a selection, and the two indicated came over to them, settling to their knees gracefully by the officers' sides. The older woman then declared that for the standard time, half an hour, there would be a charge of two packs of cigarettes per person, or 2,160 yen. The transaction was completed with the handing over of the two packs apiece, and the two girls guided them out, each heading into one of the many small private rooms in the house.

Both men later reported that they had enjoyed their time with the girls, the first half of which had been spent learning words in each other's language and playing children's games, such as "rock, paper, scissors," and the latter half under a quilt on a mat. They each gave their girl a gift of another pack of cigarettes after the session was over, which was accepted gratefully and enthusiastically. They dressed, returned to the reception room, said good-bye to their girls and to Mama-san, and promised to return. They then retrieved their shoes and headed for the officers' club bar, happier than they had been a scant hour earlier.

After relaxing at the bar, they visited the staff officer whom we had met previously. He told them that starting on October 1, we would officially be free to go to Atami and stay at the European hotel he had earlier recommended. He also confirmed that the girls in the officers' "geisha house" were regularly inspected by naval medical officers. Having more than satisfied their objectives for the day, Snowden and Gearhart took the next boat back to the *Cotten*, eager to share their newly gained intelligence.

After supper they reviewed their experiences with Drake and me in detail, including instructions on how to locate the geisha house. Pleased as the two of us were at the prospect of going to Atami on October 1 for what would be a two-night-and-three-day pass, the unforeseen information about the geisha house in Yokosuka made a visit there a higher priority.

At the break of dawn the next morning, September 27, however, the weather turned nasty. Captain Linehan asked me to stay aboard as duty officer for the next two days, during which he and Snowden had business off the ship. They were to attend a meeting of the captains and execs of DesRon 50 with the new squadron commander, Capt. H. T. Deutermann, who had relieved Capt. E. R. Wilkinson on August 31, 1945. Linehan instructed me to keep a close watch on our anchorage, considering how susceptible the destroyers had been to dragging anchor in winds of only twenty-five knots. I optimistically told him I would take care of things while they were gone.

There was no trouble on September 26, but during the late afternoon of the following day the wind began to kick up in earnest. The *Cogswell* had left our nest in the morning; the *Cotten* had then dropped its starboard anchor with seventy-five fathoms of chain. At 1635 *Cogswell* returned, mooring to our port side. I had stood the 2000 to 2400 watch that evening, but an hour later, at 0100 of September 28, I was called to the bridge by the OOD, Ens. Dan Hrtko. The wind had increased in force; it was now steady at twenty-five knots but with gusts up to forty knots. Checking our bearings to landmarks ashore, I found that we had already dragged two hundred yards and were continuing to drag rapidly. At 0230 we lighted off another boiler, while *Cogswell* got under way to anchor separately. *Ingersoll* and *Knapp*, upwind in another nest, were now dragging anchor and drifting rapidly down on the *Cotten*.

Fifteen minutes later the *Ingersoll/Knapp* nest was within 150 yards of *Cotten*. The two ships then hauled up their anchors, separated, and got under way to re-anchor one thousand and two thousand yards, respectively, on our starboard beam. The wind was now steady at fifty knots. At 0303 I ordered the port anchor dropped, veering ninety fathoms of chain on it, only to find that the second anchor slowed our dragging but did not stop it. At 0315, I ordered the second boiler cut in and both engines to go ahead slowly. At this point, with two anchors down and the engines making "turns" for two knots, the *Cotten* finally held its ground. By the time we had stabilized the situation, we had drifted a total of 1,150 yards downwind of our assigned anchorage. Because those who had been downwind of us had dragged considerably farther than we had, we had not endangered them.

The wind continued at gale force for twelve more hours, when the storm left with customary abruptness. We then hauled up the port anchor, set the regular in-port watch routine, secured the main engines, and secured the second boiler. When the captain and Snowden returned, we re-anchored our destroyer in its assigned position. The *Cotten* was fortunate not to have sustained any damage from the storm, and I was grateful, considering the assurances I had given the captain. Not so lucky were *C. K. Bronson, Healy, Caperton, Ingersoll,* and *Knapp* of our squadron, all of which had experienced materiel losses, including seven twenty-six-foot whaleboats that had broken loose and dashed themselves to pieces on the lee shore. Tokyo Bay was indeed an inhospitable roadstead in a storm.

At 0800 the next morning, September 29, all five destroyers of DesDiv 99 got under way to proceed to the fully protected harbor at Yokosuka Ko, where the squadron had been assigned uninterrupted mooring privileges until October 9, a period of ten full days. That afternoon I went ashore to make a delayed confirmation of Snowden's and Gearhart's report, locating the geisha house without difficulty. My own experiences now verified those of the two friends as to the cheerful, well-mannered atmosphere of the establishment and the pleasant nature of the young ladies. The fact that the *Cotten* was now moored but four blocks from this newly organized club, and even closer to the relaxed conviviality of the officers' club, made the circumstances seem a miraculous improvement over the miserable open anchorage in Tokyo Bay.

The next day, September 30, Gearhart and I went ashore in our foul-weather coats, their compartments loaded with Old Gold cigarettes, to resume the buttressing of our finances for the coming trip to Atami. When we returned to the *Cotten* that evening, we each had accumulated over sixty thousand yen in cash, which we hoped to put to good use during our three-day pass.

37

Atami

After breakfast on October 1, Snowden, Drake, Gearhart, and I left the ship for the three-day excursion to Atami. We hiked to the railroad station, purchased round-trip tickets, and walked back to the platform to wait for the train. The stationmaster told one of the guards where we were headed and evidently gave him instructions as to how he wished us to be assisted. The scene on the platform was chaotic; there appeared to be twice as many riders as could be accommodated by any number of trains. It was so crowded that movement was almost a physical impossibility.

While we waited on the platform, several trains departed headed north for Tokyo. We saw the station attendants literally shoving the passengers into the cars until they could hold no more. When the doors closed, the pressure of the mass of humanity from inside the cars greatly slowed the door-closing process.

Finally a train came in heading in the other direction and screeched to a stop. The guard who was standing with us led us through the crowd, pushing and shoving to clear a path toward the engine. We stopped below the engineer's cab, and the guard shouted up to the engineer. The engineer opened the door to his cab, summoning us up to join him. The four of us with our bags managed to fit in comfortably, at least in comparison with the passengers being jammed into the cars behind us.

When the train was loaded and the doors closed, it took off toward Kamakura, which was the first stop. At Kamakura there was a major exodus of passengers behind us, and we could have moved back, but the engineer would not hear of it, so we had the pleasure of viewing the balance of the trip from his cab. The scenery was most interesting from every angle, including the ride through the long Tanna Tunnel. The train moved along at a good clip, and despite the long stop at Kamakura necessary to unload and reload the tightly packed human cargo, we arrived at the Atami station at a little after eleven o'clock. The engineer helped us remove our baggage from his cab, and we parted with mutual bowing and smiling. We left the station, hailed a taxicab—which was powered by one of the wood-and-charcoal-fueled engines—and gave the driver the name of our hotel. We headed away up a hill in the general direction of Mount Fuji, which dominated the horizon to the northwest.

It was a short drive, despite the taxi's laborious progress being hampered by the weight of four passengers, the upward grade, and a decidedly underpowered engine. The cab drove into the grounds of the hotel until the way was completely blocked by an impressive ten-foot-high pile of silver ingots stacked on the last fifty feet of the drive. We paid the cab driver, gathered our bags, and walked around the pile of silver to the hotel. We registered for rooms for two nights, indicating that we would take our meals in the hotel dining room. After carrying bags up to the four little European-style bedrooms that were assigned to us, we reconvened in the dining room for lunch.

The spacious dining room was divided longitudinally by ceiling-high folding silk screens; each section consisted of a line of tables with clean, white linen cloths, each table comfortably accommodating eight diners. We were pleased to find European utensils as well as chopsticks, the latter being of little use to us. The meal, served by cheerful waitresses attired in impeccably clean kimonos, consisted of fish, vegetables, and rice, with fruit for dessert, all accompanied by a bottle of wine divided among the four of us. The lunch was excellent, but when we asked the waitress what kind of fish had been served, she replied, in effect, that fish was fish. This was the only answer we ever got to this question, despite the fact that no two fish dishes we were subsequently served seemed to have come from the same species. Because the cook was skilled and everything we were served was fresh and palatable, it did not matter that its exact identity would remain a mystery.

After lunch we set out on a walking tour of Atami. There was no evidence anywhere of the presence of other Americans, which led to the conclusion that we were the first occupation personnel the citizens had seen. The countless Japanese walking the sidewalks bowed and smiled in our direction when we passed by, reinforcing the impression that we were objects of polite but definite curiosity. We went into many of the boutiques in the shopping district and purchased several items apiece for future family gifts, among them pieces of laquerware, porcelain cups, items of silk, watercolor sketches, and some picture postcards with several different views of Atami.

Our tour took the afternoon, the mild exercise elevating spirits already at a high level of anticipation. The population of Atami at the end of the war was perhaps twelve thousand, and both the inhabitants and the town itself were fully up to our expectations, which had been escalating over the past month. There was no evidence of opulence, but the overall impression was one of only moderate, rather than grinding, poverty. On the other hand, the realization was bothersome that the lack of a common language was going to impede our ability to understand much of what we were seeing and doing.

Finding our way back to the hotel did not present a problem, because the town rises from the shore in the shape of a bowl, with Fuji-san as a point of reference; it was impossible to become disoriented. Gearhart and I had already determined to make an evening of it and to include feminine companionship as the major component. We assumed Snowden and Drake had similar intentions, but because our own finances, inflated by the cigarette trade, gave us more options, we decided to make our plans independently of them.

During daylight the streets had seemed completely safe, but it nonetheless seemed the better part of valor to have an escort for the intended visit to some classic geisha establishment, rather than wander about looking for one on our own after dark. With this in mind, Gearhart and I stopped by the front desk to chat with the concierge before going to join our associates for supper. Using the best of our evolving sign language, backed up by a few Japanese terms, of which *geisha* was the most important, we made an attempt to convey that it was our wish to be directed to a geisha house for an evening's entertainment after we had finished with dinner. The concierge appeared to understand what we were driving at, and we concluded that he would accommodate our request. With confidence that this chore had been accomplished, we joined Snowden and Drake.

We were four cheerful customers for supper, the main course being fish distinctly different from that served for lunch. Another bottle of wine was shared, and after dessert we were served cups of heated sake, our first taste of the famous Japanese rice wine. Snowden and Drake were also

Dinner at an Atami hotel, October 1945. From left: Robinson, Drake, waitress, Snowden, and Gearhart.

looking forward to something they had planned for later on, the nature of which they kept to themselves.

We lingered over the meal and sake until almost nine o'clock, regaling each other with sea stories until it was time for Gearhart and me to be on our way. We proceeded to the desk, where one of the clerks came out to us, asking that we follow him, speaking the word *geisha*. Our route was down the hill toward the waterfront, thence to the left parallel to the shore, the total walk being about a mile. Our guide led us to a building that was none too well maintained in appearance and beckoned us inside. We met the Mama-san, our guide explaining who we were and immediately departing.

Mama-san then ushered two pretty young ladies into the room for our perusal, and Gearhart and I briefly discussed the situation. It was inescapable, even from the limited experience gained in Yokosuka, that we had been brought to a modest waterfront bordello, with an ambiance not remotely what we expected of a geisha house. This was a considerable disappointment, but inasmuch as we were there, we agreed that we should take the bird in hand and postpone the quest for a geisha for the morrow.

This being settled, we each accepted the nearest girl and settled the financial details with Mama-san. Our young women then led us to their respective cubicles, which were not much larger than the mats they contained. I stayed for two hours, requiring two additional visits to Mama-san for negotiations of the fee. At the end of my allotted time, I gave my companion a present of two packs of cigarettes (which represented about the same market value as the total sum I had paid to Mama-san), wished her good luck, and departed from the establishment. Without waiting for Gearhart, I hiked back to the hotel in the still of the night. Reviewing the evening, which might be considered a misadventure in the quest for the elusive geisha, I persuaded myself that it had nonetheless been time well spent and that tomorrow could look after itself.

At the call for breakfast the next morning, I woke up enthusiastic about Atami and the coming day, six hours' rest having been sufficiently rejuvenating. The four of us appeared on time at our dining room table—to be joined by a fifth, a young, kimonoed Japanese girl who trailed into the dining room behind Gearhart. Everyone acted as though this were a perfectly normal situation and welcomed her to our company, as we hungrily ate a rather skimpy breakfast. She ate her meal demurely enough, handling chopsticks in a way that fascinated us, nevertheless managing to eat everything placed before her in whirlwind fashion. After breakfast she bowed good-bye to each of us and departed.

The four of us gathered in the lounge to discuss plans for the day, nothing having been previously arranged. Mulling over the limited alternatives, we decided that a walk through part of the more open countryside adjacent to Atami would be rewarding. We agreed that we would engage a cab to take us out to the site of a famous Buddhist monastery, about three miles from town. We could then take our time seeing what we could of the monastery, after which we would hike back to the hotel to get a feel for the countryside, rounding out the excursion with some fresh air and welcome exercise. We did our best to communicate this plan to the concierge, presuming that he would get a message to the monastery to advise it that we would be paying a visit. The concierge confirmed that the monastery with its adjoining temple was a noted institution in the Atami area.

Within the half hour, a cab arrived in answer to a call from the hotel. The four of us piled in, and the driver backed away from the mound of silver until clear of the driveway. Back on the street, we slowly made our way up the incline that surrounds Atami. We then proceeded through the less-dense outskirts and finally arrived in the open countryside, which consisted in the main of what appeared to be many small, individual farms. Once out in the country, we were overwhelmed by the pervasive smell of night soil, the first encounter for any of us with this ancient form of field fertilization. Like all new sensory experiences, this one took some time to get used to. In fact, there was some doubt that we could ever become acclimated to it.

The cab arrived in front of the monastery, a temple within a compound of Japanese buildings that looked to be of some antiquity. The compound was set back two hundred feet from the road, requiring that we approach on foot. At the front entrance of the monastery, we were politely greeted by a monk; he had been expecting our arrival, and he ushered us inside. Without preamble he then led us on a tour of the building, explaining in painstaking Japanese each of the many artifacts and items of historical interest. None of us understood a word, so we each did our best to concentrate on what we were seeing. A functional purpose was evident in the layout of the monastery, and the stylized art and decorative detail gave the strong impression of a cultural unity underlying everything we saw. We were beginning to appreciate that the Japanese possessed a powerful heritage that had taken many centuries to develop and now provided the basis of their national will.

When lunchtime came around, the monk ushered us in to a small room, where we sat on matting around a low, round table to be served a light noon meal. There was tea, a cold soup, rice, and fruit, apparently a typical Buddhist monk's fare. Despite having been warned by Paul Patterson, the ship's doctor, to be careful not to eat uncooked vegetables or unwashed fresh fruit, we ate everything placed before us, in deference to our healthy appetites and to avoid offending our host. Following lunch we were taken on a tour of the rest of the buildings, including a shrine, after which, not wanting to overstay our welcome, we extended our sincere thanks for the monk's gracious hospitality and made our way out to the road.

The walk back to Atami took less than an hour; we encountered on the way no traffic other than a horse-drawn wagon bringing produce to town. Hiking through the outskirts, we came upon a building that looked as though it was a public bath house. After discussion we decided to investigate, as a hot bath suddenly seemed very appealing.

Entering the building, we were pleased to find that it was in fact a public bath house, and the proprietor welcomingly invited us in. We paid a fee and were directed to a room where we deposited our clothes, toilet facilities being adjacent. We were next ushered into a shower room, where we were instructed to wash before being admitted to the bath area itself. After washing we proceeded to the room containing the hot water bathing pool, which was large enough to accommodate perhaps ten people of both sexes. The evident purpose of the pool was to sweat away while socializing with your neighbors—this being the only logical rationale, considering that bathers were thoroughly scrubbed before entering it.

We had been relaxing for about ten minutes when one of the other pool occupants, a young Japanese man, initiated a conversation in perfectly understandable English. By this time the sound of English coming from a Japanese came somewhat as a shock. However, we quickly regained sufficient composure to introduce ourselves.

Nirohiko, the young man, advised us that he was nineteen and a college student at the University of Tokyo. He was in Atami visiting his uncle, Takao Hayashi. We told him our names and that we were American naval officers from the destroyer *Cotten,* now moored in Yokosuka Ko. Snowden and Drake identified themselves as lieutenants and Gearhart and me as lieutenants, junior grade, or "jg's." We told Nirohiko that we were staying at the hotel and had spent the day on a sight-seeing hike in the country, including a visit to the monastery.

Nirohiko related in reply that his uncle was a powerful man in Japan, a former member of the Diet, and an industrialist. Takao Hayashi had manufactured sewing machines prior to the war but had converted his factories to the making of tanks, machine guns, and lastly, "baka bombs," rocket bombs with suicide pilots. Now he was making nothing and was considering how to convert his factories back to commercial ventures. His uncle, Nirohiko said, had his principal residence in Kyoto, where his first wife lived. His vacation home in Atami was the residence of his second wife, an eighteen-year-old former professional dancer. The uncle was staying with her until it became clearer just where postwar Japan was headed and how, under the new circumstances, he could best retain his properties, his wealth, and his power.

Having described his uncle to us in these terms, Nirohiko proceeded to tell us that Takao had always expressed respect for the Japanese navy but had great admiration for the United States Navy as well. He asked us if we would be interested in coming to his uncle's house, provided he could garner a formal invitation. All four of us responded that of course we would be happy to meet his uncle and honored to be invited to his house. Nirohiko said he would speak to Takao as soon as he returned home and would get back to us later in the day.

Nirohiko then related some of his experiences in Tokyo, which included a tale of his parents' house burning to the ground in one of the great firebombing raids. He and his parents had aspirations of his attending an American university as soon as possible. He gave the impression that he was not optimistic about his country's future but rather was deeply impressed by the power of the United States, which explained his unusual interest in the four of us. We also gathered, from the tone and manner of his voice, that he did not approve of Hayashi's wife number two, despite the fact that he was nominally a guest in her house.

Nirohiko was the first Japanese I had met whom I disliked as a person. However, it was now very obvious that he probably represented the only chance we would ever have to meet someone in the upper reaches of Japanese society on a personal basis; such an opportunity should not be wasted. Second and equally important, his ability to speak English made him valuable as an interpreter, which we desperately needed. My three companions had come to the same conclusions, at least with respect to taking advantage of a windfall opportunity; as a result, the four of us evinced unaccustomed tact and respectful interest, from every perspiring pore, for the benefit of young Nirohiko.

This tête-à-tête in the public bath came to an end just after two middle-aged ladies entered the water nearby, in the same state of nudity as everyone else. They paid no attention as we arose from the pool to return to the room where we had left our clothes. We toweled down and, as soon as we had stopped sweating, put our clothes back on. Nirohiko left to return to his uncle's house, and we resumed our walk back to the hotel, arriving without incident a little after four o'clock. On our arrival we adjourned to the lounge, to pass the time before dinner in conversation. We talked over the events of the day, particularly sorting out our impressions of Nirohiko and hazarding guesses as to what would happen when we met the high-powered uncle.

Just before we went into the dining room, Nirohiko appeared. He was very pleased to tell us that his uncle was eager to meet us and that he intended to make a gift to us of his family's samurai swords. General MacArthur had just ordered the Japanese people to turn in their swords to the occupation forces for destruction, considering them unacceptable symbols of Japanese militarism. Takao, Nirohiko told us, wanted us to have them, feeling that we would keep them as personal mementos of our war service, thereby ensuring their survival into the future. We listened to this speech with considerable interest. We assured Nirohiko that we were grateful for the invitation and would accept the gift of the family swords if such was his uncle's wish, keeping them with the respect they deserved. A date was set for the following morning after breakfast, when Nirohiko would return to guide us to his uncle's house.

Before he left, we asked him what the huge pile of silver ingots in the front driveway was all about. He replied that it had been in the vaults of the bank in Atami and had been ordered turned over to the occupation forces for eventual disbursement as reparations for the damage done by the Japanese army in the various countries it had occupied during the war. It was amazing to us that an uncovered pile of silver could sit out in the open for days, without guard, and yet apparently be perfectly safe.

Nirohiko then took his leave, and the dining room captain came over to advise us that dinner was ready to be served. We entered the dining room for another interesting meal, of fish (of yet a different species), vegetable, rice, wine, and fruit. We took our time, lingering after the food over sake and conversation. None of us was up to further adventure on this particular evening, so we retired at half past ten for a recuperative night's sleep.

Next morning started with a leisurely breakfast that included hard, little round balls of meat that the cook had prepared in deference to the well-known American preference for red meat. The meatballs were gamy, despite the use of unusually strong seasoning, but they were palatable enough to anyone accustomed to the fare aboard a destroyer.

Gearhart observed that the previous night he had missed the constant howling of cats outside the hotel, which had been very noticeable during our first night, although we had all slept soundly enough through the racket. When he brought the subject up, we realized that our recollections were similar. This led Gearhart to argue that our breakfast had been cat meat, a logical explanation for the double evidence of the sudden absence of the nocturnal feline mating calls and the unusual, highly aromatic nature of the meatballs. He called our waitress over and asked her, with the usual hand graphics backed up by meows for emphasis, what the Japanese word for "cat" was. The waitress replied "*Niko, niko,*" adding her customary grin. Gearhart turned to us and pronounced that we had just eaten our first, and with any luck our last, "niko burgers."

The unusual breakfast concluded, we adjourned to the lounge to await Nirohiko. About an hour later he appeared. We were ready, and with a minimum of ceremony, we departed the hotel and proceeded to walk to Takao's Atami vacation domicile, about a mile distant. It was a few minutes before ten o'clock when we arrived. We followed Nirohiko to the front door and, following his example, removed our shoes before entering. We were greeted by a very pretty young woman, whom we presumed to be wife number two, attractively dressed in an expensive-looking silk kimono. She bowed us into a sitting room through a sliding panel made of rice paper over wood framing. She invited us to sit on the matted floor around a handsome, large round table, the top of which was perhaps eighteen inches above the floor level. The five of us did as she requested, Nirohiko included.

A few minutes later the panel was opened again, and Takao appeared in the opening, wife number two standing obediently behind him. Following Nirohiko's example, we rose and bowed to our host, after which he entered the room, bowed to each of us in turn as we were introduced by Nirohiko, and sat down at the round table, indicating that we should do the same. When we were all arranged around the table, an extended conversation began between Takao and the naval officers in turn, with Nirohiko acting as interpreter. He addressed the four of us as Howie-san, Bob-san, Snell-san, and Shifty-san, respectively, all names that Takao could pronounce; he was addressed as Hayashi-san. He asked each of us how long we had been aboard the *Cotten* and what our assignments were aboard ship. He inquired into our backgrounds, what universities we had attended, and whether or not we were married, learning that he was in the company of four bachelors.

He was interested to hear of the sea battles that the *Cotten* had participated in, and we regaled him with tales of the Battles of the Philippine Sea and Leyte Gulf, confining our description of the latter to the parts played by Admiral Sherman's carrier task group and the Battle Line. Takao seemed pleased that the Battle Line had been decoyed by the Japanese carriers off Cape Engaño; he appeared to have some knowledge of the general handling of the Japanese fleet in these battles, both disasters for the Japanese. After some time had passed in this discussion, he clapped his hands, and his pretty wife appeared at the door, bowing deeply to her husband. He spoke to her briefly, after which she bowed again and left the room. Nirohiko explained that it was time for some refreshment, which was forthcoming in a moment.

A short time later Takao's wife returned, followed by a maid carrying a tray with refreshments, which she placed on the table. The maid departed, returning with a second tray with tea utensils and beautiful little teacups. The wife kneeled at the table, pouring tea for everyone and placing small cakes on plates in front of each of us. The best we could come up with in the way of proper manners was to follow the example of our host, and to that end we put forth our best efforts. When the food was gone, Takao's wife and the maid cleared everything away and made respectful departures.

The profound deference exhibited by the young wife toward the master of the house was something we Americans had never before witnessed. Nirohiko, for his part, appeared all but paralyzed with fear of his uncle. We, on the other hand, had nothing whatever to fear, which was probably evident in the way we acted. We all tried to behave in a courteous manner, with an effort that was probably equally obvious, inasmuch as such a degree of courtesy was not entirely normal to us.

Takao was not a tall man but a muscular one. He head was round as a bullet, his hair short cropped. His manner toward us was pleasant and interested, but he gave no indication that we could be of help to him in any manner. We were puzzled by this mature man, who was to remain completely inscrutable. We, on the other hand, were open and outgoing, feeling that there was no need to hide anything from him, including our less than wholly admiring view of General MacArthur. Whether this conversation with us was of value to him, there was no way to know. I have come to believe that he did gain some reassurance, specifically that the occupation of Japan by the United States, or technically by the Allied powers, would not result in Japan's destruction as a nation. I think he also satisfied himself that the United States, if we were representative of our country, would be uncomfortable in the role of conqueror and would leave the Japanese to go their own way once it was certain that Japanese militarism had been effectively dismantled. He was too worldly to think that we were privy to anything beyond our own service, but our manner alone must have suggested to him that individualism and relaxed self-assurance marked our society's basic character.

During the early afternoon, he insisted on playing a game of Go with each of us. He explained the object of the game and its moves, both of which are simple enough. However, the execution of the game is not simple; its strategy is complex and requires much long-range planning. Of course we were soon overwhelmed, giving him four easy victories. After the games there was a pause. Nirohiko explained that his uncle felt that now that he knew who we were and what we were like, and had played Go with each of us, he was comfortable with his plan to give us his family's samurai swords, the most ancient of which had been in his family's possession for over five hundred years. Takao was taking the position that he was fulfilling MacArthur's directive to turn the swords over to the American occupation forces in giving them to us, as agents of those forces. That he expected us to keep them as personal possessions did not in any way place him in defiance of the directive, inasmuch as our keeping them would be acts of our own volition, not Takao's. It was a pleasure to hear this succinct example of oriental rationalization, which apparently required no response on our part.

His wife and her maid then returned, carrying three swords, which they laid on the table in front of the master. Two swords were evidently a pair, called a *daisho*—a long sword (*katana*) and a shorter mate (*wakizashi*), the handles and scabbards matching perfectly. The third sword, also a *wakizashi*, was wrapped in a beautiful piece of embroidered silk. Takao removed this last sword from the silk and showed us the scabbard, which was very old inlaid bone, or possibly ivory. He removed the sword and displayed the blade, which was in perfect condition, sharper than the sharpest razor, and powdered to ensure it would not rust. It was this sword, according to Nirohiko's translation of Takao's speech, that was over five hundred years old, having been made some time prior to A.D. 1450, in our reckoning of time. He returned this sword to its scabbard and rewrapped it in the silk. Takao handed all three to Snowden, our senior officer and our group's representative.

Snowden accepted the swords on our behalf with a handsome speech pledging that we would do our best to give them the same respect and care that they had received at the hands of our host's family. He said we would divide the three weapons among the four of us in such a way that each of us would have an equal opportunity to own and care for one of the swords, and that the one who went without would at least have had the same chance as his luckier peers.

Nirohiko translated Snowden's comments for Takao's benefit, the latter nodding his head in satisfaction. He then clapped his hands once more, summoning his wife. She appeared as before, to receive another instruction from her husband, bowing and leaving when he had concluded. A few minutes later she returned bearing a small lacquer tray on which stood an unopened bottle of Johnnie Walker Black Label scotch whiskey, along with six beautiful small cups, which she placed in front of Takao. At a nod from the master, she opened the whiskey bottle and returned it to the tray.

Takao filled the six cups with whiskey, retaining one in front of himself along with the bottle and directing his wife to pass the others on the tray to the four of us and Nirohiko. When the whiskey was in front of each of us, Takao raised his cup to his lips, indicating that we should do the same. After we had downed the scotch, which tasted like nectar, Takao wished us good luck with the swords, stating that they represented the spirits of the samurai who had worn them with honor during their long histories.

At this moment another person arrived at the main entrance and was admitted to our presence by the maid. The new arrival was a beautifully kimonoed woman, apparently in her later thirties, turned out and coiffured in a way that seemed little less than perfect. She bowed to Takao, who stood and bowed to her as well, with the first smile on his face that we had seen. It seemed obvious that they were close friends and held each other in great esteem. We, along with Nirohiko, also rose, following our host's example. They conversed for a minute, Takao explaining the circumstances of our presence as well as of the swords and whiskey reposing on the table. When he had finished, he turned to Nirohiko, directing him to introduce us to his friend.

Again we were introduced as Howie-san, Bob-san, Snell-san, and Shifty-san; her name was Lanko-san. Nirohiko then sent a thrill through each of us by announcing, with respect, that Lanko-san was one of the head geisha at the House of the Golden Wave, the preeminent geisha house in Atami. You could have heard a pin drop. We each bowed to Lanko-san, whose flashing eyes and spirited smile made it unmistakable that we were in the presence of a remarkable personality.

The previous formality of our becoming acquainted with Takao and the ceremony of the swords now disappeared under the combined effect of two more cups of twelve-year-old straight scotch whiskey and the presence of the scintillating geisha Lanko. When it was opportune, I moved toward Lanko, indicating to Nirohiko that I needed his services. Gearhart and I had previously agreed that the two of us would return to Atami on October 13, spending the night at the hotel and returning to Yokosuka the next day.

Lanko was the easiest person to talk to I had yet encountered, even though we had to speak through an interpreter. She conveyed the feeling that she had an interest in you that was absolutely genuine and utterly without guile. This put me so at ease that I was able to come right to the point. Without embarrassment or feeling that I was in any way abusing Takao's hospitality or Lanko's preeminent position, I told her that Gearhart, or Shifty-san, and I were going to return to Atami on October 13 for one night and that we both would consider it a tremendous honor if she would sponsor us for a visit to her geisha house on that occasion.

She let out a peal of laughter, patted my arm, and said that nothing could give her greater pleasure. She asked Nirohiko to give me a piece of paper with a note on it for the hotel concierge, so that we could get in touch with her after supper the night of October 13. She said that she would arrange to introduce us to the geisha house; such an introduction was required, as well as a reservation for a party, all of which she would be happy to arrange for Hayashi's friend Snell-san. I confirmed that I would get a message to her when we arrived on the thirteenth and assured her I was looking forward to seeing her then. Lanko then, with practiced art, took control of the conversation, leaving me with the feeling that she was one of the most interesting persons I had ever met. Having taken care of me, she moved on to the others, charming each in his turn.

Unfortunately for us, the time to catch the train back to Yokosuka was at hand. Nirohiko pointed this out to his uncle and Lanko, so that farewells could proceed, breaking up what had been a wonderful party. Each of us said good-bye to Takao, Lanko, Takao's wife, and Nirohiko, with much mutual bowing, which had become second nature to us in this group. With swords in hand, we left at last, walking briskly back to the hotel to pay our bills, which were considerable, and to gather up our bags. We then hiked down to the station, arriving about ten minutes before the train was scheduled to appear.

By prior agreement, the swords were to be allocated by a simple roll of two dice, each of us getting but one roll, except if there was a tie. The person who rolled the highest number would get first choice, the second-highest second choice, and third-highest third choice, with the low roll getting nothing. In case of a tie, the two would roll again, high man getting the sword.

We deposited the swords on the station platform, and Snowden produced the two dice. My roll was two sixes, the only time in my life that I remember winning anything with such a roll. I selected the five-hundred-year-old *wakizashi*. Snowden got the second-highest roll, choosing the long *katana*. Gearhart got the third-highest roll and the smaller sword, which matched Snowden's in style. The dice had chosen for us, and each winner picked up his treasure, after a proceeding that had been a matter of great interest to some fifty Japanese standing with us on the platform, waiting with us for the train to Yokosuka.

A few minutes later the train pulled in, right on time, and we boarded along with a crowd, but nothing like the masses who had come down to Atami with us previously. There were enough seats for everyone, including the nursing mothers, who were not at all unusual on the trains, and we were delivered to Yokosuka in under two hours, but well after dark. We walked over to the Yokosuka naval base and returned to our ship and our shipmates. Because of the uniqueness of the experience, we did not advertise what we had encountered in Atami. Gearhart and I were especially secretive about our coming appointment with Lanko and the House of the Golden Wave.

38

The House of the Golden Wave

From October 4 to 9, the *Cotten* remained snug and secure in its berth in Yokosuka Ko, surrounded by breakwaters. I carried out most of my shipboard duties in a perfunctory manner during this period, concentrating instead on sorting out the experience gained in Atami, writing my parents a detailed letter about the trip and the characters I had encountered, and contemplating and preparing for the next excursion, some ten days in the future.

The original foursome now broke up into twosomes, Snowden and Drake having one set of priorities, and Gearhart and I another. Gearhart and I had made reservations for our own return to the hotel when we paid our bills, without comment to our friends. Snowden and Drake, for their part, made an unannounced return to Atami only two days after we had all come back from the first trip. They called on Takao Hayashi, presumably having received an invitation at the sword ceremony. Drake was given a very fine fourth sword by Hayashi, who regretted that he had given us only three swords initially. When the two of them returned to the *Cotten*, we were delighted to hear about Drake's sword but made no inquiry concerning the geisha Lanko, not wishing to encourage any competition on that score.

Gearhart and I, our plans being identical, concentrated on further accumulation of cash, which entailed three trips ashore to liquidate all but the last six cartons of our Old Golds. This involved one foray by train as far afield as Kamakura, to negotiate a better price for the merchandise, the price in Yokosuka having dropped by one-third due to an increase in the supply as more military personnel entered the cigarette trade.

Atami was a protected environment compared to Yokosuka and Kamakura, but the difference in the cost of living between essentially free room and board on the *Cotten* and expensive private rooms and three meals a day at a seaside resort hotel was causing us to plan carefully. The only way we could consider continuing with our ambitious plans for our return to Atami was by realizing the maximum value of the hoard of Old Golds. Lanko had laughingly told me, as interpreted by Nirohiko, that entertainment at the geisha house was very expensive, to which I had replied that I understood, that Shifty-san and I could afford the cost because we had money set aside just for such an experience. This was all well and good, but simple arithmetic showed that our plans for patronizing the House of the Golden Wave on top of our other expenses in Atami were going to require every cent we could accumulate.

While the necessary preparations for the trip were occupying Gearhart's and my nearly undivided attention, the crew of the *Cotten* was also being diverted by increasingly diverse activities ashore. The prospect of the *Cotten*'s returning to the anchorage three miles out in an open roadstead, scheduled for October 9, was an unacceptable obstruction to easy access to the dock, even with the speedboat to augment the two slow-moving whaleboats.

When we first moored in Yokosuka Ko, some of our men had noticed a fifty-four-foot Japanese power cruiser tied up at the dock and had had the good sense to inquire as to its ownership. Discovering that it was the property of the Japanese navy and had been reserved for the personal use of a newly "retired" Japanese vice admiral, they immediately requisitioned it and tied it up alongside the *Cotten*'s port quarter. The carpenter's mate, boatswain's mates, and motor machinist's mates turned to, returning the craft to full service with new paint and all "brightwork" (brass fittings) shining like jewels. This impressive craft was dubbed the "number 1 motorboat," it being understood that it was for the exclusive use of the ship's crew. Now that the prospect of the *Cotten*'s returning to the anchorage in Tokyo Bay would not limit future liberty parties, the members of the crew could concentrate on what they were going to do for diversion ashore, as heady a prospect for them as it was for Gearhart and me.

On the morning of October 9, the squadron left Yokosuka Ko to return to the open waters of Tokyo Bay. When the *Cotten* anchored, we dropped both anchors in precautionary anticipation of more heavy weather within the next twenty-four hours. As it turned out, a typhoon, and a big one, hit the Okinawa island chain head on, with reported winds of 130 knots. Tokyo Bay was too far away to feel more than twenty-five-knot gusts, which were not sufficient to cause us to drag the two anchors. The storm did pull some cold weather into the Tokyo area, in no way an inconvenience to us but a hardship for the Japanese, due to their lack of fuel and housing.

When October 13 rolled around, Gearhart and I were primed and ready for another trip to Atami. Wearing our blue uniform topcoats for warmth, we were comfortably protected from the cool fall weather. We left the *Cotten* after lunch and took the gig to Yokosuka, thence walking the short distance to the train station. A small bag apiece sufficed for clean clothes for the evening and the next day, along with toothbrushes and shaving gear. This time we boarded the train with the Japanese in one of the passenger cars, which required standing for the first part of the trip, hemmed in by the other riders like fish in a tin. Despite the crush, everyone remained in good humor, a characteristic of the Japanese that I was beginning to believe was universal.

We arrived at our hotel in Atami a little after three o'clock, checking in and depositing our gear. We handed our note addressed to Lanko to the concierge with a request that it be delivered to her, which he assured us would be attended to.

Later we both cleaned up, shaved, and dressed in pressed khakis for our coming dates. Suitably prepared, we returned to the dining room at suppertime, enjoying a pleasant meal—another breed of fish as the main course, and a shared bottle of wine—to start off the evening's entertainment. After dinner we drank some heated sake, whiling away the time. At about eight o'clock a now respectful concierge appeared at our table to advise us that Lanko-san had arrived at the hotel and was waiting for us in the lounge.

A resplendent Lanko, in another fabulous kimono, rose to greet us with a flashing smile. We exchanged bows, and I told her that she looked beautiful, in English of course, which she clearly understood from the look on my face, if not the spoken word. She suggested we hire a taxi, as she was not dressed for a walk. The concierge, hovering on the sidelines, heard the request and sped away to take care of the matter. Within minutes the wood-powered taxi had appeared, and the three of us climbed in. The ride in the cab was in itself a treat, the obviously appreciative American audience being entertained by the vivacious Lanko in the close confines of the back seat.

Our destination was less than a ten-minute drive from the hotel, so we soon arrived in front of the House of the Golden Wave. We paid for the cab and got out in front of a very nice-looking Japanese building, proceeding with Lanko to the front entrance. She opened the door with her key, and we followed her in, taking off our shoes in the place provided in the entrance foyer.

We were greeted by a maid. Following instructions from Lanko, she led us to the office of the head geisha, who was expecting us. We entered and all sat on the mat while Lanko introduced us to the head geisha, a well-presented lady in her fifties, and to an older gentleman sitting next to her. The gentleman spoke to us in very halting English, explaining that he was a regular patron of the geisha house and had been requested by the head geisha to join us to act as an interpreter, if that was acceptable to us. He held up an English-Japanese dictionary to confirm that he was prepared to solve any communication problems that might arise. Gearhart and I said that we thought that this was very thoughtful and helpful, and that we would be pleased to have him join our party. At this point Lanko rose and took her departure, saying good-bye to Gearhart and me, while we thanked her profusely for having gone to so much trouble for us. Lanko then left the room, once again bestowing on us her million-dollar smile.

Gearhart and I sat down, and the head geisha spoke to us with the halting aid of the gentleman companion, telling us what the format for our party would be, it having been planned by Lanko according to what she thought we would enjoy. At this point a maid brought in the tea service. In a formal way, the four of us—the head geisha, the gentleman interpreter, Gearhart, and myself—proceeded to drink a leisurely cup of tea.

The geisha told us that we had been scheduled for two hours' entertainment by two geisha in training, who had not yet attained the full rank of geisha. We would have a musician, proficient on the *samisen*, the three-stringed Japanese lute, who would accompany the girls when they sang songs and danced the pantomime masterpieces in which the geisha had been trained since they were children. When the entertainment was completed, we would go to private rooms with our geisha to rest and talk in an intimate environment, following which the four of us would rejoin, to refresh ourselves in the bath and enjoy the society of our ladies. This was the program, she advised us, and she named the price, which was at the high end of the range that we had anticipated. We both said this sounded fine and handed over our money.

At this point I said that this was a perfect program for our first visit, but that Shifty-san and I had it in our hearts to come back on October 16 for a party with two fully accredited geisha, including dinner and the privilege of spending the night in the House of the Golden Wave. The head geisha smiled and nodded. She turned to the other gentleman, asking if he could be with us again on that evening to act again as our interpreter, to which he replied in the affirmative. This attended to, she turned to us: yes, she would arrange such a party, with two of her most recently accredited geisha, with two older geisha to play the *samisen* and join in the entertainment. We would be served supper and would stay through the night with our geisha, although we were to understand that the ladies were under no obligation to take lovers, that being up to them on a personal basis. We told her that this was just what we wanted to experience and that we would be grateful for the opportunity.

She nodded with a smile, stating that this entertainment would cost us three times as much as we were paying for the present evening, and that the price would also include the expenses of our gentleman interpreter. We would also be expected to give our geisha generous presents as a personal matter, this being the custom. She said that if we had extra money presently with us, she would accept a deposit for the other party in advance, as the preparations were expensive, and she wished to ensure that everything would be first class. Because of our recent commercial efforts, we had enough extra money and duly handed some of it over.

With our financial arrangements completed, she rose and bade us follow her to another section of the house into a comfortably sized and attractively decorated room. We seated ourselves on the floor at a table to wait for the geisha.

In a minute the two young geisha and a third young lady, the musician carrying her *samisen*, entered. Introductions were made around the room, after which one of the geisha came over to sit beside me, the other sitting by Gearhart. They were both dressed in beautiful kimonos, though not of the high and expensive quality of those that Lanko wore. Their hair was styled in the geisha fashion, and their faces were made up according to the geisha tradition.

The girl who had chosen me had very oriental facial features, which were far from beautiful to the occidental taste. Lanko's facial features were very fine and delicate, and the young geisha that had picked Gearhart also had a fine, beautiful face, to my way of thinking. However, I was not about to show disappointment at my companion's lack of beauty, vowing instead to be as attentive as possible, to make her feel appreciated, and to seem eager to have her look on me with favor.

Our interpreter explained first for Gearhart and then for my benefit what our girls were saying to us, which amounted to almost a ritual form of flirtation mixed with wit. We, in turn, made generous compliments to them for their beautiful presentation of this initial stage of the entertainment.

The next event was musical, consisting of a series of songs, duets sung to the accompaniment of the *samisen*. These songs are lovely, creating an oriental mood that made the stylized entertainment completely natural and enchanting. Following the songs there was more flirtatious byplay and verbal interchange, which we managed to understand largely through intuition and the interpretive aid of our companion. There was an interlude for another cup of tea. Fortunately, the cups were so small that we were in no danger of floating away despite what seemed an inordinate number of pauses for tea.

The next entertainment consisted of a series of dances, each telling a short classic geisha story to the wailing plinking of the *samisen*. When this routine was concluded an hour had passed, and it was time for us to enjoy the companionship of our young ladies in privacy. With a fair amount of kidding back and forth the party broke up, and my geisha led me by the hand down the hall to a private room, where there were mats side by side on the floor and quilts and wooden pillows on the mats, which she identified as beds.

I had already learned that Japanese culture furnished easily available sex at very low cost, so the very high cost of entertainment at a geisha house was not reflective of a low commodity value of sex. With this in mind, I spent the hour with my geisha in a flirtatiously friendly manner, and I trust we both passed the time in mutual enjoyment of our privacy. The intimate interlude was too quickly over, and we then proceeded, clothed only in towels, to the hot bath, where we were shortly joined by Gearhart and his geisha. The time in the bath with the four of us as naked as jaybirds was hilarious, and it also was over too quickly. We returned to our rooms to get dressed, and I took the opportunity to give my companion a present that I hope seemed as generous to her as it did to me, after which we went to say good-bye to the head geisha. The latter was sitting with Gearhart and our interpreter, who I now gathered was an old friend of hers. They had ordered us a taxi, and as we said good night, they said they would see us again soon. We put on our shoes, went out the door, and stepped into the taxi, which returned us in its leisurely manner to our hotel.

Gearhart and I coaxed some sake from the night attendant, so that we could discuss our first evening among the geisha. I told Gearhart that I hoped he appreciated his girl, who represented my ideal of oriental femininity, in appearance at least, and he agreed that she was spectacular. Although I had also enjoyed the evening thoroughly, I felt that he had enjoyed both intriguing art and exquisite beauty, all in one petite package. Finally having exhausted the possibilities of self-congratulation on our initial success at savoring the pleasures of the Far East, we headed for our rooms and a good night's rest.

The next morning after breakfast, Gearhart and I met an army captain in the lounge and stopped for a chat. When we had arrived on the previous day, we had noted that the pile of silver in the front drive had disappeared, prompting me to ask if he knew what had happened to it. He said that he had personally supervised the loading of it into army trucks for delivery to MacArthur's command headquarters, where all gold and silver specie was being accumulated pending its distribution in settlement of Japan's reparation payments to the Asian countries it had occupied in the war. He then told us that an entire army regiment was going to be based in the Atami area within a few weeks, and he hoped to be attached to it on a permanent basis. This came as an unwelcome shock, as it meant that our unsullied haven was about to be desecrated. Certainly the environment would be ruined for us. I felt that we had been well advised to make our next date at the Golden Wave as soon as we did, well before the appearance of MacArthur's hordes.

We checked out of the hotel shortly afterward and made reservations for the night of October 16, now just two days off. While we would be sleeping elsewhere, we needed the rooms in order to dress for our party to ensure that this occasion, which would probably be our last experience in Atami, would go off in style.

Carrying our bags, we walked over to Takao Hayashi's house to pay a courtesy call, knowing that Lanko would be there as well. When we arrived we were invited into the main room with Takao, Lanko, and Nirohiko for the usual cup of tea. We were questioned about the geisha party and were effusive in our comments, slipping in the fact that we were to return for another party two days hence. Both Takao and Lanko were genuinely pleased that we had enjoyed the entertainment and that we were going to return so quickly. Lanko asked us to be sure to stop by the morning after our next party, as she had a surprise for us. Of course, we assured her that we would do as she suggested.

We did not linger long after tea, and Lanko, being dressed in an everyday kimono, insisted on walking to the train station with us. The walk was invigorating in the cool late-morning air, Lanko chattering away and the two of us, attentive as usual, almost understanding her sallies. She came out on the station platform with us when the train pulled in, waving a warm good-bye.

Our return aboard the Cotten late in the afternoon of October 14 was unnoticed by our shipmates, everyone by now being immersed in their own adventures. At supper no one asked where Gearhart and I had been, although we did tell Snowden and Drake that we had learned that the army was about to descend upon Atami in overwhelming numbers. I noted that they appeared as distressed at the news as we had been, indicating that quite possibly they had something going there that they were keeping to themselves, much as we were.

The next day Gearhart and I returned to Kamakura to sell another cargo of our Old Golds, which had now reached the bottom of the case, concealing the cigarettes as usual in the lining of our coats. This trip was successful enough financially to ensure that we would be able to give generous presents to our next geisha, personal gifts being a previously unforeseen expense. It was now painfully evident that our coming trip would be the last, as our resources were drying up for anything as elevating and costly as life on the geisha circuit.

The next morning I wrote another letter home, reciting some of the further experiences in Atami, and I hoped my parents would add it to the letters I had asked them to save for the enlivenment of later years. After packing the necessities for the coming party, Gearhart and I had lunch in the wardroom and then left for Yokosuka.

We arrived at the hotel in Atami about five o'clock, checked in, then bathed and dressed for the party, which for my part I did with unusual care. After completing the preparations, I joined Gearhart in the lounge for a preparatory glass of wine before setting off for the Golden Wave in the same venerable taxi, and with the same driver, as had served us the last time. We arrived at the Golden Wave at seven, paid the driver, and knocked at the door to announce our presence.

We were greeted by the maid, who welcomed us with a smile. We were led to the head geisha's office, where our previous interpreter companion and the head lady were locked in conversation. They both greeted us as though we were old friends, and we reciprocated in kind. If there had been any reserve in our manners at our initial meeting, it was now replaced by a subtle feeling that we were all there for the same purpose, to have a terrific evening. We sat down to the ritual cup of tea and the passing of the balance of the money to cover the night's activities before departing for the room that had been set aside for us.

Because there would be an additional musician, this room was a bit larger and, if anything, more elegantly decorated. After we had entered the room the rest of the party made their entries—two older geisha, perhaps in their forties, carrying *samisen*, followed by the two younger geisha who would be our hostesses, entertainers, and companions. Introductions were made by the head geisha, after which she wished us happiness and departed.

The two younger geisha then positioned everyone around the table. One of them had selected me as her companion for the evening, indicating where I was to sit and taking her position beside me. The other was

Gearhart's date, the two of them sitting on the same side of the table as we were. The two older geisha, flanking our interpreter friend, were placed opposite us, with the space behind them free for the artistic presentations. My geisha's name was Koko. She was attractive, slender, and beautifully attired and made up in classic geisha fashion. This time I had no eyes for Gearhart's companion; my own carried an aura of self-confidence, art, life, and coquetry that commanded my whole interest and attention.

At Koko's request our interpreter now asked us whether we would prefer wine or tea with supper. We both chose wine and asked the interpreter to offer the same choice to all of the others as well. He and the two older geisha were happy to be served wine, but the two younger women declined, with the explanation that geisha who were performing were forbidden to drink anything stronger than tea. Koko then chatted with me, asking the interpreter for assistance in translation, as I did in turn when replying. Gearhart and his girl were also conversing, so the interpreter was hard pressed to keep up, making frequent recourse to his English-Japanese dictionary.

Koko's mature self-assurance seemed indicative of a long and demanding education in the art of the geisha, prompting me to ask her how long she had been in her profession. She replied that she had been in training for fourteen years, including the past two years as a fully accredited geisha. This placed her age between twenty-four and twenty-six years, so she was probably two or three years older than I. In turn, she asked me my age. I answered that I was twenty-three and followed up with a summary of my history to date, including a recap of my education and the fact that I had been aboard a destroyer for the past two years and four months.

Koko then embarked on a teaching session covering the pronunciation of some Japanese phrases or short sentences. After a bit of coaxing I picked up two that I could remember, that in fact I long remembered. However, the rascal would not tell me what they meant, and since she giggled each time I repeated them, I suspected they were meant for the privacy of the bedroom rather than for public display. The two young women then performed a series of story dances accompanied by the two *samisen* before supper was served. Their execution and dramatic presentation seemed perfect to me and was obviously much more polished, with many more nuances, than the younger girls had been able to accomplish three nights before.

Supper was now served, it being a bit after eight o'clock. The meal was very delicate, with the customary fresh, unknown fish, and even a small portion of meat to accompany the rice and vegetables. The wine was fine to my undiscerning palate and certainly livened up the two older geisha and our interpreter. Koko fed most of my dinner to me with chopsticks, as I had very little facility with them. I am still amazed at how easy the technique looks when someone else is using them, but they have always remained beyond me. Between courses our geisha performed, alternating singing and dancing as the meal progressed. For the dessert course we were served grapes and little cups of hot sake, both of which I managed to consume without assistance.

Because of the interludes of entertainment, the meal was leisurely as well as delightful. I have no idea how long it took us to eat, but eventually the table was cleared, and we all were given hot towels by the maid to clean our hands and faces, cleanliness clearly being a priority with the Japanese. At this juncture there was a short break, to give everyone a chance to make a trip to the washroom, and of course, for the girls to make certain that their makeup, clothes, and coiffures were in proper order.

When the party reconvened, it was time for serious dancing and singing, the sessions interspersed with more conversation and flirtation between Koko and me, and I hoped between Gearhart and his girl as well, though I failed to take notice. In this manner the evening continued until about eleven, when, after a beautiful, final song, the geisha announced that the party was ended.

Good-nights were exchanged with our faithful interpreter and now friend, and with the two geisha who had accompanied our hostesses while they were singing and dancing. We gave the two ladies presents, which was fortunate, as it had been expected, and offered one to the interpreter, who definitely did not either expect or want one.

Koko and I then said good night to Shifty-san and his date, and we left them to head for our own room for the night. Our bedroom was small but attractive. There were two adjacent mats and wooden pillows on the floor, with a beautiful quilt that covered both mats. Koko handed me a light, knee-length silk robe with instructions that I was to remove my clothes and dress in it. She indicated that I could clean up in the bathroom and that she would leave for a moment to remove her makeup and prepare for the night herself. I did as bidden and sat down on the mat to await her return.

Koko returned in about ten minutes, also dressed in a light silk wrap, with her hair down and her face makeup scrubbed off. She gave me a big smile, then kneeled beside me on her side of the mat. We removed our wraps and climbed under the quilt. We did not go to sleep for some time, but eventually sleep came to us.

We awoke early enough and after awhile arose to visit the washroom, and then to sink into the large bath, the water not being scalding hot at that hour of the morning. Koko was in rare form, giving me a constant line of chatter that seemed designed to get me to loosen up, which she achieved with complete success. Gearhart and his girl appeared a bit later, and the two girls then joined in to give us both a royal ribbing, which by now we were able to return in kind, something I would have not dreamt possible just twelve hours previously.

While it had been the terms of our contract with the head geisha that we were to leave that morning at half past five, neither Koko nor Gearhart's companion was ready to see us depart. After the bath, we dressed; the girls put on light robes and insisted on giving us breakfast. Gearhart and I had both given the girls our personal presents before getting dressed, mine being every cent I could part with, so impressed was I with Koko's art and femininity. I felt certain that the presents had nothing to do with the tender care they took of us after the bath, during the breakfast that followed, and until we finally were allowed to leave at something after half past nine. When Gearhart and I left the House of the Golden Wave, we were decidedly poorer in worldly possessions but considerably richer in knowledge of the ways of men and women.

We were both mindful of the appointment we had with Lanko, so we walked briskly to Takao Hayashi's house to meet her there as planned. It was a good half-hour's walk, but the day was made for walking, and we were both feeling on top of the world. We arrived at ten sharp, finding Nirohiko waiting for us; Lanko had not yet arrived. In about ten minutes she blew in and apologized for being late, which we assured her was completely unnecessary. We then told Lanko and Nirohiko about our wonderful night at the Golden Wave, and I told her in particular how delightful I thought Koko was, both as an artiste and as a person. Lanko beamed with pleasure and said she was glad that I had found Koko to be so charming, since she was, in fact, one of the finest geisha in Atami.

I then reminded Lanko that she had told us that she had something she wanted to show us. A twinkle appeared in her eyes as she got to her feet, saying that she most certainly did. First, however, we had to walk to her house, which was about a twenty-minute hike from Takao's, generally up the westward slope of the volcano remnant. The four of us took off together in the fresh, cool morning air.

We arrived at Lanko's home, a very nice little Japanese house with beautiful dormant planting surrounding the front exposure, on the slope of the hill facing Sagami Wan. She left us standing in the street to go inside. Nirohiko told us that she had gone in to get her daughter and two of her daughter's friends, all of whom were twelve years old and had recently started their training to become geisha. Nirohiko now spilled the beans—Lanko was Takao's lover and the acknowledged father of her little girl, which explained a lot about all the relationships, and also in large measure why Gearhart and I had received such preferential treatment ever since we had met Lanko. That Nirohiko disapproved of his uncle Takao was again evident, although I did not feel that this disapproval extended to Lanko.

Lanko emerged a bit later, bringing with her the three young girls, delightful, bright-looking youngsters, smartly decked out. Lanko introduced them, proudly singling out her little daughter. Because this child was, after all, Nirohiko's first cousin, it was not surprising that there was obvious affection between the two.

Nirohiko then took his leave, telling us that Lanko intended to take us on a walk with the little girls all the way to the seashore, but that he was unable to come along. Without an interpreter, therefore, the six of us then took off on the walk toward the sea. At Lanko's instruction, her daughter took me by the hand, while her two little friends nestled alongside Gearhart and Lanko as we strolled down the hill toward the bay. These children were wonderful company, befitting the lady who was their patroness and, in the one special case, her mother as well.

Our destination was the top of a precipice that plunged down several hundred feet to the rocks on the shore of Sagami Wan. We sat together on little benches looking at the majestic scene spread out before us, with snow-covered Fuji-san looking over us from behind. The girls snuggled up against us, and we put our arms around their shoulders to protect them from the cool wind. I do not know how long we stayed, but needless to say, the moment is indelibly etched in my memory.

Like all such moments, this one had to end, and we walked back up the rise to Lanko's house. The farewell was a tender one, for my part coming from the depths of my soul. Lanko and the three girls stood in front of her house waving good-bye to us as we left them to return to the hotel. When we got back we had a quick lunch, settled up our bills, collected our bags, and headed for the station to catch the train back to Yokosuka.

Neither Gearhart nor I had much to say for the rest of the day, instead internally husbanding memories of the recent days. I believe I knew that just as the war had ended with unforeseen suddenness, so now the one month's hiatus when our victory could be savored had similarly come to a close. In this mood of reflection we returned to the *Cotten*.

39

Squadron 50 Leaves the Occupation Force

The *Cotten* remained anchored in Tokyo Bay from the time that Gearhart and I returned from our latest—and as it proved, our final—trip to Atami until November 1, 1945. During this period the demobilization of the navy gathered speed. Married officers and leading petty officers were being sent home to be released to inactive duty, which required some shuffling of assignments so that each ship would have enough key personnel to operate. An example of this process was the transfer of Mike Czarowitz from the *Cotten* to the *Healy* to become the executive officer; another was the return of Paul Patterson to the states for release from active duty, all medical officers being removed from destroyers (which normally rated only hospital corpsmen) as part of the conversion to peacetime standards.

Another bad storm hit the Tokyo Bay anchorage October 25. Again we dragged both anchors and had to operate the main engines in order to hold our ground. This time, however, we lost both the gig and the fifty-four-foot Japanese power cruiser, which broke loose and were smashed to pieces on the shore. The loss of these boats, especially the cruiser, which had been a source of pride to the crew, cut down on the liberty parties and now left the men more or less cooped up on the ship.

More important than the destruction of the two boats was the feeling that while our luck had been in the ascendant when we had acquired the speedboat and then the vice admiral's "barge" (as boats assigned to flag officers are known), the loss of the barge and our own gig was a portent of the end of our good luck. Superstition is part of a sailor's creed and is not to be taken lightly.

On November 3 the *Cotten* returned to Yokosuka Ko, remaining inside the small harbor for the following ten days. Unlike our last stay, however, new regulations imposed by MacArthur were to restrict the freedom of action that we had enjoyed for the entire month of October. The first change concerned the now-pervasive black market involving American servicemen and Japanese civilians, with which Gearhart and I had an intimate familiarity. Without warning, navy personnel were now forbidden to sell cigarettes to the civilians; that cut off the sole source of spending money other than naval pay, which was woefully insufficient for the victor's lifestyle we had become accustomed to.

The next new regulation concerned the so-called "geisha houses" that had been set aside for the navy in Yokosuka. The highest-ranking navy chaplain, a rear admiral, had visited Japan in October and had been shocked by the navy's sponsorship of these establishments. On the strength of his formal complaint to the Chief of Naval Personnel in Washington, they were immediately closed to all naval personnel, with armed marine guards posted to enforce the prohibition.

These changes in the rules transformed the previously open activities in these specific areas into illegal acts subject to military discipline. It was only a matter of days before members of the *Cotten*'s crew began to be apprehended by the shore patrol and returned to the ship under armed guard with charges preferred against them for doing what they had earlier been free to do. By the middle of November, the interest that everyone had been taking in Japan and things Japanese had come to an end. This was certainly noticeable in my own attitude. The privileged experiences enjoyed in Atami were so far removed from what we could expect to enjoy under the new regulations that there appeared to be no sense in trying to develop new plans.

Fortunately, rumors began to circulate that DesRon 50 would be leaving Japan shortly after December 1, only some two weeks hence. On November 19 Snowden went home on emergency leave to visit his mother, who was seriously ill. He told Drake, Gearhart, and me that he would see us on the West Coast at the end of his leave, reinforcing our hopes for an early departure from Japan. On November 18, Walter Walborn was detached to return home and be released from the navy. With Walborn and Snowden gone, the *Cotten*'s officer roster had been reduced to Captain Linehan,

Spencer Beresford, Bob Drake, Ralph Gearhart, Tom Wood, myself, and fourteen ensigns, including John Bock, the supply officer. The experienced petty officers were similarly reduced in number, leaving the ship with barely enough expertise to get it home, and without the skills needed to fight.

All nine destroyers of DesRon 50 were released from the occupation forces as of December 5, at which time we were to proceed as a unit to San Diego, with stops at Eniwetok and Pearl Harbor. The intervening two weeks dragged, but December 5, 1945, eventually arrived, and the nine destroyers set forth together from Tokyo Bay. The voyage across the Pacific Ocean was uneventful, and on the afternoon of December 21 the squadron steamed into San Diego Harbor, where the *Cotten* remained until January 3, 1946.

Captain Linehan and his wife owned a small house in Coronado, and they were very hospitable to the *Cotten*'s officer contingent over the Christmas and New Year's holidays. Snowden had rejoined the ship when we arrived, so he, Drake, Gearhart, and I renewed the socializing that we had enjoyed together in Japan; this camaraderie became the major rallying point of our lives during the few months remaining on active duty.

While the squadron was lying over in San Diego, it was officially transferred to the Atlantic Fleet, its designation being changed from DesRon 50 to DesRon 14. This change was another symbolic event in the winding down of the active career of the *Cotten*. The disappearance of Destroyer Squadron 50 from the active naval registry of ships had a ring of finality about it.

On January 3, 1946, the squadron got under way from San Diego and set a course for the Panama Canal. We traversed the canal on January 11–12 and then headed for New York Harbor. On arrival, the ships of our division unloaded all ammunition at the depot in Earle, New Jersey, on January 17, following which the *Cotten* moored to the north side of the Thirty-fifth Street Pier in New York Harbor. We stayed there until January 25, when we were moved to Pier 26, also on Manhattan Island, residing there until February 28. Then we moved again, this time to the Brooklyn Navy Yard, where preparatory work for the mothballing process was begun.

During these weeks, when our duties had all but disappeared, I passed my evenings ashore in company with Snowden, Drake, and Gearhart. No one was under any illusions; we were all about to have to begin the serious business of supporting ourselves, and the future was a little unsettling. I advanced in rank to lieutenant on April 1, and I knew that my new higher salary was much more than I would be likely to receive when I got my first civilian job—another vision of the future.

In the middle of April, the *Cotten* steamed to the Charleston Navy Yard in South Carolina, arriving on April 16. My duties aboard ship officially came to an end on April 20, when the final mothballing process began.

Lt. C. Snelling Robinson at the time of his release from active duty, April 1946.

This would culminate in the *Cotten's* decommissioning and removal from the navy's roster of active warships. I said farewell to the *Cotten* and to my friends and departed for Chicago and the Great Lakes Naval Station, where I was to be released to inactive duty. There I received a final check amounting to ten weeks' salary, most of which represented accrued but unused leave.

With uniforms permanently set aside and some immediate time off, I now had an opportunity to reflect on the preceding three years, as well as to consider what course to take for the future. With respect to the high adventure enjoyed by those of us privileged to have served with the Pacific Fleet, I believed that nothing could possibly ever diminish the monumental grandeur that had been the hallmark of the drive across the Central Pacific. Whatever the political result of World War II proved to be, the naval war against Japan would remain as it had initially appeared to the contestants, the greatest naval war ever fought—in terms of the immensity of the battle area, the size and complexity of the forces involved, and the tenacity of the combatants.

On a personal level, I came to appreciate the accomplishments of my shipmates, accomplishments achieved as members of a well-trained crew serving the *Cotten* during our extended tour of duty with the Pacific Fleet. I was certain that we would remember our experiences for the rest of our lives, probably with increasing fondness in the years to follow.

Epilogue

During the immediate postwar years, the U.S. government acted with unprecedented generosity toward its returning veterans, enacting legislation that made college and professional educations available to those who wanted them. Low-interest and low-down-payment mortgages were underwritten by government agencies, thereby making home ownership possible for the millions of new families, which produced more millions of young children. The long-pent-up civilian demand for goods and services finally put the Great Depression to rest, and few veterans had difficulty finding a respectable and livable niche in the nation's economic framework. Also, however, social inequities inherited from the past had become more apparent in the services, pointing to the need for substantive changes in the social contract itself.

In addition to providing assistance to their own veterans, the American people eventually treated the civilian populations of the recent adversaries (with the notable exception of their wartime leaders) with sympathy, and more importantly, financial assistance in rebuilding their shattered economies. This was done with the intention of breaking the cycle of aggression and wars of revenge between the powers.

On the dark side, overhanging everything was the fact that the genie of nuclear weapons was now out of the bottle. No one pretended to understand what this meant for the future, except that the risks for civilization seemed to have increased exponentially. Equally unnerving, it became painfully evident that the Soviet Union, so recently our ally in arms, had an agenda that was in opposition to, and would quickly come into conflict with, that of the United States. This development was to shatter the illusion that world peace could be taken for granted as a result of our victory in World War II.

The "Cold War" Era, 1948–60—*Cotten* Recommissioned

Starting with the Soviet blockade of Berlin in 1948, the confrontation between the Soviet-occupied and satellite countries and the United States and its allies steadily became more hostile. It culminated in the 1950 invasion of South Korea, an ally of the United States, by North Korea, a puppet of the Soviet Union. The United States quickly came to the defense of South Korea, resulting in the Korean War (1950–53).

By 1950 the United States had largely disarmed, so the Korean episode required a rapid rearmament of major proportions. Because of the rapid need for air support, the U.S. Navy deployed a major part of its active carrier forces to the Korean area on a continuing basis. This meant bringing carriers out of mothballs as an immediate way to replace naval air power on the U.S. East Coast. As a part of this reexpansion of the navy, the *Cotten* was taken out of retirement, restored to combat readiness, and recommissioned in July of 1951, with an entirely new complement of officers and men. For over a year it remained in East Coast waters, training and serving in the Caribbean before being sent to the western Pacific for patrol duty off Korea. The ship returned to the United States through the Mediterranean Sea, arriving home in early 1954. During 1955 it spent six months in the Indian Ocean, and during 1957 it joined the Sixth Fleet in the Mediterranean for a two-month cruise. During 1959 the ship again served in the Mediterranean, this time for six months, before returning for good to be again decommissioned and placed in reserve on May 2, 1960, this time in Norfolk, Virginia. Fifteen years later, an annual inspection revealed that the now-aging ship would not be worth the expense of another restoration. As a result it was sold to the Consolidated Steel Corporation and was towed away in August of 1975 to be broken up for scrap, the fate of all but a few of the faithful warships of World War II.

At the close of the twentieth century there remain three *Fletcher*-class destroyers, preserved as memorials: *The Sullivans* (DD 537), *Kidd* (DD 661), and *Cassin Young* (DD 793).

The Crew

In 1982 two former World War II crew members, Walter Shollmier and C. W. Stephenson, formed the "USS *Cotten* DD 669 Reunion Association." Under their fine leadership that organization at one time had 232 dues-paying members, representing both the World War II crew and, to a lesser degree, the 1951–60 crews.

While officers have been welcome members of the reunion association, it has been the former enlisted men of the various crews, particularly those of World War II, who have provided the leadership, time, and enthusiasm necessary to make it a success and a continuing tribute to the memory of the *Cotten*. Since its inception the association has held annual reunions each summer, as recently, at this writing, as 1998.

I have attended three of the reunions and enjoyed seeing Capt. Philip Winston, executive officers Joseph Wesson, Alexander Early, and Robert Rothschild, and supply officer Fred Butler, all prominent in this narrative; they have been faithful in their attendance. Another regular attendee has been Capt. John Strane, one of the two naval aviators rescued during the battle off Cape Engaño and today a vocal booster of the USS *Cotten* association. While the World War II officers still alive are now retired, it is notable that at least five—Smythe, Beresford, Stokey, Early, and Gearhart—became lawyers. Of my personal friends, Gus Smythe, Howie Snowden, Ralph Gearhart, and Bob Drake, all have died without my having had the chance to see them once again, to my great regret.

Appendix A

USS Cotten (DD 669): *Specifications and Manpower Requirements*

The USS *Cotten* was a *Fletcher*-class destroyer, a new-construction type built in large numbers during the early war years (1942–1943) to provide screens for the fast carrier task groups being built for the Pacific War. *Fletcher*-class destroyers were 376 feet six inches long, a maximum of 39 feet eight inches wide, and displaced 2,050 deadweight tons.

Main Battery

There were five 5-inch, 38-caliber, rapid-fire guns in five single centerline mounts, all dual purpose—that is, they were antisurface and antiaircraft weapons. When firing in rapid-continuous mode, each gun could fire between fifteen and twenty rounds per minute, depending upon the skill of the mount's team in getting the projectiles and cartridges loaded. The guns were aimed and controlled by a main battery director, located at the highest point of the ship and containing a fire control radar as well as an optical range finder. The director was, in turn, connected to the fire control computer, located directly beneath the director behind the pilothouse.

The computer received inputs as to range, and change of range, bearing, and rate of changes in deflection (and elevation) from the director, plus inputs concerning wind, humidity, own ship's course and speed, and condition of the guns (hot, cold, number of rounds fired). From this data the computer produced a fire control solution, which was transmitted on a continuous basis back to the director. When (and if) this solution was correct, the director's cross hairs would remain on the target automatically, the ship's roll and pitch being eliminated by gyro stabilizers built into the system. This solution, in the form of correct aim and elevation, was then transmitted to all of the 5-inch guns (with corrections allowing for the distance of each mount from the director), which were normally locked into the director's control and were thus aimed automatically.

These 5-inch guns were the main battery of the destroyer and were the principal antiaircraft defense, aside from the combat air patrols, of the carrier task groups. The destroyers would be positioned at equal intervals on a circle whose radius was anywhere from twenty-five hundred to nine thousand yards from the theoretical center, depending upon the number of destroyers in the screen.

The 5-inch projectiles used for antiaircraft firing contained a special fuse, at the time a top-secret device, that was controlled by a tiny very high-frequency radio transmitter and receiver. When the shell got within twenty to thirty feet of a large-enough object, the reflected signal would activate the fuse, and the shell would explode. Thus, if the gun could be aimed with sufficient accuracy to guide the shell within twenty to thirty feet of an enemy aircraft, the shell would explode, ideally within killing range. This device was new at the time of the *Cotten*'s commissioning, and the navy was enthusiastically predicting that air defenses were getting a leg up on the advantage attacking aircraft had possessed up until this point.

Heavy Automatic Weapons

The next grade of the *Cotten*'s armament consisted of a secondary battery of five twin-barreled, 40-millimeter, automatic weapons, each barrel capable of firing 160 rounds per minute, and seven single-mounted 20-millimeter machine guns, each capable of firing 450 rounds per minute. A separate Mark 49 visual director controlled each 40-mm mount, aiming and firing the guns electrically. The 40-mm guns were manually loaded at the mounts. The aiming, firing, and servicing of the 20-mm guns was entirely a manual operation.

Accurate fire control of these heavy machine guns depended entirely upon the skill of the personnel; an adequate level of accuracy demanded continuous practice. Anything short of a direct hit was a useless miss with these guns. It was, in the end, similar to the effective aiming of a shotgun against birds or clay pigeons, where natural ability plus a great deal of practice determines who does the best job.

Torpedoes

Fletcher-class destroyers were built with two centerline torpedo mounts, each containing five torpedoes of twenty-one-inch diameter. These torpedoes were powered by steam turbine engines fueled by compressed air and alcohol. At their high-speed setting, they could travel at over forty knots for a limited range, under ten thousand yards. The warhead contained some 450 pounds of high explosive. The intended use for these torpedoes was in a surface fleet action, wherein destroyers were to be deployed ahead of the battleships and cruiser forces, and a massive torpedo attack might have some positive influence on the course of the battle.

A major difference existed between Japanese and U.S. torpedo doctrine and tactics. The Japanese navy had developed night optical equipment so superior to American optics that it was hard for us to believe. It was a fact, however, that during night operations, the Japanese could see U.S. ships at twice the range that we could see them; in early battles that ability often equalized any advantage we might have had in the latest surface search radars that a few of our newer ships had. In addition, Japanese torpedoes had a diameter of twenty-four inches, carried a 770-pound warhead, and could travel over sixteen thousand yards at over forty-five knots. Because their fuel was oxygen and alcohol, instead of air and alcohol, the torpedoes left so little exhaust as to be invisible at night. Japanese nighttime torpedo doctrine and tactics were an unpleasant surprise to our navy, and they wreaked havoc during the several major nighttime surface actions of the Guadalcanal campaign. It may have been because Admiral Lee had had firsthand experience with the superiority of Japanese nighttime torpedo warfare that he was perhaps reluctant to commit Task Group 58.7, the Battle Line, to a nighttime search for the Japanese fleet prior to the Battle of the Philippine Sea, as related in the body of the narrative.

Depth Charges

Fletcher-class destroyers carried two racks of six-hundred-pound depth charges at the very stern of the ship, with seven depth charges in each rack. These weapons were dropped off the stern, on direction from the bridge. They contained pressure-activated fuses, which were set manually upon order to detonate the explosive when the predetermined depth had been reached.

On both sides of the ship, alongside 5-inch mount number 4, were three K-guns with storage racks alongside, containing four three-hundred-pound depth charges each. When ordered from the bridge, the K-guns would fire these charges some two hundred feet away from the ship, the detonators on these weapons being identical to the larger charges dropped from the stern. By doctrine, a major depth charge attack on a submarine consisted of a pattern of eleven depth charges, five of the six-hundred-pound charges over the stern and three of the three-hundred-pound charges each to port and starboard. The depth charges would be set to explode at the estimated depth of the submarine, and each charge would be approximately two hundred feet from the next when it exploded. This was a rough form of attack; its effectiveness was dependent upon skillful use of the ship's sonar equipment by the sound crew and on a practiced estimate of the submarine's evasive capabilities by the officer conducting the destroyer's attack, usually the captain.

Radar

The *Cotten* was equipped with the latest radar development, the SG surface search radar, as well as the older fire control radar on the main battery director, and the SC air search radar. The SG radar literally changed the nighttime tactics of the U.S. Navy to the equivalent of daytime tactics. The officer of the deck could maneuver the ship with confidence that he knew the locations of all of the other ships in the formation, and he could see minute by minute how relative positions were changing when nighttime maneuvers were carried out. SG radar had not been distributed to the navy's combat ships at the start of the war, and it became generally available only at the time the *Cotten* was being constructed.

Propulsion

Fletcher-class destroyers were powered by four high-temperature, high-pressure boilers capable of producing fifteen thousand horsepower each. Two boilers were located in each of two separated boiler compartments located in the central portion of the ship. The boilers could be connected by various "cross-connect" arrangements to the two steam turbine engines, one in each of the engine rooms, adjacent to the boiler rooms. Each engine drove one of the two propeller shafts through a massive set of reduction gears, turning the propellers at up to about 340 revolutions per minute ("turns") in the forward direction, or drastically slower in reverse. With both propellers, each ten turns ahead would produce about one knot of ship's speed. Thus, 250 turns ahead on both screws (propellers) would produce a ship's speed of twenty-five knots (which was referred to as "Speed 5," or flank speed for the carrier task groups—standard speed, or "Speed 3," being fifteen knots).

Total fuel oil tank capacity was 492 tons, or 3,346 barrels. The designed cruising range at fifteen knots, using two boilers, was 4,500 miles, or theoretically twelve and a half days averaging 360 miles per day. With two boilers on the line (half the available horsepower), the *Cotten's* maximum speed was twenty-seven knots, which was five knots above maximum hull speed. With all four boilers on the line (battle conditions), top speed was thirty-one knots. Thus, fuel consumption per mile was more than doubled when speed was raised the last four knots, a vital factor in the logistics of battle conditions encountered far from the advance fleet bases.

Maneuverability

Because of its length-versus-width configuration (long and pencil thin), a destroyer was not easily maneuvered. For example, at flank speed the *Cotten* would move one thousand yards ahead on its track before it would start turning after the rudder had been put over at right or left standard rudder (fifteen degrees). Once this turn had started, the diameter of a complete 360-degree turn was also one thousand yards. A turn with a diameter of less than one thousand yards required a much slower speed, accompanied by a reversing of the engine on the side of the ship toward which the turn was being made, while continuing ahead on the outboard engine. This device was used by conning officers when maneuvering to go alongside a dock or moored ships, to anchor in a restricted area, or finally, when maneuvering to make an attack on an enemy submarine. This maneuvering limitation of destroyers, coupled with the strong force that the wind exerted on the bow when maneuvering at slow speed, made experience in this area the highest requirement. The captain normally took direct control of the ship in this type of situation.

Wartime Operating Conditions When Under Way

General Quarters

During the war, a U.S. Navy destroyer required all of its officers (16–18) and men (310–325) to man and operate the ship, its machinery, and weaponry at 100 percent effectiveness. This 100 percent manning mode is referred to as "battle stations" or "general quarters." Normally, in combat areas, the ships of the U.S. Navy went to general quarters at dawn and dusk for about an hour, these being the most dangerous times vis-à-vis enemy land-based air attacks. The fleet also went to general quarters whenever enemy attack was anticipated, day or night.

Condition of Readiness III

During the balance of the time, one-third of the enlisted men were on watch, manning the engineering spaces, the bridge, one-third of the guns (all calibers), the main battery director and fire control computer, and the sound gear. In the combat information center (CIC), the radars were operated, a plot was kept of the task group and of enemy forces when they appeared on radar, and the various voice communication circuits were monitored. This level of readiness was called "Condition III" (general quarters being Condition I). Officers stood Condition III watches on the bridge (an officer of the deck, in charge of the ship, and an assistant, the junior officer of the watch), in CIC, in the main battery director (control), and in the forward engine room (the engineering watch officer).

Appendix B

USS Cotten (DD 669): *World War II Awards and Commendations*

Letter of Commendation

F. T. Sloat, Commander, USN — Commanding Officer
R. I. Rothschild, Lieutenant, USNR — Executive Officer
R. H. Snowden, Lieutenant, USNR — First Lieutenant
R. T. Blackburn, Lieutenant, USN — Engineering Officer
A. C. McCullough, CBM, USN

Bronze Star

P. W. Winston, Commander, USN — Commanding Officer
G. A. Williams, Cox (T), USNR
R. L. Smith, MM3c (T), USNR

Navy and Marine Corps Medal

P. L. Richards, Cox (T), USNR

Purple Heart

C. Bennett, StM1c, USNR
L. Booker, StM1c, USNR
J. L. Cornatzer, SM1c, USNR
A. J. Gifford, SM2c, USNR
L. E. Griffis, MM2c, USNR
R. W. Hein, MM3c, USNR
L. M. Rhoads, GM3c, USNR
C. T. Siracusa, F1c, USNR

Appendix C

Notes on Maps

Six preliminary maps were prepared by the author by tracing over general charts of the areas of the Pacific Ocean mentioned in the text. In the cases of the two great sea battles, the movements of the major naval elements that are referred to are shown for both the Japanese and American forces, concentrating on those with which the *Cotten* was directly or peripherally involved.

The author's original sketch drawings were then redrawn on a computer to conform to the publisher's requirements, by Mary Craddock Hoffman. Mrs. Hoffman completely redrew the artwork and rescaled the tracks, lettering, and icons.

Notes Concerning Maps

Map 1 Track of the USS *Cotten* from Pearl Harbor to Tarawa (November 10–24, 1943), including location of the sinking of the Japanese submarine. The track represents the average daily noon positions of the *Cotten* as entered in the deck log. During the period that the marines were struggling to seize Tarawa, the *Cotten* and the two escort carriers remained in the area east of the beachhead while providing air support.

Map 2 The date and location of each of the islands that were involved with the various operations and strikes of Task Force 58 between January 31 and March 29, 1944.

Map 3 Simplified, approximated, and averaged tracks of the Japanese Combined Fleet and Task Force 58 during the Battle of the Philippine Sea, from June 11, 1944, up to and including the two days of the battle, June 19–20, 1944. These tracks are not intended to show the many actual maneuvers, because such detail is confusing to anyone except a trained tactician. The losses of combat ships suffered by the Japanese Combined Fleet prior to and during the battle itself were not known by the men of Task Force 58; this map, which shows no such losses, therefore reflects the situation as it was understood by the crew of the *Cotten* at the time.

Map 4 The tracks of Task Group 38.3 (Sherman), Task Force 34 (Lee), and Task Unit 38.3.3 (DuBose), to which the *Cotten* was assigned in sequence from 2400 of October 23 until 2115 of October 25, in the Battle of Leyte Gulf (northern part) and the Battle off Cape Engaño. The tracks of these groups were developed from the daily positions contained in the war diary of Commander Destroyer Squadron 50 (Wilkinson). The tracks of all other groups, both enemy and U.S., are anecdotal and general rather than specific. They are, however, a good summary of the actual movements.

Ships shown on the map as sunk, the *Princeton* and the Japanese carrier and heavy destroyer, were those seen at close range from the bridge of the *Cotten*. The many other ships that were sunk, both Japanese and American, are not shown, as the *Cotten* did not know about them until much later. None of the naval forces involved in the southern action, the Battle of Surigao Strait, October 24–25, 1944, are shown, as they had no bearing on the activity of the U.S. Third Fleet.

Map 5 Action between U.S. destroyers *Cotten* and *Dortch* and Japanese patrol ships *PC* 321 and *PC* 326 on March 14, 1945. The track of *Cotten* and *Dortch* on March 13–14, 1945, shows the search for, engagement with, and sinking of the two Japanese ships halfway between Iwo Jima and Tokyo.

Map 6 Shows the location of various places in Japan referred to in the chapters covering the first months of the occupation (southern coast of Honshu and Tokyo and Sagami Bays), September–November, 1945.

Glossary

Chronometer rate-of-change cards Cards identifying the rate at which a given chronometer gains or loses time (for example, number 1 loses one second every thirty days). By using three chronometers, one main and two secondary, and consulting the daily-rate-of-change cards to adjust for the regular fractional inaccuracy of each, it is possible to determine when one of the three chronometers is out of adjustment, at which point a spare can be brought into use.

Degauss To make a steel ship nonmagnetic by means of electrical coils carrying currents that neutralize the magnetism of the ship itself and thereby prevent the detonating of magnetic mines.

Dog watch Either of two watches of two hours that extend from 1600 to 1800 and from 1800 to 2000. They make an odd number of watches in a day, so that crew members who work on a rotating watch system will not stand the same watches every day.

Fantail Main deck area at the stern of a ship. Formerly that part of the stern of a ship that overhung the water.

Fighter sweep A fighter sweep was an all fighter carrier-based strike, the objective of which was to target enemy aircraft, whether airborne or on the ground. This is not to be confused with a normal carrier-based air strike, the objective of which was to destroy designated targets, such as enemy carriers, land-based military targets, etc.

General quarters The term for a ship at battle stations, in which every crew member has a specific assigned responsibility, and the watertight integrity for the entire ship is at its most secure level.

IFF An electronic device identifying aircraft as friend or foe.

Lie to Hover in one position without anchoring.

Offset firing A main battery live firing exercise at a target ship with a deflection error entered into the director so that shells fall a predetermined distance to the right or left of the target.

Repeater A circular cathode ray screen on which outgoing and target-reflected radar signals appeared, in World War II, as lines and blips respectively. The screens were divided into 360 degrees relative to the ship's heading, with concentric circles indicating the various ranges.

Stadimeter A handheld instrument for triangulating short distances. With the distance between the waterline and the top of the foremast entered on the instrument, the exact distance between two similar ships can be quickly and easily read off.

Bibliography

Alexander, Joseph H. *Storm Landings*. Annapolis, Md.: Naval Institute Press, 1997.
———. *Utmost Savagery*. Annapolis, Md.: Naval Institute Press, 1995.
Bottomley, Ian, and Anthony Hopson. *Arms and Armor of the Samurai: The History of Weaponry in Ancient Japan*. New York: Crescent Books, 1988.
Dull, Paul S. *A Battle History of the Imperial Japanese Navy (1941–1945)*. Annapolis, Md.: Naval Institute Press, 1978.
Fukudome, Shigeru. "The Air Battle off Taiwan." In *The Japanese Navy in World War II*, 2d ed., edited and translated by David C. Evans, 334–54. Annapolis, Md.: Naval Institute Press, 1986.
Koyanagi, Tomiji. "The Battle of Leyte Gulf." In *The Japanese Navy in World War II*, 2d ed., edited and translated by David C. Evans, 355–84. Annapolis, Md.: Naval Institute Press, 1986.
Lockwood, Charles A., and Hans Christian Adamson. *Battles of the Philippine Sea*. New York: Thomas Y. Crowell, 1967.
Morison, Samuel Eliot. *The Two Ocean War: A Short History of the United States Navy in the Second World War*. Boston: Little Brown, 1963.
Nomura, Minoru. "Ozawa in the Pacific: A Junior Officer's Experience." In *The Japanese Navy in World War II*, 2d ed., edited and translated by David C. Evans, 278–333. Annapolis, Md.: Naval Institute Press, 1986.
Raven, Alan. *Fletcher-Class Destroyers*. Annapolis, Md.: Naval Institute Press, 1989.
Roscoe, Theodore. *United States Destroyer Operations in World War II*. Annapolis, Md.: United States Naval Institute, 1953.
Torisu, Kennosuke, and Masataka Chihaya. "Japanese Submarine Tactics and the Kaiten." In *The Japanese Navy in World War II*, 2d ed., edited and translated by David C. Evans, 440–52. Annapolis, Md.: Naval Institute Press, 1986.
United States Navy Department, Office of the Chief of Naval Operations, Naval History Division. *Dictionary of American Naval Fighting Ships*. Vols. 1 and 2. Reprint with corrections. Washington, D.C.: Government Printing Office, 1970, 1969.

Index

sweeps against, 116, 160; invasion of, 158–60; task groups covering, 120, 122, 139–40, 144

MacArthur, Gen. Douglas, 226, 236; landings in the Philippines, 113–14, 121, 138, 158, 160; and liberation of Philippines, 88, 144, 175; naval support for, 50, 56–60, 148, 169; in occupation of Japan, 242, 244–47, 271–72, 274, 291; other landings by, 59, 149, 152; sailors' opinions of, 100–101, 208

Machine guns. *See* Heavy automatic weapons

Mail: censorship of, 34; to *Cotten* crew, 188–89; Snelling's letters home, 278, 285

Main battery guns, 299–300; exercises with, 12, 67–68, 224; in fire support for Iwo Jima, 185–87; firing at Japanese boats, 78, 192–93; 5-inch, 58–59, 82, 105

Maine, training in, 12–13

Majuro Atoll: as advance base, 46–49, 57, 59, 61–62, 69; marine landing at, 44–45

Makin, Task Force 52 to seize, 21–31

Manila, Philippines: attacks on, 109–10, 159; Japanese airfields around, 122, 140, 151

Maneuvering: of cruiser-destroyer group, 134–35; and cruising formations, 43–44, 46; defensive, 58–59, 116, 124, 150–51, 228; of destroyers, 12–13, 27–28, 303; for flight operations, 28, 65–66, 172–73; during night fighting by surface ships, 94–95; during refueling, 24–25; of task groups, 109, 151, 158, 175–77; training in, 224, 228

Manus Island, 50, 56–57, 104

Mare Island, 201, 222

Marianas, 85–86, 91; in Central Pacific strategy, 56–57; and Japanese fleet, 77–78, 87; mission against, 47–49, 69–85, 88–90

Marines: determination of, 32; at Eniwetok, 47–48; at Iwo Jima, 175–80, 185–87; at Majuro, 44–45; in occupation force, 234–35, 237, 257; at Peleliu, 108; and prisoners, 6; at Saipan, 78, 88; at Tarawa, 26–27, 38; at Tinian, 92; at Ulithi, 110

Markob (destroyer tender), 63

Marshall Islands, 33, 41–47, 96

Maryland (battleship), 25–26

Massachusetts (battleship), 44, 129; and destroyers, 45–46, 139; in Task Force 38, 104–6, 112

McCain, Adm. J. S., 137–38, 149, 151, 163–64

McCracken, Bob, 198, 208

McCullough, Chief Boatswain's Mate Albert C., 90, 257–58, 259

McGhee, Ens. C. M., 160–61

Merrimack (oiler), 235

Miami (cruiser), 67, 92, 95–96

Midget submarines, 145–47, 257–58

Midway, Battle of, 42

Miller (destroyer), 96

Mindanao, air strikes on, 105

Mindoro, landing on, 149, 152

Minefields, 159, 165, 257; in Tokyo Bay, 235–36, 242–43

Mini, Cdr. J. H., 125, 136

Mississinewa (oiler), 145–47

Missouri (battleship), 236, 242

Mitscher, Rear Adm. Marc, 70, 105–6; canceling air strikes, 110, 182; command of, 103, 137–38, 166; and damaged ships, 117, 124; and Japanese fleet, 80, 83–85, 87, 131; operations orders from, 41, 46, 74, 93, 113, 174; and subordinates, 71, 136; and Task Force 38, 100, 106, 137–38; and Task Force 58, 41, 47, 71, 166

Moale (destroyer), 181–82

Mobile (cruiser), 47, 92, 95–96, 115, 131, 136

Molala (attack transport), 257–58

Monaghan (destroyer), 31, 154–55

Monastery, Atami, 268–69

Recreation (*cont.*)
  See also Liberty
Reeves, Rear Adm. John W., 46, 74–75,
  78, 79, 85; command of, 41, 90; and
  Task Group 58.3, 71, 76; in Task
  Group 58.1, 47, 50; and torpedo
  bomber attacks, 58–59, 76
Refueling, 24–25, 35–36, 75, 136, 173;
  attack during, 165; in bad weather,
  142, 152–53, 161–63; from battleships
  vs. oilers, 111; by destroyers, 31, 235;
  nighttime, 45–46; Snelling as OOD
  during, 250–51; speed of, 37–38, 85;
  trying to maintain schedule for, 157,
  162–64
Reno (light cruiser), 91–92, 123, 150
Repairs: after destroyer collision, 167, 174;
  after typhoon, 157; to *Cotten*, 66, 99,
  145; during overhaul, 197, 199; by
  tenders, 48–49; at Ulithi, 117, 142, 148
Resupplying, 224; with ammunition, 31,
  92, 110, 188, 222; delays in, 111–12; at
  Eniwetok, 89, 99; with food, 31, 185;
  at Iwo Jima, 185, 188; at Majuro, 69;
  at Pearl Harbor, 228; at Saipan, 92,
  110; in Tokyo Bay, 243; at Ulithi, 137,
  142, 144
Richards, P. L., 146
Robinson, Ens. C. Snelling, *1, 17,* 293; in
  Atami, 267; on leave, 203–5, 207–8;
  as OOD, 89, 225
Robinson family, *1;* and Snelling's leave,
  197, 199, 203–5, 207–8; Snelling's
  letters to, 278, 285
Rodgers (destroyer), 251
Rodney (British battleship), 2
Room and board, 5, 20, 209
Roosevelt, President Franklin D., 2–3,
  57; death of, 199, 207; and liberation
  of Philippines, 88, 144
Ross (destroyer), 224, 229, 230
Rothschild, Lt. Robert I. ("Rocky"), 213,
  226, 229, 297; as executive officer,
  100, 102, 107, 216; and Japanese
  patrol boats, 192–94; during overhaul,

197, 209–10; and Snelling's watches,
  148, 171
Ryukyu Islands, 40, 114

Sagami Bay, 236, 242, 243
Saipan, 92, 110; air strikes against, 74–76;
  bombing raids from, 170, 190;
  invasion of, 78, 80, 87–88, 89, 91
Salaries: as ensign, 5; increased with
  promotion, 105; for lieutenants, 226,
  292–93; in military scrip, 252; sending
  home, 35
Salt Lake City (heavy cruiser), 44, 189
Samar, 108, 122, 137, 148
Samurai swords, Takao Hayashi's, 271,
  274–75, 277–78
San Bernardino Strait, 121–22, 126–27,
  131–32
San Diego, California, 224, 292
San Diego (cruiser), 171
San Francisco, California, 18, 211; fog
  around, 200–201; overhaul in, 197–
  200, 223
San Jacinto (light carrier), 153; striking at
  Japanese air bases, 150, 158; in Task
  Group 58.3, 71, 90, 92
Sangamon (oiler), 31
Santa Fe (cruiser), 47, 131; in Battle Line
  fleet exercises, 95–96; and cruiser-
  destroyer group, 134, 136; destroyers
  screening for, 171, 175
Schmidt, Corporal, 253–54
Scouting line: for air strikes against
  Honshu, 170–72; for approach to
  Tokyo, 173–74
Screen commander, at Iwo Jima, 183–84,
  196
Screening, 26, 38; on approach to home
  islands, 170, 174; for Battle Line, 79,
  94, 104; for carrier groups, 165, 174,
  179; of damaged battleships, 46, 123,
  143; by destroyers, 31, 58, 72, 171, 174,
  235, 299; and formation changes, 110,
  164–65; at Iwo Jima, 178, 188, 190;
  Japanese, 134–35; maneuvering to

200,000 *Miles aboard the Destroyer* Cotten

was designed and composed by Christine Brooks

at The Kent State University Press

in 10.5/13 Fairfield Light with display text in Stone Informal

on an Apple Power Macintosh system using Adobe PageMaker;

printed on 50# Turin Book stock;

Smyth sewn and bound over binder's boards in Brillianta cloth,

and wrapped with dust jackets printed in two colors

by Thomson-Shore, Inc. of Dexter, Michigan

and published by

The Kent State University Press

KENT, OHIO 44242 USA